Crime and Its Modification
(PGPS–77)

Pergamon Titles of Related Interest

Crime and Its Modification

A Social Learning Perspective

Michael T. Nietzel

Pergamon Press

New York • Oxford • Toronto • Sydney • Frankfurt • Paris

179068

Pergamon Press Offices:

U.S.A.   Pergamon Press Inc., Maxwell House, Fairview Park, Elmsford, New York 10523, U.S.A.

U.K.   Pergamon Press Ltd., Headington Hill Hall, Oxford OX3 0BW, England

CANADA   Pergamon of Canada Ltd., 150 Consumers Road, Willowdale, Ontario M2J 1P9, Canada

AUSTRALIA   Pergamon Press (Aust) Pty. Ltd., P O Box 544, Potts Point, NSW 2011, Australia

FRANCE   Pergamon Press SARL, 24 rue des Ecoles, 75240 Paris, Cedex 05, France

**FEDERAL REPUBLIC Pergamon Press GmbH, 6242 Kronberg/Taunus,
OF GERMANY**   Pferdstrasse 1, Federal Republic of Germany

Library of Congress Cataloging in Publication Data

Nietzel, Michael T
    Crime and its modification.

    1. Rehabilitation of criminals. 2. Behavior modifi-
cation. 3. Corrections. 4. Correctional psychology.
I. Title.
HV9275.N53   1979   365'.6   78-23984
ISBN 0-08-023878-5
ISBN 0-08-023877-7 pbk.

Printed in the United States of America

CONTENTS

PREFACE

I have one major aspiration for this book: that its audience will have as many of its beliefs about crime and psychology challenged as its author did. I suspect that most readers will not experience a fully satisfying sense of closure after finishing the book. I know I haven't, because the changes I've experienced do not all lead in one direction. In some cases I have become more encouraged about the potential impact of behaviorally oriented corrections. In other instances, my pessimism grows.

For example, I am not sanguine about the ability of social learning theory to explain adequately the complexity of crime which it must confront. Theoretical misgivings aside, I am reasonably convinced that, for many types of criminal conduct, behaviorally oriented techniques offer a better chance of durable rehabilitation than almost any other correctional alternative.

I am optimistic that behavioral techniques can be delivered in accord with the growing ethical and legal requirements that must guide correctional interventions. I think this is particularly true for behavioral programs that are delivered in noninstitutional settings. At the same time, I am not at all sure that treatment (regardless of theoretical perspective) is morally, socially, or ethically preferable to punishment in every instance. I would argue (see Chapter 8) that one of the crucial tasks for correctional psychologists is to devote the fullest measure of their ability to rehabilitative programs while still recognizing that punishment is a legitimate response of society to illegal conduct.

I am not disappointed with the lack of closure experienced personally or projected to my audience, because I am convinced that this book represents a fair appraisal of the current achievements of behavioral corrections. I shall be much more disappointed if this book fails to stimulate some of the theoretical and practical advances that would enable a more consistently positive appraisal in the future.

There are several people who helped me in writing this book, and I take this opportunity to thank them for making it a better product than it would have been without them. First, to Steven Kaiser, friend and student, who performed every task, from the most mundane to the most demanding, with absolute quality and an unyielding enthusiasm, my thanks for being the type of student who can make teaching a fine privilege. Also, I would like to pay special tribute to my colleague, Juris Berzins, for his careful reading of the manuscript, his steady and true editorial hand, and most important, the warmth of his friendship. Finally, my appreciation to Arnold Goldstein for his guidance and support on this project.

I am grateful to Sheri Graham, Ruth McKee, and Priscilla Confer for using all their patience and skill in transforming some truly rough drafts into the manuscript's final form and to Sylvia Halpern at Pergamon Press for her excellent editing. Lastly, I wish to thank my wife Deedra for her professional guidance regarding the sometimes bewildering workings of the criminal justice system, and for her personal understanding and devotion throughout this project.

Chapter 1
Behavioral Community Psychology and Problems of Adult Crime

Nothing can you steal,
But thieves do lose it.

—Shakespeare

Psychologists have long been active in applying their science to the resolution of social problems. Among such problems, few have sustained more of a consistent professional interest than crime and delinquency. As early as the first part of this century, with Hugo Munsterberg, often considered the founder of applied psychology, psychologists have striven to establish a practical interface between their profession and the law as well as a more specific expertise on the nature, cause, and correction of criminal behavior (Munsterberg, 1908). Other proposals for collaboration between psychology and law have occurred repeatedly since Munsterberg (e.g. Burtt, 1931; Marshall, 1966; Murchinson, 1926; Riesman, 1951; and Toch, 1961), although the most frequent and consistent interest has become obvious only since the late 1960s (Tapp, 1976).

The legal profession's perception of psychology's repeated excursions into matters pertaining to the criminal law has been mixed. Munsterberg (1908) himself lamented that of all professionals, attorneys seemed the most "obdurate" in seeing psychology as a source "of help and strength for them." For the most part, the legal profession has welcomed the contributions of psychology to an understanding of criminal conduct, particularly in instances of extreme deviance or seemingly inexplicable violence (see Bazelon, 1973 for a thoughtful and critical examination of psychologists' contributions to the criminal justice system).

1

The most prominent illustration of this collaborative relationship is the trial testimony by both psychiatrists and psychologists concerning criminal defendants who claim insanity as a defense to their alleged crimes.[1] Psychologists' interest in the criminal and civil justice systems is revealed by numerous other areas of activity, including the development of special courses (Monahan, 1974), training programs in forensic psychology (Gormally & Brodsky, 1973; Spielberger, Megargee, & Ingram, 1973), the application of psychological theory to jury selection (Rokeach & Vidmar, 1973), the understanding of jury behavior (Davis, Bray, & Holt, 1976), consultation to law enforcement agencies (Bard, 1969; Barocas, 1971), overall evaluations of the adversary system of justice (Thibaut & Walker, 1975), particular courtroom procedures (Bermant, Nemeth, & Vidmar, 1976), and the provision of psychological services in correctional facilities (Brodsky, 1973; Scharf, Kohlberg, & Hickey, 1976).

Taken together, these pursuits suggest that over the past decade forensic psychology has enjoyed a burst of professional interest which has given the field considerable visibility among both the public and other justice system personnel. At least three organizations now exist for psychologists with specific forensic interests; the American Psychology-Law Society, the International Academy of Forensic Psychology, and the American Association of Correctional Psychologists. The total number of psychologists actually employed in the criminal justice system is difficult to determine. Gormally and Brodsky's (1973) survey of male correctional facilities in 31 states revealed 221 fulltime and 40 parttime psychologists, yielding a ratio of one psychologist for every 400 inmates. The United States President's Commission on Law Enforcement and the Administration of Justice (1967) reported that 385 psychologists were employed in correctional facilities, a figure which was only about one-third of the recommended staffing level. No doubt the passage of time since these surveys, as well as the inclusion of psychologists employed in noncorrectional criminal justice system positions, would increase the present number of forensic psychologists considerably.

One particular development which has spurred the involvement of psychologists and other mental health professionals in the criminal justice system is the presumed relationship between crime and mental illness (Nietzel & Moss, 1972). If it is true that a substantial proportion of criminal activity is causally related to mental-emotional difficulties (Blinder, 1974), then, the reasoning follows, the ultimate rehabilitation of such criminals should reside with the psychologists and the psychiatrists who have the special expertise to identify and treat the underlying disorders.

This psychologizing of illegal behavior has at least two important sources. First, the role of the individual processed by the criminal justice system has much in common with the role of the individual traditionally serviced by the mental health system. Both systems label the person with whom they come into contact as deviant in some manner; both, then, assume the task of changing the individual so as to remove, or at least reduce, the deviance; and finally, due to the alleged dangerousness of the mentally disturbed or the criminal, both systems accommodate their interventions to the strictures and requirements of public protection. Second, it is often assumed that the offender's better interests will be served by replacing the methods of the penal institution with the programs of the psychiatric hospital. This preference for psychological interventions stems from the opinion that they are more effective and more humane than their correctional counterparts. This belief has prevailed in the face of both data and polemic (Foucault, 1965; Kittrie, 1971; Szasz, 1965, 1970) that suggest a consistent historical overemphasis of the therapeutic, benevolent characteristics of psychiatric treatment relative to its coercive and punitive elements.

One unfortunate counterpart of psychology's desire to demonstrate its relevance has been the willingness of its practitioners to assume an attitude of expertise concerning certain social problems which greatly exceed the empirical, theoretical, or experiential foundations on which a real expertise should be based. This professional "overreach" reveals itself in many current attempts to modify the behavior of criminals; but, like psychology's general interest in the criminal justice system, it is not a particularly modern phenomenon. For example, in *On the Witness Stand*, Munsterberg (1908) warned: "if experimental psychology is to enter its period of practical service, it cannot be a question of simply using the ready-made results which were not in view during the experiments. What is needed is to adjust research to the practical problems themselves and thus, for instance, when education is in question to start psychological experiments directly from educational problems. Applied psychology will then become an independent experimental science which stands related to the ordinary experimental psychology as engineering to physics" (pp. 8-9).

A similar sentiment was proposed years later by Kurt Lewin's succinct directive that nothing was so practical as good theory. Our need for good theory has not diminished. In fact, a dominant perspective of this book is that most behavioral interventions for problems of crime are plagued by the lack of a theory which is sufficiently appreciative of the multivariate determinants of criminal behavior. Although some successful interventions may occasionally be atheoretical, a functional science of psychological influence for criminal conduct will require the development of a coherent and unique theory of criminal behavior. At present, a completely adequate, behaviorally oriented theory of criminal conduct is not available. Rather, most behaviorists have appeared content to translate a social learning theory derived from the animal laboratory, human learning research, and clinical analogues into conceptions bearing only a superficial relevance to the complex phenomena of crime.

BEHAVIOR ANALYSIS AND COMMUNITY PSYCHOLOGY

For the past two decades, there have been two major paradigms for which many of psychology's interventions for social problems including crime have emerged.[2] The first of these paradigms is applied behavior analysis or, more broadly, social learning theory,[3] a movement which has enjoyed dramatic growth and considerable prominence among mental health professionals. The second paradigm is community psychology, a perspective with its most immediate origins in the professional and social discontent of the 1960s.

Applied Behavior Analysis

The general theory (Bandura, 1969; Rimm & Masters, 1974; Ullmann & Krasner, 1969, 1975) and application (Kazdin, 1975; Craighead, Kazdin & Mahoney, 1976; Rimm & Masters, 1974; Ullmann & Krasner, 1969, 1975) of behavioral principles are probably well known to the readers of this book, therefore will not be addressed here except to highlight the most distinctive qualities of this approach. First, from a theoretical perspective, behavioral interventions depend on an amalgam of several orientations, including operant and classical conditioning (Skinner, 1953; Wolpe, 1958), social learning theory (Bandura, 1969) and experimental social psychology (Goldstein, Heller & Sechrest, 1966), resulting in several major theoretical differences among those who would willingly share a behaviorist label.

Despite this conceptual diversity, behaviorists voice an almost unanimous commitment to experimentally derived data and the empirical confirmation of any technique's effectiveness. This experimental tradition has been a hallmark of both "basic" and "applied" behavioral research. Behavior is "understood" when it is demonstrated that particular procedures or processes are responsible ("functionally related") for specific behavioral changes. At an applied level, experimental methods are used to validate the impact of a given technique on a specified target behavior. Behavior modifiers have sought an integration of service and research (Winett, 1976) by including data collection as an integral part of their efforts at behavior change.

A third characteristic of behavior applications is the relative simplicity of their terminology and procedures. This quality has been championed as a major contributor to behavior modification's proliferation and popularity by enabling both non- and paraprofessionals to use behavioral techniques successfully (Tharp & Wetzel, 1969). Additionally, behavior modification appears to necessitate less of the cognitive insight or psychological mindedness upon which many other therapeutic approaches place a premium, thereby allowing its efficacious use with a broader range of clients than that usually achieved by other therapies (O'Leary & Wilson, 1975). Its emphasis on action, direct advice, and observable behavioral changes probably renders behavior modification a more acceptable intervention for clients whose economic constraints, verbal limitations, or cultural differences diminish the possible impact of the more "conventional" psychotherapies (Goldstein, 1973; Lorion, 1974).

A fourth feature of behavioral techniques is their relatively unique pattern of success with clinical problems otherwise known for their unmanageableness or refraction of treatment attempts. For example, problems associated with retardation (Gardner, 1971), chronic psychoses (Ullmann & Krasner, 1975; pp. 380-387), infantile autism (Lovaas, Koegel, Simmons, & Long, 1973; Margolies, 1977), psychosomatic illnesses (Shapiro & Schwartz, 1972), health jeopardizing habits such as smoking (Bernstein, 1969) or overeating (Leon, 1976), and seizure disorders (Efron, 1956; Ince, 1976) have all yielded somewhat to behavioral intervention.

The obvious popularity of behavior modification among American psychologists in particular should pose no surprise. In its broadest historical origins, behavior modification resides squarely within Western "mainstream" psychology. Its emphasis on experimental verification, its functional, utilitarian orientation, and its preference for behavior as the primary data for psychology are qualities which have helped distinguish American versions of psychology from their European predecessors and contemporaries (Boring, 1950). As we shall see throughout this book, these same qualities, in conjunction with fair amounts of political and philosophical compatibility, account for the generally favorable reception afforded behavior modifications by many correctional officials.

Community Psychology

Community psychology was a product of the mid-1960s representing a culmination of two sets of developments which had been unfolding for the previous 10 to 15 years. One set of developments was internal to the profession of psychology itself while the other entailed more extensive social-political changes. Among the within-profession stimulants the following issues were the most prominent: (a) a pervasive disenchantment with the theory and practice of a clinical psychology dominated by the intrapsychic emphasis of the medical model of psychopathology (Rappaport, 1977; Zax & Specter, 1974); (b) an accompanying skepticism about the positive effects of psychotherapy (Eysenck, 1952, 1966), as well as the reliability and validity of psychological diagnosis and evaluation (Rosenhan, 1973; Temerlin, 1973); (c) prophesies of impending manpower shortages given the prevalent one-(professional) to-one (client) style of delivering mental health services (Albee, 1959); and (d) dissatisfaction with the training models and role requirements for clinical psychologists (Iscoe, Bloom, & Spielberger, 1977; Korman, 1974; Peterson, 1968; Seidman & Rappaport, 1974).

Several influential forces external to the profession contributed to the origins of community psychology. First of all, the growth of social and political activism in this country during the 1960s was a force which dramatically affected almost all those who experienced it. Psychologists were no exception. Rappaport (1977) identifies the Civil Rights Movement, black separatist ideology, urban crises, Lyndon Johnson's War on Poverty, and the unrest and demonstrations of university students as particular, but related, events which produced a willingness, perhaps even an enthusiasm, for psychologists to expand their conceptions of what the helping profession should do.

A second external force was legislative. The passage of the Mental Health Study Act in 1955 established the Joint Commission on Mental Health and Illness. The final report from this commission in 1961 is often regarded as the direct impetus of the start of the community mental health and community psychology movements recommending as it did the construction of multiservice comprehensive care centers to serve the mental health needs of local communities. Subsequent legislation empowering the construction and staffing of these centers was passed in 1963 and 1965 (see Bloom, 1973).

A final influence occurred at the general governmental level. One emphasis shared by the Democratic administrations of both Kennedy and Johnson, was on social reform and domestic liberalism which contrasted with America's conservative, colonial stance in foreign affairs during the 1960s (Halberstam, 1969). A consequence of this emphasis was an escalation in the stature and employment of social scientists who were extended primary responsibilities in the formation and administration of the "Great Society" programs. In the midst of this programmatic professionalism, many psychologists were confronted with models of intervention that demonstrated more breadth and impact than they had previously encountered with strictly psychological approaches.

The field of community psychology has evolved enough of an identity, or self-consciousness, to struggle with its own definition. For example, in one of the first attempts at description, Bennett, Anderson, Cooper, Hassol, Klein, and Rosenblum (1966) proposed that: "community psychology. . . is devoted to the study of general psychology processes that link social systems with individual behavior in complex interaction. Conceptual and experimental clarification of such linkages were seen as providing the basis for action programs directed toward improving individual, group, and social system functioning'' (p. 7).

A more recent definition took the following form: ''Community psychology is regarded as an approach to human behavior problems that emphasizes contributions made to their development by environmental forces as well as the potential contributions to be made toward their alleviation by the use of such forces'' (Zax & Specter, 1974, p. 3).

Perhaps a more informative characterization of community psychology would be provided through an enumeration of the concepts or practices that community psychologists consensually regard as requisite for their field. Among these essential attributes, the following are most often emphasized: (1) the dominant conceptual perspective of community psychology has been the ecological viewpoint, ''. . . an orientation emphasizing *relationships* among persons and their social and physical environment. Conceptually the term implies that there are neither inadequate persons nor inadequate environments, but rather that the fit between persons and environments may be in relative accord or discord . . .'' (Rappaport, 1977, p. 2). This ecological perspective is the paradigm alternative to the medical model of clinical psychology and psychiatry which stresses intra-individual determinants and the sociological model which neglects the individual by its almost exclusive emphasis on social vectors. (2) Not surprisingly, the preferred interventions of community psychologists have taken one of two forms both of which are compatible with the ecological viewpoint. Cowen (1973) has labeled these two types of interventions ''person oriented'' (individual or small group treatments, crisis intervention, case consultation), and ''system oriented'' (the analysis and modification of social systems so as to maximize human adaptation).

Regardless of their target, the interventions of community psychologists often have a special style. Most community psychologists eschew the one-to-one service delivery which typifies clinical psychology and psychiatry, preferring instead opportunities to enlist the services of various kinds of assistants such as nonprofessionals, paraprofessionals, or indigenous helpers. For this reason, consultation, supervision, and education are frequent role requirements for the community psychologist. These activities are often pursued in a very activist manner with the community psychologist assuming the role of advocate and organizer for the population which he or she is serving. The combination of consultive relationships with a preference for activism is intended to produce social benefits beyond mere improvement in the immediate problem. Often, the objective is to amplify a community's internal resources for change or to enhance the strength of a community by creating effective alternatives to its existing social institutions. Sarason (1974) has referred to this emergent, shared sense of social competence as the ''psychological sense of community.''

Finally, an overarching goal for most community psychologists is *prevention* of social problems. *Primary prevention* involves the reduction and ultimate elimination of disorders by either altering the pathogenic parts of the environment or strengthening interpersonal-individual resources to the point where disorder does not occur. Examples of primary prevention include compensatory education (Cowen, 1969), job training projects (O'Conner & Rappaport, 1970), and family intervention and parent education (Bolman, 1968). *Secondary prevention* seeks a reduction in the prevalence of disability through the coordinated activities of early detection and rapid, effective intervention. Secondary prevention efforts have often been directed at young school children because of the demonstrated relationship between later adjustment problems and early school maladaptation. An example of this approach is the Primary Mental Health Project of Cowen and his colleagues at the University of Rochester (Cowen, Dorr, Izzo, Madonia, & Trost, 1971).

Behavioral Community Psychology

Although behavior modification and community psychology were initiated and developed independently of one another, they share numerous similarities. For example, both perspectives display a strong resolve for relevance to important social problems. Both emphasize applied research as a method which combines data generation with intervention. Both have regarded the "medical model" of deviance with substantial impatience or disdain. And both have espoused an environmentalist etiology of psychosocial problems to the virtual exclusion of intrapsychic, "internal" determinants.

Beyond these commonalities, a careful contrast of behavior modification with community psychology reveals a very important pattern of relative strengths and weaknesses. Almost without exception, the strengths of one paradigm can be viewed as the weaknesses of the other. Consider these comparisons. A continuing deficiency of the community psychology movement has been its inability to translate its rhetoric and activist attitude into original, programmatic techniques for producing measurable social change. Unfortunately, most community psychologists are unified, not by their shared creation of an effective technology for problem prevention or social change, but by their critical attitudes about the inadequacies of past approaches to these problems. On the other hand, behaviorists have developed a host of specific procedures (e.g., systematic desensitization, modeling, behavioral rehearsal, aversive conditioning, covert sensitization) capable of reliably influencing important human behaviors. A related difference involves the fact that while there is considerable uncertainty about the unique functions of the community psychologist (i. e., what is it that he or she does particularly well), behavior modifiers, or behavior therapists, are frequently identified as experts for helping people to reduce their anxiety, control their smoking, drinking, or overeating, and to become more socially assertive.

When evaluating behavior modification as it has been applied to social problems such as crime, one discovers a profile of limitations which mirrors many of community psychology's most vital components. At least four such constraints can be identified (see Nietzel, Winett, MacDonald, & Davidson, 1977, pp. 345-359).

First, behavior modifiers have exhibited neither a strong commitment to principled, provocative social activism as a style of intervention nor an interest in professional or paraprofessional consultation. Still, the social action dimensions of community psychology have been a very prominent feature of this movement, and one to which some of its most decisive effects have been attributed.

Second, behavioral theories remain rather provincial and austere by minimizing such major psychological traditions as social psychology, individual differences, organic-physiological bases of behavior, cognition, and perception. The tendency for behaviorists to focus on individual variables, such as behavioral deficits, reinforcement contingencies, and learning histories, has obstructed the development of more ambitious, multidisciplinary theories of community problems. However, a primary characteristic of the ecological paradigm for community psychology is its deliberate attention to the functional relationships between social-environmental systems and the official creation of problems, deviance, and victims within certain populations.

Most examples of applied behavioral analysis have not displayed much affinity for preventive interventions. ''Too often they have appeared content to discourage individuals from continuing their littering, drinking, stealing or bizarre behavior. As a result behavioral interventions have been tertiary and sporadic, with neither the etiological understanding nor breadth of focus necessary for primary prevention'' (Nietzel, et al., 1977, page 347). As already mentioned, a cardinal element of the community psychology movement has been its search for interventions that seek to prevent (either primarily or secondarily), rather than to ameliorate improper human behavior such as crime (Cowen, 1973, 1977; Kessler & Albee, 1975). With this focus, community psychology has often been regarded as a type of ''mental health engineering.''

Finally, the usual delivery system for behaviorists has remained largely a hierarchical one in which services are delivered directly to consumers by the expert or professional. There have been some recent indications of a greater sensitivity to ''spreading'' an intervention's influence through the use of *in vivo* agents or nonprofessionals, but for the most part such efforts are rare. Community psychologists have usually aimed for a more lateralized type of

Table 1-1

A Comparison of the Behavioral and Community Psychology Paradigms: Similarities and Complementary Differences

Paradigm Characteristics	Behavioral Paradigm	Community Psychology Paradigm
Intervention Technology	1. Preference for direct-limited interventions which minimize verbal fluency as a prerequisite for success. 2. Development of several techniques for specific, predictable behavior	1. Preference for direct, time-limited interventions which minimize verbal fluency as a prerequisite for success. 2. Lack of consistently effective change technology
Role Recognition and Definition	1. Commitment to be relevant to social problems. 2. Clear role definition with specific recognition of professional expertise.	1. Commitment to be relevant to social problems 2. Uncertainties about the special competencies of a community psychologist.
Style of Intervention	1. Hesitancy to become involved in social activism. 2. Only occasional use of paraprofessionals and consultive relationships. 3. Not oriented toward primary prevention; occasional examples of secondary prevention.	1. Social activism often considered *sine qua non* of the movement. 2. Active attempt to disseminate impact through use of nonprofessionals, paraprofessionals and consultation. 3. Strong orientation toward both primary and secondary prevention.
Conceptual Components	1. Dissatisfaction with psychodynamic and medical models. 2. Emphasis on individual learning variables as most important etiological influences. 3. Infrequent interdisciplinary theorizing.	1. Dissatisfaction with psychodynamic and medical models. 2. Emphasis on ecological variables (the person in the environment) as most important influences in social problems. 3. Frequent use of political, sociological, and economic theories.
Research	1. Emphasis on applied, naturalistic research. 2. Research often seen as integral part of intervention.	1. Emphasis on applied naturalistic research. 2. Research often seen as integral part of intervention.

intervention with the identification of goals, selection of techniques, and actual implementation of the program all being responsibilities to be shared by the psychologists, the nonprofessional participants in the program, and the individuals within the target populations.

Given their aforementioned similarities, but more importantly the complementary quality of their differences (see Table 1-1), the synthesis of the behavioral paradigm with community psychology should not be unexpected. Stated more affirmatively, it is a merger that should be encouraged. The alliance of social learning techniques with the philosophy and style of community psychology has been proposed in a previous volume (Nietzel, et al., 1977) which surveyed the application of this "behavioral community psychology" (a term originally used by Briscoe, Hoffman, & Bailey, 1975) to problems in the schools, juvenile delinquency, crime, alcoholism, drug abuse, aging, social skills acquisition, environmental problems, unemployment and community mental health.

The advocation of a behavioral community psychology is founded on the belief that an integration of community psychology with the behavioral paradigm will be more productive than either model practiced in isolation from the other. Behaviorally oriented interventions have not addressed the social-environmental-political determinants of behavior that are not reduceable to a mere collection of reinforcement contingencies or to purely personal behavioral excesses and deficits. For this reason behavior modification persists as a technology whose application is largely restricted to either one-to-one treatment with moderately distressed individuals of average or better financial means, or programmatic efforts with more seriously/chronically disturbed individuals residing in closed institutional settings. Behavioral methods have infrequently aimed for a preventive impact with populations of people who may have only marginal social standing.

The other side of this issue would suggest that our prototypical community psychologist needs ". . . to develop, adapt, or embrace a technology that provides empirically based methods for promoting these system oriented changes. Currently the rhetoric of the community psychology camp has not been matched by validated, concrete demonstrations of effective changes" (Nietzel, et al., 1977). In short, the aspiration of behavioral community psychology is to wed the professional activism and perceptive social analyses of community psychology with the several techniques for human behavior change afforded by social learning theory.

The specific goal of this book is to review and to evaluate the application of social learning theory and techniques to criminal conduct. My orientation to this task is that this area is an excellent example of the overreach which I had earlier claimed sometimes plagues applied psychology, leading in this instance to behaviorally oriented psychologists' misperception that they possess a more complete understanding of crime's causes and solutions than is actually the case.

An effective behavioral community psychology of criminal conduct is more of a future idea than a present reality. It does not mean we won't encounter instances of important achievement in this area both conceptually and practically. There are several such examples of success which should stir our enthusiasm. For the most part, however, behavioral approaches to crime leave the unsatisfying, but unfortunately familiar, taste of old wine in a new bottle, because they have yet to incorporate either the stylistic or the theoretical ingredients of community psychology that could render them both more effective and more conceptually adequate.

This attempt to evaluate behaviorally based approaches to the problems of crime will rely on essentially the same standards against which behavioral applications to a greater diversity of social problems were analyzed previously by Nietzel, et al., (1977). The following criteria are considered to represent the major features of an effective community psychology intervention when pursued from a behavioral orientation: (a) the interventions seek a preventive (at least at the secondary level) impact; (b) the interventions are applied in the ecological settings where the problems exist, and where desired changes must be manifest; (c) the interventions are intended to produce institutional change rather than, or at least in addition to, personal adaptation; (d) the interventions are designed and delivered in ways which maximize the prospects for generalization of changes across time and settings; and (e) the interventions are enriched by an active consideration of legal, sociological, political, economic, and organizational variables.

In addition to a review of behavioral corrections, and an evaluation of this domain on the above criteria, an initial section of this book is devoted to some basic issues pertaining to the measurement and etiology of crime (Chapters 2 and 3). In Chapter 4, a more detailed attempt is made at integrating various social learning factors that have been offered as explanations for criminal behavior.

The specific content and emphasis of each chapter is summarized below.

Chapter 2 surveys the various indicators of the extent of crime. Four strategies for measuring the amount and impact of crime are reviewed: police (F.B.I.) statistics, victimization surveys, self-reports and unobtrusive measures. Each method is evaluated with respect to the particular types of distortion and measurement error that threaten its accuracy. A preference for one type of crime statistic depends on the uses to which it will be put. Generally, official police statistics will be the most helpful source of data for program-policy decisions. They may be less recommendable for purposes of theory construction and evaluation.

This chapter also includes a brief discussion of the economic cost of crime. Recent, comprehensive data on this topic are scarce; however, a brief inspection of cost estimates from the 1960s suggests the probable magnitude of expense associated with crime in this country.

There is a tremendous diversity of theoretical explanations for crime. Following a discussion of the historical antecedents of modern criminological theory, a review of sociological, biological, and psychological formulations of crime is presented in Chapter 3.

Sociological theories are divided into two categories: structural and subcultural. Examples of structural explanations include Cloward and Ohlin's (1960) differential opportunity theory, Albert Cohen's (1955) reactance theory, and the modern conflict theories of Austin Turk (1969) and Richard Quinney (1974). The subcultural variety of sociological theories stresses the importance of inherent subcultural differences in the development of crime, and is best exemplified by Walter Miller's theory of focal concerns.

A second type of theory is the biological, which regards biophysical factors as predisposing influences to crime. Biological theories of crime are divided into those which emphasize genetic inheritance, chromosomal abnormalities and constitutional determinants.

The final type of theory considered in this chapter is the psychological, which regards crime as the result of personality attributes possessed in some unique degree by the potential criminal. Among those psychological theories considered in this chapter are the psychoanalytic, Yochelson and Samenow's (1976) notion of criminal thinking patterns, and the concept of psychopathy.

Sociopsychological theories of crime are discussed in Chapter 4. All these positions share the basic tenet that crime, like other forms of behavior, is a learned phenomenon. Some sociopsychological theories emphasize that crime results from a failure to learn how *not* to offend. This "control" variety of explanation is represented by Walter Reckless's (1961) Containment theory and Hans Eysenck's (1964) theory of differential conditionability, as well as other conceptualizations of moral development.

The other major variety of sociopsychological theory concentrates on the direct acquisition of criminal behavior. Sutherland's (1947) theory of differential association is the best known example of this view. Operant conditioning, social learning theory, and social labeling are other forms of the "direct" sociopsychological position.

Feldman's (1977) recent attempt to integrate the psychology of individual differences, theories of moral development, the direct learning of offending behaviors and social labeling theory is proposed as a particularly comprehensive sociopsychological approach to the understanding of criminal behavior.

Chapter 5 reviews three types of behavior modification procedures conducted in penal institutions. First, a number of behavioral approaches to remedial education are surveyed. Second, the following six examples of prison token economies are discussed in considerable detail. The Walter Reed Project; the Cellblock Token Economy at the Draper Correctional Center;

START, Virginia's Contingency Management Program; the Patuxent Institution; and the Junction City Treatment Center. Finally, Chapter 5 examines several types of aversion therapies delivered in institutional settings.

Chapter 6 presents the results of attempts to treat adult "outpatient" offenders with a multitude of behavior therapy techniques. The bulk of these interventions have been applied to sexual offenses such as fetishes, voyeurism, exhibitionism, pedophilia, sexual assault, and rape. In addition to the literature on sex offenders, Chapter 6 also reviews nonresidential behavior treatments for theft, assault, drunkenness and drug abuse.

The clinical adequacy and methodological status of the nonresidential behavior therapy literature also are discussed in this chapter. The major clinical limitation of this work is its excessive reliance on aversion therapy as the primary treatment. A number of developments which could enable clinicians to offer more sophisticated interventions are discussed. From a methodological standpoint, there is a need to move beyond the current proliferation of case-study demonstrations. The most promising avenue of progress is likely to involve the use of single-subject designs, especially the multiple-baseline variety.

Behaviorally based interventions occurring in community correctional settings is the topic of Chapter 7. Following a brief discussion of the history of probation and parole, this chapter discusses the augmentation of these services with behavioral techniques. Particular emphasis is placed on contingency management as an adjunct to usual probation and parole programs. Other issues relevant to community corrections such as probation subsidy, residential community programs and the indeterminate sentence are also considered in this chapter.

Chapter 8 is concerned with the ecological settings in which correctional behavior modification approaches to criminal rehabilitation have usually been conducted. It concludes that behavioral approaches to criminal rehabilitation are characterized by "ecological conventionality" which refers to the fact that behavior modification is applied typically in institutional or in one-to-one therapy settings and lacks an intention to prevent illegal conduct. Three components of community-based corrections (deinstitutionalization, decriminalization, and diversion) are presented, and the degree to which behavioral interventions approximate these standards is discussed.

A final section of Chapter 8 argues that prisons cannot be institutions of both rehabilitation and punishment. The concept of punishment by incarceration is recognized as a necessary element of our current criminal justice system; however, its existence requires that psychologists develop alternative roles for themselves other than those imposed by institutional versions of corrections. Several such roles are proposed at the conclusion of the chapter.

On both conceptual and methodological grounds, behavioral approaches to criminal rehabilitation have yet to attain a full measure of sophistication. The first part of Chapter 9 presents six principles intended to increase the conceptual adequacy of correctional behavior modification. The areas where improvements are required are cognitive control, increased individualization of treatment; constructional (as opposed to pathological) orientation toward rehabilitation; programmed generalization and prevention, and system-level interventions. The last portion of this chapter suggests remedies for a number of specific methodological deficiencies revealed by much of the research presented in Chapters 5, 6 and 7.

The ethical and legal status of behavior modification as a treatment strategy for adult offenders are surveyed in Chapter 10. Case law relevent to the legality of correctional behavior modification is presented according to six types of legal challenges: the right to treatment, informed consent, due process protections, the right to physical and mental privacy and autonomy, prohibitions against cruel and unusual punishments, and an assortment of substantive, constitutional rights.

Ethical challenges to behavior modification with offender populations are also considered in this chapter. Ethical issues are addressed under the following five topics: ethical misconceptions, behavorists' implicit "image" of man, behavior control, aversion techniques, and the "prompting" of ethical decisions.

The final chapter reviews the book's numerous suggestions intended to bolster the efficacy of behaviorally oriented approaches to the correction of criminals. An overarching consideration of these recommendations is that the legal-ethical requirements that are emerging in this field are usually compatible with the needed conceptual-ecological innovations. For this reason, it is argued that simultaneous responsiveness to both sets of demands (legal-ethical, and conceptual-ecological) is not only possible, but is likely to yield new procedures with a greater capacity for influencing criminal conduct than has previously been the case.

NOTES

[1] Actually there are a number of insanity defenses or "tests" including the *McNaughten Rule* [10 Cl. and F. 200, 8 Eng. Rep. 718 (H. L. 1843)], *Durham v. U.S.* [214 F. 2d 862 (D. C. Cir. 1954)], *irresistible impulse* [*U.S. v. Pollard*, 171 F. Supp. 474 (E. D. Mich. 1959)], *diminished responsibility* [*People v. Goedecke*, 65 Cal. 2d 850, 423 P. 2d 777, 56 Cal. Rptr. 625 (1967)], and the American Law Institute's *Model Penal Code Test* [*U.S. v. Freeman*, 357 F. 2d 606, 622-625 (2d Cir. 1966)]. Since a comparison and evaluation of these various approaches are obviously beyond the purpose of this book, the reader who has further reason to examine this area should consult Arens (1974), Brooks (1974), Diamond (1961), Fingarette (1972), Goldstein (1967), Jacobs (1971), Jeffery (1967), or Livermore and Meehl (1967).

[2] The applications of psychotherapy, group therapy, crisis intervention techniques, and other types of clinical interventions are not considered here because they are usually aimed at the remediation of problems of an individual or small group of people rather than the type of aggregated, shared distress which can be viewed as a social problem.

[3] Throughout this chapter, the terms *social learning theory, behavior modification, behavior therapy,* and *applied behavior analysis* are used interchangeably despite the frequent distinctions which have allowed each term to evolve a unique meaning (see e.g. Franzini & Tilker, 1972; Lazarus, 1972, 1977; Locke, 1971; Rimm & Masters, 1974).

Chapter 2
The Measurement of Crime

Our most common techniques for measuring the various parameters of crime
are notorious for their inaccuracies and disagreements. Despite this deserved
reputation, statistical assessments do permit at least one unanimous verdict
about the frequency of crime: there is too much of it.

Beyond this less than startling revelation, there are several other agreed-
upon criminal statistics. For example, the frequency of reported crime has
increased dramatically since 1960. Over this same period, the economic cost
of crime has risen steadily. Third and fourth parameters of criminal behavior,
about which there is mostly agreement, are age, and sex. Generally, crime,
especially serious crime, is an activity performed by young males.

These types of agreements are far outnumbered by disagreements among
crime statistics, and the many attempts to explain the discrepant data. This
state of affairs moved one critic to complain, ''the United States has the worst
crime statistics of any major country in the Western world'' (Sellin, 1957).

In this chapter I wish to discuss the common procedures that have been used
to classify and to quantify crime in this country. Of course, the major issue has
been how much crime there is, and much of the controversy surrounding crime
statistics involves the adequacy of the methods for measuring crime frequency.
Additionally, questions such as: Is the crime rate increasing? and, What is the
economic cost of crime? are also examined in this chapter.

METHODS FOR MEASURING CRIME

There are four basic techniques for measuring amounts of crime: the Federal

Bureau of Investigation's Uniform Crime Reports (*UCR*), the United States Census Counts and other victimization surveys, observations and interviews, and unobtrusive measures. This section will review these methods by describing the historical development and current methodology of each. Special attention will be paid to identifying the limitations of the techniques, particularly their most common sources of measurement error.

Police Statistics

By far the oldest and best recognized crime figures are those collected by the F.B.I. and published in its *Uniform Crime Reports*. By an act of Congress, the F.B.I. began publishing the *UCR* in 1930 and, while the form of the reports has been modified since then, the general procedure for collecting crime data has remained largely unchanged. Data sources for the *UCR* are local police departments who record those violations of a state's criminal law which become officially known to them (violations of federal law are not included in the *UCR*). Cooperation by local police departments is entirely voluntary; the F.B.I. has no authority to compel their participation. By 1976 more than 12,000 law enforcement agencies had contributed data for these reports (Uniform Crime Reporting Handbook, 1976). These agencies represented about 95 percent of the nation's population.

The F.B.I. does provide some technical/instructional assistance in the form of its *Uniform Crime Reporting Handbook* on how to complete the reporting forms but the decisions which determine whether a criminal incident is reported remains a local police decision. After collecting the data on the incidence of certain crimes known to them, and having discounted all unfounded complaints, local police departments forward these figures to the F.B.I. which in turn classifies them according to certain categories and computes quarterly and yearly frequencies, both of which are then published.

The scheme by which crimes are classified has undergone some modification. Prior to 1958 the F.B.I. recorded crimes under two broad categories: Part I and Part II Crimes. Part I crimes were considered to be "major" or "serious," and included criminal homicide, forcible rape, robbery, aggravated assault, burglary, larceny-theft in excess of $50, and auto-theft. Part II crimes were lesser offenses and included other assaults, arson, forgery and counterfeiting, fraud, embezzlement, buying or receiving or possessing stolen property, vandalism, carrying or possessing weapons, prostitution and commercialized vice, sex offenses, narcotic drug laws, gambling, offenses against the family and children, driving under the influence, liquor laws, drunkenness, disorderly conduct, vagrancy, runaway, suspicion, curfew and loitering laws, and all other offenses. Arrest information is still reported for these Part II offenses.

Since 1958 the F.B.I. has concentrated on the Part I crimes which have come to be known as the "index crimes" so-called because they ". . .

establish an index to measure the trend and distribution of crime in the United States" (F.B.I., 1959; reported by Seidman & Couzens, 1974). The index crimes also are considered those to be reported most consistently to the police. Index crimes are further divided into the violent crimes, or crimes against persons (criminal homicide, forcible rape, robbery, aggravated assault) and the crimes against property (burglary, larceny-theft, and auto-theft). See Table 2-1 for definitions of the seven index crimes. It is well known that this index is seriously overweighted by crimes against property, which, in fact, account for 90 percent of all index crimes. In 1973, 89.9 percent; in 1974, 90.5 percent; in 1975, 90.9 percent; and in 1976, 91.3 percent of the total index crimes were property crimes.

Of course, index crimes themselves represent but a small portion of the total crime in this country. Only one-fifth of all nontraffic arrests are for index offenses and approximately one-half of all arrests are for the so-called crimes without victims (prostitution, gambling, and narcotics violations), and disturbances of the public peace (drunkenness, disorderly conduct). One of every three arrests is for simple public drunkenness (Morris & Hawkins, 1970; United States President's Commission, 1967; see also Chapter 8 of this volume for a discussion of victimless crime).

The UCR has been subjected to a multitude of criticisms, running the gamut from statistical unsophistication to politically motivated distortion. Whether the UCR is as misleading and inaccurate as the weight of these denunciations would suggest is doubtful. There is some evidence, to be presented later, which reveals the UCR to be a more adequate method of measurement than is typically assumed. Nonetheless, many negative evaluations of the method remain, and deserve our attention.

1. **Underestimation of Crime.** It is obvious that UCR statistics underestimate the actual amount of criminal activity because all criminal events are not observed and, of those observed, not all are reported to the police. Such underestimation is common to many measurement problems where the task is to choose some index that will accurately represent some universe of events whose dimensions are not completely known. In the case of the UCR the issue is not so much that the underestimation occurs but that it is so strikingly large.

Perhaps no more than 50 percent of all criminal acts are detected. Of these, approximately half (Kalish, 1974; Maltz, 1975) may be officially reported to the police. Even these figures may be too conservative. The detection rate has often been estimated to be as low as 10 percent with the percentage of crimes reported to the police placed at only four percent (e.g., Biderman, 1967). The underestimation would be even larger if the figures were based on arrests, or convictions, since there is a large decrement in the number of retained cases as one moves through the usual criminal justice sequence.

2. **Selective Underestimation.** The problem of underestimation is com-

Table 2-1 Definitions of F.B.I. Index Crimes*

Index Crimes	Definitions
Murder and nonnegligent manslaughter	Murder is defined as the willful killing of another. The classification of this offense, as well as other index crimes, is based solely on police investigation as opposed to the determination of a court or other judicial body.
Aggravated assault	The unlawful attack by one person upon another for the purpose of inflicting severe bodily injury, usually accompanied by the use of a weapon or other means likely to produce death or serious bodily harm. Attempts are included, since it is not necessary that an injury result when a weapon is used which could result in serious injury if the crime were successfully completed.
Forcible rape	The carnal knowledge of a female through the use of force or threat of force. Assaults to commit forcible rape are also included; statutory rape (without force) is not included.
Robbery	The stealing or taking of anything of value from the care, custody or control of a person in his presence, by force or the threat of force. Assault to commit robbery and attempt at robbery are also included.
Burglary	The unlawful entry of a structure to commit a felony or theft. The use of force to gain entry is not required to classify a crime as burglary.
Larceny-theft	The unlawful taking of property without the use of force, violence or fraud. Included are crimes such as shoplifting, pocket-picking and purse-snatching. Excluded are ''con'' games, forgery and the issuing of worthless checks.
Motor Vehicle Theft	The unlawful taking or stealing of a motor vehicle, including attempts. This definition excludes taking for temporary use by those persons having lawful access to the vehicle.

*Source: F.B.I. *Uniform Crime Reports*. U.S. Department of Justice, Washington, D.C., 1976.

pounded by the fact that it occurs selectively. Some types of crime are more seriously underreported or underrecorded than others. The reasons for this are rather straightforward. First, the context in which a criminal act happens will exert some influence on the probability of its being officially reported. There are many variables which discourage, or encourage, the reporting of certain crimes. For example, a theft or burglary is more likely to be reported if the stolen items are insured. On the other hand, assaults in which the victim and the perpetrator are related are probably less likely to be made known than incidents in which the participants were previously unacquainted. The extent of the victim-offender relationship is of extreme importance since the majority of crimes against persons occur in a context where offender and victim are either related or well acquainted (U.S. President's Commission, 1967).

A general social factor contributing to increased crime reporting is the rising expectation and demand by people, especially poor people and members of minority groups, that the police provide effective law enforcement and protection for them. One byproduct of the activism and the Civil Rights Movement of the 1960s appears to be a decreasing tolerance for violent, criminal behavior in those urban areas where violence had been an accepted, almost normal way of life.

The nature of the crime is also related to reporting practices. Murder and auto theft are reported quite faithfully and accurately. However, such "deviant acts" as window-peeping may involve a victim who not only fails to report the event but, to some degree, even encourages its repeated occurrences.

A second reason for selective underestimation is that police records are not merely impassive archives but are quite reactive measures for many purposes. The increasing professionalization of police departments, combined with the introduction of centralized complaint centers, or bureaus, has produced more effective reporting programs, thereby greatly increasing, not the frequency of crime, but the frequency of investigating and reporting it. One of the most notorious examples of internal, administrative changes in police reporting is that in the immediate year after New York City replaced its previous policy of precinct-by-precinct processing of complaints with a centralized reporting system, robberies increased 400 percent and burglaries rose 1300 percent (U.S. President's Commission, 1967). It would require an overwhelming demand on our imagination to attribute that magnitude of increase to the greater activity of New York City's robbers and burglers rather than to the modified reporting practices of its police.

The other obvious impetus for selective crime reporting is political or financial expedience. It is not at all uncommon to discover shifting criteria for the categorization of crime, depending on the manner in which a police chief or mayor or governor wishes to portray the incidence of local crime. If there is a desire to substantiate the effectiveness of anticrime legislation or police programs, crime may be underreported or reported under categories reflecting lesser severity than that represented by the actual event. An audit of one Philadelphia police district showed that the police had handled 5000 more complaints than they had reported (U.S. President's Commission, 1967). Increases in reported crime can also serve such purposes as documenting the need for additional police, federal assistance, weapons, etc. Seidman and Couzens (1974) have summarized the reactive nature of official police statistics as follows: the ". . . uses of crime statistics create pressures to have the statistics show certain things. Sometimes the pressure is to show that crime is being reduced. Sometimes the pressure is to increase the number of crimes. These pressures impinge upon the data generating system, the police department, and in some cases affect the statistics, entirely apart from the effects of the number of crimes which are actually committed'' (p. 484).

Contrary to the prevailing opinion, extralegal factors do not appear to exert a major biasing influence on what is officially recognized as a crime. Nettler's (1974) review of research on police-citizen interactions reveals that, even for nonserious crime, factors such as ethnicity (Goldman, 1963; McEachern & Bauzer, 1967), or social class (Black & Reiss, 1967) do not appear to produce prejudicial police actions. The most reliable, extralegal factor which may differentiate formal (arrests) versus informal (no arrests or reports) police action in the case of nonserious offenses is the common sense notion that being respectful toward a policeman may result in more lenient treatment (Piliavin & Briar, 1964).

3. Variable Reporting Policies. Much of the error variance in the *UCR* is due to the differing reporting procedures of participating departments, a deficiency recognized at the very beginning of the *UCR* system (Warner, 1931). The problem is still a serious one, as illustrated by Beattie's (1955) observation that records collected from thousands of individual police departments in "different criminal jurisdictions, each varying from the other in definitions of crime, in organization of law enforcement operations, and in methods of maintaining basic records, raises a real question as to how homogeneous and accurate the facts collected and published in this series may be" (reported by Wolfgang, 1963, p. 711). The F.B.I.'s publication of a *Uniform Crime Reporting Handbook* has been a deliberate attempt to remedy this problem by specifying criteria for classifying offenses, for "scoring" (counting) offenses after they have been classified, and for estimating the value of stolen property.

Despite this welcomed improvement, the technology of data collection remains problematical. Such a basic figure as the number of participating departments fluctuates from one year to the next. In 1957 approximately 7,000 police departments supplied data; by 1964 this number had increased to 8,000 (Mitford, 1974). In 1976 there were more than 12,000 participating agencies.

4. Inadequate or Misleading Presentation of Data. Probably the most severe indictments of the *UCR* have been reserved for the last stages of the reporting process, the format in which crime statistics are released to the public. These criticisms have focused on the following three deficiencies which are discussed more fully below:

- Confusion between absolute frequency of crime and rate of crime per population unit

- Inadequacies in the computation of a population base for determining the rate of crime
- Uncertain relationships between various data categories in addition to unclear relationships between data sources and published categories

Number of crimes versus rate of crime. Counting the number of crimes known to the police from year to year is an almost meaningless index of the "true" incidence of crime since such a number is completely confounded by population increases. It is necessary to compute a rate of crime which is based on the number of known offenses per population unit. In the case of the *UCR* the crime rate has been computed as the number of known offenses per 100,000 inhabitants.

Throughout the history of the *UCR*, the standard practice has been to report both number of offenses and crime rate per population base. Despite this dual reporting the F.B.I. has consistently paid more attention to the absolute frequencies. Without exception, the consequence of this emphasis has been to inflate artificially the reported volume of crime. (Harris, 1968).

A number of examples will illustrate the extent to which the emphasis on absolute frequencies can distort the actual rate of reported crime. In 1960, the *UCR* reported that there were 98 percent more serious crimes than in 1950. However, as Morris and Hawkins (1970) indicate when the crime *rates* per 100,000 inhabitants for those two years are compared, the 1960 rate is actually 22 percent greater than that for 1950. Even more startling is that the *rate* of willful homicide during the mid-1960s was actually about 30 percent less than that during the 1930s (U.S. President's Commission, 1967).[1]

Wolfgang (1963) has provided a more detailed example by comparing the percent change of index crimes according to total volume and according to crime rates. These data, comparing crimes for the years 1940 and 1950, are reproduced in Table 2-2. Column C of this table contains the percent change using the typical *UCR* method of computation by number of offenses while Column D contains percent change based on computations using crime rates. In every instance of comparison (Column E), percent change based on number of offenses exceeds that based on crime rate. Across the nine comparisons, the average amount of overestimation using number of offenses as the basis is 17.7 percent. The traditional *UCR* computation reveals an increase in the amount of crime for every category, while the rate-based computations indicate a rise in the amount of crime increases in only two of the nine categories (Column F).

The most objectional presentation of crime data in the *UCR* is the "crime clock" which the F.B.I. continues to publish despite statisticians' incisive objections to it. An example of the crime clock from the 1976 *UCR* is presented in Fig. 2-1. As can be seen, the essential ingredient is the pictorial representation of the number of minutes or seconds that elapse between every murder or rape or auto theft.

Table 2-2 Comparison of Percent Change of Crimes According to Total Volume and Crime Rates—1940 and 1950 for 353 Cities

Part I. Offenses	(A) Number of Crimes[1] 1940	(A) 1950	(B) Crime Rate per 100,000[2] 1940	(B) 1950	(C) Traditional UCR Expression of % Change of 1950 over 1940[3]	(D) % of Crime Rate Change of 1950 over 1940[4]	(E) Absolute % Diff. of Col. C minus Col. D	(F) Direction of UCR % Change
Murder and Nonnegligent Manslaughter	2,208	2,370	6.1	5.5	+7.3	-9.8	17.1	Incorrect
Negligent Manslaughter	1,469	1,544	4.0	3.6	+5.1	-10.0	15.1	Incorrect
Rape	3,207	4,994	8.8	11.6	+55.7	+32.0	23.7	Correct
Robbery	25,269	25,909	69.3	57.9	+2.5	-16.4	18.9	Incorrect
Aggravated Assault	20,312	32,350	55.7	75.7	+59.3	+35.9	23.4	Correct
Burglary	146,361	170,708	401.1	399.6	+10.4	-3.7	14.1	Incorrect
Larceny	391,812	425,325	1073.8	995.6	+8.5	-7.3	15.8	Incorrect
Auto Theft	71,350	73,521	195.5	172.1	+3.0	-12.0	15.0	Incorrect
Total	661,988	736,721	1814.0	1724.0	+11.3	-5.0	16.3	Incorrect

[1]Crude data are from 1956 UCR 80-81. The 1940 population for the 353 cities was 36,488,430; the 1950 population was 42,719,693. These are "offenses known to the police."

[2]Offenses divided by population multiplied by 100,000.

[3]The difference between the number of offenses in 1950 and 1940, divided by the number of offenses in 1940.

[4]The difference between the rate in 1950 and 1940 divided by the rate in 1940.

(Reprinted with permission from Marvin E. Wolfgang, "Uniform Crime Reports: A Critical Appraisal," *University of Pennsylvania Law Review* 1963 III, 708-38, © 1963.)

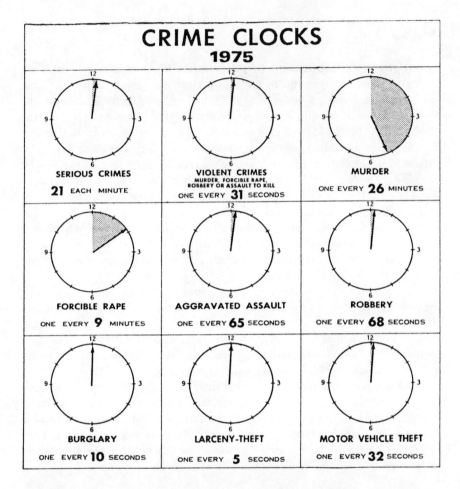

CRIME CLOCKS
1975

SERIOUS CRIMES
21 EACH MINUTE

VIOLENT CRIMES
MURDER, FORCIBLE RAPE,
ROBBERY OR ASSAULT TO KILL
ONE EVERY 31 SECONDS

MURDER
ONE EVERY 26 MINUTES

FORCIBLE RAPE
ONE EVERY 9 MINUTES

AGGRAVATED ASSAULT
ONE EVERY 65 SECONDS

ROBBERY
ONE EVERY 68 SECONDS

BURGLARY
ONE EVERY 10 SECONDS

LARCENY-THEFT
ONE EVERY 5 SECONDS

MOTOR VEHICLE THEFT
ONE EVERY 32 SECONDS

Fig. 2-1. 1975 Crime Clocks. The crime clock should be viewed with care. Being the most aggregate representation of UCR data, they are designed to convey the annual reported crime experience by showing the relative frequency of occurrence of the Index Offenses. This mode of display should not be taken to imply a regularity in the commission of the Part I Offenses; rather, it represents the annual ratio of crime to fixed time intervals. (From the FBI Uniform Crime Reports.)

There is little doubt that this type of data fulfills an obvious purpose, to convince citizens of the need for more law enforcement resources in order to protect them and their property. There should also be no doubt that the statistical basis for this device is absolutely unjustifiable. Consider these possibilities. The "crime clock" would advance if the population were increasing, but the rate of crime, actually, would remain stable. On the other hand, if the volume of crime remained stable, and the population were decreasing, the crime rate would increase, but the crime clock would reveal no change (Wolfgang, 1963).

Inadequate computation of population base. For many years, the *UCR* computed the crime rate by collecting each year's reported index crimes, then adjusting by using the official decennial census figure. Therefore, the 1940 census served as the base figure for each year's crime rate during the 1940s. The official 1950s census would be the base for each year during that decade. This procedure produced a curious, but logically quite expected, pattern in which the rate of crime would "increase" each year during a given decade only to "decline" during the census year in which the population figure was updated. Beginning in 1958 this problem was remedied by computing the crime rate on the basis of annual population estimates supplied by the Census Bureau. Certainly, this yearly updating is a considerable improvement over the previous practice. Nonetheless, the nature of the population base for computing crime rates remains quite crude and, in some cases, inappropriate (Hindelang, 1974).

It is important to compute rates using population bases that include those persons who are most likely to be "at risk" for committing a criminal offense. For example, it makes little sense to include females in the population base used to compute rape rates. A more accurate, meaningful rate of car theft would require an age-standardized population base. Retired persons infrequently steal automobiles; juveniles are far more likely to do so. Computation of more adequately standardized crime rates is complicated by at least one primary obstacle: standardization of population bases requires a knowledge of the dimensions, demographics, or environments differentiating vulnerable from nonvulnerable populations. In the cases of rape or auto theft, sex and age are obvious dimensions to consider; however, for other offenses (e.g., murder) refinement of crime rates is more problematic.

Unclear relationships between data categories. The form in which the data are presented in the *UCR* makes it virtually impossible to assess accurately the interrelationships of various figures. For example, one rule of classification is that in multiple-offense incidents (e.g., several crimes are committed by one individual or group of individuals) only one crime is counted. The rest are ignored. Determination of the crime to be counted is based on the index crime hierarchy, as follows: criminal homicide, forcible rape, robbery, aggravated assault, burglary, larceny-theft and motor vehicle theft. The F.B.I. rule is succinct: "locate the offense that is highest on the list and score that offense and ignore the other offenses involved in the incident" (*UCR handbook*, 1976; p. 36). This practice makes it very difficult to translate data on "offenses" into data on "offenders." Since the raw data for offense incidents are not made available, it is not possible to follow the classification of the event from one stage to the next (offenses known to the police, arrests, final disposition for offender on each possible charge). Of course, the *UCR* format also ignores such parameters as circumstances of the offense, the extent of harm or loss, and the nature of the victim-offender relationship. More extensive discussions of the validity of various inferences drawn from *UCR* statistics can be found in Robison (1966), Wolfgang (1963), and Zeisel (1973).

5. Classification by Seriousness. One of the most frequent objections to the *UCR* is that it deals inadequately with the varying seriousness of different crimes (Robison, 1966; Sellin & Wolfgang, 1969; Wolfgang, 1963). The index offenses are considered as the most serious crimes because they cause physical harm. However, crimes such as kidnapping, arson, and assault and battery also inflict physical harm and are excluded from the index. Similarly, the loss associated with "white-collar" or "business" crimes such as embezzlement, price-fixing, and loansharking probably exceeds the dollar value of property loss due to theft, but white-collar crimes are not included in the index. The most striking empirical demonstration of this problem was provided by Sellin and Wolfgang's (1964) development of an index of delinquency. The Sellin and Wolfgang index is an attempt to produce a severity weighting of criminal events. It differs from the *UCR* approach in several ways.

The data base for this index was a 10 percent sample (1,313 cases) of juvenile offenses in Philadelphia during the 1960s. Each event was analyzed in terms of every violation of law which occurred during it, rather than just the most serious one. Offensive incidents were classified into categories defined, not by the traditional legal labels, but by the bodily harm, theft of property, or damage to property which resulted from the occurrence. Each event was then scaled according to severity on various rating and magnitude scales completed by students, police officers and judges. These scaling results have been well replicated (Akman & Normandeau, 1968).

Comparisons of the Sellin and Wolfgang Index with the *UCR* classification system revealed the following contrasts: only 38 percent of the Philadelphia cases resulting in bodily injury would have been classified as an index crime in the *UCR*; further, 54 percent of the Philadelphia cases resulting in either bodily harm, loss of property or damage to property would not have been listed in the F.B.I. index of serious crimes.

In addition to the exclusion of many other crimes that produce substantial personal harm or property damage, the lack of any seriousness weighting among the index crimes makes the total amount of index crime a very misleading figure. To choose the most extreme contrasts: a $50 theft is treated equivalently to a murder in the first degree; a forcible rape is identical, statistically, to an instance of car theft. Because offenses against property show the greatest correlation with total index crime (Hindelang, 1974), it is not surprising that total index crime is more indicative of the rate of less serious offenses. The total sum of index crimes is misleading in one other important manner. Attempted acts of crime (e.g., attempted rape, attempted robbery) are considered the same as actual offenses and are included among the index crimes despite the fact that no bodily harm, property loss or property damage has resulted.

While the logic of using a seriousness-weighted index is appealing, Hindelang (1974) has demonstrated that available weighting schemes result in very similar rank orderings of the magnitude of crime problems as those obtained with the unweighted *UCR* index. Table 2-3 presents the intercorrelations of offense rates using the unweighted *UCR* index and five of the best recognized weighting strategies. With the exception of the President's Commission weightings, the unweighted *UCR* rates are almost interchangeable with the rates derived from the remaining weighting systems.

6. Atheoretical Quality of the UCR. Several reviewers of the *UCR* have objected to the fact that it was constructed independent of any underlying criminological theory. Wolfgang (1963) has offered a pointed critique of the *UCR'S* atheoretical quality: "designed without theory, without testing of hypotheses in a research project, without establishment of operational definitions for empirical analysis that inductively could lead to significant conclusions but, instead, based upon assumed administrative utility and presumed uniformity in collection of statistics, the classification (the *UCR*) lacks adequate criteria for understanding the volume and quality of criminal activity" (p. 724).

A further objection is that criminologists have exerted minimal influence on the conceptual improvement of these statistics, preferring instead to rely on,

Table 2-3 Intercorrelation of Indices Resulting from
the Use of Various Weighting Schemes 3,141 United States
Counties or County Equivalents, 1969

		1	2	3	4	5	6
Unweighted UCR rates	1	1.0000	.9883	.9995	.9816	.9960	.1731
McEachern-Bauzer weightings	2		1.0000	.9832	.9645	.9848	.1645
Robin weightings	3			1.0000	.9831	.9953	.1794
Sellin-Wolfgang weightings	4				1.0000	.9913	.2938
National median time served weightings	5					1.0000	.2110
President's commission disutility weightings	6						1.0000

(Reprinted with permission from Michael Hindelang, "The Uniform Crime Reports Revisited," *Journal of Criminal Justice*, 1974, 2, © 1974, Pergamon Press, Ltd.)

rather than to refine them. So basic an issue as the different definitions of certain crimes from one jurisdiction to another is obscured by the practice of classifying offenses according to their legal labels, rather than the common behavioral and situational elements of certain crime events. In addition, there is little or no appreciation for the shifting social sentiment about what activities should and should not be considered criminal. A sizeable reduction in the incidence of crime could be effected by the expedient method of decriminalizing the ''victimless'' offenses. While such redefinitions would not solve the social and individual problems that contribute to drug abuse or prostitution or compulsive gambling, they would allow some conceptual purification of what is ''criminal'' by restricting the purview of the criminal law to the activities that cause harm to persons or property.

Data from the UCR

Although F.B.I. crime statistics have been subjected to numerous theoretical and empirical criticisms, they remain the principal data by which the public monitors the amount of crime as well as any important crime trends. As Table 2-4 reveals, over the past decade and a half, a number of quite distinctive trends in the UCR index crimes have occurred. First, the total number of index offenses known to the police has increased a dramatic 234 percent, from 3,384,200 offenses in 1960 to 11,304,800 offenses in 1976. This increase has been more pronounced for violent crimes (murder, forcible rape, robbery, and aggravated assault) which have increased 242 percent compared to the crimes against property (burglary, larceny-theft, and motor vehicle theft) which have increased 233 percent over the same period.

As we have already learned, any increase in the frequency of crime is confounded by an increase in the population. Therefore, a rate-of-crime per population unit is a more meaningful indicator of ''actual'' increases in crime. Table 2-4 also shows the change in crime rate per 100,000 inhabitants from 1960 to 1976. Again, a large increase in crime is apparent although it is less imposing than that which results from using total number of offenses. Violent crimes still show the larger increase from 160.9 offenses per 100,000 persons in 1960 to 459.6 offenses per 100,000 persons in 1976. This is an increase of 186 percent compared to a 178 percent change in property crime rates from 1960 to 1976. For particular crimes, the largest 1960-1976 rate increases were for robbery, burglary, and forcible rape. Murder and nonnegligent manslaughter had the smallest percentage increases.

Figure 2-2 presents the year-to-year percent increases in the rate of index crimes for 1960 to 1976. This figure indicates that the largest increments in index crime rates occurred during the 1960s especially during the latter half. However, in the past few years, the index crime rate began to stabilize. In fact, the rates for some types of crime have already started dropping. For the past two years the reported number of murders and nonnegligent manslaughters has

Table 2-4 Index of Crime, United States, 1960-1976

				Number of Offenses*						
Year	Total Index Crime	Violent Crime	Property Crime	Murder and Manslaught.	Forcible Rape	Robbery	Aggravated Assault	Burglary	Larceny-Theft	Motor vehicle Theft
1960	3,384,200	288,460	3,095,700	9,110	17,190	107,840	154,320	912,100	1,855,400	328,200
1961	3,488,000	289,390	3,198,600	8,740	17,220	106,670	156,760	949,600	1,913,000	336,000
1962	3,752,200	301,510	3,450,700	8,530	17,550	110,860	164,570	994,300	2,089,600	366,800
1963	4,109,500	316,970	3,792,500	8,640	17,650	116,470	174,210	1,080,400	2,297,800	408,300
1964	4,564,600	364,220	4,200,400	9,360	21,420	130,390	203,050	1,213,200	2,514,400	472,800
1965	4,739,400	387,390	4,352,000	9,960	23,410	138,690	215,330	1,282,500	2,572,600	496,900
1966	5,223,500	430,180	4,793,300	11,040	25,820	157,990	235,330	1,410,100	2,822,000	561,200
1967	5,903,400	499,930	5,403,500	12,240	27,620	202,910	257,160	1,632,100	3,111,600	659,800
1968	6,720,200	595,010	6,125,200	13,800	31,670	262,840	286,700	1,858,900	3,482,700	783,600
1969	7,410,900	661,870	6,749,000	14,760	37,170	298,850	311,090	1,981,900	3,888,600	878,500
1970	8,098,000	738,820	7,359,200	16,000	37,990	349,860	334,970	2,205,000	4,225,800	928,400
1971	8,588,200	816,500	7,771,700	17,780	42,260	387,700	368,760	2,399,300	4,424,200	948,200
1972	8,248,800	834,900	7,413,900	18,670	46,850	376,200	393,200	2,375,500	4,151,200	887,200
1973	8,718,100	875,910	7,842,200	19,640	51,400	384,220	420,650	2,565,500	4,347,900	928,800
1974	10,253,400	974,720	9,278,700	20,710	55,400	442,200	456,210	3,039,200	5,262,500	977,100
1975	11,256,600	1,026,280	10,230,300	20,510	56,090	464,970	484,710	3,252,100	5,977,700	1,000,500
1976	11,304,800	986,580	10,318,200	18,780	56,730	420,210	490,850	3,089,800	6,270,800	957,600

Table 2-4 (Cont.) Index of Crime, United States, 1960-1976

Number of Offenses*

Rate per 100,000 inhabitants*

Year	Total Index Crime	Violent Crime	Property Crime	Murder and Manslaught.	Forcible Rape	Robbery	Aggravated Assault	Burglary	Larceny-Theft	Motor vehicle Theft
1960	1,887.2	160.9	1,726.3	5.1	9.6	60.1	86.1	508.6	1,034.7	183.0
1961	1,906.1	158.1	1,747.9	4.8	9.4	58.3	85.7	518.9	1,045.4	183.6
1962	2,019.8	162.3	1,857.5	4.6	9.4	59.7	88.6	535.2	1,124.8	197.4
1963	2,180.3	168.2	2,012.1	4.6	9.4	61.8	92.4	576.4	1,219.1	216.6
1964	2,388.1	190.6	2,197.5	4.9	11.2	68.2	106.2	634.7	1,315.5	247.4
1965	2,449.0	200.2	2,248.8	5.1	12.1	71.7	111.3	662.7	1,329.3	256.8
1966	2,670.8	220.0	2,450.9	5.6	13.2	80.8	120.3	721.0	1,442.9	286.9
1967	2,989.7	253.2	2,736.5	6.2	14.0	102.8	130.2	826.6	1,575.8	334.1
1968	3,370.2	298.4	3,071.8	6.9	15.9	131.8	143.8	932.3	1,746.6	393.0
1969	3,680.0	328.7	3,351.3	7.3	18.5	148.4	154.5	984.1	1,930.9	436.2
1970	3,984.5	363.5	3,621.0	7.9	18.7	172.1	164.8	1,084.9	2,079.3	456.8
1971	4,164.7	396.0	3,768.8	8.6	20.5	188.0	178.8	1,163.5	2,145.5	459.8
1972	3,961.4	401.0	3,560.4	9.0	22.5	180.7	188.8	1,140.8	1,993.6	426.1
1973	4,154.4	417.4	3,737.0	9.4	24.5	183.1	200.5	1,222.5	2,071.9	442.6
1974	4,850.4	461.1	4,389.3	9.8	26.2	209.3	215.8	1,437.7	2,489.5	462.2
1975	5,281.7	481.5	4,800.2	9.6	26.3	218.2	227.4	1,525.9	2,804.8	469.4
1976	5,266.4	459.6	4,806.8	8.8	26.4	195.8	228.7	1,439.4	2,921.3	446.1

*Estimates for 1960-1975 are based on 1975 F.B.I. figures; 1976 figures are based on the 1976 *Uniform Crime Report*.

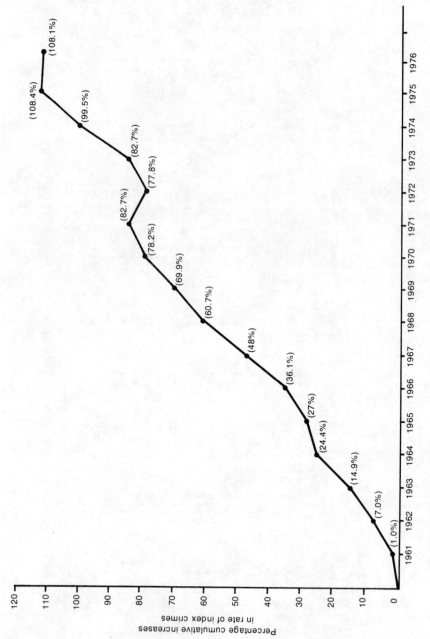

Fig. 2-2. Cumulative increases in rates of **FBI** index crimes from 1960 - 1976. (From Nietzel et al. (1977).)

32

decreased. In 1976, the rates of murder, robbery, burglary, and motor vehicle theft declined from their respective 1975 levels. In 1976 the rates of all violent index crimes decreased (4.5 percent) for the first time since 1960. Total index crime remained about even with the 1975 total.

Preliminary figures for 1977 reveal a continuation of this stabilizing trend. For the first quarter of 1977 the crime index was down 9 percent, and a *Wall Street Journal* survey of 20 major U.S. cities revealed that 17 continued to report a decline in serious crimes for the second quarter of 1977 (Schellhardt, 1977). There are a number of possible explanations for this improvement in the crime rate. The cold weather of that winter may have discóuraged some law breaking, although the decreases have extended into the warmer months of 1977. A second alternative would be that crime prevention programs have attained a degree of success in making crime more difficult to accomplish. Third, longer mandatory sentences for habitual offenders may be producing their intended effect of keeping those criminals who commit the majority of serious crimes off the streets.

The most likely reason for the lowered crime rate may be what Schellhardt (1977) has called the "maturing of the U.S. population." This concept refers to the decreasing percentage of young people in this country, a decrease of great importance since it is young people who commit a disproportionately large number of serious crimes. Schellhardt (1977) quotes Harvard criminologist James Q. Wilson as saying, "the babies born in the baby boom of the early 50s are starting to age. Some of the young men who helped produce the crime wave of the 60s are getting too old for that nonsense."

The crime-reducing advantage of this demographic trend should continue for a number of years. By 1990, the number of Americans between 14 and 25 will be approximately 16 percent less than in 1975 (Schellhardt, 1977). This projection has given rise to the expectation that, unless there is some dramatic economic upheaval in the next decade, crime rates should continue slowly to decline.

Victimization Surveys

Next to the *UCR*, surveys that interrogate a sample of persons about their crime victimization experiences over a limited time period are the most frequently used source of crime statistics. Victim surveys are thought to circumvent some deficiencies of the *UCR*, the major one being the reluctance of victims to report criminal offenses to the police. The initial national victimization survey was conducted by the National Opinion Research Center (NORC) for the United States President's Commission on Law Enforcement, and the Administration of Justice (Ennis, 1967). Additional victim survey projects in Washington, D.C. (Biderman, 1967), and in selected areas of Chicago and Boston (Reiss, 1967), also were launched by the Commission. A second series of victimization surveys was initiated by the Law Enforcement Assistance

Administration (LEAA) in 1972. This series, known as the National Crime Survey (NCS), involved interviews of persons, in a sample of 60,000 homes across the United States, about the crime victimizations which they had personally experienced (see Maltz, 1975; Skogan, 1975 for extended discussions of these surveys, as well as comparisons of their results to that contained in the *UCR*).

The NORC study (Ennis, 1967) surveyed a sample of 10,000 households in the continental United States. An initial screening interview was conducted with an adult member of each household to determine if anyone in the house had been criminally victimized within the preceding 12 months. A more intensive interview was then conducted, with each victim identified during the screening interview. Each interrogation attempted to assess the general nature of the crime, where and how it took place, the extent of loss, damage or injury, whether the police were notified of the crime, reasons for not reporting the incident, a description of the offender, and the judicial outcome of the case.

Table 2-5 contrasts the 1965-1966 rates of index crimes as estimated by both the NORC survey and the *UCR*. Two facts should be emphasized. First, with the exception of auto theft, the rank order of frequency for index crimes is identical for both sources of data. This similarity is confirmed further by Table 2-6, which shows the percentage of total index crime represented by each of the seven component crimes as assessed by the NORC survey and the *UCR*. Second, the NORC data substantiate the belief that much more crime is committed than is reported to the police. The rates of homicide and auto theft are quite similar and represent the only exceptions to the conclusion that criminal incidents are very much underreported. Rape appeared to be four times more frequent than indicated by police records. Across the seven index offenses there would seem to be at least twice as many crimes as that reported to the police.

Biderman's (1967) victimization data for Washington, D.C. are presented in Table 2-7, which also contains the number of offenses actually known to the police. In this case, the underreporting is of a much larger magnitude than that reported by Ennis. For the 13 crime categories, one incident was reported for every 23 occurrences. The rate of underreporting varies by offense category, but the validity of these data is called into question by the unprecedented discrepancy of experienced versus reported homicides. The suggestion that there were 30 more homicides than the one officially reported to the police seems highly improbable, unless murderers in Washington, D.C. are unusually skillful in "covering up" their victim's corpses. Once again, as with the NORC survey, the rank order for index crimes is quite similar, whether one examines victim reports or police records. Furthermore, as Nettler (1974) has observed, "the social conditions associated with high rates of serious crimes known to the police are also, with some qualification, associated with high rates of reported victimization" (p. 72).

Table 2-5 Estimated Rates of Part I Crimes: 1965-66

Crime	NORC Sample Estimated Rate per 100,000 Population	Uniform Crime[1] Reports: 1965 Total per 100,000 Population	Uniform Crime[2] Reports: 1965 (Individual or Residential Rates) per 100,000 Population
Homicide	3.0	5.1	5.1
Forcible rape	42.5	11.6	11.6
Robbery	94.0	61.4	61.4
Aggravated assault	218.3	106.6	106.6
Burglary	949.1	605.3	296.6
Larceny ($50+)	606.5	393.3	267.4
Vehicle theft	206.2	251.0	226.0[3]
Total	2,119.6	1,434.3	974.7

N (32,966)

[1]*Crime in the United States, 1965 Uniform Crime Reports*, Table 1, p. 51.

[2]*Crime in the United States, 1965 Uniform Crime Reports*, Table 14, p. 105, shows for burglary and larcenies the number of residential and individual crimes. The overall rate per 100,000 population is therefore reduced by the proportion of these crimes that occurred to individuals. Since all robberies to individuals were included in the NORC sample regardless of whether the victim was acting as an individual or as part of an organization, the total UCR figures were used as comparison.

[3]The reduction of the UCR auto theft rate by 10 per cent is based on the figures of the Automobile Manufacturers Association *(Automobile Facts & Figures, 1966)*, showing 10 percent of all cars owned by leasing-rental agencies, and private and governmental fleets. The Chicago Police Department's auto theft personnel confirmed that about 7-10 percent of stolen cars recovered were from fleet and rental sources and other nonindividually owned sources.

Evaluation of Victimization Surveys. As we have already seen, comparisons between *UCR* statistics and victim surveys are probably inevitable despite uncertainty about which source should serve as the criterion for accuracy. Because victim surveys yield a much greater number of reported incidents for most crimes, they are usually considered a more sensitive indicant of the total amount of crime. However, victim surveys are subject to several types of distortion and measurement error that should call their criterion status into question. Some of these limitations are discussed briefly below.

1. *Victim Unawareness.* With some types of crime, a person may not be aware that he or she has been victimized, and would be unable to report the

Table 2-6 Comparison of Victim Survey Estimates and
Uniform Crime Reports, Frequency Profile,
Part I Crimes, 1965-1966

Crime	NORC Sample Percent of All Part I Crimes Known	Percent of All Crimes Reported to Police	Uniform Crime Reports (1965)*
Homicide	0.1	0.2	0.5
Forcible rape	2.0	2.3	1.2
Robbery	4.4	4.6	6.3
Aggravated assault	10.3	10.4	10.9
Burglary	44.9	41.6	30.5
Larceny ($50+)	28.6	27.5	27.4
Vehicle theft	9.7	13.4	23.2
Total	100.0	100.0	100.0

(From P.H. Ennis, *Criminal Victimization in the United States (Field Survey II): A Report of a National Survey*, President's Commission on Law Enforcement and Administration of Justice, 1967.)

*Corrected for individual and residential and larcenies and car thefts.

critical incident. This type of error commonly occurs with certain kinds of business theft, white-collar crime, and even personal theft.

2. Sampling Error. An obvious consideration for victim surveys involves the adequacy of their sampling methods. Simply stated, the problem here is to insure that different crime victims have equivalent chances of being interviewed. But in many surveys this standard is not achieved because it is common practice to interview only one adult member of a household who is then requested to report both personal victimization as well as the victimization experiences of other household members. This procedure is problematic because of the well-known difference in recall for crime events: personal victimization is remembered more often than the victimization of even close acquaintances.

A second sampling deficiency involves the exclusion of certain types of individuals from the survey. For example, Skogan (1975) has argued that the systematic elimination of conventioneers, tourists, and commuters from central city samples underestimates certain crimes (e.g., auto theft, robbery, rape) for which these very people are at risk. Similarly, young males, a group who are disproportionately represented as victims of certain crimes, are likely to be underincluded in household samples.

Table 2-7 Offense Classes in Survey and Police Data

Class of offense	Incidents mentioned by survey respondents		Actual offenses known	
	N	%	N	%
Part I:				
Criminal homicide	31	*	1	*
Rape	46	*	4	1
Robbery	1,082	11	35	8
Aggravated assault	457	5	20	4
Burglary	2,174	22	110	25
Larceny	1,832	18	116	26
Auto Theft	1,381	14	21	5
Part II:				
Other assaults	675	7	30	7
Arson, vandalism	112	1	47	10
Fraud, forgery, embezzlement	143	1	8	2
Other sex offenses	48	*	12	3
Offense against family	3	*	—	—
All other offenses	2,009	20	39	9
Total	9,993	100	443	100

*Less than 1%
(From A.D. Biderman et al., *Report on a Pilot Study in the District of Columbia on Victimization and Attitudes Toward Law Enforcement*, Field Survey 1: President's Commission on Law Enforcement and Administration of Justice, 1967.)

3. Selective Underestimation. Victim surveys suffer one of the same limitations that has plagued the *UCR*: certain types of crimes are underreported by victims. There is differential recall for victimization according to the nature of the crime. Recall is very high for auto theft, it is relatively low for assault. The relationship between victim and offender may also affect recall of a criminal event. Respondents are relatively reluctant to report clashes or thefts incurred at the hands of relatives, or close acquaintances. It is interesting that these characteristics are the same ones which are thought to decrease citizen willingness to report certain criminal incidents to the police.

4. Inaccurate Reporting. The fact that victim surveys occur in an interpersonal context (interview) introduces the possibility that respondents may distort their victimization reports in any number of ways. Victimization experiences may be either fabricated, or deliberately underreported for the purpose of creating a desired impression on the interviewer, such as the elicitation of sympathy, or the support of a fraudulent insurance claim. Unlike incidents reported to the police, there is no opportunity to establish independently the validity of victim reports through interviews with witnesses or official investigations.

In addition to motivated distortion, there may be a number of unintentional sources of reporting inaccuracies. Many criminal events have what Biderman (1967) has called "low salience" for the victim, resulting in very low recall rates. There are considerable data to show the recall rate is lower for crime incidents that are more distant in time (Biderman, 1967; Ennis, 1967). A third basis for inaccurate victim reports is the notion of "forward telescoping" which is the "tendency of respondents to recall events which occurred outside of the reference period of the survey and to claim that they occurred within the specified interval" (Skogan, 1975, p. 25).

Self-report Measures of Crime

A third method for assessing the extent of crime is to ask individuals to report on their own criminal conduct. This self-report methodology is quite similar to victim surveys except that participants are asked to report on the crimes they have committed rather than suffered. These measures usually take the form of anonymous, self-administered questionnaires (Dentler & Monroe, 1961; Voss, 1963) or individual interviews (Gold, 1966; Waldo & Chiricos, 1972) which often are then validated against official records (e.g., Erickson & Empey, 1963).

In most cases, the respondents are juveniles; however, college students (Waldo & Chiricos, 1972) and adults (Wallerstein & Wyle, 1947) have also been questioned about their illegal activities. Usually respondents are asked whether they have committed any of a number of criminal acts, how often they have committed the acts, whether they were detected or arrested or convicted for the offense, and under what circumstances the act was committed. Much care is taken to assure participants that their responses will be treated anonymously and confidentially in the hope that their answers will be honest.

Self-reports of criminality yield some consistent, if not monotonous results. Repeatedly, they confirm the almost universally accepted suspicion that crime is not restricted to officially designated criminals. Without exception, these studies indicate that the majority of any respondent sample have committed an act which, if detected, could have justified their arrests. Erickson and Empey (1963) reported that 92 percent of juvenile males with no court or police record had committed a theft while 32 percent admitted to at least one act of breaking and entering. Another very frequently cited study (Wallerstein & Wyle, 1947) surveyed 1,698 New Yorkers, 91 percent of whom admitted committing at least one criminal offense since the age of 16. If the reports were valid, 64 percent of the males and 29 percent of the females could have been convicted of a felony ranging from auto theft to robbery. Across eight general categories of crime self-admitted by juvenile males (e.g., traffic, property, alcohol and narcotics), Erickson and Empey (1963) found that more than 90 percent of the offenses went undetected. The empirical fact of an enormous amount of "hidden delinquency" or undetected crime[2] is often interpreted inaccurately. Because large proportions of juveniles admit to having committed a criminal act, it is not necessarily true that all juveniles are equally delinquent. It is important to distinguish between those who admit to isolated, usually minor, transgressions and those who repeatedly commit serious offenses against property or persons. There are data that clearly document that official delinquents (youths with at least one official court appearance) commit criminal offenses much more frequently than other juveniles. Further, a much larger proportion of official delinquents commit more serious offenses (e.g., grand theft or armed robbery) than the average juvenile (Erickson & Empey, 1963).

Gold's (1966) interview data for 522 male and female juveniles from Flint, Michigan support the notion that official delinquents are more likely to be repeat offenders. Table 2-8 shows that while only 16 percent of the total sample of boys reported being arrested for at least one offense, the most delinquent youths (more than eight offenses) were far more likely to be arrested than the least delinquent boys (not more than one offense).

Self-reports of criminality have often been used as crucial tests for certain theories of crime emphasizing sociological, or class variables as major behavioral determinants (see Chapter 3 for a review of such theories). These studies are conducted to determine if the actual frequency and/or severity of

Table 2-8 Frequency of Offending and Police Apprehension

Proportion of boys at different levels of delinquency
who report being caught by police at least once

Number of Index F* Offenses	N	% report being caught
0-1	52	2
2-4	87	10
5-7	62	12
8+	56	19
Total	257	16

*Index F refers only to offenses which would have warranted police action if the offenses had been detected.

(Reprinted, with permission of the National Council on Crime and Delinquency, from Martin Gold, Table 7 from "Undetected Delinquent Behavior," *Journal of Research in Crime and Delinquency*, January 1966, p. 39.)

delinquency (presumably measured by self-reports) is related inversely to social status, or whether only official delinquency (as judged from court or police records) is so related. The self-report methodology has not yet resolved the issue, for one regularly encounters a type of *instrument effect*: interviews usually reveal an inverse relationship between social status and confessed delinquency (Erickson & Empey, 1963) while self-administered checklists or questionnaires do not (Clark & Wenninger, 1962; Dentler & Monroe, 1961; Hirschi, 1969).

Evaluation of Self-report Methods. Self-report measures of criminality have not proven as useful a corrective of official statistics as their proponents have hoped. There are several reasons for this, the most obvious being that people are most likely to distort their reports of their own behavior when that behavior is incriminating, embarrassing, or socially condemned. Intuitively, it would seem that people are likely to suppress reports of illegal conduct, especially when that conduct involves very serious or violent crime. On the other hand, aggressive, illegal behavior is not necessarily contranormative among juveniles, especially males. For this reason, it may be socially desirable, at least from a limited peer perspective, to inflate the reported amount of one's criminal activity. Hirschi (1969) reported that 55 percent of the white boys and 24 percent of the black boys who said that they had been arrested did not, in fact, have any police record.

In general, the reliability (retest and internal consistency) of self-reports has been at least acceptable (see Nettler, 1974, pp. 87-88 for a selective summary of reliability estimates in this research). However, empirical attempts to establish the validity of self-reports have produced mixed results. Gold (1966) investigated the validity of self-reported criminality gathered in interviews with 125 juveniles about whose delinquent acts relatively reliable information had already been obtained from youthful informants. The interviewed youths were unaware of this information, which was accepted only if the informant had witnessed the activity in question or had heard it directly from the interviewed delinquent. Using this method, the author classified 72 percent of interviewees as "truth-tellers" and 17 percent as "concealers." The validity of reports was regarded as questionable for 11 percent of the youths.

Similarly impressive validity figures are reported by Voss (1963) who found that less than 5 percent of the known police apprehensions were denied by respondents on an anonymous questionnaire. Erickson and Empey (1963) reported no instance of denying offenses for which there was an official record.

On the other hand, substantial invalidity has been suggested by Hirschi's (1969) previously mentioned documentation of inflated crime reports (*denial* of known offenses occurred for many respondents also), and McCandless, Persons, and Roberts' (1972) discovery of a .12 rank-order correlation between admitted and committed crime in a sample of institutionalized juvenile males.

In addition to the questionable psychometric properties of these methods, self-report surveys are overweighted by minor, almost trivial crimes or activities which are not even proscribed by law. For example, Erickson and Empey (1963) included "skipping school," "smoking (habitually)," and "defying parents" among their list of violations. Nye and Short (1957) ask "have you ever had sex relations with a person of the opposite sex" as an item on their delinquency scale (one might argue that a negative response indicates as much delinquency proneness as an affirmative one).

The routine inclusion of these types of items detracts from the usefulness of the self-report methodology as a basis from which to evaluate the impact of law enforcement or correctional programs. The increasing sentiment that the criminal justice system should concern itself primarily with the more serious, predatory, or costly types of crime is difficult to reconcile with any major emphasis on a data system that taps an almost indiscriminate range of transgression.

Unobtrusive Measures

Since the publication of Webb, Campbell, Schwartz, and Sechrest's (1966) seminal volume on unobtrusive measures, researchers within several of the social sciences have sought to supplement their reactive questionnaires with nonreactive measures that "do not require the cooperation of a respondent and that do not themselves contaminate the response" (Webb, et al., 1966, p. 2). Most unobtrusive measures are characterized by considerable face validity (e.g., estimating children's activity level by measuring the rate at which they wear out their shoes) and the potential for acceptable test-retest reliability. Of course, they have limitations, not the least of which is a poor imagination on the part of a potential investigator. Perhaps more importantly, unobtrusive measures are only minimally controlled by an experimenter, therefore it is difficult for him or her to know the conditions under which they occurred, the purposes for which they were originally intended, and the selective survival, erosion, or accretion to which they might be subject. Unobtrusive measures appear less appropriate for certain types of phenomena than others. For example, in mental or physical health research, the most important source of information is, and probably should be, the patient; the direct consumer of service, the individual with the most immediate access to change in physical or in psychological functioning. Occasionally, unobtrusive measures have been used in mental health research (Palmer & McGuire, 1973), but they have yet to attain a status upon which a systematic program of mental health evaluation could be founded.

There are a few isolated examples of the unobtrusive measurement of crime. Perhaps the most obvious is the public's purchase of weapons, alarms, security systems, private guards, and big frightening animals in order to be better defended against criminal victimization. Nettler (1974) cites the following data as unobtrusive support for the notion that crime is increasing: "sales in the United States of protective devices for the home, principally electronic burglar alarms, increased over the past decade; and the number of American companies selling security services and equipment jumped from some 100 to 900 during the later 1960s" (p. 5). Another example of an unobtrusive indicant of crime might be the rate at which families move from certain high-crime areas.

Evaluation of Unobtrusive Measures. Of course, unobtrusive methods could never qualify as an acceptable, independent measure of crime. For some crimes (arson) it would be foolish to search for some indirect or uncontaminated measure when the direct, physical evidence of deliberate fire-setting can be established with little uncertainty.

The more fundamental objection to unobtrusive criminal statistics is that they are probably influenced, not so much by actual criminal events, but by crime as it is portrayed to the public in official crime statistics such as the *UCR*. Data, such as the number of burglar alarms purchased, are actually unobtrusive measures of the effectiveness with which official crime statistics convince the public that crime is increasing. It would be unjustified to view these data as very much other than an index of the successful manipulation of public opinion.

ECONOMIC IMPACT OF CRIME

Although there may be some lingering skepticism about the increasing volume of crime, there is no doubt that the financial costs associated with crime are enormous, and steadily increasing. A total cost is not easily determined, but even if it were, the figure would not be very meaningful (Morris & Hawkins, 1970). The major reason for collecting cost data is to enlighten policy makers, agency directors, and the public about "which crimes cause the greatest economic loss, which the least; on whom the cost of crime falls, and what the costs are to prevent or protect against it; whether a particular or general crime situation warrants further expenditures for control or prevention and, if so, what expenditures are likely to have the greatest impact" (U.S. President's Commission, 1967, p. 123). A total cost figure aggregated across different sources of loss and expenditure could not provide the necessary enlightenment. Rather, what is needed is a series of cost estimates for different types of crime, for the operation of different components of the criminal justice system, and for private expenditures relating to crime prevention or protection.

There are no current, comprehensive investigations of the economic costs of crime. The initial effort at measuring the national cost was undertaken by the Wickersham Commission (U.S. National Commission on Law Observance and Enforcement) in 1931. The most recent attempt was supported by the President's Commission on Law Enforcement and Administration of Justice (1967; see *"The Economic Impact of Crime," Task Force Report; Crime and Its Impact*) which estimated the costs for (a) four general categories of crime, (b) the administration of the criminal justice system, and (c) private costs associated with crime.

Figure 2-3 presents the estimated annual cost of different types of crime. A portrayal of crime in economic terms results in a distinctly different picture from one based on frequencies of offenses known to the police. Organized crime, a category not included among the index crimes, and one for which relatively few arrests occur, accounts for more than twice the criminal income of that achieved by all other criminal activities combined. Homicide, while the least frequent in occurrence, is the most costly of the index crimes. Property offenses not included among the index crimes (e.g., fraud, embezzlement, commercial theft) have much greater financial impact than the index property offenses.

In addition to personal losses from crime and revenue accruing to criminals from their illegal activities, the economic impact of crime must include the public's financing of criminal justice system functions on the local, state, and federal levels. In the mid-1960s, the cost of collective services from these agencies was estimated at more than $4 billion per year (U.S. President's Commission, 1967). Figure 2-4 contains a breakdown of public expenditures for the prevention and control of crime. As can be seen from this representation, the funding of local police agencies is the single most expensive function followed by state corrections, an area whose operating costs are increasing very rapidly.

Quite understandably, as crime has increased so have the institutions and the interventions intended to rehabilitate its perpetrators. Official figures for the mid-1960s placed the number of adults in our more than 4,000 jails and prisons, or on some type of supervised release, at over 1.3 million (Fox, 1977; U.S. President's Commission, 1967); 10 years later, the number has increased to an estimated 1.8 million offenders (Reid, 1976). About 2.5 million are processed through the correctional system in the course of a given year (U.S. President's Commission, 1967). The total budget for corrections is over $1 billion, most of which purchases purely custodial goods and services such as the guarding, feeding, and clothing of inmates (Morris & Hawkins, 1970). Torok (1971) estimated that the cost of maintaining one inmate in a state correctional institution was approximately $6,000 for a single year.

These estimates do not consider the thousands of offenders in hospitals, short-termed detention centers, clinics, and special treatment programs, nor do they include the expense of numerous examples of social legislation and programs, many of which are justified in part on the basis of their potential for crime prevention and control.

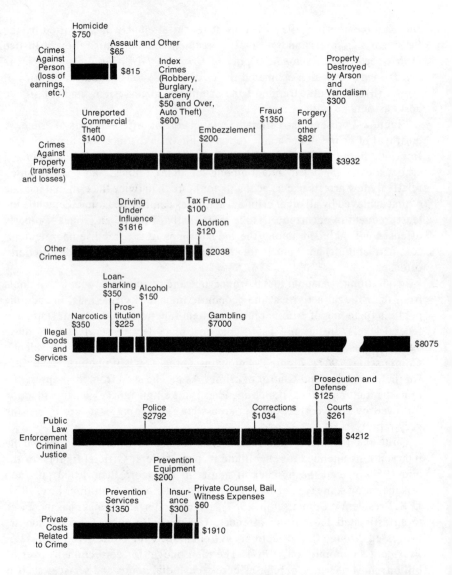

Fig. 2-3. Economic impact of crimes and related expenditures, estimated in millions of dollars. (Reprinted from *The Challenge of Crime in a Free Society*, published by Avon Books, New York, 1968. Reprinted by permission of Avon Books.)

The third category of crime-related costs involves the use of private or personal resources which the U.S. President's Commission (1967) estimated at more than $1.9 billion per year. Most of this money was used for the purchase of prevention services ($1.3 billion) in the form of security firms, bodyguards and private detectives. Approximately $200 million went toward

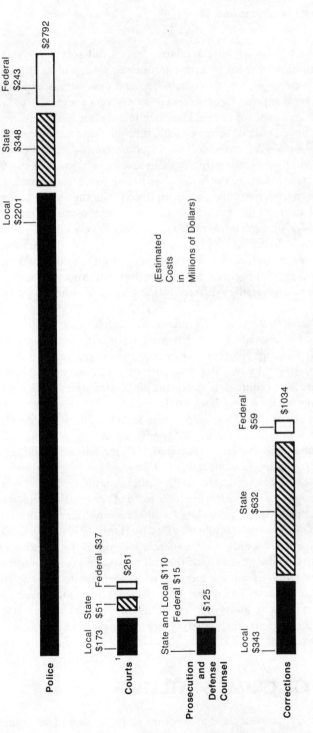

Fig. 2-4. Public expenditures for prevention and control of crime. Source: Bureau of the Census, Division of Governments (corrections and police); Bureau of the Budget (courts); Commission studies. All figures are for fiscal year ending June 30, 1965. (Reprinted from *The Challenge of Crime in a Free Society*, published by Avon Books, New York, 1968. Reprinted by permission of Avon Books.)

¹Total court costs are estimated at $782 million — $109 Federal, $155 State and $518 local; criminal court costs were estimated at one-third of the total based on studies in several jurisdictions.

Police

Local $2201   State $348   Federal $243 $2792

(Estimated Costs in Millions of Dollars)

Courts¹

Local $173   State $51   Federal $37 $261

Prosecution and Defense Counsel

State and Local $110   Federal $15 $125

Corrections

Local $343   State $632   Federal $59 $1034

protective equipment such as burglar alarms or special security systems. Another $300 million was spent on crime insurance, while $60 million was used to secure private legal counsel, obtain bail and pay witness expenses.

We can be certain that these figures represent only very rough approximations of the economic impact of crime. The direction of error is also apparent. Available figures underestimate crime's costs, if for no other reasons than the two most obvious ones—a greater volume of crime from year to year and steady economic inflation. Underestimates can also be attributed to the fact that economic figures seldom assess certain "radiating" effects of crime. For example, both the offender and the public are faced with the financial hardships of enforced unemployment and the resulting decrements in earnings following an offender's incarceration, or a victim's injury or death. Moreover, increasing amounts of financial support are being extended to the victims of crime. The recent development of victim compensation (Schafer, 1968) and restitution (Laster, 1970) programs has directed attention to the very real personal and economic adversities suffered by the victims of either property or violent crime.

It remains that, as with statistics on crime incidence, the most troublesome limitation of cost-of-crime data is that they are guided insufficiently by conceptual principles. Reusing our previous example involving shifting definitions of deviance, it is obvious that the cost of crime depends on what behaviors are regarded as criminal. If marijuana possession were legalized, the former cost of enforcing these drug laws would be eliminated. The problems of drug abuse would remain, and so would their social costs. It is doubtful, however, whether we could find a more expensive alternative for handling drug abuse problems than the cost associated with the current practices of arrest, prosecution, and imprisonment.

At a different level, cost-of-crime studies often confuse "cost" with a reduction in community welfare. However, the price of certain illegal goods or activities need not necessarily be equated with economic loss or financial waste. Consider the following example provided by Hann (1972): "the market value of goods stolen bears only a tenuous relationship to the reduction in potential community welfare because of theft. The accounting value of bets placed in illegal gambling is more a measure of the benefits to society from bookmaking than of the cost. Tax revenue lost is a measure of the loss to the government—not to the community. If the government would have spent it less productively than the bookmakers, society might even have benefited from the bookmaker's tax evasion" (p. 27).

SUMMARY OF CRIME STATISTICS

Among their several purposes and uses, crime statistics should serve three crucial functions. First, they should promote the construction and evaluation of theories about crime's origins and causes. This function usually takes the form of establishing certain correlates of crime (location, climate) or criminals (age, sex, social status) which are then assumed to reflect the processes by which differential rates of deviant behavior are produced. As we shall see in the next chapter, this use of crime statistics has been especially important for sociological theories of crime which have concentrated on explanations of *collective* behavior. To be sure, this use of criminal statistics is a hazardous venture. As this chapter has repeatedly indicated, all statistics on the incidence of crime, regardless of their source, bear an unknown relation to the "actual" amount of crime. Most scholars recognize this fundamental weakness of official criminal statistics which involves numerous sources of error that intrude between the actual occurrence and the recording of deviant behavior. However, despite this problem, they continue to use some type of official statistics to support or to reject the particular criminological theories in which they are invested.

At the present time, victim surveys have not attained the methodological sophistication nor the measurement accuracy that would justify their use as standards against which to measure the adequacy of police statistics. The more profitable approach would be to use both police records and survey data conjointly in the spirit of multimethod assessment. The specific advantage of employing multiple types of crime statistics is captured by Skogan's (1975) recommendations: "Comparisons of victim self-reports with police records allow us to pick optimal recall periods for accurate survey measures, and to estimate the magnitude of patterned nonrecall and its social origins. Comparisons of survey-generated and official crime rates will enable us to gauge the impact of bureaucratic processes upon the recording and releasing of crime data . . ." (p. 30).

A second use of criminal statistics, official or otherwise, is to evaluate the effectiveness of a vast number of criminal justice system programs or practices. Do certain kinds of police patrolling practices reduce incidents of street crime? What effect does special antinarcotic legislation have on drug related crime? Do alternative correctional programs differentially reduce recidivism? Is there a general deterrence value associated with mandatory prison sentences? Many of these uses of criminal statistics are illustrated in later chapters in this volume.

The unknown amount of error interposed between the commission of crimes and their official recordings is no less of a limitation for evaluation research than for theory construction. However, the use of cost-of-crime or incidence-of-crime data for justice system evaluation is plagued by an additional source of measurement error. The persons who collect the data are usually not unaware of the purposes for which the data will be used. As any budding researcher is well aware, the presence of a nonnaive investigator introduces the possibility of both fortuitous and intentional experimenter artifacts (Rosenthal & Rosnow, 1969) which may ensure obtaining one's most desired results.

Finally, crime statistics can be used to guide policymaking, the setting of priorities, and the rational allocation of limited resources within the separate components of the criminal justice system. Wilkins (1965) speaks of the utility value of crime statistics in terms of their informational power for directing social action. He advocates that crime statistics which have no utility (i.e., identical policy decisions are made with or without them) should no longer be collected.

The scope of this chapter does not permit the presentation of additional data that would examine the specific, empirical correlates of particular crimes. Because of limited space, I have concentrated on the most general types of crime statistics: incidence and cost of crime. Data relevant to more refined questions, such as who are the most likely victims of certain crimes, what environmental conditions are the most criminogenic, and what types of individuals are most likely to perpetuate certain crimes have not been included. There are, however, burgeoning literatures in each of these areas, evidence that criminologists and criminal justice system researchers are increasing both their interests and abilities in generating specific, socially useful crime statistics.

The reader interested in pursuing any of several subtopics in criminal statistics should consult the following references: (1) demographic characteristics of offenders (Reasons & Kuykendall, 1972; and the UCR); (b) socioeconomic status of offenders (Cohen, 1955; Miller, 1958; Reiss & Rhodes, 1961; Shaw & McKay, 1931; and Wolfgang, Figlio, & Sellin, 1972); (c) victimization patterns (Ennis, 1967; Glaser, 1970; and Schafer, 1968); and (d) environmental-ecological correlates of crime (Bloom, 1966; Clinard, 1960; and Harries, 1974).

NOTES

[1] In most categories of crime the actual rate of known index offenses during the 1960s is considerably higher than during the 1930s. This is especially true for property crime.

[2] Participant observation is an alternative method for assessing the magnitude of hidden delinquency. Miller's (1967) observation of theft, and theft-related acts among urban gangs is illustrative of this approach which, like self-report methodology, indicates that criminal activity occurs far more often than is reported. In part, the high rate of undetected crime is an artifact of this method. Groups are selected for observation because it is already known that they have high rates of criminal activity within them.

Chapter 3
Theories of Crime: Sociological, Biological, and Psychological

Poverty is the parent of revolution
and crime

—Aristotle

Opportunity makes a thief

—Francis Bacon

Theories of crime are nearly as old as the phenomena they try to explain. The first implicit theory of crime was probably hatched by the original crime victim who, discovering that his cave had been burglarized or his favorite club filched, grappled with the general question, ''Why?'' or struggled with the more personal, but equally vexing puzzle, ''Why me?''. More formal descriptions of crime had a religious tone, being primarily concerned with transgressions of God's rather than man's law. From this perspective, crime was either equivalent or due to sin.

During the 1700s and 1800s, naturalized accounts of man's relationships with his brethren concerned moral issues and were the turf of social philosophers and social critics such as Voltaire and Rousseau. Several social and legal concepts were emphasized by this group of thinkers, including the philosophy of free will, in which behavior was directed by rational choices, based on hedonistic decisions, and the social contract doctrine which advocated that individuals surrender some autonomy to the state so that liberties could be protected for the greatest number of people.

This movement has come to be known as the *classical school* of criminology, and its two major components were the Italian intellectual Cesare Beccaria and the British philosopher Jeremy Bentham. The classical school did not provide a theoretical explanation of crime beyond the moral judgment that criminals were individuals who, faced with the decision of doing right or wrong, freely opted to do wrong. The major intent of the classical school was reform. The targets of reform were the harsh and arbitrary administration of law in post-Renaissance Europe, the corruption and incompetence of legal officials and, most importantly, the apparent enthusiasm with which inventive forms of torture and capital punishment were administered for even trivial offenses. The core reformist principle of the classicists was the concept that the punishment should fit the crime. Punishment should be tailored to the offense it follows, but punishment should never be severe. The aim of punishment should be deterrence, which is best accomplished by making penalties certain and prompt. In this way rational man would be discouraged from committing acts that would result in his punishment. The current importance of the classical school is not to be found at the level of theoretical criminology but in the domain of correctional philosophy where Beccaria and Bentham's ideas still exert a notable influence.

Explicit theories of crime owe their origin to what is termed the *positivist school* of criminology.[1] The positivists substituted the concept of *determinism* for the classicist *free will* and therefore sought scientific explanations for why certain individuals behaved criminally. The positivists' determinism took many forms. Some emphasized social factors, others preferred physical, psychological, or environmental variables.

The first important positivists were three Italians: Cesare Lombroso, Enricho Ferri, and Raffaele Garofalo. Physical characteristics were most strongly emphasized by Lombroso, although Garofalo also suspected a congenital contribution to crime. Ferri stressed social determinism, while acknowledging the role of physical factors. All the positivists championed the empirical approach and saw themselves as scientists. By today's metrics, their science was crude: they included no control groups, they relied exclusively on small samples of institutionalized offenders, and they lacked adequate measuring instruments. Although the positivists produced further reform in prison methods (their advice was the punishment should fit the criminal, not the crime —an antecedent to today's notion of the indeterminate sentence), their major impact has been on theoretical criminology. Almost all contemporary theories of crime are derived from the spirit if not the concepts of the eighteenth century positivists.

There are many modern theories of criminal behavior. Virtually every field of scholarly inquiry, including biology, genetics, psychology, sociology, economics, anthropology, and religion, has generated at least one plausible theory of crime. The empirical status of these attempts to explain proscribed conduct varies as much as the types of concepts on which they rely. Most remain unconfirmed; many are unconfirmable. However, each theory of crime has attracted its own appreciative audience which continues to offer rational justification for the theory's validity or individual examples of criminal behavior that appear to confirm the theory's major propositions.

There is at least one simple reason why so many theories of crime enjoy professional or public favor. Most of them are true, albeit in some very circumscribed way. Each contains certain truisms, such as "people who disrespect the law are likely to break it." Each provides descriptions or justifications of crime that are likely to be confused with empirically verifiable explanations. Each possesses a range of convenient explanations whereby a particular category of offense (e.g., property crime) is more adequately explained by one kind of theory than any other kind. Each offers a view of crime that is well-tuned to a favorite political ideology. Conservatives may favor explanations which stress individual variables and the personal responsibility for offensive behavior. Liberals are likely to champion socially or culturally deterministic explanations that suggest the need for political or economic reform. Each suggests correctional remedies (punishment, redesign of society, rehabilitation) that are already favored for a host of other reasons.

Unfortunately, the principal implications suggested by these theories are often conflictual. The collective impact of our criminological doctrines on questions involving the prevention or control of crime has been negligible. The field of criminology still awaits a well articulated, empirically supported theory from which specific principles of realistic crime prevention or correction can be derived (Peterson & Thomas, 1973).

Theories of crime are classified under one of four general categories. First, there are *sociological* explanations; historically, probably the most common and popular form of criminology. Sociological theories assume many forms, as we shall soon see, although they all presume cultural conflict to be a root cause of crime. In general, they describe criminogenic conditions that exist in the social or cultural environment shared by certain populations. The sociological emphasis is on factors that are *external* to any particular individual, that are *prior* to any specific criminal act, and that are *emergent* from the social class, political, geographical, or environmental structures that affect large groups of people (Nettler, 1974). In most sociological theories, individual difference variables are relegated to a minor, if not trivial, status in favor of influences that are thought to homogenize a collection of individuals into a population at risk for crime. At-risk populations are produced when social-cultural conditions combine to lower some group's endorsement of legal norms and prohibitions.

Typically, sociological theories are subdivided into *subcultural* and *structural* explanations (Nettler, 1974; Reid, 1976). Most structural theories emphasize the basic equality of personal interests and abilities on the one hand, and the fundamental inequality of opportunities to actualize these talents in socially legitimate ways on the other.[2] This discrepancy between aspiration and the means of attainment is offered as a sufficient criminogenic condition. Structural theories usually search for the social structures or factors that most vigorously and reliably thwart legitimate attainment, thereby compelling people to rely on illegitimate (illegal) methods.

Subcultural theories assume more socially determined variations in people's attitudes, beliefs, and aspirations than do the structuralists. The subcultural perspective holds that the conflict of norms, which engenders criminal behavior, is due to the fact that various class or ethnic groupings of people adhere to cultural patterns of behavior which are inconsistent with the dominant injunctions against certain types of crime. These illegal patterns of behavior are supported by the particular subcultural norms that actually exert pressure toward deviation from the consensual norms underlying the criminal law.

A second type of theory is the *biological* or physiological variety. Like their sociological counterparts, biological explanations of crime have a long and popular history. Shakespeare betrayed a tendency for physiological explanation with his warning about the dangers of people with lean and hungry looks.

Lombroso, often considered the father of criminology, emphasized biological causes and correlates of crime, although not to the total disregard of environmental factors, as his critics unfairly claim. Lombroso believed criminals to be physically inferior to noncriminals, commenting on the similarity of criminals to savages, the insane, and epileptics, as well as various anatomical oddities of criminals such as big ears and small craniums.

Biological theories of crime can be divided into those which emphasize genetic inheritance, chromosomal abnormalities, physiological irregularities, and constitutional (body type) determinants. All these theories regard biophysical factors as predisposing influences to crime; however, they retain a healthy respect for the importance of environmental and sociological influences. In fact, most physically oriented explanations reveal a greater appreciation for sociological concepts than sociological theories show for potentially important biological factors.

Psychological explanations constitute a third type of criminological theory. These theories are unified by the basic belief that crime is the result of some personality attribute uniquely possessed, or possessed to a special degree, by the potential criminal. In some cases the causal attribute is an extreme one, as when crime is thought to be the result of mental illness or personality disorder. The work of William Healy, the famous founder of Chicago's Juvenile Psychopathic Institute, is an early illustration of the personality defect model (Healy & Bronner, 1936).

Psychoanalytic theory has been frequently employed to explain criminal behavior. There are many variations on the basic psychoanalytic theme that crime is the result of an immature personality, one in which ego and superego are insufficiently strong to control the aggressive, predatory instincts of the id. Psychoanalytic theories can be distinguished most reliably on the importance they extend to the social environment in patterning aggressive instincts into specific forms of criminal behavior.

A host of studies have sought to paint a psychological portrait of the "criminal type." Personality trait research has revealed a number of traits that have differentiated delinquents, including dependency and impulsivity

(Glueck & Glueck, 1959), conditionability and extroversion (Eysenck, 1964), psychopathy (Cleckley, 1964), and self-control (Megargee, 1966). Unfortunately, the methodology of most of this research does not allow adequate grounds for belief in cause-effect conclusions involving specific personality traits. A recurring problem is that delinquent vs. nondelinquent status is typically based on official police, court, or prison records, resulting in the confounding of delinquent status with other status indicators such as institutionalization, official labeling of behaviors, and social class. Further, the large number of personality traits on which officially designated criminals or delinquents and noncriminals or nondelinquents are contrasted are so numerous that statistically significant differences may arise on a chance basis alone.

One theory of recent vintage which pursues the elusive identification of the criminal personality is Yochelson and Samenow's (1976) description of characteristic criminal thinking patterns, and how these cognitions are translated into criminal acts. This is a theory that has elicited much controversy in modern criminology. It will be presented more fully later in this chapter.

Sociopsychological theories constitute the final type of criminological theory which we shall consider. Ultimately, all sociopsychological explanations are learning theories, and it is for this reason that social learning or behavioral theories of crime are classified under the sociopsychological rubric. There is, of course, considerable diversity among these theories. Differential mechanisms, and conditions of learning are proposed, personality characteristics are given differential weight, and the role of cognitive and mediating responses receives variable emphases. The most important distinction, however, involves *what* is learned. As we shall see in the next chapter some theories focus on the learning of a repertoire incompatible with criminal conduct. This is what Feldman (1977) has called "learning not to offend." Others focus on the learning of criminal behavior itself (in Feldman's terms, "learning to offend").

The emphasis of this book is on behavioral methods. For this reason our review of nonpsychological, nonbehavioral theories must be limited. This chapter and the next are not attempts at a comparative criminology. There are many sources which offer a comprehensive comparison of major theories of crime, and the reader with an interest in pursuing this area should consult Mannheim (1965), Nettler (1974), Reid (1976), Schafer (1969), Sutherland and Cressey (1974), Taylor, Walton, and Young (1973), and Vold (1958).

The present chapter discusses sociological, biological, and psychological theories of crime. I have selected several examples for each perspective. Those included do not begin to exhaust the set of such available theories, but they do illustrate the distinguishing features of each type of thought. Also, the selected theories are well known among professionals within the respective disciplines, and have provoked a large body of debate and empirical inquiry which, in some cases, has allowed the refinement or extention of the original theory.

In the next chapter, we will turn our attention to sociopsychological formulations of criminal behavior, and attempt to integrate the several positions which are committed to the principle that most forms of crime are learned behaviors. The major example of sociopsychological thought, differential association theory, will also be presented in the next chapter along with the various explanations of crime proposed by behaviorally oriented psychologists.

SOCIOLOGICAL THEORIES: STRUCTURAL TYPES

The Theory of Differential Opportunity

Differential Opportunity theory was proposed by Cloward and Ohlin (1960) in their book, *Delinquency and Opportunity*. This is one of the most prominent theories of crime, employing the concept of anomie as a principle construct, and attempting to integrate it with Sutherland's (1947) concept of differential association.

Emile Durkheim, the famous French sociologist, emphasized the fundamental social nature of man by stressing the functional necessity of moral bonds and restraint between men. Durkheim thought that life without moral obligations or social rules and requirements would become intolerable and result in *anomie*, a feeling of rulelessness, or normlessness, which may precede such destructive behaviors as suicide or crime. One of the many implications of anomie theory was that unlimited aspirations or conduct produces a pressure for deviation from important social norms.

Modern sociologists have given a somewhat more limited meaning to Durkheim's anomie, emphasizing the fact that society often presents conflicting demands in terms of its endorsed goals of conduct and the available means of achieving these goals. Merton (1957) relied on Durkheim's original use of anomie to explain deviant behavior. Merton restricts the use of the anomie concept to situations where the social structure stimulates certain common aspirations (e.g., wealth, property ownership) at the same time that it limits the means of acceptable attainment. In Merton's words (1957), "it is only when a system of cultural values extols, virtually above all else, certain common success-goals for the population at large while the social structure rigorously restricts or completely closes access to approved modes of reaching these goals for a considerable part of the same population, that deviant behavior ensues on a large scale" (p. 146).

There are numerous barriers to legitimate opportunities. This theory concentrates on the obstacles most often suffered by the lower class: cultural differences, economic adversities, and the limited availability of resources crucial for upward mobility. Special emphasis is placed on class differentials in the availability of educational opportunities. Educational achievement is the channel to most forms of legitimate social attainment. However, lower-class youth are unable to pursue the goal of advanced education because they are unable to afford it. Therefore educational "expectations are scaled down to accord with the realistic limitations on access to educational opportunities . . . these cultural orientations, once crystalized, persist as major obstacles to the utilization of opportunity" (Cloward & Ohlin, 1960, p. 103).

Cloward and Ohlin's differential opportunity theory, a direct derivative of anomie theory, is an attempt to explain youthful crime, especially as it occurs in a gang context. Criminal conduct is thought to emerge from the web of social and individual factors that limit a person's access to both legitimate and illegitimate roles. Employing Sutherland's notion of differential association, Cloward and Ohlin suggested that crime depends on differential access to legitimate and illegitimate opportunities for adjustment. When legitimate opportunities are blocked, available illegitimate means are cultivated and crime results. The core hypothesis is relatively straightforward: "the disparity between what lower-class youth are led to want and what is actually available to them is the source of the major problem of adjustment. Adolescents who form delinquent subcultures, we suggest, have internalized an emphasis upon conventional goals, and unable to revise their aspirations downward, they experience immense frustrations; the exploration of nonconformist alternatives may be the result" (Cloward & Ohlin, 1960, p. 86).

This perspective views most crime as functional or instrumental because it is aimed at achieving conventional goals. The distinctive feature of crime is not its ends, but its unconventional (illegal) means.

The topography of delinquency depends on the types of illegitimate norms, models, and activities to which the young person has the most access. Illegitimate resources are developed into characteristic law-violating ways of life by membership in one of three distinctive kinds of delinquent subcultures.

First, there is the *criminal subculture*, the pattern to which Cloward and Ohlin devote most of their attention. This subculture is committed primarily to crimes of acquisition, theft, extortion, and the illegal obtaining of money. It is "achievement oriented," and is transmitted through many readily available adult-criminal models to whom lower-class youth are exposed. These older criminals instruct their youthful pupils in both the techniques of crime as well as the attitudes and norms which support illegal behavior. The learning of unconventional norms that justify crime is similar to what Sykes and Matza (1957) have termed the "techniques of neutralization."[3]

Second, there is the *conflict subculture*, where a premium is placed on violence as a means of winning status. "The immediate aim in the world of fighting gangs is to acquire a reputation for toughness and destructive violence. . .it represents a way of securing access to the scarce resources for adolescent pleasure and opportunity in under-privileged areas" (Cloward & Ohlin, 1960, p. 24). Unlike the criminal tradition, conflict subcultures do not involve a strong identification with adult role models.

Finally, there is the *retreatist subculture*, a pattern which Cloward and

Ohlin equate with the drug culture. Members of retreatist groups are preoccupied with indulgent, expressive, offensive behaviors that may be deviant, but not necessarily criminal. Retreatists "perceive themselves as culturally and socially detached from the lifestyle and everyday preoccupations of members of the conventional world" (Cloward & Ohlin, 1960, p. 25). Retreatists also perceive themselves as persistently inadequate, having failed to achieve their goals through either legitimate or illegitimate means. They have experienced what Cloward and Ohlin term "double failure."

Although most crime is seen as functional in this theory, the inclusion of the conflict and retreatist subcultures allows for a more reactive type of crime. Some illegal conduct may be the means for delinquents to express their intense anger and frustration at the unfair constraints on their opportunities.

Evaluation of Differential Opportunity Theory. Differential opportunity theory has enjoyed much popularity, particularly among individuals who advocate the expansion of social service projects and government programs intended to increase the legitimate opportunities for potential or actual youthful offenders. Despite this popularity, the theory is an inadequate one for several reasons which are explored very briefly below.

1. Lack of empirical support for the theory's description of delinquents. The most fundamental objection to differential opportunity theory is that its descriptions of juvenile delinquents are inconsistent with the available research. The assumption of initial, individual similarities in educational attitudes and abilities between delinquents and nondelinquents flies in the face of much evidence to the contrary. Serious delinquents display many differences from other youths *in addition to* differential educational opportunities.

Both attitudinal and ability differences have been observed. Nettler (1974) summarized the relevant data in the following manner: "a multiplicity of studies tells us that juvenile offenders, and particularly the more serious offenders differ from their less delinquent counterparts in their greater resistance to schooling. They hate school work and they hate their teachers. They more frequently ditch school and destroy school buildings and equipment. They do poorly in academic work, are more frequently retarded in grade and score low on tests of mental performance. They are perceived by both their teachers and their classmates as troublemakers and they are, in general, disliked by both. This dislike is, of course, reciprocated" (p. 164).

A further difficulty is the theory's focus on crime as a phenomenon of the lower class. While the theory doesn't view crime as *uniquely* lower-class, it does imply that crime is concentrated in this particular economic stratum of society. Such a view ignores the several types of crime which are either rather egalitarian, with respect to social class indicators (e.g., murder), or are almost uniquely middle or upper class (e.g., embezzlement).

2. The lack of logical coherence. Even if the relationship between academic underachievement and criminal behavior was confirmed empirically, differential opportunity theory's focus on crime as a lower-class response to blocked academic accomplishment would be logically unsatisfying. There is no evidence that lower-class youth find their limited educational achievement to be more frustrating than do middle-class youngsters. On the contrary, one could expect the exact opposite to be true. Feldman (1977) has argued that "a criminal response to low achievement should surely be more likely by low achieving *middle-class* boys than by low achieving working-class boys—the former seem *a priori* both more likely to have acquired middle-class values and to be rejected for failure, both by parents and teachers" (p. 196). The theory may be correct about the wrong populations!

An additional, obvious objection to differential opportunity theory is that it begs the question of what causes certain youths to become gang-affiliated and, in turn, subservient to the injunctions of one of the three delinquent subcultures. This is not merely a rhetorical question, since it is well known that the majority of youths from any socioeconomic class do not become official or serious delinquents. At a more specific level, one is uncertain about what influences could account for the fact that only certain lower-class youths, who may also be educational underachievers, develop a criminal behavior pattern. This limitation is not specific to differential opportunity theory. It is shared by all sociological theories that emphasize culture conflict or the localized erosion of social controls to the exclusion of those individual difference factors which specify who will be most adversely affected by what type of social deregulation.

3. Inadequate operationalization of theoretical terms. Many commentators have criticized differential opportunity theory for the poor operationalization of its major theoretical concepts. "Aspiration," "frustration," "opportunity" are given vague definitions which frequently do not exceed their meanings as used in everyday language. While this may facilitate some types of communication, it hinders the extent to which the hypotheses of the theory can be confirmed or verified by empirical methods.

Nettler (1974) claims that the conceptual imprecision of this and other structural theories is due, in part, to the too ready acceptance of an individual's verbalizations as an adequate, univocal measure of key terms such as "aspiration" and "opportunity." The concepts of the theory require a multiple operationism in which at least one of the operations is procedurally independent of the individual's self-report, and also involves observations different from the outcomes which the concept is used to explain.

Cohen's Reactance Theory

Albert Cohen's (1955) *Delinquent Boys: The Culture of the Gang* proposes another structural hypothesis in which crime and delinquency are thought to be related to social class differences and their effects on social status. Cohen's theory has not been uniformly christened with a formal designation. I have used the title ''reactance theory'' because Cohen emphasizes the *reaction* of lower-class youth to the goals of the middle class which, being unattainable, are ultimately repudiated through the vehicle of destructive, vandalistic crime.

According to Cohen, lower-class youths are evaluated repeatedly by the ''middle class measuring rod.'' These evaluations occur in institutions in which the lower class must function (e.g., the schools). The schools, however, are operated by middle-class individuals who require the lower-class youth to accept their values and standards, and to attain the goals suggested by their orientation.

The lower-class juvenile lacks the necessary prior socialization experiences that would prepare him for successful middle-class achievement. Instead, he has been reared in an environment which values immediate gratification and physical aggression. While he has been trained by the media and his parents, who wish that his future achievements will exceed their present accomplishments, to endorse middle-class values, he is ill-equipped to translate these aspirations into effective actions. The lower-class youth is therefore deprived of a viable social status.

The frustration and lowered self-esteem caused by these failures stimulate the formation of a delinquent subculture in which the standards of the middle-class measuring rod are vigorously repudiated. Cohen explained the formation of delinquent subcultures using the psychoanalytic concept of *reaction formation*—the norms of the previously accepted middle-class orientation are rejected and defied by replacing them with their most recognizable and offensive opposites.

''The hallmark of the delinquent subculture is the explicit and wholesale repudiation of middle class standards and the adoption of their very antithesis'' (Cohen, 1955, p. 129). Reaction formation involves only an apparent rejection; the delinquent may still secretly desire what it is he openly repudiates. According to Cohen (1955), ''may we assume that when the delinquent seeks to obtain unequivocal status by repudiating, once and for all, the norms of the college-boy culture, these norms really undergo total extinction? Or do they, perhaps, linger on, underground, as it were, repressed, unacknowledged but an ever present threat to the adjustment which has been achieved at no small cost? There is much evidence from clinical psychology that moral norms, once effectively internalized, are not lightly thrust aside or extinguished'' (p. 132).

Within the delinquent subculture, a special kind of crime is developed by which the gang member can express his resentment and anger toward the denial of middle-class respectability. Cohen described six characteristics of delinquent-gang crime. The most emphasized quality is the *nonutility* of the activities which often involve crimes that are not goal-oriented. In Cohen's (1955) words, ''there is no accounting in rational and utilitarian terms for the effort expended and the danger run in stealing things which are often discarded, destroyed, or casually given away'' (p. 26). These crimes are also *negativistic* (''the delinquent's conduct is right, by the standards of his subculture, precisely because it is wrong by the norms of the larger culture,'' p. 28) and *malicious* (''enjoyment in the discomfiture of others, a delight in the defiance of taboos itself,'' p. 27).

Delinquent activities are motivated primarily by *short-run hedonism*, a characteristic often attributed to members of the lower class. This lack of planning may contribute to the *versatility* of delinquent crime (''stealing tends to go hand-in-hand with 'other property offenses,' 'malicious mischief,' 'vandalism,' 'trespass,' and 'truancy,''' p. 129). Finally, delinquent gangs are disciplined only by ''the informal processes within the group itself,'' an influence which Cohen identified as *group autonomy*.

Reactance theory agrees with differential opportunity theory in viewing social stratification, and the accompanying loss of status, for lower-class persons as frustrating and even criminogenic. However, the two theories diverge on the quality of crime which such sociocultural conflict produces. Reactance theory describes crime which is nonutilitarian, gratuitous, and expressive, rather than the rational, acquisitive, utilitarian, criminal responses described by the differential opportunity theorist.

Evaluation of Reactance Theory. Reactance theory is blessed by a degree of intuitive charm. At one level, it provides little more than a restatement of the obvious. One would be hard-pressed, for example, to disbelieve the assertion that people behave hostilely when frustrated by social limitations that they regard as unjustified or arbitrary. As with differential opportunity theory, however, there is insufficient empirical support for the propositions of reactance theory.

1. The unproven assumption that lower-class juveniles aspire to middle-class membership. The most glaring deficiency is the assumption that members of the lower class initially accept and adhere to middle-class values. This was one of the first criticisms leveled at Cohen's analysis. As an example Kitsuse and Dietrick (1959) argued ''Cohen's image of the working class . . . standing alone to face humiliation at the hands of middle class agents is difficult to comprehend'' (p. 211). Similarly, Cloward and Ohlin (1960) criticized Cohen's assumption that disenchanted lower-class youth internalize middle-class attitudes and then seek to affiliate with the ''carriers of middle-class values. We submit . . . that this may be true of *some* discontented lower-class youth but not all. It is our view that many discontented lower-class youth do not wish to adopt a middle class way of life or to disrupt their present associations and to negotiate passage in the middle class groups'' (p. 92). If social class influences are as powerful as sociologists argue, it would be more reasonable to suppose that socialization practices of the lower class would insulate its members against insidious indoctrination into middle-class preferences.

2. The inaccurate portrayal of the delinquent subculture as nonutilitarian and malicious. Kitsuse and Dietrick (1959) also pointed out that the descriptions of typical gang-affiliated crime were not entirely accurate. Most lower-class delinquency has an instrumental quality to it. By contrast, middle-class crime often involves random, expressive destruction and vandalism motivated by seemingly noninstrumental aims. This evaluation is reminiscent of the previous objection to Cloward and Ohlin's theory—the description may be partially right about the wrong group of people.

3. The limited variety of crime explained. This objection should be obvious. Even if empirically verified, Cohen's theory applies to a rather restricted range of illegal conduct: vandalism,. wanton destruction, and the resentful disruption of public order. Instrumental crime in which the offense is motivated by a rather obvious economical incentive lies outside the boundaries of this theory's explanatory convenience. Subsequent extension of the theory (Cohen & Short, 1958) has identified additional categories of subcultures that would include a broader range of criminal conduct. These subcultures are the *conflict oriented* (physical violence), the *drug addict* (obtaining and selling narcotics), and the *semi-professional theft* (economic theft).

Conflict Theories

The structural theories we have reviewed to this point are characterized by the *consensus* model of society which assumes that in every society there is "a basic consensus of values reflected in the totality of social demands" (Chambliss & Seidman, 1971, p. 18). This view is attributed to the original work of Talcott Parsons and the "structural-functionalist" school of American sociology whose principal assertions Chambliss and Seidman (1971) summarize as follows:

(1) Every society is a relatively persisting configuration of elements.

(2) Every society is a well-integrated configuration of elements.

(3) Every element in a society contributes to its functioning.

(4) Every society rests upon the consensus of its members.

The most radical alternative to the consensus model is the *conflict* model of society proposed by Ralf Dahrendorf (1959). Contrasted with the consensus model, the four principal assertions of the conflict model are:

(1) Every society is, at every moment, subject to change; social change is ubiquitous.

(2) Every society experiences, at every moment, social conflict; social conflict is ubiquitous.

(3) Every element in a society contributes to its change.

(4) Every society rests on constraint of some of its members by others (Chambliss & Seidman, 1971, p. 18).

George Vold (1958) was one of the first criminologists to view crime as a persistent product of social conflict, a reflection of the inevitable political and social inequality of stratified social systems. The two most important, contemporary examples of conflict theorists are the American criminologists Austin Turk and Richard Quinney whose views were developed during the 1960s, a period of American life where social conflict touched, and in some cases changed, many of this country's important institutions.

Austin Turk's major statement on the nature of crime is contained in his *Criminality and Legal Order* (1969), a work owing a considerable intellectual debt to Dahrendorf's *Class and Class Conflict in an Industrial Society* (1959). According to Dahrendorf, society was stratified, not on the basis of economic classes as Marx argued, but by the differential possession of *authority*. In this postcapitalist society there are two levels of position—*domination* or the possession of authority, and *subjection* or the deference to this authority. Turk's theory of crime focuses on the role-differentiation between authorities (those who dominate) and subjects (those who are dominated). In his words, "the study of criminality becomes the study of relations between the statuses and roles of legal *authorities*—creators, interpreters, and enforcers of right-wrong standards for individuals in the political collectivity—and those of *subjects*—acceptors or resistors but not makers of such law creating, interpreting and enforcing decisions" (Turk, 1969, p. 35).

A stable social order depends on the acceptance of authority-subject relationships which are governed by two types of norms: *norms of domination* and *norms of deference*. Violations of law are an indication that authority has failed: that the stable authority relationship between the dominators and the dominated has been disrupted. As it turns out, certain people (young, male, black) are more likely to resist submitting to authorities because they lack the "sophistication" or the realism to perceive the negative consequences of their nondeference. The status of criminal is assigned to these "norm resistors" who actually represent a failure of the authorities to enforce the norms of domination and deference.

Richard Quinney has authored several critiques of the legal order which rely primarily on the Marxist philosophy that crime is the product of economic class struggle. Actually, "crime" conceived of as individual acts of deviance is a fiction, an irrelevancy which prevents the criminologist from studying the crucial phenomenon: the oppressiveness of the criminal justice system and "crime as a product of the authority that defines behavior as criminal" (Quinney, 1974, p. 27).

In tune with the above formulation, Quinney's most recent statement is not so much a theory about the causes of criminal behavior as it is a critical analysis of the utilitarian quality of the criminal justice system in a capitalist society. In outline form this critique consists of the following six propositions:

(1) American society is based on an advanced capitalist economy.

(2) The state is organized to serve the interests of the dominant economic class, the capitalist ruling class.

(3) Criminal law is an instrument of the state and ruling class to maintain and perpetuate the existing social and economic order.

(4) Crime control in capitalist society is accomplished through a variety of institutions and agencies established and administered by governmental elite, representing ruling class interests, for the purpose of establishing domestic order.

(5) The contradictions of advanced capitalism—the disjunction between existence and essence—require that the subordinate classes remain oppressed by whatever means necessary, especially through the coercion and violence of the legal system.

(6) Only with the collapse of capitalist society, and the creation of a new society, based on socialist principles, will there be a solution to the crime problem (Quinney, 1974, p. 16).

This conception of crime bears a strong resemblance to the social labeling theory of deviance, which is a topic to be discussed in the next chapter. In fact, Quinney's conflict theory can be characterized, not too unfairly, as a highly politicized version of social labeling theory fueled by evidence that the criminal law is often enforced selectively (see Chapter 2), the author's own preference for a socialist society, and the usual Marxist rhetoric about the omnioppressiveness of Western capitalism. For example, in *Critique of Legal Order* (1974), Quinney devotes nine pages to brief, *selective* biographical sketches of the 19 members of the very influential President's Crime Commission in an effort to substantiate the "class bias" of the commission. There is a paradoxical similarity between Quinney's objection to the Commission's composition on grounds of occupation, class, and past government service, and former Vice-president Agnew's attempt to discredit an unsympathetic press on the basis of political party, education, and geographical origin.

Evaluation of Conflict Theories. The chief value of the conflict theories is that they provide an intellectual or philosophical corrective to the staunchly positivistic theorists that insist on the biological, psychological, or sociological pathology of the criminal as the efficient cause of his or her deviance. The conflict theorists offer a more pervasive, energetic criticism of Western society than the previous structural theorists (e.g., Cloward & Ohlin, 1960, or Cohen, 1955) who focused on certain criminogenic aspects of society without advocating the need for "socialist revolution" (Quinney, 1974).

A second advantage of the conflict theorists is that they bring a sense of history to the study of crime. Applauding this perspective, Taylor, Walton and Young (1973) concluded: "in particular, we can hope to see studies of law and crime which are informed, not by a static conception of pathological and/or anomic individuals colliding with the simple and taken-for-granted set of institutional orders, but rather by a conception of the complex interaction between developments in institutional and social structures and the consciousness of men living within such structures'' (pp. 266-267).

Evaluated on the basis of the formal requirements of good theorizing, conflict theories are found lacking. Quinney's ideas are less a theory of criminal behavior than a somewhat rhetorical indictment of economically stratified societies in general, and the inadequacies of the criminal justice system in particular. A glaring weakness of Quinney's formulation is that it is selectively immune to data which are inconsistent with Quinney's angst over the legal system. For example, how does one explain crime among the ruling class or economic elite, or, conversely, the lack of crime among many members of the ''ruled'' classes? While few would dispute the evidence that the criminal law is often enforced selectively, the progress in reforming the procedures in the criminal justice apparatus, especially so as to make them more fair to racial minorities and to the poor, seems equally indisputable. Over the past 20 years, the American criminal justice system has displayed a consistent self-correcting quality which has promoted the interests of criminal defendants, especially the indigent and the young. Possibly, Quinney would attempt to discount such reforms by arguing that they are trivial trappings intended to mollify the masses into accepting a legal system whose corruption can be ended only by social revolution. Of course, this type of response insures that the theory cannot be disconfirmed; there are no data, no changes in the criminal justice system that could contradict the belief that the criminal law is an instrument of class oppression.

The logic of Turk's position is also frequently dissatisfying. It is highly tautological to explain crime by ascribing it to violations of authority. This amounts to little more than explanation by redefinition.

Conflict theories stimulate our impatience because of their tendency to be more concerned with the reasons for making certain laws than the reasons for breaking them. We can agree that the status of deviance is socially created, and that such creations may occasionally serve vested power interests, without being misled that we have adequately explained the effective cause of the deviant behavior itself. (Additional evaluation of created deviance theory is provided in the next chapter's section on labeling theory.)

Rational Crime

One special form of structural theory involves what Nettler (1974) has termed ''rational crime.'' As this description implies, rational crime involves illegal behavior that ''makes sense'' because it is materially reinforcing, and can be committed with a relatively low risk of detection. It is crime encouraged by some nearly irresistible ''golden opportunity.''

Nettler discusses four contexts in which rational crime might occur. First, there are situations where objects or money are easy targets for theft. Shoplifting, thefts by employees, and embezzlement are examples of this type of offense. Second, there are circumstances associated with otherwise legitimate work that "demand" certain crimes. Price fixing, fraud, and business crime are the outstanding illustrations of this sort of illegality. Third, there is crime as a preferred livelihood. Included here are theft rings, all "organized crime," and computer crime. The final example of rational crime is crime organized into an "enterprise engaged in to fulfill the demands of the market" (Nettler, 1974, p. 187). These activities involve what is usually regarded as the major domain of organized crime: the illegal provision of liquor, drugs, prostitution, and gambling.

Evaluation of Rational Crime. Rational crime is very similar to other types of structural theories. It applies only to limited, albeit different, categories of offense. It also characterizes crime as functional and utilitarian. The major distinction is that, while most structuralists see crime as an understandable reaction to social disadvantage, the "rationalist" position views crime as an understandable reaction to the advantages of particular social arrangements.

SOCIOLOGICAL THEORIES: SUBCULTURAL TYPES

As the first two examples of this chapter illustrate, most structural theoris localize crime within the lower class and the culture conflict that attends structurally enforced class differences. To this extent, structural theories become incidental or second-order subcultural theories. The structural-subcultural theories differ from "pure" subcultural theories in that the latter emphasizes the *inherent* subcultural qualities which (1) typify the shared practices of a certain social group, and (2) maintain and even promote the acceptability of certain types of crime. On the other hand, the structural variety of subcultural theories emphasizes the *emergence* of lower-class support systems of crime as a reaction to the limited opportunities which the structure of society imposes on lower-class individuals. The structuralists assume that subcultures are formed because the aspirations "we" all share become thwarted by the structures of society. The subculturalists assume a different distribution of aspirations and preferences that directly places a member of a particular subculture in jeopardy of law violations.

Miller's Theory of Focal Concerns

The best known example of a "pure" subcultural theory is Walter Miller's (1958) theory of "focal concerns." Miller (1958) attributes the criminal activities of lower-class adolescent gangs to "the attempt to achieve ends, states, or conditions which are valued, and to avoid those that are disvalued within their most meaningful cultural milieu, through those culturally available avenues which appear as the most feasible means of obtaining those ends" (p. 17). While it may be true that achievement or success or accomplishment, defined by lower-class concerns, violates middle-class norms, such violation, for the sake of itself, is not the major ingredient of motivation (as Cohen suggested), but is merely the byproduct of a well-established adherence to the traditions of lower-class culture.

Lower-class culture[4] generates criminal activities because its own influential standards or "focal concerns" are automatically in violation of certain legal norms, which are derived, typically, from middle-class focal concerns. The six focal concerns that typify lower class culture are *trouble, toughness, smartness, excitement, fate,* and *autonomy.* Table 3-1 presents a schematic version of the focal concerns. Each is to be considered a dimension along which a great range of behavior may occur depending on *"which* of its aspects is oriented to, whether orientation is *overt* or *covert, positive* (conforming to or seeking the aspect), or *negative* (rejecting or seeking to avoid the aspect)" (Miller, 1958, p. 7).

For example, with the concern of *toughness* which Miller considers the dominant feature of lower-class culture, an individual may express an overt commitment to the law abiding alternative of column A while behaving according to the covert conviction that "getting into trouble" can achieve such desired ends as peer group prestige or a reputation for courage and risk. To a lesser extent, commitment to the column A alternatives (Table 3-1) for *toughness, smartness, excitement, fate,* and *autonomy* may demand responses that involve the commission of illegal acts.

Most lower-class crimes occur in "one sex peer units" (sociological jargon for "gangs") which Miller thought were the most stable social units in lower class communities. These gangs are organized around two additional "concerns"—*belonging* and *status. Belonging* is achieved by demonstrating a knowledge of, and a commitment to, the valued aspects of toughness, smartness, etc. *Status* is maintained in the same way—demonstrations that one possesses the crucial value of his culture. Once again it is a positive commitment to the immediate group's concerns of *belonging* and *status* that fuels the motivation for criminal behavior.

Other Subcultural Theories

There are, of course, several other relatively "pure" subcultural theories of crime, none of which represent enough of an extension of Miller's thesis to warrant very much of our attention in this chapter. Mays (1963) suggests that subcultures with high rates of offending socialize their individual members according to standards that are deviant from middle-class norms. Similarly, Banfield (1968) discusses a lower-class propensity to crime.

Table 3-1 Focal Concerns of Lower Class Culture

Area	Perceived Alternatives (state, quality, condition)	
1. Trouble:	law-abiding behavior	law-violating behavior
2. Toughness:	physical prowess, skill; "masculinity"; fearlessness, bravery, daring	weakness, ineptitude; effeminacy; timidity, cowardice, caution
3. Smartness:	ability to outsmart, dupe, "con"; gaining money by "wits"; shrewdness, adroitness in repartee	gullibility, "con-ability" gaining money by hard work; slowness, dull-wittedness, verbal maladroitness
4. Excitement:	thrill; risk, danger; change, activity	boredom; "deadness," safeness; sameness, passivity
5. Fate:	favored by fortune, being "lucky"	ill-omened, being "unlucky"
6. Autonomy:	freedom from external constraint; freedom from superordinate authority; independence	presence of external constraint; presence of strong authority; dependency, being "cared for"

(Reprinted with permission from Walter B. Miller, "Lower Class Culture as a Generating Milieu of Gang Delinquency," *Journal of Social Issues*, vol. 14, no. 3 (1958).)

Evaluation of Focal Concern Theory. Although Miller's theory is less conflict-oriented than the structural examples of sociological theories, it is subject to many of the same criticisms. By now the reader should be familiar with this litany of objections. Obviously, the theory applies to a restricted range of crime, a limitation which probably would not have dismayed Miller who acknowledged that his theory applied to only "one particular kind of delinquency." Nonetheless, the failure to explain how crime is acquired by individuals who are not socially disadvantaged is a rather unnecessary deficiency of Miller's theory.

As with other sociological theories, this one suffers from the vagueness of its key concepts. There is insufficient precision to allow empirical evaluation of such questions as: How do cultural standards originate? How are they transmitted from generation to generation or from adult to juvenile? And how do they control the behavior of any particular individual? These are questions which the social learning approaches to be examined in the subsequent chapter have attempted to answer more satisfactorily by proposing the learning mechanisms by which individuals, or collections of individuals, learn to offend.

The most troublesome concept is the theory's central one, *subculture*. Some critics deny essential differences in values or behavior between groups. Nettler (1974) cites Rossi's (1971) argument that "there is little firm evidence that there are many people, black or white, who are permanently hedonistically present-oriented." A related objection is that while there may be some important subcultural differences, these differences are temporally bound. Subcultures change. There is little reason to believe that the characteristics of the lower-class subculture of the 1950s have not been modified in some dramatic ways by the political, technological, and economic changes of the past 20 years.

BIOLOGICAL THEORIES OF CRIME

The belief that criminals are biologically or genetically inferior to the "general population" persists, despite the paucity of data that favors such a conclusion. The likely reasons for the lingering popularity of biological theories rests with two of their essential qualities. They are simple. And they justify a partitioning of the world into people who are obviously cut from the criminal cloth, and people who obviously are not. Almost all biological theories search for types of people who, because of certain genetic deficiencies, physiological excess, or constitutional deficits, are then uniquely disposed to criminal behavior. This disposition is translated into actual offensive behavior through the impact of a stressful environment. As we have already learned, the early positivists were advocates of biological theories, particularly Lombroso with his concept of atavism which held that the criminal was a biological anomaly, a congenital degenerate, a reversion to a primitive, savage type of man.

One of the most ambitious organic views of crime was developed by the famous Harvard anthropologist, Ernest A. Hooton in his remarkable volume *Crime and the Man* (1939). Hooton sought to discover the racial-anatomical distinctions between different types of criminals, and between criminals and "civilians" (his noncriminal controls). While some sociological and demographic contrasts were performed, the major intention of the work was to measure anthropometric variations in the criterion and contrast groups. The list of morphological features selected for measurement was quite astounding, and included beard thickness, lip seams, ear lobes, chin and shoulder shapes, physique, wrinkles, and even freckles. Measures were taken on more than 17,000 persons. The approximately 14,000 criminals were drawn entirely from prison and jail populations in ten geographically dispersed states. The more than 3,000 civilians, of whom more will be said later, came from numerous work and recreational settings in Tennessee, and in Massachusetts.

It should come as no surprise that Hooton reported a surfeit of physical differences between the groups of interest. A multitude of offender-group differences was discovered. For example, burglars were found to possess short heads, golden hair, and undershot jaws. Robbers, on the other hand, were conspicuous by their long wavy hair, high heads, short ears, and broad faces. Sex offenders were a particularly disgusting lot physically. They "include among the rapists no few of full-bodied and probably over-sexed ruffians, but also, and especially in the other sex category, a majority of shrivelled runts, perverted in body as in mind, and manifesting the drooling lasciviousness of senile decay" (Hooton, 1939, p. 374).

Comparisons of criminals with civilians led Hooton to his primary conclusion that crime was the product of an initially inferior creature made even more evil by the stress of its environment. "I think that inherently inferior organisms are, for the most part, those which succumb to the adversities or temptations of their social environment and fall into antisocial behavior, and that it is impossible to improve and correct environment to a point at which these flawed and degenerate human beings will be able to succeed in honest social competition. The bad organism sullies a good environment and transforms it into one which is evil" (Hooton, 1939, p. 388).

Hooton prescribed several remedies for the criminal type. The lesser impaired offenders should receive educational and vocational training and be returned to have another go at civilian life. More incorrigible delinquents should be permanently ensconced on enclosed and well-supervised reservations with "good natural resources" and the exclusion of "extraneous politicians, criminologists, and up-lifters" (Hooton, 1939, p. 392). Finally, bottom-of-the-barrel criminals ("hopeless constitutional inferiors") should be permanently incarcerated and never allowed to breed. This should be done humanely.

Hooton's "criminal anthropology" (Cohen, 1966) has not weathered well either the test of time or the patience of his more environmentalistic colleagues who have come to dominate American behavioral science. Certainly, the major objection has centered on the inadequacies of his sampling procedures, limitations of which Hooton was not entirely unaware. In a bit of an understatement, Hooton admitted that his research had not achieved a truly random sample. The following description of how the civilian control group was recruited confirms his judgment: "we set up an anthropometric booth at Revere Beach; we were unwelcome guests at the drill halls of the militia, we insinuated ourselves into the dispensories of public hospitals; we interrupted firemen at their games of checkers and students in their more or less intellectual pursuits; but still we did not secure really satisfactory civilian samples with which to compare our criminals" (Hooton, 1939, p. 108).

The weight of time and the disrepute into which Ernest Hooton's work has fallen have had one minor, but unfortunate, consequence. Students are exposed to the work only through secondary sources which generally have dismissed it as a fatality of some prescientific era. While this judgment misses the mark only a little, students who take the time to peruse this book may find themselves enriched by its engaging style and good humor, as well as an absolutely extraordinary set of drawings by the author intended to portray and to satirize the cultural-physical qualities of certain criminal types. One of these gems is reproduced in Fig. 3-1 for your enjoyment.

Fig. 3-1. A typology of crime according to Earnest Hooton. (From Earnest Albert Hooton, *Crime and the Man*, New York: Greenwood Press, 1968, p. 263. Copyright © 1939 by the President and Fellows of Harvard College; renewed 1967 by Mary C. Hooton.)

Constitutional Theories

Both a psychologist and a physician, William A. Sheldon was best known for his somatic typology which was composed of three dimensions of physique and their corresponding temperaments (Sheldon, 1942, 1949). Sheldon thought there were three somatotypes, or types of body builds: the *endomorph* who tended to be obese, soft and rounded, the *mesomorph* who was muscular, athletic and strong, and the *ectomorph* who was tall and thin but had a well developed brain. Each somatotype was associated with a particular dominant temperament. Endomorphs were funloving, sociable, and jolly. Ectomorphs were introverted, sensitive, and nervous. Mesomorphs were assertive, vigorous, and bold.

Based on his comparative analysis of 200 delinquents and 200 nondelinquents, Sheldon proposed that the mesomorphic somatotype was best suited for criminal behavior. He thought the mesomorph's aggressiveness along with a lack of inhibitory controls combined to produce a predatory person who was a prime candidate for criminality. Sheldon did not believe that a mesomorphic condition was a sufficient cause of crime; obviously, not all mesomorphs became criminals. He did not believe that environment was unimportant; however, he was convinced that physical variables were being unwisely neglected in most attempts to explain crime.

Evaluation of Sheldon. Today Sheldon's ideas are largely ignored or occasionally ridiculed. His sampling methods have been criticized. His definition of delinquency is too vague to be meaningful. Perhaps the most persistent objection is that Sheldon's theory was conceptually unsatisfying. His somatotypes are actually little more than stereotypes which enjoy a misleading face validity that is very resistant to disconfirmation.

The search for a constitutional predisposition to delinquency has persisted. In their classic study, *Unravelling Juvenile Delinquency* (1950), Eleanor and Sheldon Glueck compared 500 chronic delinquents with 500 nondelinquents. The two samples were matched on a host of demographic variables (Glueck & Glueck, 1950, 1956). The research involved several types of contrasts —sociocultural, psychological and physical. Using Sheldon's classification scheme, plus a fourth typology they called *balanced*, the Gluecks claimed that significantly more delinquents were predominantly mesomorphic than nondelinquents. However, a substantial percentage of delinquents were not mesomorphic. In their interpretation of these data, the Gluecks avoided the excesses indulged by the early somaticists. They eschewed a grand theory of biological determinism and suggested, instead, that constitutional factors may play some contributory role in concert with many other nonphysical factors. "It is quite apparent that physique alone does not adequately explain delinquent behavior, it is nonetheless clear that, in conjunction with other forces, it does bear a relationship to delinquency'' (Glueck & Glueck, 1956, p. 246). They were also careful not to restrict the predisposing influence of physique to only the mesomorphic condition: delinquency in other than mesomorphs may be a ''. . . reactive, or compensatory phenomena when (it) occur(s) in the naturally sensitive (ectomorphic) and obese (endormorphic) body types'' (Glueck & Glueck, 1956, p. 271).

The most recent attempt to include constitutional factors in conjunction with sociocultural variables is Juan Cortes' *Delinquency and Crime* (1972). Using his own method of somatotyping on a sample that included 100 delinquents, 100 nondelinquents, and 20 convicted felons, Cortes discovered significant relationships between delinquency, predominant mesomorphy and certain self-evaluated traits of personality, particularly need for achievement, risk-taking, and extraversion. Cortes was not convinced that a mesomorphic condition was a necessary or sufficient impetus to crime. He, like William Sheldon and the Gluecks, however, was persuaded that constitutional influences should not be overlooked nor prematurely relegated to the role of psuedo-science, as many modern social scientists seem to prefer.

Genetic Theories

Genetic explanations of behavior are nearly irresistible. All sorts of conditions, good and bad, have been attributed to a person's inheritable components. So it is with criminals who have often been thought to suffer an hereditary taint which either singly, or in collaboration with a pernicious environment, produces antisocial behavior.

The earliest methodology for studying genetic contributions to criminality was the genealogy or the study of family lines. This procedure is straightforward but can be painstaking and fraught with errors. Basically, what is required is the completing of a record that traces the ancestry of a certain individual or family, or alternatively charts the descent of various offspring from one common ancestor. The most famous ''pedigree analyses'' in criminology are Henry Goddard's study (1916) of the fictitiously named Kallilak family and Richard Dugdale's (1942) examinations of the Jukes. Both families were cursed by a large progeny of scoundrels, leading the investigators to suspect a not-so-negligible influence of heredity. This suspicion was particularly strong for Goddard who believed that mental defect or ''feeblemindedness'' could be inherited and associated perhaps 50 percent of the time with eventual criminality. Dugdale was less certain, and decided that both heredity and environment played very important roles in determining the character of an individual.

The genealogical method suffers from several limitations, not the least of which is the unreliability of birth and court records, as the investigator traces back his or her subjects in time. Of course, the major problem with the method is that it does not permit an unambiguous untangling of what it is exactly that the family transmits, genetic predisposition or psychosocial characteristics, or both.

A preferred research strategy is the twin study in which the researcher compares the *concordance rate* (the percentage of twin pairs sharing the characteristic or behavior of interest) for monozygotic twins (genetically identical twins), and dizygotic twins (commonly called fraternal twins who share the same amount of genetic material as brothers and sisters born at different times). The usual procedure is to calculate the concordance rate for monozygotic and dizygotic twins separately, and then to compare the rates. If the monozygotic concordance rate is significantly higher, the investigator is likely to conclude that the behavior in question is genetically influenced, because of the fact that monozygotic twins are genetically identical while dizygotic pairs are not. This method assumes that intrapair environmental differences are equivalent for the two types of twins, an assumption which may, in many cases, be quite inaccurate. Finally, the discovery of any discordant monozygotic twins indicates that some nongenetic factor is an influential agent in producing the behavior being studied.

The first twin study of crime was conducted in Germany by Johannes Lange (1930). Lange obtained data on 30 pairs of same-sex twins from the Institutes for Criminal Biology. There were 13 monozygotic pairs and seven dizygotic. In each twin pair, one member, the twin first studied had been imprisoned. The criminality concordance rate for the monozygotic twins was 77 percent compared to a dizygotic rate of 12 percent leading Lange to conclude that inherited tendencies play a "preponderant part" in causing crime.

Lange's study was followed by two more studies, both of which reported consistently higher concordance rates for monozygotic twins than dizygotic twins. Legras' (1932; cited by Rosenthal, 1970) data were particularly striking: monozygotic twins were 100 percent concordant while 20 percent of the dizygotic twins were concordant.

Kranz (1936) obtained a sample of 32 monozygotic twins, 43 same-sex dizygotic, and 50 opposite-sex dizygotic. The concordance rate for having a criminal record was 66 percent for monozygotics, 54 percent for dizygotics of the same sex, and 14 percent for opposite-sex dizygotics. The difference between the identical and same-sex fraternal twins was not significant. Rosenthal (1970) interprets the substantial difference between same-sex and opposite-sex dizygotics as evidence "that environmental factors are of overriding importance with respect to the legal criterion of whether or not one obtains a criminal record" (p. 134). A second study by Kranz (1937) replicated the lack of a significant difference between monozygotic versus dizygotic concordance, although the rate was again somewhat higher for the identical twins.

Christiansen (1968; cited by Reid, 1976) was one of the first investigators to obtain a complete, unselected series of twins born during a specific time period. He reported that 66.7 percent of identical twins were concordant for criminal behavior compared to 30.4 percent of fraternal twins.

The most effective strategy for unconfounding genetic from sociocultural influences, both of which are transmitted within a familial context, is the adoption study, where the adopted offspring of parents who manifest the disorder being observed are compared to the adopted offspring of parents who do not. Schulsinger (1972) compared the records of biological relatives of adoptees, whom he had diagnosed as psychopathic on the basis of the adoptees hospital records, with the diagnoses of the adoptive relatives, and members of the adoptive families. A greater proportion of biological relatives were diagnosed as psychopaths or as having "psychopathy spectrum" disorders (alcoholism, drug addiction, character deviations, etc.) than either of the two adoptive-relative groups. Crowe (1972) compared 52 adopted offspring of a group of female offenders, 90 percent of whom were felons with a control group of adoptees matched for age, sex, race, and age at adoption, with the index cases. Nonparametric contrasts revealed the probands to have significantly more arrests, convictions and incarcerations than controls. While these differences were significant they were relatively small in magnitude; e.g., eight of the probands had been arrested compared to the arrests of two adoptee controls. A number of possible confounds prevent total confidence in a conclusion that heredity predisposes to antisocial behavior. First, the equivalence of the adoptive homes of the two groups is assumed in the absence of any data bearing on the point. Second, children were not separated from their biological mothers in some cases until after one year of age. Third, it was uncertain what percentage of the adoptive parents were aware of the criminal status of the biological mother, and whether this knowledge might have affected their treatment of the child. Finally, there are no data on the biological fathers of the two groups.

Any decision that crime is even partially determined by genetic factors begs the obvious question: what, exactly, is the criminogenic liability that is inherited? There is a lengthy list of likely candidates, but Rosenthal (1970) in his recent review concentrates on four possibilities.

1. *Constitutional predisposition.* This is ground already covered. As we have seen, the data are inconclusive and do not carry us much beyond the obvious intuition that strong, athletic, muscular youths are better suited to be topnotch bullies than either their portly or puny peers.

2. *Cortical abnormalities.* Rosenthal suggests that the high rate of abnormal EEG patterns in prison populations may be related to crime through the association of EEG irregularities with poor impulse control and impaired judgment. Many studies have reported a greater frequency of abnormal EEGs among certain types of criminals. The most characteristic pattern is a diffuse slow-wave pattern although temporal-area spiking has also been reported. Ellingson's (1954) review of 14 studies indicated that 13 of them had revealed an EEG abnormality in at least 31 percent of the sociopaths studied. The

importance of this finding is not certain. It is well known that there is a high base rate of EEG abnormality in the general population, a problem which limits the diagnostic or predictive utility of the electroencephalogram. Further, there are some studies that have failed to find a significant relationship between EEG pathology and delinquent behavior (Loomis, 1965).

3. *Intellectual deficit.* This view can be traced to Goddard's notion that feeblemindedness was inherited, and was characteristic of about 50 percent of criminals. In addition to his previously cited research on the Kallilak family, Goddard assembled detailed case histories of three feebleminded murderers[5] and published his notions of how intellectual deficit contributed to their offenses in a little book not so charmingly titled *The Criminal Imbecile*.

4. *Genetic Anomaly.* In 1965, Patricia Jacobs and her colleagues (Jacobs, Brunton, Melville, Brittain, & McClemont, 1965) reported the results of a survey at a Scottish state hospital, containing mentally subnormal patients with dangerous, violent or criminal tendencies, in which they discovered seven men (of 197 patients studied) with an XYY chromosomal constitution. A second study (Jacobs, Price, Court-Brown, Brittain & Whatmore, 1968) on a population with average or above average intelligence from the same hospital found nine males with the 47 XYY karyotype out of 315 patients examined.

The XYY male has 47 chromosomes instead of the normal complement of 46, the extra one being a Y chromosome. The extra Y chromosome was associated with a trio of characteristics: tall stature, subnormal or borderline intelligence, and episodic aggression. The relationship between the XYY condition and aggressive conduct soon became a very popular topic, and it was thought, in some circles, that the XYY anomaly might possibly explain some crimes of violence whose unpredictable and grisly quality seemed resistant to simple explanation.

The data supporting this suspected relationship are far from compelling. In some cases, XYY criminals were found to have committed fewer crimes of violence than a group of XY inmates (Price & Whatmore, 1967). Kessler and Moos (1969) evaluated the evidence for XYY aggression and concluded that it was "a myth promoted by the mass media."

One of the most comprehensive reviews of the effects of the XYY karyotype was conducted by Jarvik, Klodin, and Matsuyama (1973) who compared the rates of various kinds of genetic anomalies (XYY; XXY, also known as Klinefelter's Syndrome; and mongolism) among different populations of males. These comparisons summarized in Table 3-2 indicate the following sets of conclusions:

(1) The incidence of Klinefelter's, mongolism and XYY is virtually equal among newborns.

(2) The incidence of XXY and XYY karyotypes is approximately the same among normal men.

(3) The incidence of an extra sex chromosome among mental patients is greater than among men or newborns in general, but there is about the same probability that the extra chromosome will be an X as a Y.

(4) The frequency of the XYY condition among criminals is approximately 15 times greater than among men in general, and about three times greater than among mental patients.

(5) The XXY condition occurs about as frequently among criminals as among mental patients.

Jarvik, et al. (1973) conclude that since criminals are the only population in which the extra Y chromosome occurs significantly more often than the extra X chromosome, "an extra Y chromosome predisposes to aggressive behavior" (p. 680). Although this is one of the strongest statements about chromosomally determined aggression that one is likely to encounter today, the authors do admit that most crimes of violence are committed by chromosomally normal people. Further, it is quite apparent that the majority of XYY males are neither criminal nor unusually plagued by an aggressiveness which they are unable to control.

Evaluation of Genetic Theories. There is no reason to equivocate about the relationship between genes and crime. *The present data indicate that genetics play a very small role in determining criminal behavior.* Methodologically, most studies are unable to separate heredity from the psychological, cultural, and social influences transmitted from the family of rearing. In the isolated instances where such separations may be made with slightly greater confidence, the data suggest only a possible genetic potential for a very select range of criminal behavior.

However, the most basic deficiency of a genetic theory of crime is conceptual. It is simply unreasonable to assume that there is a direct link between genetics and the enormous array of legally deviant behavior which the criminologist tries to explain. The specific pattern by which deviant behavior is enacted, whether it be stealing a car, forging a check, stabbing or shooting an enemy, embezzling funds, molesting a child, or cheating on income tax, is no

Table 3-2 Incidence of Genetic Anomalies
in Various Populations*

Population	Number of Studies	Incidence of Genetic Anomaly		
		XYY	XXY	Mongolism
Newborn males	5	.13%	.14%	.13%
Normal adult males	10	.13%	.35%	—
Mental patients	6	.70%	1.00%	—
Criminals	20	1.90%	.86%	—

*Derived from Jarvik, Klodin & Matsuyama (1973).

more inherited than the specific patterns by which socially useful behaviors, such as performing surgery, fighting fires, teaching high school, or writing memorable music, are performed (Cohen, 1966).

PSYCHOLOGICAL THEORIES

Psychoanalytic Theories of Crime

Psychoanalytic theories of crime have played a prominent role in psychological and psychiatric circles, and continue to be the dominant orientation of many mental health professionals who seek to explain criminal conduct. Basically, psychoanalysts assume that crime is a manifestation of some type of personality disturbance in which internal (ego and superego) controls are unable to restrain the primitive, aggressive, antisocial instincts of the id. While the unique biography of the individual should reveal the particular factors that have produced a defective superego, the most common factor is thought to be a faulty identification by a child with his or her parents. Crime is seen as a means of maintaining, or rectifying, psychic balance. It serves a function similar in nature to the neurotic defense mechanisms, the primary difference being that, in the case of crime, the conflict is externalized or acted out.

Freud himself offered little specific speculation about the psychodynamics of the criminal. His basic position appeared to be little different from his theory of neurosis. The criminal suffers from a compulsive need for punishment to alleviate the guilt feelings stemming from the unconscious, incestuous feelings of the Oedipal period. Crimes are committed so that the perpetrator will be apprehended, punished, and cleansed of his guilt. "In many criminals, especially youthful ones, it is possible to detect a very powerful sense of guilt which existed before the crime, and is therefore not its result but its motive. It is as if it was a relief to be able to fasten this unconscious sense of guilt onto something real and immediate" (Freud, 1961, p. 52). The need to be punished for lingering Oedipal guilt remains a popular concept among current psychoanalysts (see, for example, Glover, 1960).

Franz Alexander (Alexander & Healy, 1935; Alexander & Staub, 1931) was more prolific in applying a psychoanalytic interpretation to criminal behavior. He viewed the criminal as someone who was unable to postpone immediate gratification in order to obtain greater rewards in the future. The criminal could not orient his behavior in line with the "reality principle," a basic lesson to be learned during the anal stage of development through the social (parental) demands of toilet training. It is not surprising that Alexander regarded the antisocial activities of the adult as exaggerated anal characteristics acquired in childhood. In fact, the initial prototype of the criminal act was the child's defecation in an undesirable location violating what Yochelson and Samenow (1976) refer to as the "prescription for cleanliness" (p. 81). Like many other psychoanalytically oriented theorists, Alexander did not ignore the etiological significance of environmental and social factors. In addition to genetic and early acquired tendencies, he thought family and general social forces contributed to the emergence of criminality. In his very influential *Roots of Crime*, written with William Healy, Alexander (1935) argued that "criminal acts are not always committed by certain individuals who can be defined and characterized psychologically or in terms of personality as specifically inclined to crime, but neither are criminal acts restricted to certain social groups which can be characterized and defined sociologically . . . both personality and sociological factors are active at the same time; either of them may be predominant in one case, negligible in another . . ." (p. 273).

Other psychoanalysts have suggested that criminal behavior is a means of obtaining substitute or compensatory gratification of basic needs such as love, nurturance, and attention which should have been normally satisfied within nuclear family relationships. Maternal deprivation has received the most attention, although the effects of paternal inadequacies have not been completely neglected.

Bowlby's work (1949, 1953, Bowlby & Salter-Ainsworth, 1965) is the best known illustration of the maternal deprivation theory which holds that the biological-emotional bond between mother and child is a requirement for normal socialization. In one of his most specific statements about the relationship of crime to maternal contact, Bowlby claimed that "maternal separateness and parental rejection are believed together to account for a majority of the more intractable cases (of delinquency) including the 'constitutional psychopath' and the 'moral defectives'" (Bowlby, 1949, p. 37).

A recent psychoanalytic view stresses that the antisocial conduct of an individual may stem from the unconscious permissiveness of his parental figures, by which the parents themselves obtain vicarious gratification of id impulses from their offsprings' violations. In the course of identifying with parental figures who give at least tacit approval to delinquent behavior, the child develops a partially formed superego ("superego lacunae," or a superego with holes) which has a diminished capacity to control socially forbidden conduct (Johnson & Szurek, 1952).

Evaluation of Psychoanalytic Theories. In the eyes of many beholders, psychoanalysis remains the most comprehensive statement about the nature and processes of human personality which is available. As the few examples of this section illustrate, the breadth of psychoanalytic explanations is impressive, involving several types of etiological factors. If we were to locate the above four psychoanalytic theories along a continuum of locus of influence, we would discover that the theories move from a position of exclusive concern with internal, psychodynamic events (Freud's unconscious guilt theory) to a point where social, especially familial, factors play a great part (superego lacunae theory).

In the eyes of many other beholders, psychoanalysis is one of the most inadequate statements about the nature of human personality, suffering from numerous logic-of-science errors, as well as the lack of empirical verification. Evaluations of psychoanalytic criminology have concentrated on several logical and empirical deficiencies of which only a few can be mentioned here. More thorough critiques are available in Cohen (1966; see especially pp. 59-62) and Yochelson and Samenow (1976; see pp. 85-89).

One of the most common objections is that psychoanalytic theories are spun in ways that trap their adherents in tautological circles. Cohen (1966) has criticized the notion of impulsive antisocial instincts as inventories which are merely alternative names for the behaviors they are intended to explain. ''Aggressive or acquisitive acts are often explained by underlying aggressive or acquisitive impulses. The evidence for these impulses . . . turns out to be the aggressive or acquisitive act to be explained'' (p. 61). This is a little like claiming that anxiety is due to nervousness. It may be true but it is also meaningless.

Equally troublesome is the fact that psychoanalytic interpretations of crime are vastly discrepant from patterns of actual criminal conduct. Freud's allegation that the criminal commits crimes in order to be caught and punished flies directly in the face of the obvious extremes to which offenders will go to avoid detection of their wrongdoings. Further, much of the evidence discussed in Chapter 2 indicates that criminals are very successful in their efforts to prevent detection or, if detected, elude official prosecution and conviction. Most offenders do not appear unduly frustrated or further guilt ridden by the fact that their ''crime pays'' at least some of the time. In fact, the success of their crimes seems to be one of the major gratifications in their lives (Cleckley, 1964). Finally, psychoanalytic descriptions are at odds with the observation that many forms of crime are more calculated than compulsed, more orchestrated than overdetermined, and more devised than driven.

Psychopathy

One of the most captivating concepts of psychological criminology has been that of the *psychopath*. Psychopathy is not so much a theory of criminal behavior as it is a description of individuals who are involved in frequent and repetitive criminal activity. The concept of psychopath has a long history. McCord and McCord (1964) identified Pinel's diagnosis of *manie sans delire* as an early antecedent of the label of psychopath. Ullmann and Krasner (1975) reported that Pritchard used the term *moral insanity* in 1835 to describe a patient with perverted moral principles, and Benjamin Rush spoke in 1812 of *moral derangement*, a condition manifested by vicious actions and ''the morbid operations of the will.''

Psychopathy is not an official diagnostic category. The official designation of the psychopath is found in DSM-II as *antisocial personality*, a term "reserved for individuals who are basically unsocialized and whose behavior pattern brings them repeatedly into conflict with society. They are incapable of significant loyalty to individuals, groups, or social values. They are grossly selfish, callous, irresponsible, impulsive and unable to feel guilt or to learn from experience and punishment. Frustration tolerance is low. They tend to blame others or offer plausible rationalizations for their behavior. A mere history of repeated legal or social offenses is not sufficient to justify this diagnosis" (DSM-II, p. 43).

Ullmann and Krasner (1975) list ten generally recognized characteristics of the psychopath: (1) a failure to play by the rules of society; (2) a facade of charming competence and maturity; (3) impulsive performance of illegal or unusual behavior; (4) repeated commission of petty, deceitful crimes; (5) chronic untruthfulness accompanied by a false sincerity of remorse; (6) a lack of anxiety or guilt over past misdeeds; (7) failure to learn from past experience; (8) repeated conflict with authorities; (9) inability to sustain close, meaningful interpersonal relationships; and (10) unwillingness to delay gratification.

Psychopaths are sometimes further divided into certain subcategories. One common clinical distinction is between a *primary* psychopath who manifests little or no anxiety to typical, anxiety-illiciting situations, and the *anxious* psychopath who does develop emotional reactions (including anxiety) to the environment or his specific behavior.

Arieti (1967) identified two types of psychopaths: the *simple* psychopath who doesn't delay gratification, and experiences very little anxiety, and the *complex* psychopath who is emotionally similar to the simple psychopath, but who is able to construct more elaborate plans for achieving what he wants.

There are a multitude of etiological theories of psychopathic behavior emphasizing a host of psychological, physiological, and sociological factors. A common view is that psychopaths suffer a cortical immaturity making it difficult for them to inhibit behavior that is likely to lead to punishment. This maturational retardation results in a perseveration of the most dominant responses in given situations. Hare (1970) has been a major proponent of this position, the primary evidence for which is the relationship between a high rate of EEG abnormality among institutionalized adult criminals (see above, this chapter).

Psychopaths are usually thought to be deficient in emotional arousal, thereby producing their characteristically reduced anxiety level. In addition to the observation that autonomic correlates of fear subside more quickly in psychopaths than in normals, GSR results suggest that psychopaths are relatively underaroused in the resting state as well. This combination of low cortical and autonomic arousal results in a high need for stimulation in which the psychopath displays a preference for novel situations and has a tendency to "shorten" stimuli, thereby being less influenced or controlled by them. Quay (1965) has advanced a *stimulation-seeking* theory which claims that the exciting, and disruptive, behavior of the psychopath serves the function of increasing sensory input and arousal to some minimally tolerable level.

One result of this thrill-seeking is that the psychopath may be "immune" to, or short-circuit, many of the social cues that govern behavior. Eysenck (1964) has proposed a similar theory which emphasizes the slower rate of classical conditioning for psychopaths. Eysenck argued that socialization and conscience development depend on the acquisition of classically conditioned avoidance responses, and that psychopaths' conditioning deficiencies may account for their difficulties in normal socialization. (See Chapter 4 for additional discussion of Eysenck's theory.) There are some recent data (Chesno & Kilmann, 1975) that confirm psychopaths' relatively unsuccessful acquisition of avoidance responses.

Probably the most popular explanation for the antisocial personality involves some variety of familial disturbance. Parental rejection and parental absence, brought about by divorce or separation, are frequently suspected causative factors. Some theorists emphasize maternal rejection, others concentrate on rejection by fathers. Coleman (1976) cites Greer's research (1964) in which 60 percent of a group of psychopaths had lost at least one parent during childhood, contrasted with 28 percent for neurotic, and 27 percent for "normal" controls.

McCord and McCord (1964) concluded that emotional deprivation and rejection by parents were primary causes of later psychopathy. Inconsistent, erratic discipline was also considered to be a potential source of psychopathic conduct. It is important to recognize that the McCords did not advocate an exclusively familial theory of psychopathy. They thought that disturbed familial relations may interact in some cases with certain kinds of physiological damage to produce eventual antisocial tendencies.

Buss (1966) identified two patterns of parental behavior which might foster psychopathy. First, there are parents who are cold and distant in familial and interpersonal relations. The child who imitates this parental model will develop a cold, detached, interpersonal style that gives the superficial appearance of social involvement, but which actually lacks the empathy or emotional commitment required for stable, satisfying relationships. Second, there are parents who are inconsistent in their behavior as they reward and punish, making it difficult for the child to imitate a stable role model and develop a definite, consistent self identity. Buss felt that a child in this situation learns how to avoid blame and punishment, rather than learning what is right and wrong behavior. The development of psychopathic characteristics results from the parents rewarding both "superficial conformity" and "underhanded nonconformity." Maher (1966) offered a similar description in which the psychopath is portrayed as a person who learns how to avoid the negative consequences of his behavior, rather than how to control or eliminate the misbehavior itself.

Ullmann and Krasner's (1975; pp. 551-554) social learning formulation of psychopathic behavior also stresses the learning experiences that occur in a familial context. As a result of inconsistent discipline and erratic parental models, the potential psychopath finds himself in a series of situations where the effects of his behavior are unpredictable. His behavior appears to be "inconsequential." As a result, other people do not become effective social or secondary reinforcers for the psychopath, resulting in the extinction of pro-social behaviors. Additionally, since people are not meaningful long-term reinforcers for the psychopath, his behavior is more likely to be controlled by short-term, material gains or the opportunity to escape the more humanizing qualities of interpersonal relations.

The psychopathic personality is relatively easy to detect, difficult to understand, and extremely troublesome to treat. Unraveling the etiology of psychopaths, and modifying their distressing conduct are extremely challenging tasks. We should not, however, lose sight of the fact that psychopaths account for a very small percentage of our law violators. A successful theory of psychopathy will have limited relevance to most offenders.

Yochelson and Samenow (1976)

One recent position which defies easy classification is contained in Yochelson and Samenow's (1976) *The Criminal Personality*, a work which has evoked heated debate among correction officials. Yochelson and Samenow's book, the culmination of 15 years of intensive interview, therapy and follow-up studies, rejects traditional psychological and sociological theories of crime and their accompanying "permissive" techniques of rehabilitation.

Yochelson and Samenow claim that criminals possess a unique set of cognitive patterns ("criminal thinking patterns") which, while internally logical and consistent, are erroneous, according to responsible thinking. Before outlining the major thinking patterns characteristic of the criminal personality, it is important to understand what Yochelson and Samenow mean by criminal: "we do not use 'criminal' in a legal sense. Our emphasis is on *thinking processes* that the irresponsible but nonarrestable person, the petty thief, and the 'professional' criminal all manifest, but to different degrees and with different consequences" (p. 253). Although most people define "criminal" in some legal sense with emphasis on breaking the law, and/or apprehension, and prosecution, these authors seem to define criminality in terms of responsibility and thinking patterns which are conducive to lawbreaking.

Yochelson and Samenow (1976) picture a continuum of responsibility to illustrate their concepts, with the extreme criminal at the far end of the irresponsible pole, and the nonarrestable, but irresponsible, person located midway between "responsible" and "irresponsible" (p. 253). The responsible person is seen as accepting and fulfilling obligations, considerate of other persons, and hard-working. Persons at the other end of the continuum are the extreme criminals. They are not only irresponsible in the sense that they avoid obligations, are inconsiderate of people, and avoid work; they are irresponsible in terms of the law. They see no obligation to keep within the legal limits society has outlined. Yochelson and Samenow argue that a person can be irresponsible and yet not break the law, but the extreme criminal who constantly breaks the law cannot be responsible.

There are a number of thinking patterns which are characteristic of extreme criminals. These cognitive patterns are usually manifested and ingrained by an early age. It is these patterns, coupled with irresponsibility, which mold lives of crime. Unless these patterns are completely irradicated or destroyed, the person will inevitably commit crimes again. Crime is like alcoholism: "once a criminal, always a criminal." There must be complete abstinence from criminal activity for there to be any kind of enduring rehabilitative effect.

The following criminal thinking patterns can be isolated: suspiciousness, self-seeking, manipulative, impulsive, simplistic, concrete and compartmentalized thinking, excitement-sensationalism seeking, hyperactive, shutoff mechanism, compulsive lying, power-oriented, angry, sentimental, prideful, and average intelligence. Although some theorists may prefer to view the above list of thinking patterns as personality traits, thereby qualifying the theory as psychological in nature, Yochelson and Samenow's choice of "thinking patterns" reflects the authors' emphasis on conscious volition in crime more than does the notion of personality characteristics.

In many ways, this formulation resembles control theory, or a theory of moral development (see Chapter 4), more than psychological theory. The essential concept involves *responsibility*. "Our stance has gradually been changing from an amoral one to an emphasis on moral living, in very strong terms . . . we sought to broaden the meaning of responsibility, so that it could be taught and then implemented as a *set of mental processes*" (Yochelson and Samenow, 1976, p. 37).

The criminal must be regarded as someone responsible for his, or her, life, who has chosen a life of crime. "It is not the environment that turns a man into a criminal. Rather, it is a series of choices that he makes starting at a very early age . . . crime does not come to him; he goes to it, often traveling far outside his neighborhood to do so" (Yochelson and Samenow, 1976, p. 247).

Evaluation of "The Criminal Personality". Yochelson and Samenow's theory is more concerned with the description of irresponsible criminal thinking patterns than an etiological account of how these deviant cognitions originate. Their theory does not provide an intellectually satisfying explanation of how criminal thinking is acquired in the first place. This is a task which a comprehensive formulation of crime should not avoid. In fact, one might wonder whether the description of the "criminal personality" offers very much beyond that provided by the older concept of the psychopath. Much like the rediscovery of the wheel, a redefinition of the psychopath will yield few benefits unless the redefinition possesses some major heuristic value.

Conceptually, the theory suffers from an imprecision of terms. For example, the definition of crime is rather idiosyncratic "in this volume we use the term criminal far more broadly . . . as we describe patterns of thought and action, the emphasis being upon the former . . . some of the thinking patterns described here and called 'criminal' are shared by responsible people. However, while in the criminal they eventuate in crime, they do not have that outcome in the responsible person (although they may contribute to his irresponsibility). For example, as we point out, the consequences of a lie told by a criminal and of a lie told by a noncriminal are very different. The same is true of anger, perfectionism, and all other patterns described" (Yochelson & Samenow, 1976, p. viii).

From a methodological standpoint, the Yochelson and Samenow study cannot provide an adequate basis for drawing unambiguous cause-effect conclusions. The "design" consists of intensive and extensive interviews with a relatively small number of offenders, the majority of whom were incarcerated, "hard core," adult, male criminals. No control groups of any sort were included, thereby precluding confident judgments about the possible influence of incarceration itself or the prevalence of irresponsible thinking patterns within noncriminal samples. While case histories can serve as a fertile source for theoretical hypotheses, they alone are an insufficient base for a theory which attempts to generalize its principles to all types of criminally offensive conduct.

The data were derived largely from personal interviews and exhaustive case histories. Interrater reliabilities of these data are not provided, neither are their attempts to validate these data with formal, concurrent measures. Rather, the validation procedure is described as follows: "We recorded early self-serving accounts, but we have been able to correct and update them, because, as a criminal progresses in the program for change, he has less and less need to justify what he does and he presents us with a different picture. Our changing people have reviewed and revised what they told us earlier. We have also talked with family members, many of whom were at first instructed by the criminal to lie. We took information from criminals who were changing and from their families and presented it to totally unchanged criminals. In part, we did this to establish the validity of that material" (Yochelson & Samenow, 1976, pp. 117-118). This is not a satisfactory validation method, because it does not include a data source which is independent of the self-reports offered by the criminals themselves.

NOTES

[1] For a critical analysis of positivistic criminology see Taylor, Walton and Young (1973).

[2] One exception to this general description is what Nettler (1974) terms rational crime in which particular social structures provide almost irresistible opportunities for illegal behavior. Rational crime is described more fully on pp. 63-64 of this chapter.

[3] Matza (1964) theorized that adolescents "drift" into delinquency motivated by an adherence to "subterranean" values of adventure, excitement and thrill, and unchecked by the conventional norms to which these same adolescents are sometimes committed. Matza (Sykes & Matza, 1957) did not believe that delinquents totally rejected the norms of society. Rather, the delinquent can temporarily suspend the norms of social control through various techniques of neutralization that allow him, or her, to remain basically committed to most social imperatives. There are five important techniques of neutralization: Denial of responsibility, denial of a victim, denial of injury, appeal to higher authorities, and condemnation of the condemners.

[4] Miller concentrates on what he terms the "hard-core lower class," a group comprising about 15 percent of the American population. The critical attributes of this culture are the "female-based" household as the basic childrearing unit and "serial monogamy" as the primary marital pattern.

[5] The characters were Jean Gianini, Roland Pennington and Fred Tronson who confessed to the murders of Lida Beecher (schoolteacher), Lou Pinkerton (farm manager), and Emma Ulrich (stenographer) respectively.

Chapter 4
Sociopsychological Theories of Crime

> Crimes, like virtues, are their
> own rewards.
>
> — George Farquhar

> Crimes, like lands, are not inherited.
>
> — Shakespeare, *Timon of Athens*

In this chapter we discuss theories that view crime as *learned* behavior. While some of these theories emphasize sociological influences and others emphasize the role of individual, even genetic, differences, they all exemplify the position that specific patterns of crime are learned by the process of social interaction. As a group, these formulations are sometimes identified as *social process* theories (Reid, 1976, Chapter 8) in order to call attention to their concern with the processes by which an individual becomes criminal.

In contrast to structural theories, social process theories stress those reciprocal transactions between people and their social environments which would explain why some individuals consistently behave criminally while others do not. Social process theories attempt to bridge the gap between the abstract environmentalism of sociological theories and the narrow individualism of psychological or biological theories, a feature which has led to their alternative designation as *sociopsychological* theories (Nettler, 1974, Chapters 8 and 9).

The sociopsychological emphasis on crime as a learned phenomenon was anticipated by earlier scholars. Munsterberg (1908), whom we discussed in Chapter 1, argued that crime was acquired through imitation of the many examples of illegal conduct in society. Many years earlier, Gabriel Tarde, a French judge and social philosopher, had proposed a very similar view: crime, like many other kinds of behavior, is learned through imitation.

Modern sociopsychological theories can be divided into two categories. First, there are the *control* theories. This variety assumes that people will frequently behave antisocially unless they are trained not to. Nettler (1974) claims that the basic aim of control theories is to explain "not so much why we behave badly as how we can be induced to behave well" (p. 216). Lawful behavior requires successful socialization and the growth of a conscience which restrains potentially criminal patterns of behavior. This self-controlling value of the conscience was recognized by the English novelist W. Somerset Maugham who declared it "the guardian in the individual of the rules which the community has evolved for its own preservation" (1921). Ultimately, all control theories are explanations of faulty moral development in which the conscience fails to control the crime to which a person is tempted.

The second variety of sociopsychological theory includes a number of formulations that focus on the learning mechanisms by which criminal behavior is directly acquired and maintained. There is no umbrella term identifying this category although it includes several influential theories, such as Sutherland's differential association theory, social learning theory and social labeling theory. Among the learning processes proposed by the theorists in this group are symbolic interaction, classical conditioning, operant conditioning, modeling, cognitive processes, and social labeling.

This chapter will be organized into three sections. First, we shall review the most prominent examples of the control theories. Following this, a number of direct learning hypotheses will be summarized. Finally, Feldman's (1977) recent attempt to integrate the elements of conscience development, learning, and social labeling, will be presented. Feldman's analysis relies on very eclectic learning theory encompassing data from laboratory and field experiments on transgression, aggression, attitude change, and moral development.

CONTROL THEORIES

Hans Eysenck

Hans Eysenck is a British psychologist whose professional contributions cover several areas of behavioral science. Although he is best known by American students for his published skepticism regarding the positive effects of psychotherapy, our attention in this chapter is limited to the use of his personality theory as an explanation for criminal behavior.

Eysenck views most social behavior as the result of both situational learning experiences and relatively stable, inherited dimensions of personality. In the case of crime, "heredity plays an important, and possibly a vital part, in predisposing a given individual to crime" (Eysenck, 1964, p. 55). Socialization practices translate these innate predispositions to criminality into reality, the specific topography of particular criminal acts.

Socialization depends on two kinds of influences. First, there is instrumental (operant) learning in which behavior is acquired and maintained by virtue of its consequences. This is learning according to what Thorndike originally termed the *law of effect*: responses followed by rewarding consequences will be strengthened, while responses followed by aversive consequences will be weakened. It is the psychologists' equivalent to the classical hedonism of Bentham: men act to seek pleasure.

Actually, Eysenck proposes a short-term hedonism. One of the cardinal principles of operant conditioning is that the immediate consequences of a response are more influential than its delayed consequences. According to Eysenck, the immediate effects of behavioral consequences account for the fact that instrumental learning is ineffective in restraining antisocial conduct. The negative effects of punishment are "long delayed and uncertain; the acquisition of the desired object is immediate; therefore, although the acquisition and the pleasure derived from it may, on the whole, be less than the pain derived from the incarceration which ultimately follows, the time element very much favors the acquisition as compared with the deterrent effects of the incarceration" (Eysenck, 1964, p. 101).

Because of the ineffectiveness of punishment, restraint of antisocial behavior becomes the task of the second kind of influence, the conscience, whose development depends largely on classical (Pavlovian) conditioning. Eysenck contends that conscience is simply a conditioned reflex, produced by close temporal contiguity of some undesirable behavior by a child with the almost immediate punishment of that act by a parent, teacher, or other child. The proscribed act is the conditioned stimulus which, when associated frequently enough with the unconditioned stimulus of the punishment, will come to produce some sort of unpleasant autonomic response.

Eysenck continues, "we would expect a fairly general reaction of fear and autonomic 'unpleasure' to become associated with all antisocial activities, because of the process of stimulus generalization . . ." (Eysenck, 1964, p. 107). Conscience, then, becomes an inner control whose agents of punishment are the autonomically mediated emotions of anxiety and guilt.

So much for the role of learning in Eysenck's theory. The extent to which conditioning can build a strong conscience is largely dependent on the inherited sensitivity of the autonomic nervous system. Here, there are large individual differences. In some people, conditioned responses are slow to develop and easy to extinguish; in others, conditioning progresses rapidly and there is strong resistance to extinction.

Underlying these differences are the two major dimensions of Eysenck's personality theory; *extroversion* and *neuroticism*.[1] The extroversion dimension is composed of two relatively independent components; *sociability* and *impulsiveness*. One extreme of extroversion is high extroversion, the other extreme is low extroversion or alternatively, high introversion. The neuroticism dimension runs from high neuroticism to low neuroticism or high emotional stability.

High extroverts are likely to be outgoing, very active and optimistic, and quite impulsive; conversely, high introverts are more withdrawn, unsociable, passive, and cautious. High neuroticism is associated with restlessness, emotional lability, and hypersensitivity; emotional stability (low neuroticism) is characterized by greater emotional evenness, reliability, and potential for leadership.

The extroversion and neuroticism dimensions are also associated with important, and relatively stable, physiological differences which are very significant for Eysenck's theory of conscience formation. High extroverts are seen as having low levels of cortical arousal which retard their ability to acquire conditioned responses and also renders those responses, which are developed, much less resistant to extinction. Conditioning is also impaired because inhibition increases more quickly and dissipates more slowly among high extroverts.

Neuroticism, too, is thought to be related to autonomic nervous system reactivity. Feldman (1977) summarizes this relationship in the following terms: "persons high on neuroticism are considered to have a highly labile ANS (autonomic nervous system) and to react strongly with excessive fear reaction to painful stimuli. When neuroticism is high it interferes with the efficient learning of responses, particularly to unpleasant stimuli, because of the irrelevant anxiety evoked" (p. 145).

With respect to socialization, Eysenck thought that high scores on both neuroticism and extroversion would result in poor conditionability and, consequently, inadequate socialization. The person who fails to develop moral and social responses because of low conditionability is likely to become the criminal. Additionally, high degrees of neuroticism and extroversion will provide a higher drive to carry out the specific crimes. In brief, then, the potential criminal is someone whose genetically influenced personality predispositions make it difficult to acquire the classically conditioned avoidance responses which Eysenck held were the elemental components of human conscience and the ability to resist temptations to antisocial conduct.[2]

Evaluation of Eysenck's Theory. Eysenck's theory has been subjected to severe criticism. Perhaps the most scathing attack was offered by Christie (1956, p. 450; quoted by Taylor, Walton & Young, 1973, p. 58) who observed, "errors of computation, uniquely biased samples which forbid any generalizations, scales with built-in biases which do not measure what they purport to measure, unexplained inconsistencies within the data, misinterpretations and contradictions of the relevant research of others, and unjustifiable manipulation of the data. Any one of Eysenck's many errors is sufficient to raise serious questions about the validity of his conclusions. *In toto*, absurdity is compounded upon absurdity, so that where the truth lies is impossible to determine."

The data concerning the empirical relationships among extroversion, neuroticism, and criminal offending are mixed. Feldman (1977) summarized the relevant literature through 1975 as (1) confirming the positive relationship between elevated extroversion and increased offending among female, but not male prisoners, and strongly confirming the relationship among adolescents of both sexes who were asked for self-reports of their offending; (2) supporting the prediction that high neuroticism would be related to increased offending among prisoner and nonprisoner respondents; (3) finding a consistent, positive relationship between psychoticism and increased offending; and (4) confirming a strong association between criminal behavior, and scores above the medians on all three personality dimensions. "Expressed another way, those scoring high on all three *tend* to be consistent in carrying out a range of illegal behavior; those scoring low on all three *tend* to be consistent in not carrying out a range of such behaviors" (Feldman, 1977, p. 149).

Of course, these associations may be mediated by the relationship of extroversion and neuroticism to other, noncriminal aspects of social behavior. For example, as Feldman observes, the positive correlation between neuroticism and increased offending may be due to the tendency of anxious persons to admit more readily to deviant conduct. As another example, highly extroverted persons are likely to be exposed to more opportunities for learning or for committing deviant behaviors because of their greater general level of social activity.

Another objection posed by many behaviorally oriented theorists is that moral behavior is specific to the particular situation in which it is expected to occur. Mischel (1976), perhaps the best known advocate of the specificity position, claims that different components of moral behavior are only minimally interrelated; verbal standards of right and wrong, resistance to temptation, and guilt feelings after transgression show meager correlations one with another. Further, within each of these types of morality, moral conduct is specific to the task at hand. Mischel (1976) concludes, "the data on self control and moral behavior do not support the existence of a unitary, intrapsychic moral agency like the superego, nor do they suggest a unitary trait of conscience or honesty" (p. 461).

A similar, and perhaps more troublesome criticism would be that Eysenck has not been able to separate a differential predisposition to be conditioned from the different quality of conditioning opportunities which children will experience. Another way of saying this is that genetic differences probably will be accompanied by different conditioning histories. A family of extroverts may transmit its potential criminality not through inherited personality features but through an accompanying *laissez faire* policy of discipline, where conditioning trials are scarce, inconsistent, or specific to only certain kinds of misconduct. Certain families may even inculcate criminal tendencies through conditioning episodes that strengthen antisocial behaviors. In these instances, introverts would be predicted more likely to behave criminally since they would acquire conditioned "antisocialness" more strongly.

In fairness to Eysenck, these are objections of which he is quite well aware. His attempts to answer such criticisms generally involve the strategy of admitting to the importance of specific learning environments, while still maintaining that predispositional differences account for the major portion of potential antisocial variance.

Containment Theory

"All the reasons given for high crime and delinquency in the United States as well as the description of the new 'pitch' or component of crime and delinquency in America can be summed up conveniently into the phrase: *lack of containment*" (Reckless, 1961, pp. 4-5). Lack of containment is the central theme of Walter Reckless' very influential explanation of crime known, appropriately enough, as containment theory.[3]

Reckless rejected what he called the predominant "pressure" criminology of American sociologists, and its emphasis on such criminogenic conditions as class inequity, poverty, unemployment, and lack of education, also, the "pull" theories, and their stress on conflicting cultural affiliations and differential identification with various social norms. He preferred containment theory as a central position between the conceptual extremes of sociological "pressures," and "pulls," and psychological "pushes." Containment was a concept that could account for both law-abiding individuals living in high crime environments, as well as the law violator who hailed from areas, or cultures, with a low incidence of norm violation.

Reckless considered the controls which could contain crime to derive from two general sources; external and internal. *External containment* consisted largely of social pressure to conform to the prevailing norms of the group. Such influences were strengthened by the stability of those social structures which perpetuate important systems of behavioral regulations. The most influential origins of external containment are a well-integrated society with well-defined social roles and limits on behavior, effective familial discipline and supervision, and the support and expectations of social groups for positive accomplishment.

Stable, external containment is strong "in undisturbed, isolated, homogeneous, unchanging, primary-group societies, such as primitive tribes, folk communities, agricultural villages, and religious sects. It was found to be absent or disappearing among peoples disturbed by change, impact, dislocation, migration, heterogeneity of the population, and cultural clash of conduct norms" (Reckless, 1961, p. 337). One example of maximum external containment is the Hutterites, a Christian sect of North America practicing communal ownership and control of property, among whom antisocial behavior, violence, and extreme symptoms of mental illness are very rare.

As external controls weaken or disappear, restraint of crime becomes increasingly a matter of *internal containments*, or what psychologists have reified as the superego. When external containment is weak, inner containment must be additionally strong to hold the line against "adversities (pressures), the subculture of delinquency, wrongdoing, and crime (pulls), as well as discontent and frustration (pushes)" (Reckless, 1961, p. 351). The most important inner containment is a good self-concept which acts as an "insulator" against delinquency. A favorable self-concept directs an individual toward lawful behavior while an unfavorable self-concept is unable to resist the pressures of adversity, the pulls of delinquent subcultures, and the pushes of psychological frustration and aggression.

Effective inner containment consists of several elements, most of which would commonly be regarded as products of a strong conscience. The presence of robust inner containment can be inferred from the following indicators: ego strength, high frustration tolerance, active goal orientation, high resistance to diversion, ability to find substitute satisfactions, tension-reducing rationalizations, and a heightened sense of personal responsibility.

Reckless and his colleagues conducted a series of investigations which compared the self-concepts of teacher-nominated "good" and "bad" boys drawn from a high delinquency area (Dinitz, Scarpetti & Reckless, 1962; Reckless, Dinitz & Murray, 1956). This research indicates a generally more favorable self-concept existed among the "good" boys. Additionally, there were significant differences, at relatively early ages, between the "good" boys and the potential delinquents on such dimensions as feelings toward authority, expectation for future breaking of the law, preferences for friends, and liking for school. Dinitz, et al.'s (1962) followup of a portion of these original samples revealed more police contacts by the "bad" boys by the age of 16 than the "good" boys.

Reckless championed containment as a concept with broad applicability. He considered it sufficient to explain most crimes, both against property and against persons. There were only two fairly rare categories of crime to which the theory was inapplicable. First, it did not attempt to explain the compulsive, illogical deviance of the psychopath and other psychologically or organically impaired individuals. Second, it did not apply to crime occurring in those narrowly drawn subcultures or social groups organized around a total commitment to deviant behavior. Because of its intermediate position between "pressure-pull" and "push" theories, containment theory should have appeal to both sociologists and psychologists. Reckless also thought that his theory could guide treatment efforts, as well as encourage prevention through its "on-the-target" focus.

Evaluation of Containment Theory. Generally, containment theory has been well received by criminologists. In particular, the self-concept research of the Reckless group has been very influential. This is not to say that his research has escaped critique. Reid (1976) identified the following recurring criticisms of the self-concept work: inadequate operationalizations of self-concept, the lack of necessary control groups, and differential attrition of "good" and "bad" boys at the time of their followup.

Containment theory is concerned primarily with the *products* of socialization. It has very little to say about the *procedures* by which one becomes either well or poorly socialized. This neglect of the differential processes of socialization reduces containment theory to the rather tautological claim that people commit crimes because of their failure to resist illegal behavior. The truth of this statement is largely definitional, rather than empirical. It is difficult to falsify the proposition that crime is due to the inability to forego temptations to behave criminally.

A major limitation of containment theory is its failure to explain why not everyone who commits a crime is treated as a criminal. As we learned in Chapter 2, the detection, arrest, prosecution, and punishment of law-breakers are occasionally moderated by several characteristics of the accused having little to do with the illegal behavior itself. Ironically, this is a weakness shared by the social-structural theories with which Reckless found so much fault. Any theory which concentrates its explanations on "official" delinquents or criminals will minimize the importance of the criminal justice system in creating some portion of the deviance it attempts to correct. This is as true of those psychological theories that restrict their attention to internal psychodynamics as it is of those sociological explanations that consistently emphasize the broad-range pressures of social disadvantage and cultural disintegration.

Finally, one might challenge containment theory's implicit assumption that evilness is an inherent characteristic of human nature. The fact that this belief is as old as the *Old Testament* notion of original sin, and is shared by almost all other varieties of control theory, makes it no less objectionable. Taking feral man for granted ignores the evolutionary importance of social altruism and personal sacrifice which some behavioral scientists are increasingly recognizing (e.g., Campbell, 1975). In the course of natural selection, social cooperativeness, and a sense of personal integrity probably have had considerably more adaptive value than either personal hedonism or innate aggressiveness.

This is not to say that virtuousness is any more natural than aggressiveness. Behavioral control and its internalized counterpart, conscience, are undoubtedly the result of socialization processes. But so are many forms of crime. As Bandura (1976) has argued, "people are not born with preformed repertoires of aggressive behavior. They must learn them in one way or another" (p. 204).

Other Control Theories

Any theory of moral development is at least an implicit example of control theory. Most psychological formulations of morality emphasize general abilities in self-control and resistance to temptation, rather than specific restraints on illegal behavior. For this reason, I will include only brief comments on several well-known theories of general moral development. Each of these have stimulated extensive research literatures which will not be summarized here except to provide references which interested readers may pursue at their own interest.

1. Kohlberg's Developmental Stage Theory. Lawrence Kohlberg has hypothesized six age-graded stages of moral development which are a function of increasing cognitive maturation (Kohlberg, 1963, 1969). Although the pace at which a child moves from one stage to the next may be accelerated by certain social experiences, Kohlberg believes that the sequence of movement is relatively invariant and even quite stable across different cultures.

At the first two stages (Preconventional Orientation), moral reasoning is typified by an overriding concern with the consequences of one's actions. Goodness is equated with explicit rewards and the satisfaction of personal desires; badness is equated with punishment and the lack of personal satisfaction. In the next two stages (Conventional Morality), moral reasoning relies on conformity to explicit social standards and laws, as well as the maintenance of authority and social order. The last two stages (Postconventional Morality) involve reasoning, which recognizes the value of orderliness, but places a greater premium on individual principles of conscience and ethics that recognize uniform standards of justice. Although Kohlberg believes in the universality of his stages, he does not ignore the important role of social interaction, and parental practices.

The primary instrument for measuring stages of moral development has been Kohlberg's Moral Judgment Scale. This scale is a quasi-projective test, consisting of nine moral dilemmas for which respondents are asked to justify their decision about whether or not the central character should perform a certain act. The best known dilemma is one in which a husband is faced with the decision of stealing a drug which he cannot afford in order to save the life of his wife.

Some of Kohlberg's hypotheses have been tested on prisoner or delinquent populations. Fodor (1972) administered the Moral Judgment Scale to matched groups of delinquents and nondelinquents. Although the delinquents scored significantly lower than the nondelinquents, the mean scores for both groups fell at the third stage, indicating that official delinquents were not associated with an overall difference in their dominant stage of moral judgment. Ruma and Mosher (1967) collected moral judgment scores, as well as several separate measures of guilt, among a group of male delinquents. Higher moral reasoning was associated with higher guilt on most of the measures. These findings applied to only the first three stages of the theory, since there was only one participant who scored above the third stage.

Kohlberg's analysis has enjoyed only limited empirical support. First of all, with the exception of adequate interrater agreement, the reliability of the

Moral Judgment Scale has not been established. In their excellent review of the literature on the Moral Judgment Scale, Kurtines and Greif (1974) were unable to find any estimates of the scale's temporal reliability, internal consistency, or standard error of measurement.

Of greater importance for a theory of crime is the uncertain validity of the Moral Judgment Scale. While there is some evidence for age-graded trends in moral development, Kurtines and Greif (1974) conclude that neither "the cross-sectional, longitudinal, nor sex-difference data support the notion of an invariant developmental sequence" (p. 467). Further, there are several experimental demonstrations that moral judgments can be altered readily in contra-developmental directions by brief social interactions with influential adults. This research will be presented more extensively in the section on social learning theories of moral development.

With respect to predictive validity, Kohlberg's theory may have little relevance to external behavioral criteria. Scores on the Moral Judgment Scale are derived from different levels of moral reasoning, not differential moral action. As Kurtines and Greif (1974) comment, "individuals at different stages can exhibit the same behaviors using different kinds of reasoning, whereas individuals at the same stage can exhibit different behaviors using the same type of reasoning" (p. 459). This is a particular limitation on the model's utility for criminology since violation of the criminal law, the ultimate subject matter of the field, requires the prediction of illegal acts, not immoral, amoral, or premoral cognitive judgments.

2. Piaget's Theory of Moral Development. Piaget's view of moral development (Piaget, 1932) is closely tied to his theory of intellectual development, since moral reasoning depends on cognitive maturation and the development of rules. Like Kohlberg, Piaget believes that moral development occurs in an ordered, relatively fixed sequence. Unlike Kohlberg, Piaget's model is much less differentiated; it is based on only two general stages of moral reasoning.

At the initial stage, children behave according to the wishes of authority figures. Rules are taken very literally, and the evaluation of an activity depends on its *objective* consequences rather than the intent which motivated the behavior. As the child matures he, or she, becomes more capable of autonomous moral reasoning where the evaluation of rightness and wrongness depends on the *subjective* intentions of the actor, as well as the particular circumstances surrounding the activity. Rules and laws are interpreted less literally and are not the ultimate criteria for moral decisions.

Conceptually, the relationship between these two levels of moral reasoning and the commission of crimes is not immediately clear. While greater sophistication in moral judgment would probably be associated with fewer violations of the law, this need not necessarily be true. Faithful adherence to a morality of naive legalism would likely be a very effective curb to any criminal behavior.

Conversely, situational ethics could be used as *ad hoc* apologies for behavior which is socially recognized, and statutorily defined, as criminal.

3. Social Learning Theories of Moral Development. In contrast to the age-graded sequence of development posed by Kohlberg and Piaget, social learning theorists argue that moral development depends on the gradual acquisition of social knowledge through observation, imitation, and direct instruction from parents, other adults, and older children. Moral behavior reflects the accumulation of these learning experiences as children are selectively reinforced for behaving in line with the expectations of the adults who supervise them.

The major evidence in support of the social learning position derives from experiments which purport to show how moral judgments can be modified through social influence. The most frequently cited example is an experiment by Bandura and McDonald (1963) in which children listened to several pairs of stories describing situations for moral judgments. Each pair of stories was based on two types of moral reasoning: *objective responsibility* and *subjective responsibility*. Objective moral judgments depended on the amount of damage done by an act, regardless of the intent of the actor, while subjective judgments required an appreciation of intent, rather than merely the material consequences of the act.

The children were divided into two groups, based on their predominant level of reasoning in responding to the stories. Forty-eight children used primarily objective criteria in deciding which of the stories contained more transgression; 36 children employed subjective criteria when deciding for the majority of the stories. Children from each of the objective and subjective groups were then assigned to one of three training groups.

In the first training group, children were exposed to an adult model who expressed opinions contrary to the predominant level of reasoning used by the children in the pretest. In other words, for "objective" children the adult modeled subjective reasoning, while "subjective" children were exposed to objective models. The adult models also socially reinforced the children who reversed their positions and used the same form of reasoning as their models. Children in the second training group also interacted with adults who modeled the contrary type of moral reasoning, but they did not receive any praise for a change in their own opinion. Children in the third training group were not exposed to adult models.

After "training," all children were retested on new stories. The children who had experienced a model's influence were significantly more likely to change the type of judgment they used than children not exposed to an adult model. This was true, regardless of the form of reasoning used prior to the training; "objective" children progressed to subjective judgments, and primarily "subjective" children reverted to objective judgments. Social reinforcement did not facilitate the effects of modeling alone.

These results pose a challenge to the cognitive-stage theories of moral development. Apparently, children of a certain age use different criteria for their moral judgments; further, the level of these judgments can be increased or decreased by rather simple, abbreviated social interactions.

The results of the Bandura and McDonald (1963) study are complicated by a partial replication by Cowan, Langer, Heavenrich and Nathanson (1969) which indicated that children who shifted from primarily objective to primarily subjective judgments maintained these changes at a two-week followup, while children who were induced to shift to objective judgments from their earlier subjective preferences returned to their original subjective judgments at the followup. Of course, these results are just what would be predicted by stage theorists who would regard the progression from objective to subjective morality as the result of cognitive maturation, not easily changed by isolated opportunities for contramaturational imitation.

4. Hogan's Cognitive-affective Theory. Robert Hogan's (1973) view of moral conduct is a complex five-factor theory that emphasizes the natural, evolutionary value of the rules which people make and follow. The first factor, *moral knowledge,* is a cognitive variable which refers to a person's knowledge of moral principles. A person would not be expected to behave morally unless he, or she, knew the operating rules of conduct. The second factor is *socialization.* This is the process by which rules become personally meaningful and mandatory; in the psychological vernacular, socialization produces the internalization of rules. *Empathy,* the third factor, is often identified with the ability of role-taking, or considering the effects of one's actions on another. Hogan's fourth factor is *ethics,* and involves the basis upon which a person regards rules to be useful in controlling human conduct. Two forms of ethical justification for rules have been emphasized. There is the "ethics of conscience," which is derived from higher laws of justice that are recognized by human reason and intuition. Hogan considers the ethics of conscience to be the "dominant viewpoint of the contemporary American intellectual establishment" (p. 225). The second position, the "ethics of responsibility," is a product of utilitarianism and eighteenth century legal positivism which saw law as a necessity for promoting social welfare, order, and predictability. Finally, there is *autonomy,* or the extent to which people choose to govern their behavior out of a personal sense of duty and principle.

Various kinds of moral conduct can be predicted from the differential development of these five factors, each of which can be measured independently. Deficits in both socialization and empathy will probably result in a high propensity to delinquency. However, an undersocialized, unempathic person may resist transgression if he, or she, believes strongly in the instrumental value of laws for making the world orderly and safe. Individuals who are high in empathy but somewhat deficient in socialization may feel free to break certain rules, as long as their behavior causes no harm to another person.

Within this model, moral maturity involves a combination of compliance with recognized social rules, as well as a sensitivity to the rights and feelings of others. Preliminary data (Hogan & Dickstein, 1972; cited in Hogan, 1973) has yielded substantial correlations between the model's major factors and the maturity of moral judgment among college students.

THE DIRECT LEARNING OF CRIMINAL BEHAVIOR

The remainder of this chapter is devoted to learning theories which seek to explain how criminal behaviors are acquired and maintained. We may think of these formulations as "direct" learning theories. In contrast to the emphasis of control theories on the failure to learn noncriminal modes of behavior, the theories in this section concentrate on the mechanisms by which criminal behavior itself is learned. Control theories concentrate on socialization processes that fail; direct learning theories focus on criminalization experiences that succeed. Learning explanations of the direct acquisition and maintenance of criminal behavior are exemplified by Sutherland's differential association theory, operant conditioning, Bandura's social learning theory of crime, and finally, social labeling theory. We shall now review each of these positions, beginning with differential association.

Differential Association

Edwin H. Sutherland first published the theory of differential association in 1939, presenting it in his influential textbook entitled *Principles of Criminology*. Sutherland, a descendant from the Chicago school of criminology, formulated a broad sociological theory in cultural transmission terms. In 1947 the theory underwent a slight modification, taking the form in which Donald R. Cressey, a student and colleague of Sutherland's, has continued to publish it.

Differential association has been categorized in any number of ways: Nettler (1974) describes it as a social psychological theory; Cohen (1966) classifies it as a cultural theory; Homans (1969) calls it a socialization theory of crime; Hirschi (1969) classifies it as a group conformity theory; and Sutherland and Cressey (1974) refer to it as a genetic theory. This seeming lack of congruence in interpretation is due more to biases in reviewers' evaluative dimensions than to confusion within the theory itself. It is generally agreed that the theory describes criminal behavior as the product of learning, just as any other behavior is learned. Deviance is not inherited, physiologically determined, due to deviant personality traits or a unique invention of the criminal. From association with criminal patterns, communicated through various processes, the potential criminal learns "definitions" favorable to deviant behavior. If these definitions exceed the frequency, intensity, duration, and/or priority of definitions unfavorable to deviant behavior, then the person is likely to commit a criminal act. Sutherland did not think it was necessary to associate directly with criminals or to learn specific criminal behaviors. The important factor was the definition of the behaviors in terms of their legality.

A child could learn procriminal definitions from his middle-class parents. A child might see his mother receive too much change for an article she had purchased, and observe that, even though the woman realized she had received too much money, she did not return it. The mother did this, despite the fact that she instructs her child that stealing is wrong. Similarly, upper-class business executives could consider income-tax evasion to be normative behavior but regard burglarly as obviously illegal, and deserving of punishment.

Sutherland outlined his theory in the following nine postulates:

1. Criminal behavior is learned.
2. Criminal behavior is learned in interaction with other persons in a process of communication.
3. The principle part of the learning of criminal behavior occurs within intimate personal groups.
4. When criminal behavior is learned, the learning includes: (a) techniques of committing the crime, which are sometimes very complicated, sometimes very simple; and (b) the specific direction of motives, drives, rationalizations, and attitudes.
5. The specific direction of motives and drives is learned from definitions of the legal code as favorable or unfavorable.
6. A person becomes delinquent because of an excess of definitions favorable to violation of law over definitions unfavorable to violation of law.
7. Differential associations may vary in frequency, duration, intensity, and priority.
8. The process of learning criminal behavior by association with criminal and anticriminal patterns involves all of the mechanisms that are involved in any other learning.
9. While criminal behavior is an expression of general means and values, it is not explained by those general needs and values since noncriminal behavior is an expression of the same needs and values (Sutherland, 1947).

Sutherland intended his theory to be a sociological explanation of crime. That is, he wanted his theory to explain different crime rates in the various sectors of society. However, differential association theory uses the individual as its unit of analysis, rather than a group, community or society. Sutherland and Cressey (1974) explain this apparent contradiction by asserting that since the crime rate is only a summary statement of the actions of individuals, the proper unit of analysis is the individual. Despite this they maintain that: "the postulate on which the theory is based . . . is that crime is rooted in the social organization and is an expression of that social organization. A group may be organized against criminal behavior. Most communities are organized for both criminal and anticriminal behavior, and in that sense the crime rate is an expression of the differential group organization'' (p. 77).

Evaluation of Differential Association. A multitude of criticisms have been aimed at various levels of differential association theory. Cressey (Sutherland & Cressey, 1974) has classified these into two categories: ''literary errors'' and ''popular criticisms.'' Regarding the former, Cressey maintains that since the entire theory is spelled out in just a little over two pages, there are many criticisms of the theory that are due to misunderstandings. Because Sutherland never elaborated the nine propositions, some authors have misinterpreted the meanings which he intended. One of these misinterpretations is whether mere associations with criminals are a sufficient cause of criminal behavior. If this were true, then obviously all correctional personnel should be criminals. Similarly, if it is necessary to associate with criminals in order to be a criminal oneself then it is difficult to explain middle-class delinquency or white collar crime. Cressey declares that this argument is the result of overlooking the proposition that states that there must be an excess of criminal associations in proportion to noncriminal associations for there to be delinquent tendencies.

The second misunderstanding that is common in the literature is that differential association does not explain why people have the associations they do. The theory does not address itself to the question of why some people who live in the same culture, or even the same family, learn criminal behaviors and others do not. Cressey answers this objection by claiming that the theory does not attempt to explain why people have the associations they do. The theory assumes that within the social fabric there are opportunities to associate with criminal and noncriminal types of behavior; it did not venture to say why certain individuals seem to align with one or the other.

Cressey argues that differential association theory should not be faulted for being deficient in this area, since it never intended to outline reasons for persons differentially associating with criminal or anticriminal behavior patterns. By taking this position, the proponents of the theory not only avoid the question of why people have the associations they do, but also whether people intentionally seek out certain associations, encounter them by chance, or both.

The criticisms which Cressey categorizes as ''popular criticisms'' deal with more substantive aspects of the theory. One of these has to do with the theory's scope. Several authors (Clinard, 1942, 1944, 1946; Lemert, 1953) have suggested that crimes such as naive check forging, white collar crime, and rural crime are not explained by the theory of differential association. Others (Nettler, 1974) have argued that the theory does not apply to crimes of violence or passion. Cressey maintains that until such criticisms are subjected to direct empirical tests, they should not be considered criticisms at all but ''proposals for further research.''

Another criticism centers around a supposed omission of the theory rather than lack of scope. ". . . At least a dozen authors have proposed that the (theory) is defective because it omits or overlooks the general goal of personality traits in determining criminality" (Sutherland & Cressey, 1974, p. 83). Sutherland felt that the theory might need revision to include some personality predispositions. Cressey, however, says that, in the latter part of his career, Sutherland modified this position and took the stance that advocates of trait theory needed to prove the relationship between traits and criminality. The argument between trait theorists and proponents of differential association theory may be due more to semantic preferences than to actual disagreement between the two groups. As Sutherland & Cressey (1974) and Nettler (1974) point out, both traits and criminality, as pictured in differential association theory, are the products of learning. Nettler concludes that the theory characterizes criminality as a set of attitudes and values which predispose persons to commit crimes. When differential association theory is couched in these terms, it is difficult to distinguish it from the concepts of trait theory.

A similar criticism of the theory concerns its focus on the transmission of deviant behavior from person to person, at the expense of ignoring the differential receptivity of individuals to the message. This objection is based on the observation that some people are more likely than others to learn criminal behavior. Differential susceptibility, it is argued, is the primary reason for dissimilar acquisition of crime among people in the same group. In addressing this objection, Sutherland (1956) said that the learning processes outlined in differential association theory could account for differential receptivity to criminal messages. In other words, people with criminal behavior patterns are more likely to interpret events in terms of those predispositions. Sutherland appears to be discussing differential responses once criminal patterns have already been learned. It is understandable that the perception of the situation by a criminal and a noncriminal would be different. The question being raised, however, is why some people are *initially* more susceptible to deviant messages than others.

The abstract nature of sociological theories, such as differential association, makes it difficult to test them empirically. This general characteristic is magnified in the case of differential association because of the lack of precise definitions for such key terms as "excess of definitions," or "favorable" and "unfavorable" definitions. Researchers have found it difficult to operationalize these concepts. How do you count the proportion of favorable definitions to which a person is exposed? Is it possible to measure subjective estimates of the duration, intensity, and importance of relevant communications? Questions like these plague most efforts at empirically evaluating differential association theory.

Nettler (1974) poses yet another criticism of differential association theory; it seems to completely disregard situational variables. Differential association theory treats opportunity for crime as a constant factor. Once a person has acquired criminal behavior, it is unclear what triggers a given criminal act. What kinds of situational variables compel specific incidents of embezzlement, robbery, or check forgery? The theory would have been strengthened by some general consideration of the influence of opportunity on criminal behavior.

The final criticism of differential association theory deals with its simplified treatment of the learning process. It should be remembered, however, that at the time of the original formulation of the theory, learning theory itself was relatively unsophisticated. In recent years, there have been numerous attempts to specify various learning mechanisms that accurately describe the acquisition of criminal behaviors. The remainder of this chapter reviews several of these mechanisms, beginning with operant conditioning, probably the most widely discussed variety of learning theory over the past 20 years.

Operant Conditioning

According to strict behaviorists, operant conditioning is the process by which most "voluntary" forms of behavior are developed. Of course, the most important figure in the application of operant conditioning to an understanding of human social conduct is B. F. Skinner, whose book, *Science and Human Behavior* (1953), is regarded as one of the foundations of modern behavior therapy (Rimm & Masters, 1974). The basic premise of operant conditioning is deceptively simple: behavior is learned and strengthened as a result of its consequences. The term "operant" suggests a person whose behavior acts upon the environment and changes it in some way. In turn, these environmental changes influence the probability that the behaviors which preceded them will occur in the future.

The main effect of operant conditioning is that randomly emitted, trial-and-error behaviors are progressively shaped into meaningful patterns of activity as a result of their outcomes. Positive, or rewarding, consequences (reinforcers) strengthen the likelihood of previous operants, while aversive consequences weaken the probability of future responding. Skinner's own research concentrated on the role of reinforcement as the major determinant of behavior.

There are five procedures which define the core techniques of operant conditioning. Four of these are represented in Fig. 4-1, which depicts the possible combinations of presenting or withdrawing either positive or negative reinforcers, following some emitted behavior. Presenting a positive reinforcer following some behavior is *positive reinforcement*, a process which, as the arrow in cell I indicates, strengthens the behavior. Cell II describes *(positive) punishment*, in which a negative reinforcer occurs after some behavior resulting in a decrease of that behavior's future probability of occurrence. *(Negative) punishment* (cell III) involves withdrawal of a previously available positive reinforcer after emission of some behavior. As the arrow indicates, it also decreases the future probability of that behavior. *Negative reinforcement* results in an increase in the probability of a behavior's future occurrence. As cell IV indicates, negative reinforcement involves a procedure where a negative reinforcer is withdrawn, contingent on some behavior. Reinforcement, both positive and negative, always produces the strengthening of a behavior. Punishment always decreases a behavior's future probability of performance.

The fifth procedure, not presented in Fig. 4-1, is *extinction*. Extinction refers to the withholding or elimination of consequences, following the emission of a previously conditioned operant. It results, ultimately, in the weakening of that operant.

Behaviorists recognize that many behaviors are emitted only under certain conditions. The fact that reinforcers are differentially available, depending on

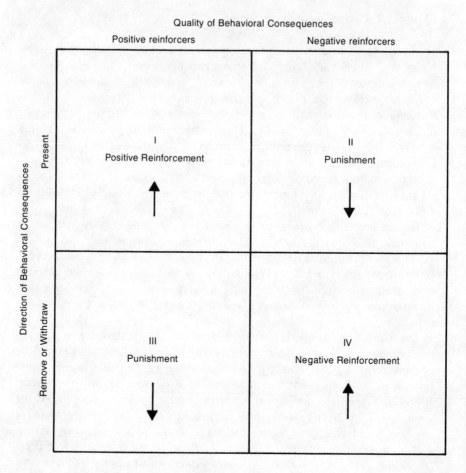

Fig. 4-1. Technique and Effect of Operant Conditioning.

certain stimuli antecedent to a given response, exerts strong control over whether that response will be performed upon the recurrence of that particular stimulus array. To choose an obvious example: we pick up the telephone and say "hello" only after the stimulus event of the phone ringing has occurred. This is not a reflective behavior; our arms do not jerk automatically to the receiver when the phone rings. However, picking up the receiver and saying "hello" in the absence of the phone ringing is seldom reinforcing, and is a very improbable response in most of our repertoires. This is an example of *stimulus control*, a process by which the situational appropriateness of most behavior is explained.

Acquisition of Criminal Behaviors. C. R. Jeffery was one of the first behaviorists to suggest that criminal behavior was learned according to the principles of operant conditioning. Jeffery's view (1965) involved a translation of differential association theory into the behavioral lingo of differential reinforcement and stimulus control: ". . . (A) criminal act occurs in an environment in which in the past the actor has been reinforced for behaving in this manner, and the aversive consequences attached to the behavior have been of such a nature that they do not control or prevent the response" (p. 295).

Shortly after Jeffery's formulation, Burgess and Akers (1966) attempted a systematic revision of Sutherland's theory into seven propositions of operant learning theory. Although several conditions of learning are recognized, Skinnerian conditions are accorded the greatest importance: "criminal behavior is learned according to the principles of operant conditioning."

Burgess and Akers claimed that operant conditioning accounted for the acquisition of original criminal acts as well as the maintenance of these behaviors. Evidence that harmful behaviors can be shaped by differential reinforcement is limited, for the most part, to the development of aggression in animals. Azrin and Hutchinson (1967) demonstrated that food rewards, made contingent on aggressive behavior, dramatically increased attacks by pigeons against one another. Aggression can also be learned rapidly when it is instrumental in allowing an animal to escape or to avoid aversive stimulation (Azrin, Hutchinson & Hake, 1967). Other data (Lagerspetz, 1964) indicate that prearranged schedules of victories and defeats can, at least temporarily, modify preexisting aggressive tendencies.

As one example of how differential reinforcement can shape aggressive behavior in humans, Bandura (1973) cites research by Patterson, Littman and Bricker (1967) which demonstrated the relationship of aggression to the consequences of children's attacks on their peers. However, it is unlikely that very many novel forms of human aggression are developed from random activities through the guidance of differential reinforcement. This would make for painful and dangerous learning. Similarly, it is doubtful whether human transgression is acquired on the basis of direct, differential reinforcement. The primary role of reinforcement is probably to ensure the continued performance of either aggressive or transgressive acts which, originally, were learned through other mechanisms.

In the next section we consider the various ways in which reinforcement can maintain antisocial behavior, transforming it from an occasional act into a more habitual repertoire of unlawfulness.

Maintenance of Criminal Behaviors. The sustained performance of most operants is regulated by their environmental-interpersonal consequences. Responses once dominant in a repertoire will cease to be performed if they are routinely followed by aversive outcomes. On the other hand, formerly low-probability behaviors will become more frequent if they regularly produce favorable results. So it is with crime. Illegal behavior will persist if the potential and actual rewards outweigh the expected and obtained costs. Criminal behaviors need not be rewarded each time they occur for this strengthening process to take place. In fact, most of the experimental literature suggests that operants (including aggressive ones) are made more durable by reinforcers delivered on an intermittent schedule.

Bandura (1973) suggests four types of direct, external reinforcers that may sustain repeated antisocial acts. First, there are tangible rewards for persistent misconduct. This is especially obvious in most property offenses, where economic rewards accrue to the successful burglar, thief, embezzler, counterfeiter, and price fixer. Repeated aggression is also related to schedules of material reinforcement. Bandura (1973) cites evidence by Cowan and Walters (1963) that boys, reinforced intermittently with marbles for striking a toy clown, performed more aggressively than continuously reinforced children during an extinction phase in which no marbles were earned for aggressiveness.

Social and status rewards are a second variety of reinforcers which will encourage the repetition of those behaviors which evoke praise, respect, or promotion. There is considerable evidence that repeated misconduct is related to the social approval and status which it gains. The value of norm violations in earning positions of leadership within juvenile gangs is well documented (e.g., Short, 1968). Social reinforcement has been shown to increase aggression by children (Patterson, Ludwig & Sonoda, 1961, cited by Bandura, 1973), and adults (Geen & Stonner, 1971; Loew, 1967).

Often, aggressive conduct is negatively reinforced because it is instrumental in terminating aversive treatment from others. Bandura (1976) refers to this as "defensive aggression" (p. 220), because it usually follows some mistreatment or coercion which the person is attempting to escape or avoid. This view of counteraggression is somewhat similar to the popular frustration-aggression hypothesis (Dollard, Doob, Miller, Mowrer, & Sears, 1939) which holds that aggression is motivated by disruption of goal-directed behavior. Regardless of the exact manner by which counteraggression is conceptualized, it tends to be rather resistant to extinction because its original success in terminating aversive treatment typically disallows any subsequent reevaluation of the threatening stimulus.

Finally, Bandura suggests that, under certain conditions, expressions of pain in victims can be reinforcing to offenders. Visible pain may be reinforcing when it is suffered by a particularly oppressive enemy, or when it is repeatedly associated with sources of pleasure such as sexual arousal. In general, however, pain cues are unlikely to be strongly rewarding. Bandura (1973) concludes, "although the scope of the experimental treatments and the populations studied are too limited to warrant sweeping generalizations, the evidence indicates that expressions of suffering serve as aggression inhibitors" (p. 198).

Social Learning Theory

Although social learning theory acknowledges the influence of differential reinforcement in the development of original behaviors, it differs from the strict operant position in ascribing more importance to cognitive factors and to the role of observational, or vicarious, learning. While social learning theory concentrates on the *behavior* of individuals, it recognizes that people actively construe the world around them in different ways, and that our expectation about the results of behavior may be as influential as the actual contingencies we experience. Social learning theory regards higher mental processes as necessary causal agents of complex human behavior (Bandura, 1969).

The most important learning mechanism in social learning theory is observational learning. Bandura (1969) claims that "virtually all learning phenomena resulting from direct experiences can occur on a vicarious basis through observation of other persons' behavior and its consequences for them" (p. 118). In fact, in many instances, learning through modeling is far more efficient and effective than learning through differential reinforcement. Observation of competent models can eliminate the hazardous and negative consequences of unguided trial-and-error behavior. Highly sophisticated behaviors, such as speech, require the presence of models as do complex chains of motor behavior, such as driving a car. For those behaviors that can be developed through direct experience, the process of learning is usually shortened by the opportunity to observe the performance of appropriate models.

In addition to the acquisition of novel responses, modeling has two other effects (Bandura, 1969). Observation of the consequences of a modeled behavior may either *inhibit* or *disinhibit* imitative behavior in an observer. Finally, observing the behavior of others can facilitate the performance of similar responses already present in the repertoire of the observer.

Observational learning depends on four components. First, one must attend to the important features of the modeled behavior. *Attentional processes* are regulated by several variables, including the utility value of models, their interpersonal attractiveness, and the affiliation preferences and opportunities of the observer. Second, for a model's behavior to be influential, the observer must be able to remember it. *Retention processes* involve the ability to encode, mentally rehearse, and store response patterns in symbolic form in long-term memory. Following the symbolic representation of modeled behaviors, the observer must attempt to perform what he or she has learned. Such *motor reproduction* depends on the behavioral abilities and the physical capacities of the observer. Vigilant attention and accurate retention will not compensate for motor deficiencies when it comes to dunking a basketball, or beating up an adversary. Finally, *reinforcement* will determine, to a large extent, whether what is learned will be overtly performed. Positive incentives will encourage the activation of previously unperformed knowledge, while unfavorable consequences for performance are likely to discourage a display of what one knows.

One obvious implication of this formulation is that learning and the actual performance of certain behaviors are not synonymous. This willingness to distinguish between learning and performance differentiates the typical social learning theorists from the modal Skinnerian who equates learning with overt performance. Bandura (1969) argues that

> the acquisition of matching responses results primarily from stimulus contiguity and associated symbolic processes, whereas the performance of observationally learned responses will depend to a great extent upon the nature of reinforcing consequences to the model or to the observer (p. 128).

This distinction is drawn later in the following terms:

> the learning analysis is concerned with the manner in which variables . . . determine the degree to which the modeled behavior is learned. The performance analysis, on the other hand, is concerned with factors governing persons' willingness to perform what they have learned (p. 129).

The most prominent attempt to apply social learning theory to human misconduct is Bandura's (1973) work, *Aggression: A Social Learning Analysis*. An abbreviated version of this theory is provided by Bandura's chapter (1976) in a book he edited with Ribes-Inesta (*Analysis of Delinquency and Aggression*). As the title of the first book suggests, Bandura's primary domain is aggressive behavior. However, there are few conceptual obstacles to applying his position to transgressive conduct as well. In this way a full range of criminal activities can be considered from a social learning perspective. Bandura's view of direct learning by differential reinforcement was presented in the previous account of operant conditioning. In this section we consider the role of other social learning variables in a theory of criminal behavior. Specifically, the presumed role of modeling and other cognitive influences in the acquisition, maintenance, and instigation of aggression are discussed.

Acquisition. According to Bandura (1976) modeling, or the "influence of example," is the most important mechanism for initiating novel patterns of aggressive behavior. Most observational learning of aggression occurs in three social contexts.

1. *Familial influences*. Aggression, which is modeled and reinforced by family members, is one primary learning source. Familial aggression may assume many forms, including child abuse at one extreme of severity to aggressive parental language and attitudes at the other. It is the arena of parental discipline however, where children are most exposed to frequent and vivid examples of coercion and aggression as the preferred style for conflict resolution.

2. *Subcultural influences*. Particular subcultures provide a rich schedule of aggression as well as social status and rewards for their most combative members. "The highest rates of aggressive behavior are found in environments where aggressive models abound and where aggressiveness is regarded as a highly valued attribute" (Bandura, 1976, p. 207). One interesting example of subculturally transmitted aggression is found in special social agencies such as the military, to whom society deliberately assigns the task of teaching effective aggression.

3. *Symbolic models*. Experimental research has demonstrated the virtually equivalent effectiveness of real-life versus pictorial, or verbally described, models in observational learning (Bandura, Ross & Ross, 1963). The major influence of symbolic models on aggression has been attributed to the mass media, particularly television.

A number of well controlled experimental (Liebert & Baron, 1972) and field (Friedrich & Stein, 1973) studies have demonstrated a *short-term* increase in interpersonal aggression associated with exposure to aggressive television fare. Evidence for a *long-term* facilitative effect of TV violence on aggression is less convincing. The most widely cited long-term study was conducted by Eron, Huesmann, Lefkowitz, and Walder (1972), who followed up a group of juveniles whose TV viewing habits had been assessed ten years earlier. Among males, there was a significant correlation between an early preference for violent television and aggression as teenagers. This outcome led the investigators to conclude that there was an enduring, independent effect of viewing violent programming on peer-rating, and psychometric measures of aggression. This conclusion may not be warranted since the research did not disconfirm the possibility that both television preferences and adolescent aggression were related to some other common etiological factor.

Evaluative reviews of the literature on television and aggression are contradictory regarding the meaning of the evidence. Bandura (1973) states, "given the abundant evidence for observational learning, there is no longer any justification for equivocating about whether children or adults learn techniques of aggression from televised models" (p. 271). Nettler (1974) cites an unpublished review by Kaplan and Singer (1972) which claims that the majority of experiments indicate that watching televised violence can instigate certain forms of viewer aggression, *given that* participants are intentionally aroused, and that ordinary negative sanctions against aggression are suspended. Singer (1971) concluded that the direct effect of media aggression on actual violence has yet to be demonstrated, although the tendency to portray great amounts of justified aggression might lower inhibitions against actual aggressive behavior.

Maintenance. In addition to direct consequences, Bandura thought that vicarious reinforcement and self-reinforcement would maintain aggressive responding.

1. *Vicarious reinforcement.* "In general, seeing aggression rewarded in others increases, and seeing it punished decreases, the tendency to behave in similar aggressive ways . . . the more consistent the observed response consequence is, the greater are the facilitatory and inhibitory effects on viewers" (Bandura, 1976, p. 223).

The maintenance-enhancing effects of vicarious consequences involve various mechanisms of influence. Observed reinforcement contingencies have informational value by indicating the topography of successful and unsuccessful actions as well as signalling the specific settings in which overt performance of certain behaviors will be well received. Vicarious successes may also motivate observers' expectations that they will enjoy similar rewards for duplicated behaviors. Observed outcomes can also result in the conditioning or extinction of fears, which would, in turn, inhibit or disinhibit aggressive and transgressive behaviors. As Bandura points out, the criminal law notion of general deterrence rests on the assumption that "exemplary punishment" will inhibit widespread criminal activity.

In special circumstances, observation of punishment can provoke aggressive responding in an audience. This is the case where the punishment is disproportionate to the offense it follows. Unjustifiably severe punishment may incite observers to intensify their aggression as a reaction against treatment which they see as illegitimate and brutal.

2. *Self-reinforcement.* Unlike most Skinnerians, social learning theorists stress the ability of people to regulate their own behaviors through self-produced consequences. This self-control extends beyond the mere "rigging" of external consequences. It includes the cognitive and affective evaluations that accompany human behavior. Individuals who derive a sense of pride and self-worth in their ability to harm or to "rip off" others will persist in these activities. Conversely, people are likely to discontinue conduct which results in self-criticism and feelings of self-contempt.

Bandura emphasizes the tendency of people to exempt themselves from their own injunctions or prohibitions of conscience, thereby allowing themselves to behave aggressively without suffering severe insults to self-esteem. These tactics of "self-exoneration" are remarkably similar to Sykes and Matza's techniques of neutralization (see Chapter 3 of this volume). Neutralization of self-punishment for aggression can assume any one of the following forms: minimizing the seriousness of one's aggression by identifying more serious or dangerous offenses; justifying aggression by appealing to the motivation of higher values; displacing the responsibility for behavior onto some legitimate authority; blaming the victims of aggression for their predicament; diffusing or sharing responsibility for aggressive offenses; dehumanizing victims as objects whose ascribed characteristics dispossess them of their human qualities; and misrepresenting the consequences of one's aggression by underestimating the injury it inflicts.

Antecedents to Aggression. Both social learning theory and operant conditioning recognize the importance of certain environmental antecedents which may increase the probability of a subsequent aggressive or transgressive behavior. Whether one prefers the operant terminology of stimulus control or Bandura's choice of behavioral '' instigators'' the effect is the same: people "tend to aggress toward persons and in contexts where it is relatively safe and rewarding to do so, but they are disinclined to act aggressively when to do so carries a high risk of punishment" (Bandura, 1976, p. 212).

1. *Modeling influences.* According to Bandura, modeling is an effective procedure for prompting others to behave aggressively. Aggressive models are particularly effective when observers have been previously frustrated or the modeled aggression is presented in a justifiable context (Berkowitz, 1965).

2. *Prior aversive treatment.* Physical assaults, verbal threats and insults, reductions in levels of available reinforcers, and thwarting of goal-directed behavior are all aversive events which may cause a state of emotional distress that precedes an increase in aggressive conduct. Contrary to the classic frustration-aggression theory, frustration need not, invariably, elicit an aggressive reaction. Rather, "aversive antecedents, although they vary in their activating potential, are facilitative rather than necessary or sufficient conditions for aggression" (Bandura, 1976, p. 217).

3. *Incentive inducements.* Both aggression and transgression may be prompted by the anticipated rewards of misbehavior. Expected incentives may motivate certain behaviors, whether these expectations are veridical or not. Bandura (1976) suggests that "aggressive actions are therefore sometimes prompted and temporarily sustained by erroneous anticipated consequences. Habitual offenders, for example, often err by overestimating the chances of success for transgressive behavior" (p. 217).

4. *Instructional control.* Milgram's (1963) famous experiment which demonstrated the widespread willingness to follow orders to inflict "pain" on another person, suggests that aggressive behavior can be instigated by commands from respected authorities. Thankfully, the potency of instructional control is not without its limits. Obedient aggression decreases under circum-

stances where participants can observe the harmful consequences of their actions or are brought into closer physical proximity with their victims (Milgram, 1974).

5. *Delusional control*. Occasionally, behavior can come under nonconsensual verbal control. This is the case where individuals respond aggressively to hallucinated commands or to paranoid suspicion. Typically, individuals who suffer delusional symptoms are also somewhat socially isolated, a factor which insulates them from potential corrective influences in the environment.

6. *Alcohol use*. Feldman (1977) specifies alcohol ingestion as a potential facilitator of aggressive affect and behavior. Although the mechanisms by which alcohol potentiates aggression are not certain, it must be reckoned with as a potent instigator to harmful conduct. It is estimated that one-third to one-half of all felons were to some degree under the influence of alcohol when they committed their crimes (Kittrie, 1971).

Evaluation of Behavioral Learning Theories. Operant and social learning formulations are both distinguished by several advantageous features. Undoubtedly, the major asset is their ability to account for how specific criminal acts are actually developed by individual offenders. No other position explains the specific topography of crime as well as behavioral learning theory.

A second strength of these perspectives is the applicability of their concepts to both aggressive and transgressive crime. Most other theories have a rather restrictive range of explanatory convenience; sociological theories are concerned predominantly with property offenses, while psychologicial perspectives are best suited for explaining crimes of violence. However, one of the major tenets of behavioral learning theory is that all behavior, criminal or noncriminal, violent or nonviolent, honest or dishonest, is acquired and maintained by identical mechanisms of learning.

Operant and social learning conceptualizations of crime are not without their limitations. The most obvious one is that there is precious little empirical evidence to support the proposition that *in vivo* criminal behaviors are learned according to the principles of behaviorism. Almost all of the relevant data have been generated in laboratory analogues, whose approximation to real life crime is very questionable. The most obvious deficiency of these experimental demonstrations is that the laboratory setting nullifies the whole gamut of social and legal sanctions which actual offenders must be willing to risk. The laboratory situation is quite different for experimental subjects, who may aggress or transgress in an environment stripped clean of those very rules and consequences that could deter offending.

The learning framework cannot explain why certain people fall prey to learning influences while others are able to resist them. Learning may be a necessary ingredient in the development of crime, but it is probably not a sufficient one. We all are quite aware of the potentially rewarding consequences of property offenses; however, few of us steal. Over 90 percent of the American population are exposed to aggressive models on television, yet only a few people go on to emulate the violence they observe.

Finally, behavioral theories do not explain why people who commit the same acts, who perform the same violations of law are treated differently. What accounts for the fact that some offenders are officially categorized and punished as criminals while others are exempted, almost entirely, from the stigmatizing imprimaturs of the criminal justice system? Labeling theory, our next topic, has devoted most of its attention to this topic.

Social Labeling Theory

Nearly all theories of criminology seek to identify prior causes of crime, whether these causes are biological, psychological, or sociological. Labeling theory, like the conflict theories of the previous chapter, is an exception. It does not emphasize the etiology of crime; rather, labeling theory argues that the proper subject matter in studying any type of deviance is the labels or special names conferred on specific individuals by social audiences.

The intellectual heritage of labeling theory owes much to George Herbert Mead who proposed that one's sense of self is largely socially constructed; the way we perceive ourselves depends, in part, on the way others have behaved toward us. There have been several important labeling theorists, not all of whom embrace each and every tenet of the labeling position with equal intensity. Among the most influential originators of the labeling hypothesis have been Howard Becker (*Outsiders: Studies in the Sociology of Deviance*, 1963), Edwin Lemert (*Human Deviance, Social Problems, and Social Control*, 1967), Kai Erikson (1962) and Edwin Schur (*Labeling Deviant Behavior: Its Sociological Implications*, 1971). Labeling theory has also been a popular approach to such phenomena as mental illness (Scheff, 1966), aging (MacDonald, 1973), retardation (Mercer, 1965), and differential educational achievement (Rosenthal & Jacobsen, 1968).

The basic assumption of labeling theory is that deviance is constructed or created by the labels society assigns to certain acts of people. Becker (1963) argues, ''deviance is not a quality of the act a person commits, but rather a consequence of the application by others of rules and sanctions to an 'offender.' The deviant is one to whom that label has successfully been applied; deviant behavior is behavior that people so label'' (p. 9). This is actually a theory of role formation. Roles are assigned and enforced by the manner in which the behavior of persons is categorized. Likewise, persons are pushed to accept and enact these roles because of social expectations which are very difficult to disconfirm. Individuals, ultimately, conform to the stereotypes which have been applied to them. The created role of ''delinquent'' or ''criminal'' enforces a progressive commitment to rule violation and deviation. Social control is the major independent variable in the creation of deviance.

Labeling theorists do not try to explain the primary deviance of a criminal's behavior so much as the secondary deviance produced by society's official reactions to offensive misconduct. This distinction between primary and secondary deviance was developed by Lemert who emphasized the function of stigmatizing labels in advancing and sustaining a deviant identity (secondary deviance) which may have borne an unsubstantial, even trivial relationship to original physical or psychological differences (primary deviance).

There are two important implications of the labeling hypothesis for criminal behavior. The first is that the criminal justice system produces much of the deviance it is intended to correct, and, in fact, that this deleterious impact increases as the defendant progresses through the system. A person arrested, but against whom the charges are quickly dropped, should be less stigmatized than one required to appear in court. A convicted person, given a probated sentence, is not stigmatized as much as one who serves a prison term.

The second implication derived from the labeling perspective is that certain types of individuals are more often stigmatized into deviance than others. Juveniles from the lower socioeconomic classes, political dissidents, and minority-group members are the most likely candidates for this discriminatory handling. As we have already seen in Chapter 2, the data do not consistently support the biasing influence of extralegal demographics with respect to official tallies of arrests. The cumulative effect of each stage of the justice system sequence might be more problematic. Feldman (1977) concludes, "at each stage following the *same initial offending behavior*—complaints, search, arrest, trial, conviction and type of sentence—there is a greater possibility that certain social groups of the population will proceed to the next stage than will other groups. Moreover, certain offenses are more likely to lead offenders into custody than others. The final composition of those in custody will be a function *both* of the facts of offending and of being detected *and* of the systematic bias in selection which occurs at each stage of the process" (p. 27).

Evaluation of Social Labeling Theories. Social labeling theory has elicited sharp criticisms. Some commentators (Gibbs, 1966; Taylor, Walton & Young, 1973) do not even consider the labeling approach to meet the minimum requirements of a formal theory. Many others (Akers, 1967; Gibbs, 1966; Taylor, Walton & Young, 1973; and Ward, 1971) have questioned most of the core assumptions of the labeling position.

Before examining its conceptual and practical weaknesses, we must acknowledge the values of the labeling hypothesis. It forces us to recognize that many of our criminal justice policies may do more harm than good by entrenching individuals in a deviant status or by escalating their occasional rule breaking into a criminal career. The labeling hypothesis formally affirms our natural suspicion that some treatments are worse than the illnesses they are prescribed to cure. In this respect, it would be more profitable to regard labeling theory as a very perceptive explanation of social reaction to deviance, and one which has many important practical implications for how to respond to offensive behavior in ways which do not exacerbate it. In fact, the major intellectual impetus for most of this country's attempts at decriminalization is provided by social labeling theory.

Labeling theorists also cause other theorists to contend with the fact that a primary determinant of future behavior is the labels assigned to people on the basis of their past conduct. The impact of this *self-fulfilling prophecy* would be especially severe on juveniles, whose behavior may become progressively more criminal because of official reactions which push the juvenile toward a more extreme delinquent self-concept, and away from a law abiding self-perception.

The most obvious limitation of the social labeling position is that it does not adequately explain the commission of the rule-breaking behavior itself. Labeling theorists confuse offensive misconduct with the social reactions to it. Differences between people and their actions exist, and will persist, independent of the names we call them. However, social labeling theorists minimize the importance of primary differences whether due to physiological, psychological, or sociological influences, preferring, somewhat paradoxically, to aggrandize each and every political or justice system difference they can identify as irresistible pressures toward criminality.

Labeling theory requires an almost total externalization of responsibility for behavior which flies in the face of the common-sense presumption that labels might just be very accurate categorizations of the individuals to which they are applied. Although social labeling theory's attitude toward society is sometimes characterized as cynically realistic (Taylor, Walton & Young, 1973), the belief that a world without labels could be a world without deviance is actually a highly romanticized portrayal of the individual.

The assertion that "no act is intrinsically criminal" (Feldman, 1977, p. 204) may be technically true, but the ultimate logical implications of this position are practically, socially, and psychologically unpalatable. It is highly doubtful that the problem of robbery would be lessened if we renamed it "enforced borrowing." Just as "a rose by any other name would smell as sweet," assault and battery under any other label would hurt as much. I do not mean to deny the value of those decriminalization efforts which might result from the social labeling perspective. I do mean to question the utility of the belief that behaviors would evaporate if only society would redefine them.

It is important to remember the principal advantage of labeling theory over the traditional positivistic, absolutist theories of crime: its recognition that social reactions to rule violations are not equivalent and that these differential reactions may sustain, or even escalate, criminal careers. Unfortunately, this value is obscured by labeling theorists' persistent tendency to substitute one sort of conceptual blindness for another. The problem of differential, official responding to antisocial behavior is in no way remediated by denying individual differences in either personality or performance.

Feldman's Integrated Learning Theory

M. Phillip Feldman's recent attempt (1977) to assimilate the perspectives of modern learning theory, individual predispositions, and social labeling theory represents one of the most comprehensive sociopsychological accounts of crime currently available. Feldman's theory is relevant to crimes against both persons and property.

Learning variables are the most influential of criminogenic factors exerting their effects on the acquisition, performance, and maintenance of criminal behavior. Individual predispositions exert most of their impact at the acquisition stage, while labeling variables predominantly effect the maintenance of agressive and transgressive misconduct. The learning component is also the most persuasive influence across different types of offenders; however, predispositions may play a more important role for persons who suffer psychological problems or are at the extremes of the major dimensions of personality.

Learning. Feldman's view of learning recognizes two different directions of influence. People may learn not to offend due to early socialization practices whose restraining power is maintained by positive consequences for rule-keeping, and negative consequences for rule-breaking. Faulty training in socially acceptable behavior can result in a repertoire dominated by legally forbidden activities.

People also may learn to offend through the direct effects of differential reinforcement, social modeling, and situational inducements to dishonest or harmful behavior. Criminal behavior will be maintained by certain cognitive processes accompanying overt performance. One such mechanism is cognitive dissonance which, like the techniques of neutralization or Bandura's techniques of self-exoneration, may self-servingly underestimate the aversiveness of one's offenses. Another is self-reinforcement for successful criminal acts which help to maintain such behaviors.

The effects of learning variables may be moderated by the broad social situations that have been emphasized by the social structural theorists. In Feldman's words (1977), "membership of a particular class or culture, or living in a particular geographical area might affect the probabilities of acquiring and performing criminal behaviors, and of such behaviors being maintained or reduced" (p. 284).

Individual predisposition. Just as social settings might lead to a greater consistency of criminal behavior among certain groups, so might individual personality differences. Successful socialization depends on an optimal match between the training techniques used and the personality attributes of the learner. Feldman chooses Eysenck's theory of personality to account for the differential acquisition of conditioned responses unfavorable to law breaking. Extroverted neurotics are thought to have the poorest personality potential for effective socialization, while people high on psychoticism may be relatively insensitive to the plight of their victims. The role of personality predispositions remains secondary to the effects of learning. Relatively small, initial differences in personality may grow into major ones through differential social shaping. "The Eysenckian personality dimensions are likely to make a useful contribution to the explanation of criminal behavior, but more to acquisition than its performance on maintenance, and much more in the case of extreme, than in the case of medium, scorers. Even in acquisition, by extreme scorers, personality will be only part of the story; situational variables will play a significant role" (Feldman, 1977, p. 161).

Social labeling. The final component of Feldman's framework is labeling theory, which "points to the important role of the social reactions of those in positions of power within the law enforcement and penal systems in maintaining, perhaps even enhancing, the criminal behavior of over-represented groups" (Feldman, 1977, p. 285). The person whose genetic predisposition, in combination with a specific learning history, produces a high susceptibility to offending may be pushed into official and progressively more permanent deviance by criminalizing contacts with the legal system.

Evaluation of Feldman's Theory. Feldman's formulation of crime satisfies the formal requirements of good theory. It applies to crimes against both persons and property. It can account equally well for the initial acquisition, overt performance, and subsequent maintenance of criminal behavior. Its emphasis on mechanisms of learning enables it to specify how aggression and transgression are actually developed. And it points the way for practical innovations in crime control and correction.

In addition, Feldman's theory surmounts many of the difficulties encountered by an exclusive reliance on social learning or on operant concepts. Basically, it confronts the social realities of crime in a more satisfactory way than does a theory based strictly on learning principles. Its inclusion of personality predispositions acknowledges a differential susceptibility to acquire a repertoire favorable to offending. In this way it accounts for the selective manifestation of the learning experiences that underlie crime. Secondly, the inadvertent amplification of some criminal careers can be explained by the harmful stereotypes imposed by the procedures of the criminal justice system. A social learning analysis of labeling theory stresses the opportunity to learn more felonious offenses from the criminal models one encounters following arrest or imprisonment or conviction. From this perspective, the most deleterious effect of official criminal labels is that they force association and identification with those people who are the most able instructors of crime — criminals themselves.

The most distinctive asset of Feldman's theory is its well-informed eclecticism. It is richly psychological, drawing on the literatures of personality theory, moral development, socialization practices, attitude change, classical and operant conditioning, social learning theory, altruism, equity theory, psychopathology, and genetics. Although most of the research from these diverse areas was generated within the confines of experimental settings, and therefore suffers reduced ecological validity, this problem should not obscure the unique integration of material that Feldman has accomplished. The limitations of experimental analogues have a remedy: conduct research on actual and potential criminal behavior occurring in the natural environment. Feldman's integrated learning theory provides an excellent framework from which to investigate the complementary influences of genetically based personality predispositions, learning, and social labeling in producing criminal repertoires.

NOTES

1. A third dimension, psychoticism, was added later and did not play a role in Eysenck's early formulation of conditioning and crime. Psychoticism would be related to criminality in some degree because of its marked similarity to the characteristics of psychopathy.

2. A very similar theory of criminality has been proposed by another Englishman, Gordon Trasler, in his book, *The Explanation of Criminality* (1962). Trasler's position is sometimes seen as a corrective to Eysenck's overemphasis on genetic determinants. Although Trasler also uses the concept of differential capacity for conditioning, he stresses child rearing practices and consequently the learning of general moral principles, rather than the acquisition of many specific inhibitions whose interrelationships depend on verbal labeling and stimulus generalization.

3. Reckless acknowledged the importance of other examples of control theory such as Reiss (1951) and Nye (1958) both of which he recast into the language of containment.

Chapter 5
Institutional Behavior Modification

> He hath evermore had the liberty
> of prison; give him leave to
> escape hence, he would not.
>
> — Shakespeare, *Measure for Measure*

Although behavior modification procedures for officially identified criminals have been applied in a diversity of settings (see Chapters 6 and 7), the greatest number of offenders have been exposed to behavioral techniques in some type of penal institution (see Chapters 8 and 9 for discussions of the compatibility of behavior modification with correctional philosophy). The objectives of these institutional programs have been far-ranging and pursued with numerous types of offenders. For the most part, the target behaviors of these applications have been components of a larger, extant rehabilitative effort which may include vocational training, group and individual psychotherapy, and educational opportunities.

This chapter reviews three types of institutional behavior modification:
1. Behavioral approaches to remedial education;
2. Contingency management programs that occur primarily at a systemic level, and involve nearly all of an inmate's behavior during his period of incarceration;
3. Institutional aversion therapy, a technology that has sparked frequent, and often dramatic, controversy regarding the ethics and the legalities of its application.

INSTITUTIONAL EDUCATION PROGRAMS

McKee (1964) and his associates (Clements & McKee, 1968) have used programmed instruction for several years at the Draper Correctional Center in

Alabama. Although programmed materials offer advantages over traditional methods of education, they have not proven successful in sustaining learning in inmate populations. In an attempt to increase the learning productivity of 16 inmates, Clements and McKee (1968) employed a combination of performance contracts and contingency management procedures. Following a three week baseline during which participants completed programmed materials at their own pace, a four week "experimenter management" phase was introduced. Each week during this period the experimenter assigned an amount of work approximately 20 percent greater than the average assigned for the immediately previous week. Successful completion of the specified materials resulted in short reinforcement periods (15 minutes) that allowed the participant to choose preferred activities from a "reinforcement menu." In the final phase of the study, the inmates specified the amounts of materials they wished to complete. The one restriction was that performance output had to be at least as great as the baseline average. The same reinforcement schedule was in effect as during phase two.

The results indicated that educational output during the two contingency periods was significantly greater than during baseline. The experimenter and self-management phases did not differ significantly in educational output. Level of performance during the last week of the "experimenter management" phase was maintained for both weeks of phase three. These changes were accompanied by greater work efficiency and improvements on periodic achievement tests.

The absence of a reversal to baseline condition in this study makes it difficult to attribute its effects to the procedures during the second and third phases. In addition, the design confounded the effects of the performance contracts with those of the contingency procedure.

Milan, Wood, Williams, Rogers, Hampton, and McKee (1974) evaluated alternative formats for the presentation of programmed instruction in a basic English course. Three methods of presentation were contrasted: a traditional programmed textbook, a teaching machine, which presented the textbook material a frame at a time, and tutoring sessions in which peer tutors presented the textbook material and then monitored student responses giving corrective feedback when necessary. The nine inmates who served as participants in the experiment received each of the formats in a counterbalanced order, and data were presented for the seven students who completed the course.

The individual tutoring method was associated with faster rates of study than the programmed text or the teaching machine, which did not differ from one another. However, the varying instructional formats did not produce any differential effects on either immediate or delayed retention measures. The different rates of study appear to be a result of minimal importance, given the author's suggestion that they may have been merely an artifact of the reduced amount of study activity required by the tutoring procedure. From a cost effectiveness perspective, the much greater cost of the tutoring format would not be justified by the rather unsubstantial differences represented by these data.

In an effort to increase participation in educational programs, Milan (1972) examined the influences of a "license" procedure in which inmates could exchange tokens for backup reinforcers only when they possessed an exchange license. While the tokens were earned by successful participation in a broad-scale token economy, licenses could be obtained only by completing specified amounts of educational material. The effect of the license procedure was substantial. Prior to the token economy .2 percent of the inmates were involved in the program for an average of .2 minutes daily. During the token-only phase (no license procedure in effect), 17.4 percent of the inmates were involved in the program for an average of 37.3 minutes per day. Participation during the license phase increased to 41.9 percent of the inmates devoting an average of 161.8 minutes per day to the program. Following termination of the licensing procedure, a second token-only phase was implemented during which only 8.5 percent of the inmates participated for an average of 25.5 minutes per day. A final baseline period resulted in no inmate participation in the educational program. Milan and McKee (1974) report other variations on the basic model such as the use of regular performance charts and financial payment for educational achievement.

Contingency-managed programmed instruction has yielded other impressive outcomes. Reviewing the Draper project, Milan, Wood, Williams, Rogers, Hampton, and McKee (1974) reported that "offenders enrolled in the projects averaged gains of 1.4 grades per 208 hours of programmed instruction. High school equivalencies were earned by 95 percent of those who qualified for and took the GED, and nine former students entered college after leaving prison" (p. 11). It is not possible to determine how these figures compared to the performance of nonprogram inmates because such data have not appeared in published form.

Bassett, Blanchard, Harrison, and Wood (1973) reported a program at an adult prison farm where expanded access to phone privileges was made contingent on attendance at a remedial education center. The results indicated that during a 17-day contingency phase, the man-hours utilization of the educational center was almost three times as great as that during baseline levels. Reinstatement of baseline conditions resulted in a return to baseline levels of use. The man-hour increase, which was associated with the contingency, was also significantly related to grade level improvement on a monthly achievement test. Methodologically, this study was an advance over the earlier work by Clements and McKee (1968) which found academic achievement to be related substantially to the introduction of a contingency program, but did not include either a control group or an attempt to reverse behavior to baseline levels.

Additional work by this group of researchers (Bassett, Blanchard & Koshland, 1975) has concentrated on increasing the occurrence of "free world" targets defined as ". . . behaviors not subservient to the maintenance of institutional harmony, but which, instead, had potentially adaptive value for the inmates once they returned to the free world" (p. 640). Two goals were selected: increasing television-news watching, thereby knowledge of current events, and encouraging voluntary attendance at an educational center. The experiments to be reviewed here were conducted within the larger context of a ward-wide behavior modification program which was a comprehensive, contingency-based system, operative apparently on an around-the-clock basis.

In experiment one, percentage of time watching television and comprehension of news content (assessed with short answer quizzes) were analyzed with a sequential design that presented a noninstructional baseline (six weeks), instructions to watch and attend to the news (six weeks), instructions plus noncontingent quizzes (six weeks), instructions plus quizzes, on which inmates earned contingency points for correct answers (four weeks), instructions plus noncontingent quizzes (four weeks), and instructions only (eight weeks). The final stage involved a return to the contingent-quiz condition. The instructional and noncontingent quiz conditions were associated with initial, but temporary, increases in television viewing. During the noncontingent quiz condition, inmate performance stabilized at about 40 percent correct responding. The contingent-quiz procedure led to clear and very durable increases in both television news viewing (approximately 80 percent) and accurate content comprehension (about 70 percent).

In the second experiment, voluntary participation in the institution's Learning Center, which utilized individualized, programmed educational materials, was the target. Percentage of free time devoted to remedial education was measured with an ABAB design where $A_1 A_2$ provided the normal 50 points for free time attendance, and $B_1 B_2$ doubled the number of contingency points available for attendance at the Learning Center. Attendance figures averaged 20 percent during the initial baseline, increased to 45 percent after the introduction of the "bonus points" conditions, returned to 20 percent during the second baseline, and stabilized at approximately 90 percent when "bonus points" was reinstated. This surprisingly high level of participation continued for the 3.5 month duration of the bonus phase.

The authors acknowledged two limitations of their intervention that prevent any conclusion about the ultimate rehabilitative impact of the procedures—in spite of the high rates of performed target behaviors, there was little evidence that these activities had acquired the "functional autonomy which would ensure their continuation in the absence of any contrived reinforcement, and related to this was the lack of data that would compel a belief in the potential generalizability of these changes to noninstitutional environments.

PRISON TOKEN ECONOMIES

The second prevalent behavioral target of correctional facilities is increasing inmate compliance with institutional rules of conduct. The published reports of such programs are rare, possibly because their implementations are quite uneven and unsystematized. Opton (1974) cites estimates that more than 20 states have used some variant of a prison token economy. As an example of these programs, one study (Von Holden, 1969; cited by Brodsky, 1973) reported an increase in inmate compliance with military prison rules after the introduction of a contingency program that utilized a variety of reinforcers (e.g., snacks, release from segregation). Maintenance of these changes was evidenced at a 60-day followup. Six additional prison token economies are described in more detail in the following sections.

The Walter Reed Project

A special ward program for soldiers classified as "character or behavior disorders" was established at Walter Reed Hospital in 1967 (Boren & Colman, 1970; Colman & Baker, 1969; Colman & Boren, 1969). The program was intended for soldiers who had had a civilian history of minor arrests, been AWOL repeatedly, attempted suicide, or evidenced difficulty with the adjustment requirements presented by military life. The program was closed to homosexuals, alcoholics, or drug addicts. Soldiers transferred to this unit for treatment were viewed as having deficiencies in educational, occupational, and social areas of functioning. Forty-eight men participated in the program during its first year of operation. The mean age of participants was 20 years; 83 percent of the men were white, the remainder were black. Three-fourths were in a low socioeconomic-class category, and half had civilian police records. A token economy was instituted as the method of behavior change. Points were provided for soldier performance in each of the following areas: military assignments, educational classes, work duty, and ward operation (e.g., attendance at meeting, appropriate attire). Points could be exchanged for the usual assortment of privileges, such as semiprivate rooms, free coffee, passes, and access to recreational activities. Deliberate efforts were directed at individualizing the behavioral skills to be developed, and the men were responsible, to some degree, for their own treatment programming.

The program had two phases. During the first ten weeks each man was required to purchase all reinforcers with his token points. After ten weeks of satisfactory performance, participants graduated to phase two, in which program rewards were contingent on positive weekly performance reviews. Soldiers in phase two also were expected to take an active leadership role in the therapeutic management of new assignees to the ward. The duration of treatment was 16 weeks.

A comparison was performed between 46 program participants who had been released for at least three months and 48 "control" participants who had, apparently, received either general disciplinary or psychiatric attention. Of those men who had been in the token economy, 69.5 percent were functioning in a regular military unit ("successes") while 30.5 percent had received either an administrative discharge from duty or were AWOL ("failures"). In contrast, 71.7 percent of the control subjects were discharged from duty or put into the stockade ("failures"), and 28.3 percent were regarded as "successes."

These limited data are difficult to evaluate because of several methodological problems. First, it was not clear, from the published version of the program, what constituted the standard treatments to which the so-called control subjects were exposed. Also, it was not clear whether program and control subjects were similar on demographic characteristics, length of treatment, or the interval between treatment and followup. Although some components of the program were analyzed with a reversal design (Boren & Colman, 1970), behavioral performance in the four targeted areas was assessed neither at baseline, nor following any reversal of program contingencies.

The Cellblock Token Economy

The major work of the Experimental Manpower Laboratory for Corrections (EMLC) at the Draper Correctional Center in Elmore, Alabama is described by Milan and McKee (1974), and Milan, et al. (1974). The Cellblock Token Economy, as this project is known, represents the most thoroughly researched, behaviorally oriented, prison program to date. Four representative Draper experiments are reviewed below (for additional examples, see Milan, et al., 1974).

Experiment One (Milan & McKee, 1974). The characteristic method of securing control of inmates is the punishment model, in which prisoners lose initially available resources and privileges contingent on their "bad behavior" or receive direct disciplinary punishment (verbal harrassment, isolation, etc.). The application of punishment is routinized in our prisons despite numerous suggestions of its limited effectiveness and adverse side effects. This first study examined the effects of the usual institutional control procedures upon prisoner conduct.

The study was conducted in a 40-bed cellblock of the Draper Correctional Center. The impact of the punishment model was assessed by the following three measures: percentage of self-management skills performed (e.g., bed-making, area maintenance, personal appearance), percentage of voluntarily performed maintenance tasks completed (e.g., cell upkeep, mopping, cleaning), and behavioral incidents (e.g., fighting, property destruction, insubordination).

The study employed an ABA design. Stage A ("laissez-faire baseline") involved verbal instructions to perform the self-management and maintenance tasks, but no contingencies were applied for noncompliance. In Stage B ("officer corrects"), the correctional officer in the cellblock applied the usual methods of institutional control (e.g., isolation, loss of good time) to increase inmate performance of self-management duties. Maintenance tasks were not targeted during this phase. Phase C involved the reinstitution of baseline procedures.

The median level of self-maintenance skills during baseline (32 percent) was almost doubled during the "officer corrects" conditions (62 percent) but slowly declined following the introduction of the second baseline. Baseline levels of self-maintenance tasks (35 percent) were relatively unaffected by the subsequent phases.

While the effects of the punishment procedures did not generalize to non-targeted areas, they were quite effective with respect to the targeted behavior of self-maintenance. As expected however, introduction of aversive control during the "officer treats" phase was coincidental with a marked increase in behavioral incidents. The number of days during baseline–one in which at least one behavioral incident occurred was only 11.8 percent, while incidents occurred on 47.8 percent of "officer corrects" days. Behavioral incidents were recorded on 28.6 percent of baseline–two days. These data are consistent with laboratory evidence that aversive control provides immediate results at the expense of increased undesirable side effects (Azrin & Holz, 1966).

Experiment Two (Milan, et al., 1974). This study examined the potential of an alternative management regime based on principles of positive reinforcement. The project was in operation during inmates' off-work hours (approximately seven hours per weekday, and 15 hours per holiday and weekend day) for a 420-day period. Reinforceable activities were restricted to those occurring on the experimental cellblock itself. "The token economy focused primarily upon those aspects of inmate performance of concern to custodial personnel: arising at the appointed hour, making the bed, cleaning the general living area, and maintaining a presentable personal appearance. A secondary objective was to motivate participation and performance in a voluntarily remedial education program in operation evenings and weekends" (Milan & McKee, 1974; pp. 32-33).

Token Points were credited to inmate checking accounts, and could be exchanged for a variety of incentives (television watching, being away from the cellblock, and the buying of commissary items) simply by writing a check for the desired item. All accounts were individualized and balanced daily. Observations of critical behaviors were recorded by a correctional officer. Independent reliability checks on project staff revealed interrater reliabilities that typically exceeded .90.

The study's design was a complex one, involving a sequence of 13 experimental manipulations in which differential levels of token points were presented contingently, or noncontingently (see Milan, et al., 1974, pp. 33-37). Three conditions (*baseline₁, officer treats, baseline₂*) preceded implementation of the token economy. During (1) *baseline₁* the scoring criteria for the target behaviors were explained to the inmates who also were informed during this period whether their behavior met reinforceable standards, and in instances when it did not, what corrections were required for an adequate performance. The (2) *officer treats* condition allowed a correctional officer to employ a variety of typical coercive procedures (threats, verbal intimidation, work details) which he had found previously successful in obtaining inmate compliance. (3) *Baseline₂* was identical to the *baseline₁* condition.

Verbal feedback, and specification of performance criteria were continued during a (4) *60 points noncontingent₁* phase which also provided 60 token points for each of the four behaviors, independent of whether an inmate had performed any of them. The (5) *60 points contingent₁* phase was the first condition to establish a contingency in which token points were given only when an inmate's behavior met the specified performance criteria. This phase was followed consecutively by (6) *90 points contingent*, (7) *60 points contingent₂* and (8) *60 points noncontingent₂* phases.

A (9) *zero points* condition compared the effects of no reinforcement with the noncontingent reinforcement of the immediately prior *60 points noncontingent₂* phase. This was followed by reintroduction of a (10) *60 points noncontingent₃* phase and a (11) *60 points contingent₃* phase. The last two phases were (12) *announced baseline₃*, which informed inmates that the token economy would be terminated in one week, and (13) *baseline₃* which was a return to *baseline₁* and *baseline₂* conditions.

The effects of these conditions on the four targeted activities (arising on time, making bed, maintaining living area and passing inspection) are summarized in Fig. 5-1. During those conditions where token points were awarded contingently performance levels always exceeded 85 percent of activities meeting criteria. In fact, on most days when the token economy was in operation, percentage of satisfactory performance of targeted behaviors surpassed 90 percent when the contingency phases were in effect, as opposed to precontingency levels of 40 percent (maintenance tasks), and 60 percent (self-management skills). For most baseline and noncontingent reinforcement phases, the percentage of all activities completed at criterion levels fluctuated between 65 percent and 75 percent. Approximately 64 percent of activities were completed during the *officer treats* days, a condition intended to approximate prototypical forms of institutional control. This was not significantly different from the level of performance for preceding or succeeding baseline conditions. In addition, Milan and McKee (1974) reported that participation in the remedial education program increased from .2 percent of inmates participating to 20 percent participating during the program.

Introduction of the final baseline condition resulted in an expected, and

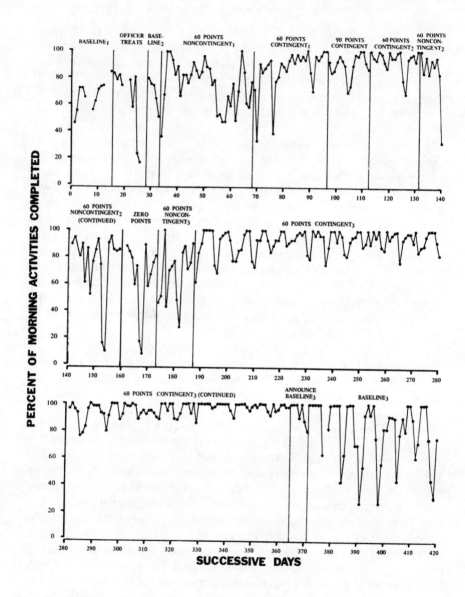

Fig. 5-1. Daily percentages of all morning activities completed under all conditions. (Reprinted with permission from Milan, Wood, Williams, Rogers, Hampton, and McKee, *Applied Behavior Analysis and the Imprisoned Adult Felon Project 1: Cell Block Token Economy*, Experimental Manpower Laboratory for Corrections, 1974.)

significant, decrease in level of completed activities. Inmate performance during the initial days of this phase was higher than that recorded during the pretoken economy baseline. However, there was no significant difference in completed activities between initial baseline and the second half of the final baseline. These data were interpreted as suggesting a steady decline in performance over the course of the final baseline condition.

Experiment Three (Milan, et al., 1974). The general success of the previous project resulted in introduction of an expanded token economy involving inmate performance across the entire day. In addition to being much more comprehensive in scope, this program, which was in effect for 390 days, substituted a punchcard system for the simulated banking system of the previous economy. The reinforcers, contingencies, and operations of this token economy were quite similar to that of the first one. Its administrators stated that the results were "as promising as those of the first. Inmate performance improved in each of the three areas under study and was maintained at high levels throughout the duration of the token economy. In addition, these changes in performance occurred without the concomitant increase in behavioral incidents witnessed during examination of the punishment model" (Milan & McKee, 1974, p. 34).

Experiment Four (Milan, et al, 1974). A further analysis of the Cellblock Token Economy evaluated the relationship between the magnitude of reinforcement and the probability that a targeted behavior would be performed. A surprising outcome of Experiment Two was that a 50 percent increase in the amount of token award (*90 points contingent* phases) was not associated with a significant increase in completed activities over either preceding or succeeding *60 points contingent* phases. The target of this specific intervention was to produce an increase in the percentage of inmates watching a televised news program, an activity thought to be conducive to a greater knowledge of current events, and social changes outside the prison. Eleven sequential experimental conditions were presented in this experiment: (1) *baseline*$_1$ (free access to the television room); (2) *pay 60 points*$_1$ (access to television required an inmate to pay 60 token points for one hour of viewing); (3) *free*$_1$ (access to television was free only during the hour of news programming); (4) *earn 60 points*$_1$ (for each hour of viewing the news program the inmate was credited 60 points). The remaining seven phases involved either increases in the amount of reinforcement or return to no reinforcement conditions: (5) *earn 120 points*$_1$; (6) *earn 240 points*$_1$; (7) *earn 120 points*$_2$; (8) *earn 60 points*; (9) *free*$_2$; (10) *pay 60 points*$_2$; and (11) *baseline*$_2$.

For the most part, the results of these manipulations were not surprising. Television newswatching was infrequent among inmates during *baseline* and *free* and *pay points* conditions, reaching a maximum of only 12.2 percent of inmates during the initial *free* phase. Increasing the magnitude of reinforcement from 60 to 120 points increased the percentage of inmates viewing television news (60 $points_1$-43.8 percent; 120 $points_1$-65.2 percent; 60 $points_2$-28.3 percent; and 120 $points_2$-61.7 percent). However, increasing the payoff to 240 points did not produce any increase in the targeted behavior (61.2 percent of inmates watched the news).

The EMLC token economies produced impressive results on almost all ''in house'' criteria. Their effect on extra–institutional indices of success was less convincing. Saunders (1974) cited 15-month followup data that revealed no differences in recidivism rates for token economy graduates from those achieved by two types of vocational training programs. In none of the summaries of the Draper program was there reference to postrelease criteria such as recidivism or employment status. Indeed the objective of the first token economy was described explicitly as ''motivating the performance of activities that administrators consider important for the orderly operation of their institutions'' (Milan, et al., 1974, p. 15). Apparently, justification of this goal was based on the contention that unless administrators develop more effective, less tempestuous means of institutional management, ''it is unlikely that they will have either the time or the inclination to turn their fuller attention to the more general problems involved in preparing the offender for his eventual return to community life'' (Milan, et al., 1974, p. 15). This logic is not compelling, especially in light of the failure to collect any data which would bear upon the point. One might just as easily suggest that implementation of an efficacious managerial system would result in levels of prisoner passivity and compliance that would be dysfunctional for present-day societal demands.

The START Tier Program

The most notorious of prison token economies was the now inoperative Special Treatment and Rehabilitative Training Program (START) developed in 1972 at the Medical Center for Federal Prisoners in Springfield, Missouri. The program was developed as a means of more effectively dealing with the most hard-to-manage residents of the federal prison system. Prisoners for whom a START placement was deemed appropriate were male inmates who were already in a prison's segregation unit because of their repetitive assaults, destructiveness, or violations of regulations. The major intention of START was to help participants gain sufficient control over their aggressive behavior to allow a return to an institution for ''training programs designed to help him make a more successful community adjustment'' (Levinson, 1974, p. 5).

START was an eight-level program with each level having certain behavioral requirements that when completed successfully were followed by institutional privileges. The levels were progressive, each succeeding one demanding more behavioral control than the previous, while at the same time increasing the range of available privileges. Promotion through the eight stages was expected in eight to nine months. (For a concise summary of the eight levels, see Kennedy, 1976.)

Residents selected for the START program have been defined by program opponents as "the few who had managed to maintain the individuality, leadership, self interest, and independence often felt to be important behaviors outside of institutions but somehow intolerable within their walls" (Holland, 1974; cited by Levinson, 1974, p. 6) and by program proponents as "destructive" and "physically assaultive" (Levinson, 1974, p,. 5). Levinson also indicated that 11 of these men had received additional sentences for offenses committed in other prisons (murder, n = 6; assault, n = 4; possession of weapon, n = 1) in addition to an avarage of 12 major disciplinary "incidents" (arson, bombing, and stabbing of fellow inmates).

The meager outcome data available for the START project are disconcerting on at least two counts. First, as detailed below, the overall impact of the program was primarily negative. But even at a more basic level, there are considerable discrepancies between the outcome figures presented in the available summaries of START.

For example, Kennedy (1976), apparently relying on a written motion (Saunders, Milstein, & Roseman, 1974) prepared for a federal district court decision on START, claimed that 21 men had been transferred to the program since its conception. According to Kennedy the final status (January, 1974) of these 21 inmates was distributed across the following categories: (1) six men remained in START; (2) three were in a separate segregation unit; (3) five prisoners had been hospitalized, presumably for psychiatric reasons; (4) five men who had demonstrated no improvement were transferred out of the program; and (5) two inmates were released, one because his sentence had expired, and another because he had completed successfully all phases of the program.

These data conflict with those presented by Levinson (1974) who reports that during the 16 months of program operation 99 offenders were considered for a START placement. Twenty-six met the program's admission requirements (see Levinson, 1974); of these, 19 individuals participated. The average program population at any one time was 12. Of the 19 participants, Levinson (1974) classified 10 as "successes" defined by their progression through the eight levels, and transfer back to an "open" institution. Six months after termination of START, six of the successes "continued to show positive behavior, including three who were released to the community" (Levinson, 1974, p. 8). Of the nine failures, eight remained in an institutional segregation unit of some kind.

It now seems apparent that START was ill-conceived for a group of inmates who had repeatedly proven resistant to the effects of similar, restrictive segregation conditions in other institutions (Kennedy, 1976). Levinson (1974) quotes the following testimony of Dr. William J. DeRisi, a court-appointed reviewer of the program: "(conditions in START) conform to bureau of prison regulations; it is little different from 'segregation' imposed at other bureau institutions. Further, it is the kind of confinement most familiar to START candidates. Most START inmates we spoke to expressed a preference for START confinement conditions." Coupled with the inadvisability of repeating a historically ineffective segregation regime was START's acknowledged emphasis on reinforcing behaviors of submission rather than behaviors of social competence. For example, Kennedy (1976) lists among the target criteria for "good days" or point reinforcers: "accepted or performed assignments, duties or tasks without needing persuasion" and "accepted designated areas to be cleaned without bickering." Additionally, the lack of any inmate input into the design or implementation of the program undoubtedly contributed to a generalized sense of powerlessness and submission.

Still, it is unlikely that a totally noncoercive treatment environment for START-suitable prisoners will be developed. To suggest that these inmates, many of whom had long histories of very violent behavior, would not benefit from learning how to become more submissive in certain situations is just as unreasonable as any claim that unquestioning obedience to the arbitrary wishes of a prison guard is a social virtue.

Notwithstanding the claims of the ACLU and many mental health professionals, it might be argued that START was, at least, less coercive than the segregation units by which it was preceded and has now been replaced. Perhaps what was most offensive were the attempts to make the program's coercive qualities more acceptable by coating them with a thin veneer of therapeutic semantics. Unfortunately, outcome data comparing START with other procedures for handling troublesome inmates are not available; however, it is questionable that a large enough difference would exist to justify START's per capita cost of $39.18 compared to the Federal Bureau of Prison's average of $14.50 (Levinson, 1974). Perhaps the most balanced judgment would be that if START was not an expensive failure, neither was it an economic success.

Virginia's Contingency Management Program

Similar in intent to START, the LEAA-funded Contingency Management Program (CMP) in Virginia was initiated in June 1973 and halted early in 1975 after state officials refused to renew the project. According to an early CMP operations manual the program was intended to "(1) receive inmates who are particularly troublesome to themselves, to other inmates, and thus to the smooth administration of correctional programs and (2) to modify the actions of such inmates so that they may be returned to the beneficial influence of correctional programs in the general population of another institution until their sentences are fulfilled" (Johnson & Geller, 1973, p. 5). Although START and CMP have been compared frequently, the program differences between the two were numerous. For example, in contrast to START, inmate participation in CMP was completely voluntary and did not include special deprivation conditions. Table 5-1 presents a fine-point comparison of other START-CMP differences.

The CMP was a four-tier token economy designed to be an alternative to the segregation units at the Richmond State Penitentiary and the Goochland County State Farm (Oliver, 1974). Inmates entered the CMP merely by requesting a credit card upon which credits for certain designated behaviors were punched and later exchanged for commissary and recreational items. Reinforceable behavior during Stage One, conducted at the Richmond Penitentiary, included educational involvement, cell maintenance, and improved personal appearance. Satisfactory performance in these areas warranted promotion to Stage Two at the state farm where inmates encountered both more freedom and more performance requirements.

The major additions at Stage Two were job training (emphasis was placed on learning rudimentary skills for data processing operations — e.g., typing), and social skills training. At this stage, contingencies were applied systematically for the acquisition of "appropriate interpersonal strategies." Stages Three and Four were located at the Saint Bride's Correctional Unit in Chesapeake, Virginia. Stage Three was distinguished by "direct training on data processing machinery," and by an increased focus on the development of social repertoires that would permit the harmonious group living that was expected during Stage Four. Beginning in Stage Three there was a gradual fading out of the CMP credit economy. By Stage Four, the credit economy was discontinued completely, and CMP residents were paid money for their work on data processing jobs. Stage Four living was virtually indistinguishable from the conditions in the general prison population; available services and privileges were greatly increased over Stage One levels. All stages provided G.E.D. courses.

In June 1974, after a site visit from a representative of the granting agency, CMP officials introduced major revisions in their program (Geller, Johnson, Hamlin, & Kennedy, 1977). First, educational opportunities were expanded by offering an alternative to the G.E.D. program in the form of individualized, written contracts that specified a wider range of reinforceable educational accomplishments (e.g., completing sections of the G.E.D. program, creative writing, developing typing proficiency).

Second, there was a marked reduction in contingencies that emphasized "institutionalized" behaviors and personal appearance. As a replacement for these contingencies, a plan was contrived whereby inmates were reinforced for presenting short (three minute) speeches to a CMP counselor. There were two weekly opportunities for such presentations, one for which the inmate selected a topic, and the other for which a topic was assigned. CMP counselors awarded credits on the basis of several criteria including overall amount of information and quality of information.

For the most part, the educational contracts and the verbal presentations

Table 5-1 Contrasts Between START and CMP

START (Special Treatment and Rehabilitative Training)	CMP (Contingency Management Program)
1. Eight stages in one building (maximum capacity = 30 inmates). Medical Center for Federal Prisoners, Springfield, Mo. Four levels of privileges: orientation, Level 1, Levels 2-6, Levels 7 and 8.	1. Four stages, each in separate facilities (maximum capacity in each unit is 70 inmates). Stage 1 — Richmond Penitentiary, Stage 2 — Virginia State Farm, Stages 3 and 4 — St. Bridges Correctional Unit Chesapeake, Va. Each successive stage added privileges and reduced environmental restrictions.
2. One-week orientation (relative deprivation) = no personal property, no commissary, 1 hr. recreation.	2. No orientation stage: inmate assigned to segregation received CMP information and could join at any time.
3. Involuntary participation. Revision provided for nonparticipation status; inmate lives in first deprivation stage (i.e., same as orientation).	3. An inmate could enter or drop CMP at any time. Nonparticipants were dealt with by the institution as regular segregated inmates.
4. Full-time staff (besides security officers): 2 managers, 2 industrial specialists, 2 counselors, 1 recreation-education specialist = total of 7.	4. Full-time staff (besides security officers): 3 counselors per building 1 data analyst per building, a vocational instructor for Stage 3 and 4 = total of 18.

(continued)

Table 5-1 (Cont.) Contrasts Between START and CMP

START (Special Treatment and Rehabilitative Training)	CMP (Contingency Management Program)
5. Part-time staff = one each of the following: chaplain, education specialist, doctor, caseworker, physician's assistant, occupational therapist = total of 6.	5. Part-time staff: four PhD psychologists, one nurse per building, one teacher per building = total of 12.
6. Muslim religious services and/or discussions were allegedly prevented.	6. No implications for religious practices.
7. Two graduates after 17 months	7. Twelve graduates after 14 months.
8. Graduates returned to the general population of a high-security prison.	8. Relocation units compatible with inmates' vocational interests; e.g., general population with reduced custody-level, prework release facility, or work release unit.
9. Vocational training = broom production.	9. Vocational training = typing, computer card keypunching.
10. Privileges existing in prior segregation status were allegedly removed during initial levels (e.g., hometown newspapers and magazines).	10. All privileges existing in segregation status continued.
11. Less than 30 inmates involved.	11. One hundred to 200 inmates were participating at any particular time.
12. Direct input from one PhD psychologist during program development and refinement.	12. Direct input from four PhD psychologists throughout program development and refinement.
13. Reduction of regular, expected privileges during orientation stage.	13. No reduction in the regular, expected privileges.

14. No immediate and tangible behavior-contingent reinforcers administered, apart from advancement to levels with more privileges.

15. Educational activities not expected in the orientation stage, and not directly reinforced at any level.

16. No personally owned property allowed during orientation and in nonparticipation status. Some property permitted in levels 1 thru 8, upon approval.

17. Recreation severely limited at orientation and nonparticipation levels (i.e., 1 hr. per week); Levels 1-6 = 1 hr. daily; Levels 7 and 8 = more than 1 hr. daily.

18. No commissary spending during orientation status and nonparticipation status.

19. Frequent use of aversive consequences; e.g., removal of status, or Good Time.

14. A ''credit-economy'' nested within the first two stages of a four-stage, progressive living plan. Tangible credits absent in the latter two stages.

15. Educational activities expected and directly reinforced at all stages.

16. All personal property normally allowed in the general prison population allowed at each stage.

17. At least three hrs. daily recreation was available at each stage except the first stage (i.e., padlock status = 2 days of 3 hrs. each per week).

18. Commissary privileges at all levels. inmates at each stage could earn credits for commissary spending (1 credit = 1 cent).

19. Minimal use of punishment; i.e., one inmate lost his CMP card for one week (timeout from credit spending) following a detection of counterfeited punches on his CMP card.

(Reprinted with permission from E. Scott Geller, colloquium presented at the Florida State University, October 1974.)

were regarded positively by both inmates and CMP counselors and "appeared to involve more than superficial, mechanistic behaviors and to preserve individuality" (Geller, et al., 1977, p. 37). The major disadvantage of these innovations was the decreased objectivity of evaluations and the awarding of credits, especially in the case of the inmate speeches. The termination of the Contingency Management Program only a few months after the introduction of the changes prevented any empirical evaluation of their program impact.

Aversive control was minimized in the CMP. "Counterfeiting" of CMP credit cards was the only punishable behavior in the program. Punishment consisted of one week restriction on the spending, but not earning, of credits. Inmates who failed to perform satisfactorily at any level could be reassigned to a lower level. While such a demotion involved a loss of available privileges, it was a mild form of punishment since cessation of program participation always remained an inmate's prerogative.

Evaluation of the Contingency Management Program is limited to preliminary data on a small number of graduates. Apparently, the level of inmate participation exceeded that of START. Geller (1974) estimated the number of Stage One and Stage Two residents to be approximately 90 per week; approximately 30 inmates graduated to Stages Three and Four. After 16 months of operation, 12 inmates had graduated from the program. Placement of these men varied, but was indicative of positive changes. "Three will remain in Stage Four as inmate-CMP staff, five will be transferred to a field unit or prework release center where they will hopefully continue their education and vocational training compatible with their interests and skills, three were recommended for parole, and one was released to the street" (Geller & Johnson, 1974, p. 17).

The originators of the CMP have discussed a number of specific problems contributing to the demise of their program, and of their own uncertainty about the possibility of applying a behavior modification technology in a penal setting (Geller, et al., 1977). In addition to the institutional obstacles enumerated by Reppucci and Saunders (1974), Geller, et al., (1977) identified the lack of support by local personnel and administrators, frequent staff turnover, and inaccurate and inflammatory labeling of the program by its detractors as major impediments to the CMP's continuation.

A particularly vexing problem concerned the attempts to make CMP participation voluntary which, in turn, necessitated the integration of participating and nonparticipating prisoners. Among other detrimental effects, "the most prominent difficulty was that opportunities to earn backup reinforcers (such as cigarettes) weakened the power of certain 'rich' social leaders and, therefore, altered peer group dominance hierarchies. Consequently, joining or quitting CMP was often a decision provoked by program-irrelevant factors, in that nonparticipants were frequently coerced by their peers to join or not join the treatment program, and some CMP participants were periodically pressured into dropping out of their treatment program. Thus, the integration of

CMP participants and nonparticipants provoked much coercive control by the. inmate peer culture" (Geller, et al., 1977. p. 29).

The first stages of the CMP have been maintained by Virginia prison officials. Apparently, its purposes no longer include the systematic preparation of inmates, either for group living or job training. Trotter (1975a) quotes prison officials' intentions as "modify(ing) the behavior of inmates who 'disrupt institutional routine by venting aggression, cowering, or simply refusing to obey rules and regulations'" (p. 10).

It is clear that START and CMP have met somewhat parallel fates. An especially ironic outcome for both programs has been that successful or threatened legal action has resulted in the departure of the professional, supervisory staff while the custodial staff still remains. Both programs continue in either truncated and disguised forms, or have been replaced by previously existing methods of securing inmate compliance.

The Patuxent Institution

The controversy surrounding the Patuxent Institution in Jessup, Maryland has rivaled the dimensions of the debates about the START program. Originating in 1955, Patuxent was designed to be a facility which embraced the philosophy of therapeutic rehabilitation rather than punishment for severe offenders. The institution's staff is composed primarily of mental health professionals including a psychiatrist as the Director, eight other psychiatrists, 12 psychologists, 17 social workers, and numerous personnel representing educational, vocational, and recreational services. This professionalization of staff is reflected by the cost of operating the institution, which was reported by Trotter (1975b) to be $12,000 annually for each inmate. Patuxent can accommodate 400 to 500 residents.

Assignment of an offender to Patuxent involves a series of legal, quasi-legal, and clinical decisions. The placement process is initiated by a judge, or in some instances a prosecuting or defense attorney, who, believing a convict to be a compulsive criminal or dangerously antisocial, refers the individual for a diagnostic evaluation at Patuxent. This evaluation typically includes a psychiatric interview, medical exam, and a battery of psychological tests and is directed at a determination of whether the offender qualifies as a "defective delinquent." Maryland statutorily defines the status of a defective delinquent on the basis of two criteria: "(1) the individual must have been convicted and sentenced for a felony, a misdemeanor punishable by imprisonment in the state penitentiary, a crime of violence or one of a number of specified sex crimes," and (2) although legally sane, the individual "reveals . . . persistent, aggravated antisocial or criminal behavior . . . and is found to have either such intellectual deficiency or emotional unbalance, or both, as to clearly demonstrate an actual danger to society" (Trotter, 1975b).

If a person is diagnosed by the Patuxent staff as a defective delinquent, he then receives a formal, *civil* commitment hearing (with the option of having a jury present) the purpose of which is to decide whether to follow the staff's recommendation for commitment. Trotter reports that of the 1,894 cases fully evaluated between 1955 and 1972, 1,163 (61 percent) were diagnosed as defective delinquents and recommended for commitment. The court has agreed, and ordered commitment in 976 cases (52 percent of those fully evaluated; 84 percent of those professionally recommended).

One of the most intensely contested features of the Patuxent program has been its use of the indeterminate sentence whereby the length of a convict's sentence is unspecified, being dependent entirely on professionals' and, ultimately, the court's decision that the individual is cured. A judgment of "cure" apparently is dependent on the inmate's development of psychological insight into his problem and the attainment of internal controls over his behavior. The primary justification for the indeterminate sentence has been its hypothesized capacity for motivating inmates to maximize their involvement in treatment programs. Yet it often has been associated with periods of confinement that exceeded what would have been allowed in a conventional prison.

The Patuxent program itself consists of three basic elements: group psychotherapy, an incentive system based on "learning theory," and the provision of a therapeutic milieu. Group therapy has been conceptualized rather conventionally as having as its objective an increased awareness by inmates of "their distorted perception, feelings and attitudes, and the part these distortions play in developing their antisocial behavior patterns" (Trotter, 1975b). The attribution of a milieu therapy quality to the institution is based apparently on its avowed rehabilitative philosophy reflected in the employment of a large number of professionals.

The major behavior change element is the graded, four-level incentive system through which an inmate is expected to progress. At level one, the prisoner is provided with only basic necessities, has limited recreational opportunities, and is assigned to the least desirable work details. Promotion through levels two, three, and four are accompanied by more freedom of movement, personal autonomy, and privileges (e.g., more use of day room, expanded visitation rights). Eligibility for opportunities such as job training and parole is introduced at the third level. In addition to advancing to higher levels on the basis of behavior changes, an inmate can be demoted within the system for a host of behavioral violations and disapproved attitudes. Decisions about inmate promotion and demotion rest with "classification committees" whose vague criteria for decision making have been previously criticized (Goldfarb & Singer, 1970). Most convicts released on an institutional recommendation are placed in a specialized parole program which provides services such as housing assistance, employment counseling, and supportive therapy.

Each inmate is evaluated once a year to determine his progress toward the goal of being cured. In its 18 year history, Patuxent has released as "cured" only 135 men. Almost three times that number (337) have been released by court decisions in the absence of a positive recommendation by the Patuxent staff. For the 135 releases recommended by professionals, the recidivism rate has been only seven percent while 39 percent of the inmates released against staff regulations have relapsed.

There can be little doubt that a recidivism rate of seven percent is lower than that achieved by almost any other program with a comparable population. However, the precise meaning of Patuxent's recidivism data is uncertain due to a number of methodological and administrative problems (Kennedy, 1976; Rappaport, 1977). First, the impressiveness of a seven percent recidivism rate is mitigated by the fact that the number of men recommended for release is very small (only 14 percent of those committed). Equally conservative release policies pursued in the usual prison undoubtedly would lower the average recidivism rate.

Additionally, as Kennedy (1976) has observed, Patuxent's intensive and extensive parole program confounds the effects of the institutional treatment in at least two ways. Unlike most systems, Patuxent does not include crimes committed during parole in its recidivism estimates. Kennedy (1976) cites one evaluation (Hodges, 1971) of Patuxent which revealed a 51 percent recidivism rate over a three year period when criminal parole violations were included. A second source of equivocation stems from the fact that those prisoners released against staff recommendations are not included in the specialized parole program. The discrepancy in recidivism between recommended (seven percent) versus not recommended (39 percent) releasees may be attributable to the differential access to parole rather than institutional treatment differences.

Finally, there is satisfactory evidence that recidivism decreases with the age of offender (Glaser, 1964). The unusually long periods of incarceration experienced by the average Patuxent inmate may be responsible for producing older inmates at the time of release who, under many circumstances, would present a lower recidivism risk.

Like similar programs reviewed in this chapter, Patuxent has stimulated inmate rebellion (Kennedy, 1976), media and professional criticism (Trotter, 1975b), and a judicial inquiry in response to an inmate law suit (*McCray v. Maryland*, 1971). In *McCray* the court held that the use of such techniques as a segregation unit (in the therapeutic vernacular: ''negative reinforcers'') constituted cruel and unusual punishment and required that the institution restructure its program around a set of written rules, with limited, well-specified consequences for infractions.

In what has become a familiar refrain for institutional behavioral modifications, the Patuxent debate culminated in demands that the institution be closed. Legislation for this purpose was passed in 1975 by the Maryland House of Representatives but stalled in the Senate which sent it to a legislative council for more study. At the time of this writing, a compromise bill has passed both houses of the Maryland legislature and is awaiting the Governor's signature. Among the important provisions of this bill is its prohibition of the indeterminate sentence. The bill, which has received the support of many mental health professionals (Monahan, 1977), also attempts to reduce the coercive quality which previously characterized inmate participation in the program. Finally, the criteria for assignment to the institution have been more carefully specified and made more stringent, thereby narrowing the range of "eligible persons" (the bill's new term for "defective delinquents") to be sent to Patuxent.

Junction City Treatment Center

One of the more systematic applications of behavioral principles to incarcerated offenders has been conducted at Ohio's Junction City Treatment Center (JCTC). Initial evaluation (McNamara & Andrasik, 1977) of this program has provided quasi-experimental data on the positive effects of different program elements.

JCTC received from other Ohio correctional facilities those convicted, male felons who had (1) evidenced some "special mental health or adjustment needs" (McNamara & Andrasik, 1977, p. 20) and (2) volunteered, via an informed consent procedure, for such a transfer. Inmates were transferred from JCTC to another correctional facility, either at their own requests or through an administrative decision. The evaluation period for the current study was August 26, 1973 to December 12, 1973, during which 50 inmates participated. Participants were 18 to 35 years of age, were at least nine months away from a parole hearing, and had I.Q.s above 85.

Three classes of behavior were identified as targets, the successful performance of which determined advancement through the program's five-step level system. The first class was the nearly ubiquitous category of self-maintenance skills that have been emphasized in START, CMP, and Draper projects, and included behaviors such as dressing properly, cleaning one's living area, etc. A second category of target activities was concerned with self-improvement, for which the inmate was expected to engage in 30 hours per week of education, employment programs, activity therapy, or counseling. The provision of these targets was important because of their presumably greater relevance to adequate extra-institutional functioning. Finally, inmates were evaluated on their ability not to engage in inappropriate behaviors, including rule infractions as well as physical or verbal aggression. Promotion through the five tiers of the behavior change system was based on weekly staff ratings and, as in similar programs, was accompanied by greater personal freedom and improved institutional living conditions.

The Step Privilege System enabled residents to earn more privileges as they progressed through the system. For example, Intake, or Step One residents had restricted access to the day room and television, could not stay up later than ten p.m., and were allowed few personal possessions. At an intermediate level (Step Three) residents were permitted to wear civilian clothes, had expanded visitation hours, and were allowed more personal possessions. Residents who had progressed to Step Five were able to attend special affairs away from the institution, had late-night privileges, and were permitted more freedom of movement within the institution.

The effects of the program were evaluated with a design that introduced two types of baselines prior to the contingency phase. For the initial four weeks, self-improvement, self-maintenance, and inappropriate behaviors were monitored during an *unobtrusive baseline* wherein the program staff monitored the three target behaviors without explicitly informing inmates that certain behaviors were being observed. This phase was followed by a seven-week *reactive baseline* during which inmates were being monitored and given feedback about their level of performance. The third phase involved the introduction of the contingency program in which inmates' progress through the tier system was determined by satisfactory completion of the three program behaviors.

The effect of the three phases on self-improvement, self-maintenance, and inappropriate conduct are presented in Figs. 5-2, 5-3, and 5-4. With the exception of "inappropriate behavior," the greatest change was associated with the introduction of the *reactive* baseline. The contingency phase produced small increments in the number of self-maintenance and self-improvement behaviors and a pronounced decrease in inappropriate behaviors. While the positive impact of monitoring and feedback (reactive baseline) is consistent with a substantial experimental literature, careful inspection of Figs. 5-2, 5-3, and 5-4 reveals that the reactive baselines were preceded in each case by a positively accelerating, unobtrusive baseline which, if continued, may have yielded nearly equivalent results. In any event, it does not appear that inmates were unaware of the behavioral surveillance taking place during the "unobtrusive" baseline, a factor which militates against the clear separation of the impact of different program components.

The JCTC program is distinguished from other penal contingency programs on several counts. First, the contingency program was applied on an institution-wide, 24-hour basis intended to provide a comprehensive, managerial system for the correctional center. Second, this was not a funded, demonstration project, therefore did not benefit from a large increase in institutional resources or therapeutic staff. Finally, from the perspective of program evaluation, this project's collection of relatively long-term recidivism data makes it almost unique among behavioral interventions in prisons.

Recidivism data were monitored for 64 released residents for the period of January 1, 1972 to May 30, 1976 (McNamara, Andrasik, & Abbott, 1977). Two types of recidivist categories were included: violations of parole conditions, and rearrest/reconviction for new offenses. The average age of this sample at the time of program entry was 24.8 years; average length of incarceration was 41.1 weeks. Twenty-eight percent of the sample recidivated within the time period. Fifty-six percent of the recidivists had violated a condition of

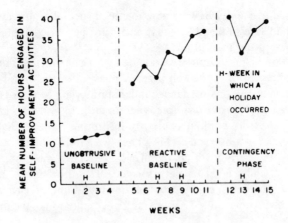

Fig. 5-2. Mean hours engaged in self-improvement activities as a function of the program phases. (Reprinted permission from McNamara, J. Regis & Andrasik, Frank, "Systematic Program Change—Its Effects on Resident Behavior in a Forensic Psychiatry Institution," *Journal of Behavior Therapy and Experimental Psychiatry,* vol. 8, 19-23. Copyright © 1977, Pergamon Press, Ltd.)

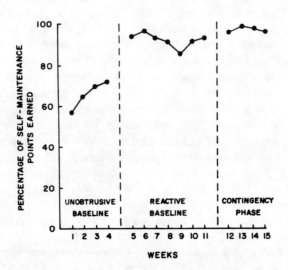

Fig. 5-3. Percentage of self-maintenance behaviors performed as a function of the program phases. (Reprinted with permission from McNamara, J. Regis & Andrasik, Frank, "Systematic Program Change—Its Effects on Resident Behavior in a Forensic Psychiatry Institution," *Journal of Behavior a Therapy and Experimental Psychiatry,* vol. 8, 19-23. Copyright © 1977, Pergamon Press, Ltd.)

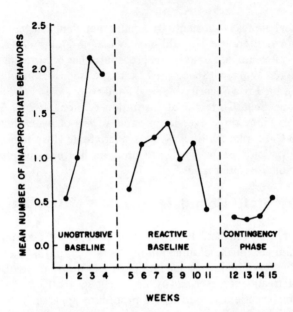

Fig. 5-4. Mean number of inappropriate behaviors as a function of the program phases. (Reprinted with permission from McNamara, J. Regis & Andrasik, Frank, "Systematic Program Change—Its Effects on Resident Behavior in a Forensic Psychiatry Institution," *Journal of Behavior and Experimental Psychiatry,* vol. 8, 19-23. Copyright © 1977, Pergamon Press, Ltd.)

parole while 44.4 percent had committed a new crime. A short-term recidivism rate of 28.1 percent is not a discouraging outcome compared to other institutional programs. As the authors acknowledge, the lack of a cohort control with which to compare these results precluded definitive conclusions about the program's specific effects.

Unfortunately, the ultimate status of this program has paralleled that of many procedurally dissimilar projects such as START and CMP. The entire JCTC institution was shut down in mid-1976 by the state of Ohio; this closure was accompanied, of course, by a discontinuation of the behavior change program.

AVERSION THERAPY IN INSTITUTIONS

Aversion therapies have been used most often in correctional institutions for the control of aggressive, sexually deviant, or uncooperative behaviors. It is not certain how widespread their use is in prison; published accounts of aversion programs are quite uncommon. The number of court cases challenging the legality of these treatments, however, makes it clear that the incidence of aversive techniques is substantially greater than that reflected by the existing professional literature. In addition to the programs described in this section, the systematic use of aversion procedures has occurred at the California Institute for Women (Spece, 1972), the Wisconsin State Penitentiary (Sage, 1974), the Iowa Security Medical Facility (*Knecht v. Gillman*, 1973), and the Connecticut Correctional Institution (Opton, 1974). The present section will examine three aversion programs, two of which have been implemented in California facilities — Atascadero State Hospital and the Vacaville Rehabilitation Center. The third program has been conducted in the Ontario Regional Penitentiaries.

Atascadero State Hospital

Reimringer, Morgan, and Bramwell (1970) reported a chemically based aversion technique for the elimination of "persistent physical or verbal violence, deviant sexual behavior, and lack of cooperation and involvement with the individual treatment prescribed by the patient's ward team" (pp. 28-29). A total of 90 male patients received the procedure apparently in lieu of the facility's traditional responses (restraint, isolation, and tranquilization) to unacceptable inmate behavior.

The technique was procedurally quite simple. Following a predetermined schedule, the staff administered to the patient an intravenous, 20 mg. dose of succinylcholine, a neuromuscular blocking agent that produces rapid (34-40 seconds after administration) but brief paralysis of the diaphragm and suppression of breathing. Inmates remained conscious during the period of apnea. The experience was defined by inmates as an intensely terrifying one. Upon suppression of breathing, the "talking phase" of the technique was initiated. This took the form of verbal admonishments to discontinue unacceptable behaviors, along with suggestions to increase positive "constructive socialization." Suggestions were repeated until the inmate was able to respond verbally to the attending staff.

The outcome measure was frequency of acting out behavior. Sixty-eight percent of the patients were classified as improved (no incidents for more than three months), 18 percent were listed as temporarily improved (no incidents for up to three months), and 13 percent were placed in a "no change" category. Only one inmate increased his violent episodes over the course of the treatment. Evaluation of these data is difficult. First of all, the criteria for reported incidents were not specified, and it is doubtful that raters were blind to the experimental status of inmates receiving aversion trials. Further, no reliability data were provided, nor were there any comparisons made with suitable controls.

Conceptually, this demonstration is also difficult to classify. At times, it appeared to follow a punishment paradigm. At least some of the time succinylcholine was delivered contingent on the occurrence of some objectionable behavior. In other instances, the procedure was described as a kind of chemically assisted sensitization procedure. As a third alternative, Dirks (1974) suggested that the drug actually was not used as an aversive UCS but as a means of introducing "a state of heightened suggestibility" (p. 1328).

Whatever its theoretical paradigm, the Atascadero experiment evoked much professional criticism. At best, it represented a rather corrupted treatment. At worst, its failure to obtain informed consent from participating inmates may have made it both unethical and illegal (Spece, 1972). Intolerance for the program did result in its termination and in some efforts to replace it with more innovative treatments. One such effort was the Sexual Reorientation Program for homosexual pedophiles, a population to which succinylcholine often had been administered.

The goal of this program was to teach homosexual inmates the skills necessary for adult homosexual behavior (Keith, 1974; Serber & Keith, 1974). Its methods involved a wide range of group-based behavioral techniques including modeling, role-playing, behavioral rehearsal, and feedback. The program has been broadened by its incorporation of consciousness-raising meetings, and rational-emotive therapy. One of its most noteworthy features was its utilization of gay community volunteers as models who taught, and role-played appropriate adult, homosexual behaviors (e.g., conversational skills, "cruising," seduction). In addition, this involvement increased the amount of positive support which the gay community extended to inmates upon their release. To date, 25 inmates have received the project's services. Formal evaluation has not occurred. Apparently there are no recidivism data for program graduates. Subjective assessment (Keith, 1974) of the project's impact have included the following observations: (a) the program has been ineffective in reducing the arousal that many patients experience in relation to male children; (b) some residents have "outgrown" the program and now require assistance with the problems that accompany any intense, or long-term relationship; (c) the project has been well received by the gay community, the residents, and an unusually responsive prison administration; and (d) the overall consequences of the program have been positive, with patients learning new gay and "straight" skills, and establishing their own self-help organization. A final benefit of the program has been the opportunity it has afforded professionals to reexamine some of their traditional prescriptions for the treatment of homosexuals.

Vacaville Rehabilitation Center

The California Medical Facility at Vacaville, California is a medical correctional institution for "convicted felons who either develop mental illness during their incarceration in prison or are found by the staff of the Department of Corrections to have personality or psychological problems even though they were held responsible for their crimes." (Spece, 1972, p. 634). Sixty-four inmates were included in an 11-month, experimental, succinylcholine aversion program intended for inmates who were unamenable to other treatments by reason of their extreme aggressive or withdrawn behaviors (Mattocks & Jew, 1970; cited by Spece, 1972).

The program at Vacaville can be distinguished from the Atascadero project on two points. First, it may be that at least five Vacaville inmates were treated without their consent, while many were treated only with the consent of a relative (Spece, 1972). In any event, this contrasts with the Atascadero experiment in which no attempt to obtain informed consent was evident. A second difference is that Vacaville officials intended their program to follow a punishment paradigm; "the actual administration of the succinylcholine injection followed as temporally close as possible to the subsequent (sic) commission of one of the designated behaviors by the patient" (Mattocks & Jew, 1970; cited by Spece, 1972, p. 635). Procedurally, this "punishment" took many forms; some inmates received threats but no injection, others received injections without warning. Vacaville prisoners also received verbal admonishments, similar in kind to those used at Atascadero. This "counseling" was seen as strengthening the association between a behavior and its consequences. Evaluation of treatment involved a comparison of the incidence of proscribed acts, rule infractions, and number of patients made accessible to other treatments before, during, and after the aversion program. Of those inmates evaluated, 61 percent did not commit a proscribed act during the program, and 11 percent committed only one such act. There was also a 27 percent decrease in rule infractions for participants during this time. Twenty prisoners were made amenable to other forms of institutional treatment.

These data are not sufficient to justify a conclusion of program effectiveness. A major methodological problem was attrition. Data were supplied for only 35 of the original 64 participants; therefore, more than 50 percent of the subjects were never evaluated. Of the 35 who were, only 15 actually received an injection. Apparently, the other 20 subjects were only threatened with its use. There was no control group of any kind.

On a theoretical level, the program was as perplexingly eclectic as its Atascadero counterpart. Spece's review of the project identified operational components of classical conditioning, operant conditioning, pseudo-hypnosis, and threats of punishment. Dissatisfaction with the program appears to have been widespread. Spece (1972) reported that it was terminated sometime in 1970 because of a lack of both staff and consenting patients.

Ontario Regional Penitentiaries

Marshall and McKnight (1975) have applied a combination of behavioral techniques to sex offenders incarcerated in Ontario Regional Penitentiaries. This report summarized data for three male pedophiles (ages 31, 36, and 55) who were transferred to a hospital for the treatment program and then returned to the institution.

The elements of the treatment program were similar to those described in previous work by Marshall (1971, 1973, 1974; see Chapter 6 of this volume). The primary component of the program was electrical aversion which was paired with slides depicting deviant stimuli. Shock was terminated contingent on the presentation of slides depicting sexual intercourse with adults. Another portion of the program integrated systematic sensitization, modeling, and role-playing to teach heterosocial skills, and to reduce anxiety associated with approaching other adults in social contexts. A final ingredient was a ward-based program providing both group therapy and a series of progressively more demanding social interactions with the hospital staff, thus enabling the inmates to practice and refine the skills they were acquiring during social skill training. Total treatment time varied considerably, lasting five months for one case, eight for the second, and four months for the final case.

Multiple sources of assessment were employed to assess treatment effectiveness. Changes in penile circumference were recorded as the patient viewed erotic slides of adults and children as well as sexually neutral slides. Inmates also rated the sexual attractiveness of the slides and completed a self-report measure of sexual preferences (Sexual Orientation Method; Feldman, MacCulloch, Mellor, & Pinschoff; 1966). Finally, "each inmate was observed in a natural setting that was relevant to his particular sexual problem . . ." (Marshall & McNight, 1975, p. 134). Since the inmates were returned to the penitentiary from the hospital, it is not clear what type of natural settings were available for such observation, nor how long inmates remained in these situations.

In general, the immediate measures of outcome revealed substantial improvement. Unfortunately, there was little long-term confirmation of treatment success. Although one inmate had been released for eight months without any reported parole violations, another participant had been returned to the penitentiary for a sexual offense against a child. The third inmate remained incarcerated 18 months after treatment termination. While acknowledging these limited results, the authors concluded that the subsequent relocation of the project to an outpatient basis, in addition to several modifications in the treatment package itself, had substantially improved the success rate of the program.

Marshall (1971) treated an incarcerated child molester with a multifaceted treatment program procedurally quite similar to several of the approaches described in Chapter 6 on noninstitutional behavior therapy. Treatment was initiated with approximately 30 sessions of aversion therapy for pedophilic arousal. This was followed by 15 sessions of systematic desensitization and social skills training intended to strengthen heterosexual behavior. Outcome data on the success of this intervention were limited to the inmate's report of heterosexual fantasies and decreased anxieties during interactions with adult females. It would be expected that penitentiary confinement would virtually preclude any opportunity for child molestation; there was, however, no report on behavioral improvement of any type other than noting an increase in "spontaneous conversation" with females. No followup or postrelease data of any kind were included.

Levin, Barry, Gambaro, Wolfinsohn and Smith (1977) treated an institutionalized, 39-year-old pedophile with several variations of covert sensitization. Pedophile molestation had been occurring for almost 20 years, having been detected increasingly often in the two years prior to the man's most recent conviction for molesting his young niece. There was also a history of alcohol abuse, and convictions for robbery and shoplifting.

Following preintervention assessment of subjective ratings and penile erection to deviant and nondeviant stimuli, the client received 32 sessions of covert sensitization over a 16-week period. Aversion relief scenes (see Chapter 6) accompanied each variety of covert sensitization. Initially, the client received "regular" covert sensitization where physically aversive imagery was paired with attraction to young girls. In the second phase, covert sensitization was accompanied by exposure to valeric acid, a compound infamous for its raunchy stench. Following this, covert sensitization continued using psychologically noxious imagery. This segment was quite similar to what has been termed "shame aversion," a procedure described in more detail in the following chapter. In the final stage, mixed imagery was employed; half the scenes involved physical imagery assisted by the valeric acid, the other half employed psychologically aversive scenes.

Each phase of covert sensitization lasted four weeks, and involved instructions to practice the procedure outside of the treatment session. Covert sensitization was supplemented by marital counseling, Alcoholics Anonymous, sex education, and group therapy.

There was a significant decrease in sexual arousal to deviant stimuli, with most of this change occurring during chemically assisted covert sensitization and sensitization employing psychological imagery. Of course, the fact that type of treatment was confounded by order of presentation disallows any firm decision of treatment superiority.

Sexual attraction to mature women increased, but this change was not as strong as the reduction in deviant arousal. Followups, continuing over a ten-month post-treatment interval, suggested that the improvements during treatment had been maintained. The patient remained an inpatient, however.

A FINAL WORD

Although more comprehensive evaluations of institutional behavior modification programs are presented in Chapters 8, 9, and 10 of this volume, the common fate of almost all of these projects warrants our current attention. The premature termination of these programs, either by legal mandate or public pressure, has become virtually emblematic of penal behavior modification. There should be no quarrel with the forced abolition of projects that persist in violating inmates' constitutional rights, coercing their otherwise involuntary participation, and attempting to promote only submissiveness to the demands of the correctional staff. On the other hand, both the deficiencies and excesses of most of these behavioral programs could have been remedied by some straightforward procedural and administrative modifications that would have enabled the continuation of the program.

We can applaud the professional vigilance and legal challenges that have become prevalent in this area and that hopefully have sensitized behavior modifiers to the requirements of acceptable prison interventions. At the same time, one might remain skeptical that any meaningful advancement has been obtained by replacing behavior modification projects with programs that represent, at best, custodial, correctional "business as usual."

Chapter 6
Nonresidential Behavior Therapy

Refrain tonight;
And that shall lend a kind of
Easiness to the next abstinence;
The next more easy; for use
Can almost change the stamp of
Nature.

— Shakespeare, *Hamlet*, III

Nonresidential therapy, from any theoretical perspective, has been used infrequently with adult offenders. Lipton, Martinson and Wilk's (1975) comprehensive review of rehabilitation evaluation research for juvenile and adult offenders (1945-1967) revealed only four studies which evaluated the effects of nonresidential psychotherapy on recidivism. Each of these studies involved juveniles. Even after expanding outcome criteria to include psychotherapy's effects on such indices as vocational adjustment and educational achievement, only one study (Winick & Nyswander, 1962) evaluating psychotherapy for adults could be identified. In this instance, the recipient population was certainly an atypical one: drug-addicted jazz musicians. Since 1967, the number of controlled studies of noninstitutional psychotherapy with offenders has increased only slightly. Adam's (1975) summary of an unpublished review by Speer (1972) revealed that of 21 experimental evaluations of group and individual psychotherapy with offenders, only 11 studies collected recidivism and followup data. Five of these 11 evaluations were noninstitutional. None of the studies with adult offenders provided evidence that psychotherapy contributed to reduced recidivism.

The scarcity with which nonresidential psychotherapy has been employed with adult offenders should not be surprising. Several features of the population militate against either a recommendation for therapy, or an expectation of favorable psychotherapeutic outcome. First, many of the crimes from which serious psychopathology is inferred (e.g., rape, child molestation, violent assault) are also crimes which evoke the public's vengeance, and demands for protection and lengthy incarceration. In addition, "uncontrolled" antisocial behavior often contributes to professionals' overprediction of dangerousness which, in turn, is accompanied by the "preventive" commitment of the individual for an indeterminate period of time (Diamond, 1974; Monahan, 1975, 1976; Monahan & Cummings, 1974, Steadman, 1973). While there probably would be a general endorsement of treatment which accompanies an offender's imprisonment, there is likely to be little tolerance for psychotherapy in lieu of it.

Second, there is a sizeable literature which indicates that lower socioeconomic class is associated reliably with several parameters of treatment responsiveness, such as greater reluctance to initiate psychotherapy (Brill & Storrow, 1960; Wolken, Moriwaki & Williams, 1973); more frequent assignment to inexperienced therapists (Schaffer & Myers, 1954); shorter duration of therapy (Lorion, 1973); higher attrition rates (Imber, Nash & Stone, 1955), and greater therapist-client discrepancy of expectations concerning the appropriate nature of therapy (Heitler, 1976; Lorion, 1973, 1974).[1] Of course, as Shah (1970) has indicated, the bulk of *apprehended* or *convicted* offenders is likely to be drawn from lower socioeconomic classes, thereby constituting a group for whom the evocative, relatively passive style of conventional psychotherapy is ill-suited.

Finally, psychotherapists' enthusiasm for working with offenders is likely to be diminished by abundant clinical lore and research (Hare, 1970) that identifies acting-out, antisocial, "psychopathic" clients as generally unresponsive to most forms of psychotherapy. The absence of anxiety, the interpersonal indifference, and the refusal to postpone gratification are the characteristic features of these offenders which are thought to prevent the formation of a working, psychotherapeutic relationship.

As mentioned previously (see, e.g., Chapter 1), one prominent characteristic of behavioral approaches to therapy is their effectiveness with problems typically assumed to be relatively intractable. Additionally, behaviorally based therapy appears to be successful with a broader range of clients than those typifying the YAVIS (Young-Attractive-Verbal-Intelligent-Successful) Syndrome (Nietzel, Winett, MacDonald & Davidson, 1977; Zax & Cowen, 1972).

The factor most important in accounting for behavior therapy's frequent nonresidential application to adult offenders is its overall compatibility with modern correctional philosophy. Behavioral techniques tend to be straightforward, focused on specific, current behavior, and easily learned by a cadre of paraprofessionals, volunteers, relatives, and peers who can initiate further behavior change conditions, or can maintain conditions and contingencies that had been introduced during a prior professional intervention. Further, there is a virtual synonymity between the correctionist's goal of individual deterrence and the behaviorist's typically ascendant goal of stopping deviant behaviors and replacing them with more socially acceptable ones. At a conceptual level, behavioral treatments have the advantage of emphasizing therapeutic principles while still employing procedures not condemned as unduly permissive or nurturant by law-and-order sympathists.

The criteria for selection of cases for this chapter presented some difficulties. First, the definition of criminal offense is problematic because, in some instances, formal criminal charges were not brought against an individual despite a police arrest (e.g., Callahan & Leitenberg, 1973; Wickramasekera, 1968); in others, an individual may have been apprehended by police but not officially arrested (e.g., Reitz & Keil, 1971). Plea bargaining may also produce a conviction for an offense quite different from that recorded at the time of arrest. Second, the determination of noninstitutional status was frequently complicated by the fact that some offenders had been incarcerated previously in correctional or penal institutions. In other cases, the offender was subject to incarceration in the event of unsuccessful nonresidential treatment.

The inclusion of cases in this chapter relied on the following criteria: (1) Offender status was assigned on the basis of committing a behavior for which an arrest and formal criminal charges could have been initiated. Arrest and charges were not necessary conditions for selection; (2) The described treatment was considered noninstitutional if it was delivered outside of a penal institution. The reality of past incarceration, or the threat of it in the future, did not obviate a current treatment from being considered noninstitutional. Programs administered to hospitalized patients are included in this review. (Behavioral treatments offered officially within the context of probation or parole are described separately in Chapter 7).

There are over 30 published accounts of behavioral interventions with nonincarcerated adult offenders. In the majority of cases the targeted offense has been some repetitive, illegal sexual practice such as exhibitionism, pedophilia, or rape. In addition to the literature on sex offenders, this chapter reviews the more recent applications of behavior therapy to problems such as theft, assault, drunkenness, and drug abuse.

SEXUAL OFFENSES

As with other therapeutic approaches to certain isolated sexual deviations, behavioral treatments are generally successful in reducing future occurrences of the target problem (Bancroft, 1974; Coleman, 1976). The modal behavioral intervention for offensive-criminal sexual behavior has been a variety of aversion techniques. This popularity is due not so much to any clinical or conceptual conviction that deviant behaviors must be suppressed before more appropriate responses can be displayed (Davison & Wilson, 1974), as it is to the realization that the rapid, resolute control of behavior, often afforded by aversion procedures, is responsive to a community's expectation that nonincarceration not be accompanied by any further occurrences of the offensive behavior. Aversion techniques for offenders usually rely on either electrical aversion or verbal-imaginary aversion (often referred to as covert sensitization). Although chemical aversion is employed frequently with addictive problems, its use with nonimprisoned sex offenders is uncommon in the available literature.

In the following presentation of this research, behavioral treatments are described for several categories of sexual offenses including fetishes and voyeurism, exhibitionism, pedophilia, sexual assault, and rape.

Fetishes and Voyeurism

A fetish is the reliance on some special part of the body or inanimate object for erotic arousal. It is not commonly seen as a presenting problem in therapy, and is even less frequently encountered in criminal proceedings (Raymond, 1956). No doubt, the prevalence of fetishes is underestimated by official sources because of the private context in which it usually occurs, and the tolerance, or even encouragement, offered by sexual partners. Bancroft (1974) identifies transvestism as a specific type of fetishistic behavior in which cross-sex-dressing produces sexual arousal.

Voyeurism also involves a certain narrowing of sexual interest in the form of achieving erotic arousal through the clandestine observation of others' sexual activity. Like fetishists, the number of legally apprehended voyeurs is small. However, the voyeur's activity is usually not insulated by a cooperative relationship with his "victims," thereby introducing a somewhat greater risk of criminal prosecution in the event of being caught.

In one of the earliest published accounts of aversion therapy with an offender, Raymond (1956) reported the successful use of apomorphine-based conditioning with a hospitalized, 33-year-old male against whom numerous charges had been lodged involving malicious attacks on, and damage to, perambulators and handbags (See Table 6-1 for a summary of behavioral treatments of similar offenses[2]). The police were aware of 12 such incidents which had occurred over several years, and had evidenced considerable diversity (e.g., setting prams on fire, driving a motorcycle into them, smearing mucus on a handbag). One prosecutor was moved to label the patient "a menace to any woman with a pram."

Exposures to the fetishistic objects were paired repeatedly with apomorphine-based nausea. After several days of such treatment delivered at irregular intervals, the patient claimed to be repulsed by the objects of his former affections and even relinquished some negatives of prams he had kept surreptitiously for years. A booster session, during which a film of the fetishis-

Table 6-1 Behavioral Approaches to Fetishes and Voyeurism

| Study | Treatment | Participants | | | Treatment | |
		N	Length of Problem	Legal History	Duration	Adjunctive Procedures
Raymond (1956)	Apomorphine aversion	1	Several years	Numerous charges involving malicious damage to perambulators	Several days	—
Fookes (1960)	Electrical aversion	27 (5 of whom were fetishist-transvestites)	N.R.***	One fetishist had come "under the scrutiny of the law"	3 months	—
Kushner (1965)	Electrical aversion and systematic desensitization	1	21 Years	Two prison sentences	41 Sessions	—
Marks, Rachman & Gelder (1965)	Electrical aversion	1	25 years	N.R.***	2 weeks	—
Marks, Gelder & Bancroft (1970)	Electrical aversion	24 (12 of whom were fetishist-transvestites)	$\bar{x}$ = 18 years	N.R.***	$\bar{x}$ = 19 Sessions	Psychotherapy and marital therapy (Bancroft and Marks, 1968)

  * Case study
 ** Self report
*** Not reported

tic objects was paired with nausea, was employed six months after treatment termination.

Nineteen months after the initiation of the aversion procedures, progress reports from the patient, his wife, the police, and his probation officer were solicited. These evaluations consistently suggested that the patient had maintained his improvement in heterosexual performance, employment record, and resistance of fetishistic behavior.

Kushner (1965) reported the case of a long-time panties fetishist, who had attempted to compensate for his sexual inadequacies by engaging in a variety

Table 6-1 (Cont.) Behavioral Approaches to Fetishes and Voyeurism

| Generalization and Maintenance | Methodology | | |
	Design	Dependent Measures	Followup
Aversion booster session	C.S.*	S.R.,** wife reports, agency records.	19 months; reduction of deviant behaviors and fantasies
Booster sessions Faded treatment sessions	Group design w/o controls	S.R.**	$\overline{x}$ = 38 months; continued success reported.
Booster sessions	C.S.*	S.R.**	18 months; occasional fetishistic fantasies during intercourse
Booster sessions	C.S.*	S.R.**	3 months
Shock given on VR schedule	Group design with nonequiv- alent, un- treated controls	Clinical ratings; self and relative reports; semantic differential ratings.	2 years; isolated relapses in 50% of the cases

of aggressive and delinquent behaviors. Following two prison sentences for assault and burglary, the man sought treatment for his fetishism. Electrical shock was administered contiguously with imaginal, pictorial, and actual fetishistic stimuli during 41 sessions. Subsequently, systematic desensitization of heterosexual anxiety was employed as a treatment for the client's chronic impotence.

Two isolated instances of fetishistic behavior occurred during an 18-month followup, and were treated by single-session booster trials. Although the client reported occasional fetishistic fantasies, and at least two serious traffic violations, his posttreatment behavior appeared to justify the author's claim that ''substantial improvement over his former condition had taken place.''

Marks, Gelder and Bancroft (1970) present a thorough description of their electrical aversion therapy with a mixed group of sexual deviants (transvestites and fetishists, n=12; sadomasochists, n=5; transsexuals, n=7).[3] Data are summarized here only for the transvestites and the fetishists, the legal status of whom was not specified.

Electrical shocks were paired with two kinds of deviant stimuli — in-session performances of deviant behavior and deviant fantasies. Aversion trials were delivered twice daily for two to three weeks on a predominantly inpatient (hospital) basis.

While half of the patients had engaged in their targeted deviant behavior since treatment termination, the frequency and enjoyment of these behaviors had decreased from pretreatment levels. Similar changes were reported for deviant fantasies. Attitudes about nontargeted responses changed little, and heterosexual adjustment was related mainly to the presence of pretreatment heterosexual behavior. Despite "minor relapses," the patients were characterized as having undergone a "lasting reduction of deviant behavior" (p. 181). Improvement occurred in approximately one-third of a group of unmatched controls not receiving treatment. The authors maintained that these changes were less substantial than those experienced by treated subjects; however, statistical comparisons of treatment and control subjects were prohibited by numerous pretreatment differences.

Fookes (1960) reported an aversion technique in which five fetishist-transvestites were required to cross-dress, and were than subjected to painful electric shocks which increased in intensity with increasing amounts of inappropriate clothing being worn. Large numbers of shocks (up to 500) were delivered per session. Followups, which averaged 35 months after treatment, revealed continued success in all five cases.

Fetishes are accompanied occasionally by other sexual deviations that might complicate certain interventions. For example, masochistic behaviors, or fantasies, might contraindicate faradic aversion as a treatment for an associated fetish. Marks, Rachman and Gelder (1965) reported the successful use of electrical aversion with a shoe-boot fetishist, who also achieved sexual gratification by being kicked or beaten with various foot apparel. Although his wife was described as reluctant to perform these services, she, on one occasion, had performed them vigorously enough to have broken his coccyx.

Prior to the use of electrical aversion, an operant task was employed requiring the client to avoid shock in the presence of the fetishistic object. This he was able to do, indicating that, despite his masochistic tendencies, shock retained its aversive qualities for him. The patient then was given electrical aversion trials twice daily for two weeks. Initially, shock was delivered when the patient signalled that he was fantasizing fetishistic behavior. After two days, this fantasy aversion was combined with shocks given when the patient actually would don a pair of boots. Booster sessions were continued during a three-month posttreatment interval to prevent any behavioral relapses. Clinically, the intervention appeared to be successful; the footwear fetish had been nullified, masochistic fantasies were infrequent, and sexual intercourse became more pleasurable.

Exhibitionism

Exhibitionism is the exposure of one's genitals to an unwilling observer for the purpose of achieving sexual satisfaction. It is conceivable that this activity provided the origin for the literal use of the term, "showing off." The exhibitionist usually follows a consistent pattern in this activity, exposing in the same kind of setting, and to similar kinds of people. In western societies (e.g., United States, Europe), exhibitionism is the most frequently reported sexual offense, constituting approximately one-third of all sexual-offense convictions (Mohr, Turner & Ball, 1964; Rooth & Marks, 1974). While most exhibitionists are not considered criminally dangerous or physically assaultive, the high frequency of their behavior, and its performance before a typically unappreciative audience, increases the risk of detection and arrest.

Fooke's (1960) previously described (see section on fetishists and transvestites) aversion method had also been applied to seven exhibitionists, all of whom had been referred by legal authorities. (See Table 6-2 for a summary of behavioral treatment of exhibitionism.) In two instances, shock was delivered contingent on a signal that the deviant behavior was being fantasized. In the other five cases, shock was contingent on actual behavioral exposures performed in-session. Reevaluation, at an average of 39.5 months posttreatment, indicated continued success for the five patients who were shocked for actual exposing attempts. One of the two patients who received fantasy-contingent shocks was regarded as a failure, while the other required intensive maintenance treatment during the followup interval.

Emphasizing the consideration that deviant sexual behavior actually involves a chain of stimulating and prepatory acts, Abel, Levis and Clancy (1970) applied electric shock to audiotaped sequences of the deviant behavior of three exhibitionists, two transvestites, and one masochist. Individualized descriptions of offensive behavior were prepared for each participant. For five of the men, shock was delivered, at first, after the final sequence of the description; later shocks were delivered at progressively earlier sections of the tape. Additionally, each session (n=10) included aversion relief trials, in which participants could avoid shock by verbalizing conventional sexual behavior. Data for those participants were contrasted with the sixth individual, who received a controlled number of shocks to sexually irrelevant tapes.

Treatment efficacy was evaluated at a six-month followup from multiple sources, including penile responses to deviant and normal tapes, clinical observation, and patient reports. The five contingent-shock participants evidenced suppression of penile erection to deviant tapes but not to normal ones, reported only one relapse of deviant behavior, and were judged to display

Table 6-2 Behavioral Approaches to Exhibitionism

	Participants				Treatment			Methodology			
Study	Treatment	N	Length of Problem	Legal History	Duration	Adjunctive Procdures	Generalization and Maintenance	Design	Dependent Measures	Followup	
Fookes (1960)	Electrical aversion	27 (7 of whom were exhibition-ists)	N.R.	Prison Sentences for three Exhibitionists	3 months	—	Booster sessions faded treatment sessions.	Group design w/o controls	S.R.	x̄ = 39.5 months; 5/7 regarded as continuing successes	
Bond & Hutchinson (1960)	Systematic desensiti-zation	1	12 Years	24 charges; 11 convictions; 9 prison sentences	29 session	—	cue-controlled relaxation and in vivo relaxa-tion practice	C.S.	S.R.	None	
Wickramasekera (1968)	Systematic desensitization	1	10 Years	at least one arrest	18 sessions	Shaping of heterosexual arousal and effective sex-ual behavior.	in vivo relaxa-tion practice	C.S.	S.R. and wife report	6 and 10 months; No reported relapses	
Abel, Levis & Clancy (1970)	Electrical Aversion	6 (3 of whom were exhibition-ists)	N.R.	4 had been arrested; one had been offi-cially charged.	N.R.	Aversion relief	—	Group (n = 5) contrasted with one con-trol subject	Penile responses; Clinical observations; S.R.	6 months; one re-ported relapse	
Serber (1970)	Shame Aversion	2	21, 15 Years	N.R.	3 sessions	—	—	C.S.	S.R.	6 months; no reported relapses	

Study	Treatment	N	Duration of Problem	Legal History	Number of Sessions	Additional Techniques	Maintenance	Design	Measures	Follow-up
Reitz & Keil (1971)	Shame Aversion	1	24 Years	At least one incident reported to the police.	more than 10 sessions	—	Tapering of scheduled sessions; *in vivo* prompting	C.S.	S.R.	14 months; no reported relapse
Stevenson & Jones (1972)	Shame Aversion	1	8 Years	7 criminal charges.	12 sessions	—	Booster sessions	C.S.	S.R. and wife report	12 months; no reported relapse.
Wickramasekera (1972)	Shame aversion (aversive behavior rehearsal)	6	4-40 years	N.R.	3 or 4 sessions	Several techniques to enhance effectiveness of the basic "shame" package		Multiple C.S.	S.R. and police records	3-35 months; no reported relapses
Callahan & Leitenberg (1973)	Electrical aversion *vs.* covert sensitization	6	6-17 years	1 court commitment, 1 arrest, 1 suspended sentence	20-42 sessions	Relaxation training.		ABAB counterbalanced with-in-subject design	Penile responses, daily ratings	4-18 months; deterioration was reported for one of the exhibitionists
Rooth & Marks (1974)	Electrical aversion *vs.* self-regulation *vs.* relaxation training	12	5-40 years, x̄ = 16 years	10 of the subjects had at least one conviction	3 weeks (each treatment for one week)	Marital therapy	Self-administered treatments during last half of each week; 7 extra sessions during followup.	Latin-Square (each subject received all treatments)	S.R.; daily diaries; parole reports	14 months; 7 reported relapses, 4 convictions
Wickramasekera (1976)	Shame aversion (aversive behavior rehearsal)	20	4-25 years	N.R.	no more than four	Several techniques to enhance effectiveness of the basic "shame" package.		Multiple C.S.	S.R.; Psychophysiological recordings; interviews with significant others; police records	3-84 months; no reported relapses

fewer indications of general psychopathology. While the noncontingent shock-control patient also showed suppression of sexual response to deviant tapes, this was accompanied by the undesirable outcome of reduced arousal to nondeviant sexual stimuli.

Callahan and Leitenberg (1973) compared counterbalanced within-subject presentations of electric shocks contingent on penile responsiveness to deviant slides with covert sensitization to a hierarchy of verbally described deviant behaviors. Both techniques were tailored to the individual needs of a mixed group of sexual offenders (two exhibitionists, one transvestite-transsexual, two homosexuals, and one homosexual pedophile). Both exhibitionists, and the transvestite had encountered legal difficulties, the most serious being an 18-month commitment of the 15-year-old exhibitionist.

Numerous patient and treatment differences precluded any group presentation of outcome data. Therefore, individual outcomes were presented for each patient. Both techniques were associated with general effectiveness on multiple outcome measures; however, subjective reports of sexual arousal favored covert sensitization. At reevaluations ranging from four to 18 months after treatment, continued suppression of target behaviors was evidenced for all participants. However, the older exhibitionist reported a gradual increase in deviant fantasies and urges during the followup period.

In one of the few comparative outcome studies with sex offenders, Rooth and Marks (1974) contrasted the efficacy of electric aversion, self-control, and relaxation training. Twelve exhibitionists (all but two with prior convictions) were assigned randomly to a Latin-square design whereby each client received each treatment in one of six possible orders. Individual treatments lasted one week (eight sessions), and were delivered over three consecutive weeks by the same therapist. Midway through each treatment the clients were asked to self-administer two daily sessions of that week's treatment; one session was to take place in the hospital, while the other was to occur in a natural, high-risk environment.

A variety of self-report measures converged on the conclusion that aversion therapy was the most effective intervention, followed by self-control and then relaxation training, which proved to be ineffective. Interestingly, while the self-administered versions of the treatments did not facilitate greater improvement, there was some evidence that the effects of self-control were potentiated by prior aversion therapy.

Unfortunately, the long-term cumulative impact of all treatments was less than desirable. One year after termination, seven of the clients reported further episodes of exhibitionism. Four clients had been convicted for an exposing offense; at least four others were receiving medication; one patient had improved to the point of publicly baring his chest rather than his genitals.

One unique form of aversion therapy involves requiring the client to perform his deviant activity in front of a number of observers. Special care is taken to ensure that the client monitors his own behavior, as well as the fact that he is being observed. Demonstration of the act is made to occur for prolonged periods of time; in some cases up to 35 minutes (Serber, 1970). The success of this surprisingly simple technique has been confirmed independently by a number of investigations for several kinds of sexual offenses. It has proven especially effective with exhibitionists.

Serber (1970) has referred to his version of this technique as "shame aversion therapy." In this treatment the patient is instructed to maintain awareness of his behavior and the fact that he is being observed, but no further attempts are made to heighten the patient's embarrassment. Serber presents data for eight patients (two exhibitionists, four transvestites, one pedophile, and one frotteur) each of whom reported his problem to be of at least 10 years' duration. No data relevant to patients' legal status were presented. Five of the patients had not engaged in their problem behavior six months after treatment. An essentially equivalent form of shame aversion was effective with an exhibitionist who had previously been unable to benefit from either desensitization or electrical aversion (Reitz & Keil, 1971).

Very similar procedures have been used by Wickramasekera (1972) to treat exhibitionists that police records indicated were chronic offenders, resistant to previous psychotherapeutic efforts. While Wickramasekera has embellished the basic "shame" package with Gestalt-awareness techniques, hypnosis, and videotaped feedback, he confirms Serber's suggestion that the treatment is best suited for patients who feel very ashamed, anxious or guilty about their behavior. Six patients who received the initial Wickramasekera package maintained control over their exhibitionism for periods of up to 35 months.

Stevension and Jones (1972) supplemented their variety of shame aversion with videotaping of the client's in-session exhibitionism. These tapes then were replayed at later sessions with the client in the audience. An additional feature of this treatment was its emphasis on engaging the client in discussions of the behavior while he was performing it.

In a more recent and detailed discussion of his Aversive Behavior Rehearsal (ABR) program, Wickramasekera (1976) presents data for 20 exhibitionists who have received the basic treatment (n=16), or a variant (vicarious-ABR), in which a client observes the *in-vivo*-ABR treatment of a fellow exhibitionist (n=4).[4]

Followups, ranging in duration from three months to seven years for the *in-vivo*-ABR package, have not revealed a single relapse, even though occasional fleeting thoughts about exposure are reported to occur. No followup evaluations are available for clients receiving vicarious-ABR. Some side effects (secondary impotence, nightmares, lessened sexual interest) of the procedure have been reported but are apparently quite transient.

Despite the numerous procedural variations which characterize shame aversion packages, there is an impressive consistency to the following clinical observations of those who have used the procedure: (1) The technique is well suited for offenders who are anxious, moralistic, and embarrassed by their behavior but may be contraindicated for those who are more aggressive, or who display additional signs of serious psychopathology; (2) every attempt should be made to keep the client in cognitive and emotional contact with his behavior during the rehearsed exposure. Wickramasekera (1972, 1976) provides a theoretical justification for this verbal interaction by suggesting that exhibitionism occurs under conditions of increased fantasy involvement, thereby reducing the judgmental monitoring of the environment which would prevent exhibitive episodes.

The success associated with this relatively brief and simple technique warrants its further investigation with more methodologically adequate research. From a conceptual standpoint, shame aversion is interesting because of the several other techniques it resembles or combines: e.g., implosion, negative practice, and symptom scheduling (Stevension & Jones, 1972). At present, however, there are no data on which of these several components is most crucial to the overall package's efficacy.

Although most treatments of exhibitionism have included some aversion component, at least one study (Bond & Hutchinson, 1960) has claimed therapeutic success without any aversion component. The client had labored through a long history of unsuccessful treatment techniques, including a chastity belt into which his wife locked him each morning to prevent exposing.

Treatment involved systematic desensitization to a hierarchy of exposure-eliciting stimuli, as well as instructions in the appropriate use of cue-controlled, *in-vivo* relaxation. Although at least two incidents of exhibitionism were reported during treatment, the patient had not exposed himself during the last two months of treatment and was reporting an enhancement of his sexual relationship with his wife.

In his treatment of a once-arrested exhibitionist, Wickramasekera (1968) combined standard desensitization for heterosexual anxiety with (1) programmed reading of progressively more erotic literature and (2) a Masters-and-Johnson-like program, in which gradually more intimate sexual activity between the client and his fiancee is specified and encouraged. The description of this treatment illustrated several examples of clinical sophistication often absent in similar case histories. First, the therapist discussed his handling of the numerous religious and moral injunctions that the client originally employed to impede treatment. Second, considerable attention was given to soliciting the active participation of the client's fiancee in the treatment plan, a factor which was probably quite crucial to the treatment's ultimate success. A reevaluation of the client's status ten months after treatment termination revealed an absence of urges to expose, as well as indications of a satisfying sexual relationship within the client's recent marriage.

Pedophilia

Pedophilia involves sexual activity with a child under the legal age of consent. The actual sex act varies considerably. In come cases vaginal penetration occurs; in others, the child's genitals are fondled, or the offender may force the child to engage in oral-genital acts.

If apprehended, pedophiles are very likely to be imprisoned for their behavior. There is good reason to believe that the incidence of pedophilia is underestimated because the aggressor is often quite well acquainted with the child (Coleman, 1976). The pedophile also can select or arrange situations which minimize the risk of detection. Further, even if caught, the pedophile often avoids prosecution because of an understandable desire on the part of parents to protect the child from the additional trauma of an official investigation or trial.

Stevenson and Wolpe (1960) presented the case of a married pedophile, whose sexual molestation of children had resulted in his arrest on at least one occasion (see Table 6-3 for a summary of other behavioral interventions with pedophiles[5]). The focus of this treatment was the client's interpersonal anxiety and his reluctance to be assertive with people, particularly his father who had retained a position of dominance over the client for many years. The primary concern of therapy was to strengthen the client's resolve and ability to interact assertively with people, and to liberate himself from the strong dependence on his father. His subsequent willingness to become more assertive was accompanied by vocational advancement, expanded social relationships, and a greatly improved marital relationship. A followup, six-and-one half months after the completion of therapy, revealed no recurrences of child molestation.

Edwards (1972) combined assertion training with thought-stopping to treat successfully a 40-year-old physician who had been molesting his sons. Apparently this case had not come to the attention of legal authorities because of the private context in which it was taking place. Anecdotal evidence suggested that the thought-stopping had diminished pedophilic fantasies, while the assertion training had reduced the interpersonal anxieties which had complicated adult heterosexual functioning. These gains were maintained at a four-month reevaluation.

As with most sex offenders, pedophiles are often treated with some form of aversion therapy, either in isolation or in combination with other procedures. For example, Marshall (1973) combined electrical aversion and orgasmic reconditioning (Davison, 1968; Marquis, 1970) in an attempt to reduce sexually deviant fantasies accompanying target behaviors, such as pedophilia (five patients), fetishism (two patients), rape (two patients), and homosexuality (three patients). Five of the patients had been referred by a correctional facility; one was a court referral, and six patients were referred privately.

Electrical shocks were delivered contingent on the patient imagining six sequential segments (thinking about the deviant act through actual commission of the act) of a deviant fantasy. Initially, each imaginal segment was punished; ultimately, the shocks were faded to a 50 percent variable schedule. Concurrent with the aversion component, the patients received orgasmic recondition-

Table 6-3 Behavioral Approaches to Pedophilia

Study	Participants			Treatment				Methodology		
	N	Length of Problem	Legal History	Treatment	Duration	Adjunctive procedures	Generalization and maintenance	Design	Dependent measures	Followup
Stevenson & Wolpe (1960)	1	N.R.	At least one arrest	Assertion training	N.R.	—	—	C.S.	—	6½ months; no reported relapses
Barlow, Leitenberg & Agras (1969)	1	13 years	Apprehended, but not arrested	Covert sensitization	24 sessions	Relaxation training; sensitization relief	—	ABA design	Diary; objective card sort; GSR	None
Edwards (1972)	1	10 years	N.R.	Assertion training	13 sessions	Thought stopping	—	C.S.	S.R.	4 months; no reported relapse
Marshall (1973)	12 (5 of whom were pedophiles)	N.R.	Prison referral (n = 5) court referral (n = 1); private referral (n = 6)	Electrical aversion and orgasmic reconditioning	At least 27 sessions	—	—	Group design w/o controls	Sexual orientation method; attractiveness ratings; penile responses	3-16 months; reported that success was maintained
Kohlenberg (1974)	1	At least 8 years	2 prior arrests	Electrical aversion; *in vivo* desensitization	21 sessions	—	—	C.S.	Daily diary on frequency of target behaviors	6 months; no reported relapses; increased response to adult males
Forgione (1976)	2	5, 39 years	S_1 = one apprehension S_2 = one conviction	Electrical aversion	N.R.	Assertion training; family therapy aversion relief	Booster sessions overlearning trials	C.S.	GSR; SR; parent (S_1) and wife (S_2) reports	3 years (S_1); 2 years (S_2); no reported relapse

ing, in which masturbation was used to associate sexual arousal and ejaculation with nondeviant heterosexual fantasies. At the end of treatment, 11 of the 12 patients reported that deviant fantasies had become less arousing, while appropriate fantasies were more attractive. Discontinuance of the problem behaviors accompanied these covert changes. Followup intervals, ranging from three to 16 months, indicated that success had been maintained in 75 percent of the cases (two patients not responding to the followup assessment were assigned to a "failure" category, as was a patient whose deviant fantasies were minimally influenced by treatment).

Using a well controlled single-subject design, Barlow, Leitenberg and Agras (1969) demonstrated the effectiveness of covert sensitization in decreasing the deviant behavior of a 25-year-old married pedophile. Following a five-session baseline, an ABA format was employed in which the participant was (A) relaxed and presented with noxious sensitization scenes, as well as sensitization-relief scenes (acquisition phase, six sessions); (B) presented arousing scenes without the sensitization component (extinction phase, eight sessions); (A) again administered acquisition trials (five sessions).

Figure 6-1 presents the effects of this intervention on two measures — a daily diary in which the client recorded each incident of pedophilic arousal (total urges) and an objective scoring of the arousal properties of a number of scenes describing deviant behavior (the card sort). The obvious improvements during the acquisition and reacquisition phases were confirmed by a GSR measure of arousal, which was lowest during acquisition and reacquisition.

Forgione (1976) reported an interesting embellishment of aversive conditioning with two pedophiles. Photographic slides were taken of each client enacting typical and fantasized molesting behavior with life-size child mannequins. The procedure was successful in eliciting substantial behavioral involvement and sexual arousal. These slides were then used as stimuli in the aversive conditioning component of the treatment. Interspersed with the pedophilic slides were slides of mature females and heterosexual couples. The clients also were provided aversion-relief trials, in which they could avoid shock by verbally rejecting deviant slides within three seconds of their onset. A number of adjunctive techniques were employed including assertion training, family counseling, and overlearning aversion trials. Long-term followups of three (S_1) and two years (S_2) revealed an absence of molesting episodes, as well as generalized interpersonal and heterosexual improvements for both clients.

Kohlenberg's (1974) case history of a homosexual pedophile evoked considerable controversy (Davison & Wilson, 1974; Garfield, 1974; Strupp, 1974) regarding its goal of training the client to become sexually responsive to adult males. While the various respondents were generally appreciative of this goal, there was considerable question (Davison & Wilson, 1974) about the clinical necessity of initially using electrical aversion to decrease sexual attraction to children. However, from a practical perspective, the author's

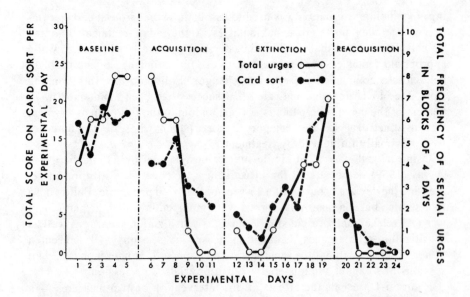

Fig. 6-1. Total score on card sort per experimental day and total frequency of pedophilic sexual urges in blocks of 4 days surrounding each experimental day. (Lower scores indicate less sexual arousal.) (From Barlow, Leitenberg & Agras, "Experimental Control of Sexual Deviations through Manipulation of the Noxious scene in Covert Sensitization," *Journal of Abnormal Psychology*, 1969, *74*, 596-601, Copyright 1969 by the American Psychological Association. Reprinted by permission.)

justification that aversion was used to prevent the likely legal consequences of any further molestation seemed defensible.

Following a four-week baseline, electric shock was paired with imaginal scenes of prowling and thoughts of pedophilic behavior. Aversion was discontinued after only four sessions because its suppressant effects diminished after the first session. The next 13 sessions were devoted to a Masters-and-Johnson-type program for which the client recruited the help of an adult, male sexual partner. A graded hierarchy of progressively more intimate sexual behaviors (sensate pleasuring, genital touching, genital contact without orgasm, and genital contact with orgasm) was developed, and the client was instructed to continue through the hierarchy at a pace that produced minimal anxiety.

At a six-month followup, the client reported more age-appropriate fantasies and sexually arousing episodes with adults. No incidents of molestation were reported.

Rape

Along with child molestation, rape is one of the most heinous and terrifying sex offenses. In recent years, societal and legal reactions to rapists and their victims have been critically examined from several sources, the most impassioned usually being drawn from a feminist perspective (Brownmiller, 1975). The law recognizes two basic types of rape. The first, forcible rape, involves two essential elements: vaginal penetration, and force or threatened force which compels the victim to submit to the act. The second, often referred to as statutory rape, consists of the act of sexual intercourse with a female who has not reached the age of consent. It does not involve force or the threat of it, but still presumes a lack of consent to the act because of the victim's age.

In recent years the frequency of rape has increased more than almost any other violent crime. The F.B.I. reported more than 56,090 cases of forcible rape in 1975. Almost all authorities agree that the actual number of rapes committed is far greater than official statistics indicate because of the pressures on the victim to let the incident go unreported. Of the total forcible rapes known to law enforcement agencies in 1975, only 51 percent were cleared by an arrest (F.B.I., 1975). A similar concern involves the low conviction rate of those charged with rape. Abel, Barlow, Blanchard and Guild (in press) cite Horos' (1974) report of a survey in which convictions had been obtained in only 13.3 percent of 1000 rape trials. Coleman (1976) describes rape as a repetitive activity rather than an isolated act, and suggests that most rapes are planned acts that usually take place in a setting with which the rapist is familiar. The typical victim-offender relationship is consistent with this pattern; most surveys have indicated that the rapist was well acquainted with his victim.

Neither incarceration nor treatment, even in their most intensive forms, has been completely successful in deterring the rapist from repeating his offense. Abel, et al. (in press) reported an average recidivism rate of 35 percent following simple incarceration. Recidivism after treatment is quite variable. Abel, Blanchard and Becker's (in press) review of eight treatment programs for sexually aggressive offenders revealed a 0-36 percent range of recidivism rates (see Table 6-4).

One of the earliest accounts of behavior therapy with a sexually aggressive individual was Mees' (1966) presentation of the case of a young, hospitalized male who previously had physically assaulted a woman. The focus of the aversive treatment was a set of long-standing sadistic fantasies, accompanied by sexual arousal and masturbation. Following an unusually long (six months) baseline, shock was administered, contingent on the patient's signal that he was fantasizing the deviant images. Shocks were delivered for 14 weeks, the last six of which the patient self-administered the shocks.

Improvement for this patient was slow. Sadistic fantasies were only gradually replaced by normal ones. Events extraneous to the aversion treatment, such as intercourse with an older woman and practice in developing normal fantasies, may have facilitated nonsadistic sexual fantasies. A six-month followup indicated isolated sadistic images which were not used for sexual arousal; however, satisfactory heterosexual activity had continued.

As Abel and Blanchard (1974) have indicated, this study was unique

Table 6-4 Treatment Center Outcomes for Sexual Aggressives

Program	Treatment Population	Outcome
Atascadero State Hospital, Atascadero, California	106 sexual aggressives with adult or child victims	22 percent recidivism rate at 5-year followup for pedophiliacs, 36 percent for adult rapists
Center for the Diagnosis and Treatment of Dangerous Persons, Bridgewater, Massachusetts	82 physical or sexual aggressives	6 percent later committed assaultive crime
Herstedvester Center, Denmark	11 rapists	No recidivism for sex crimes at 11-year followup
New Jersey State Diagnostic Center, Menlo Park, Edison, New Jersey	200 sexual deviates, 29 percent of whom were rapists	"Very small" recidivism
Philadelphia General Hospital, Philadelphia, Pennsylvania	92 sexual deviates, some of whom were rapists	1 percent arrests for sex crimes at 2-year followup
South Florida State Hospital Coral Gables, Florida	75 rapists	7 percent recidivism at unspecified followup
Western State Hospital, Ft. Steilacoom, Washington	658 sexual deviates, 11 percent of whom were rapists	9 percent rehospitalization rate at unspecified followup
Wisconsin Sex Offender	475 sexual deviates, some of whom were rapists	9 percent recidivism at unspecified followup

(Reprinted with permission from Abel, Blanchard & Becker, "Psychological Treatment of Rapists," in Walker, M. & Brodsky, S. (Eds.), *Sexual Assault*, Lexington, Massachusetts: Lexington Books, 1976.)

because of its careful, naturalistic assessment of both deviant and nondeviant fantasies, and of its suggestion of the critical role that sexual fantasy plays in the etiology of sexual deviation. Unfortunately, the patient's development of nondeviant fantasies occurred without any precise therapeutic procedures or instructions, thereby making it difficult to know the extent to which the new fantasies were a direct, rehabilitative element.

The most comprehensive outpatient treatment program for rapists is the one based on the Behavioral-Measurement Model developed by Abel and his associates at the University of Tennessee at Memphis. This program is noteworthy, not only because of its multicomponent emphasis (described below), but for its unique pretreatment entry requirements. First, treatment is offered to only those rapists whose participation is fully voluntary. Offenders under any legal coercion to receive treatment are not eligible for the program. For example, a parolee will not be accepted for treatment if a condition of his parole is that he must seek therapy. In fact, some program participants have not experienced any interface with the criminal justice system. Also, although professional expectation is that treatment may last as long as nine months, participants are free to discontinue therapy at any time they choose. The program is available on either an inpatient (hospital) or an outpatient basis, apparently another prerogative of participants.

Abel, Blanchard and Becker (in press) identified five elements of treatment that were common to several remedial approaches for sexual aggressives. The first two components are the most generalized, being characteristic of virtually all treatments, regardless of their theoretical origins. The last three ingredients are derived more specifically from a behavioral perspective, and are the key factors of the Abel treatment program.

(1) *Formation of an empathetic relationship.* The development of a warm, accepting relationship between the therapist and the offender is regarded uniformly as an important treatment factor. This element is emphasized particularly in psychodynamically oriented treatments and in group therapy, despite an absence of data about its specific contribution to clinical improvement.

(2) *Confrontation of the rapist with his own responsibility for his behavior.* The goal of the confrontation methods used in behavior modification, group therapy, institutional programs, or analytic therapy is to convince the offender that only he can stop his raping. As with the previous component, there is no controlled research to support a specific therapeutic contribution from these procedures although, at an intuitive level, the importance of any client accepting responsibility for his behavior seems undeniable.

Based on extensive physiological[6] (e.g., Abel, Barlow, Blanchard & Guild, in press) and behavioral assessment (e.g., Barlow, Abel, Blanchard, Bristow & Young, in press), the Abel model proposes that aggressive sexual deviations are comprised of three basic categories of behavioral excesses or deficits: excessive arousal to rape stimuli; deficient heterosexual arousal (or arousal to non-rape stimuli), and deficits in a set of social skills. The treatment program itself is preceded by precise behavioral and physiological measurement of a participant's particular deficits and excesses, thereby enabling the development of an individualized treatment program tailored to the specific needs of the rapist. Such a strategy has obvious benefits over those therapies that assume a unified etiology of deviant sexual aggressiveness. A further advantage of this objectified assessment is its capability to indicate clinical progress as the patient experiences the various stages of therapy. The measurement procedures provide the basis for pre-post comparisons, as well as followup data to gauge the long-term effects of the treatment.

The three behaviorally oriented components, essentially definitive of

Abel's Behavioral-Measurement Model, are described briefly below. The model also is presented in abbreviated form in Table 6-5.

(3) *Reduction of arousal to deviant stimuli.* Because this model regards sexual arousal to deviant (rape) stimuli as the defining characteristic of the rapist, techniques designed to reduce this arousal are primary ingredients in the treatment program. A variety of aversion therapies have been employed for this purpose. The most common aversive stimulus has been faradic shock, despite very limited evidence that it is effective with rapists. One case history

Table 6-5 The Behavioral Assessment and Treatment
of Sexual Aggressives

	Assessed behavioral excess or deficits	Treatment Methods
	Excessive arousal to rape stimuli	Aversion-Supression methods 1. covert sensitization 2. electrical aversion 3. odor aversion 4. chemical aversion 5. biofeedback assisted suppression
	Deficit arousal to non-rape, sexual stimuli	Generation of arousal to non-rape cues 1. masturbatory conditioning 2. exposure 3. fading 4. systematic desensitization
Social Skills Deficits	Heterosocial skills	Heterosocial skills training
	Assertive skills	Assertive training
	Sexual performance	Sexual dysfunction treatments
	Gender Role behavior	Gender role, motor behavior training

(Reprinted with permission from Gene G. Abel, "An Integrated Treatment Program for Rapists," in R. Rada (Ed.), *Clinical Aspects of the Rapist*, New York: Grune and Stratton, in press.)

reported in Abel, Blanchard and Becker (in press) and one study using a within-subject design have suggested the effectiveness of covert sensitization as a suitable form of aversion with rapists.

In the Abel program, the decision of which form of aversion to employ is determined partly by the solicited preference of the participant. Empirical and ethical factors also influence the final form of aversion to be used.

(4) *Development of arousal to nondeviant, heterosexual stimuli.* A pattern of behavior that often accompanies arousal to rape stimuli is the inability to respond sexually to heterosexual stimuli. Although increments in "appropriate" arousal have often occurred following aversion therapy (Barlow, Leitenberg & Agras, 1969; Callahan & Leitenberg, 1973), typically, such increases have been small and insufficiently durable, thereby necessitating additional techniques aimed specifically at facilitating arousal to heterosexual cues. Techniques such as systematic desensitization, aversion relief, classical conditioning, biofeedback, operant shaping, fading and intensive exposure to heterosexual stimuli have been employed with some success in increasing nondeviant arousal. Unfortunately, the minimal data supporting the effects of these procedures have not been collected on rapist populations.

Masturbatory, or orgasmic reconditioning, has been the most popular procedure for increasing arousal, and evidence at the case study level indicates general effectiveness of this method which has taken numerous procedural forms (see, e.g., Davison, 1968; Thorpe, Schmidt & Castell, 1963). Only limited evidence supports the efficacy of this procedure with sexual aggressives. Abel, Barlow and Blanchard (1973) used masturbatory conditioning to treat an 18-year-old male with severe fantasies and urges to mutilate women that had progressed to the point where he was burglarizing homes for women's clothing, which he then would mutilate while masturbating to his sadistic fantasies.

Masturbatory sessions were conducted in which the patient was instructed to masturbate while verbalizing the content of his accompanying fantasies. In order to alter the content of the fantasies, the authors relied on Thorpe, et al.'s (1963) technique where ". . . the specific fantasy changes in a stepwise fashion from a purely deviant fantasy to a fantasy temporarily arranged with gradually expanding nondeviant descriptions 'sandwiched' in between deviant description. These nondeviant portions of fantasy were extended until the last fantasy was entirely nondeviant in content" (Abel, et al., 1973, p. 3).

Five two-minute audiotaped fantasies, ranging from totally deviant to totally nondeviant content, were prepared in addition to a nonsexual control tape (a large, green tree). One of these descriptions was played for the patient before he started masturbating, and his arousal to the content was assessed by penile erection calibration, and a card-sorting rating. Arousal was measured at a preintervention baseline, during all phases of treatment and for eight weeks after treatment. Nondeviant arousal increased from 10-20 to 60-70 percent by treatment termination, and maintained at approximately a 50 percent level across the followup period. Accompanying this change was a decrease in penile response to deviant cues from 80 percent at baseline to the 10-20 percent range at the end of treatment and during the followup.

Masturbatory conditioning was also used successfully with a patient who admitted to more than 100 rapes and had been convicted of rape on two occasions (Abel, Blanchard, Barlow, & Flanagan; 1975). Nondeviant arousal increased from 25 to 60 percent while arousal to rape stimuli decreased from 50 to 10 percent. An extensive description of the masturbatory conditioning procedures used in the Abel program is provided in Abel, Blanchard and Becker, (in press).

(5) *Training of heterosocial skills*. The final category of behaviors contributing to sexual aggressiveness involves excesses and deficiencies in a variety of social skills. Subsumed under the social skill rubric are assertiveness, knowledge of heterosexual techniques, heterosocial skills, and appropriate gender role behavior.

Assessment of any problems in this area is accomplished by a self-report check list, videotaping, and a participant's responses to contrived role-playing situations. Following a determination of particular deficiencies, various forms of social-skill training such as behavioral rehearsal, modeling, and role playing are provided to develop the needed skills. While there is ample evidence that social-skill training is an efficacious procedure for several types of interpersonal problems of different client populations, there are no current data to support its specific efficacy in remediating patterns of clinical-level sexual aggressiveness.

At both a conceptual and clinical level, the individualized, integrated treatment strategy developed by Abel and his colleagues is the most sophisticated and ambitious program available for sexually aggressive offenders. At the same time, direct empirical support for the effectiveness of the procedures is very meager. To date, the primary descriptions and evaluations of the program (Abel, Blanchard & Becker, in press) have taken the form of reviewing the extant literature on the success of behavioral techniques directed in other labs and clinical settings at a diversity of sexual deviates, the vast majority of whom were not rapists. These reviews have been accompanied by extensive transcriptions of isolated sessions with rapists participating in the Abel program. While such descriptions are extremely useful in illustrating the precise forms of various techniques, they do not provide a scientifically acceptable basis for a conclusion about the impact of the overall program, or the specific contributions of its individual components to successful outcomes. Neither are there any comparative data concerning the effects of this program relative to other available procedures. That such evaluative research apparently has been initiated (see Abel, Blanchard & Becker, in press) is an encouraging development that should allow the refinement of this well-conceived program and the evolution of other empirically based projects for the sexually aggressive offender.

THEFT

Table 6-6 summarizes three published case histories involving behavioral programs applied to offenders displaying varied histories of theft. Marzagao (1972) employed systematic desensitization with a young woman who complained of a 12-year history of kleptomania. While no criminal record was reported, stealing was occurring as often as three or four times weekly. The author conceptualized the kleptomania as an anxiety-reducing behavior which would be decreased by desensitization of the relevant anxiety-arousing situations. A followup ten months after 17 treatment sessions indicated no recurrence of stealing.

Kellam (1969) treated a hospitalized, 48-year-old woman who had ten prior arrests for shoplifting. Fines, imprisonment, probation, E.C.T., psychotherapy, medication, and electrical aversion had all been unsuccessful deterrents.

For this treatment, a ten-minute film was prepared showing a subject entering a store and commiting 19 separate thefts, each of which was interrupted by a flash of disapproving faces. To increase the personal realism of the film, the patient's face was edited into the beginning and the end of the movie. As the patient watched the film, electric shock was delivered to her to coincide on a VR3 schedule with the appearance of the faces on the film. Treatment was terminated after 40 showings of the movie. Although at the end of treatment the patient reported a generalized fear of stores and of being watched, she did experience infrequent urges to steal during the three-month followup interval. A booster session, in the form of four showings of the film, was employed after the three month reevaluation.

Self-controlled contingencies were programmed by Epstein and Peterson (1973) to treat a young, self-referred male with a history of felonious theft. In eight treatment sessions, the client was trained to self-impose both reinforcement and response-cost contingencies intended to decelerate stealing. The opportunity for the client to work at his business was contingent on his staying in high-risk settings without stealing for progressively longer time periods. Any stealing was to be followed by a two-day suspension of work privileges. While no instances of theft were detected during the intervention, the absence of any followup data leaves the durability of this improvement in doubt.

ASSAULT

Aggressive attacks against persons usually result in lengthy periods of confinement for the assailant. Although incarceration for the aggressive offender is understandable and probably justifiable, there have been a handful of reports that describe behavioral programs that have been delivered outside of

Table 6-6 Behavioral Approaches to Theft

Study	Treatment	Participants			Treatment			Methodology		
		N	Length of problem	Legal History	Duration	Adjunctive procedures	Generalization & maintenance	Design	Dependent measures	Followup
Kellam (1969)	Electrical aversion; symbolic (film) presentation of social disapproval	1	16 years	10 prior arrests	40 sessions	—	Booster sessions	CS	SR	3 months; continued urges to steal, but no actual thefts.
Marzagao (1972)	Systematic desensitization	1	12	N.R.	17 sessions	—	—	CS	SR	10 months; no reported relapses.
Epstein & Peterson (1973)	Self-control procedures	1	"since high school"	One prior felony conviction	8 sessions	—	Graduated, *in vivo* exposures to high-risk situations	CS	SR	None

prison walls. While social-skills training is prescribed often as an appropriate intervention for social passivity and unassertiveness, only recently has it been regarded as potentially useful for the expansion of the deficient behavioral repertoires which may contribute to episodic aggression and verbal assault (Foy, Eisler & Pinkston, 1975; Frederiksen & Eisler, undated; Frederiksen, Jenkins, Foy & Eisler, 1976; Wallace, Teigen, Liberman & Baker, 1973). Frederiksen and Eisler's (undated) case report is most relevant to the current chapter's focus.

The patient was a middle aged, hospitalized male with a long legacy of verbal and physical assaults, including the shooting of six men. Three of these incidents had been fatal. Not surprisingly, the patient had experienced several arrests, social disruption, and physical injury. The intervention program consisted of the following ingredients: relaxation training, to reduce the elevated levels of arousal which often accompanied violent attacks; social-skills training, to provide the patient with alternative, nonaggressive behaviors which would be instrumental for the patient; and generalization training, to help the patient construe daily, interpersonal situations in a nonthreatening manner, thereby making aggressive attacks less likely.

The results revealed improvement in such component social skills as eye contact, appropriate affect, appropriate requests and compliance. Unobtrusive assessments of these behaviors on the hospital ward also revealed generalized improvement. For the most part, positive effects were maintained well over an eight-month posttreatment interval. Ten months after treatment, the patient reported no assaultive incidents; however, he had been arrested for discharging a gun within the city.

DRUNKENNESS AND DRUG ABUSE

Drunkenness

Alcoholism is not a crime. However, intoxication in a place where the public has the right to gather is legally sanctioned by statutes pertaining to public drunkenness, disturbing the peace, and disorderly conduct. The magnitude of the problems covered by these statutes is enormous. In recent years, one of every three arrests in this country has been for public drunkenness. The more than two million arrests each year for this behavior poses staggering burdens for the criminal justice system which has been made responsible for the apprehension, prosecution, punishment, and rehabilitation of these offenders.

Therapeutic control of public drunkenness has recently been encouraged as a preferable alternative to criminal sanctions which, almost without exception, are viewed as ineffectual in controlling the problem. This preference has been formalized by one court decision which prohibited the criminalization of *chronic* public drunkenness and ruled that the jailing of inebriates whose drinking meets the medical criteria of chronicity is cruel and unusual punishment (*Driver v. Hinnant*, 1966). Another decision (*Easter v. District of Columbia*, 1966) also disallowed mandatory commitment even for purposes of treatment.

Following the successful treatment of a chronic, skid-row alcoholic who had been arrested many times for his intoxication (Miller, Hersen & Eisler, 1974), Miller (1975) developed a behavioral intervention program for public drunkenness offenders whose repeated incarceration had been prohibited by the Uniform Alcholism and Intoxication Treatment Act. The 20 participants had been arrested for drunkenness at least eight times in the past 12 months; however, their participation in the program was entirely voluntary. The project, although limited in terms of size and duration, illustrates the advantages of coordinating community agency services with systematic behavioral contingencies designed to interrupt a social problem such as drunkenness.

Contingent on sobriety, as measured by direct observation or breathalizer tests performed on a VI 5-day schedule, 10 chronic alcoholics were provided with necessary goods and services (employment, housing, medical service, clothing, meals, counseling) through existing community service agencies. Participants who evidenced gross intoxication, or alcohol concentrations exceeding 10 mg/100 ml of blood volume, were not provided these resources for a 5-day period after determination of alcohol abuse. A control group of 10 alcoholics, similar to the experimental-contingency group in terms of demographics, arrests, and duration of drinking problem, received the same goods and services whether intoxicated or sober.

Although the two groups did not differ significantly on frequency of arrest prior to intervention, only the experimental-contingency group displayed a significant pre-post decrease in arrests. Additionally, participants in the intervention significantly increased the number of hours employed following the introduction of the contingencies, while control participants showed a slight decrease in employment time.

Drug Abuse

For most of this century, the dominant American response to the unwanted use of drugs has been legal prohibition. The major direction of legal controls has been to criminally sanction individuals who sell, possess, or use illicit drugs. Criminalization of drug use began in this country in the early 1900s with the passage of the Harrison Act in 1914. Since then, this country has relied on the criminal law to suppress drug use. There were 31,752 arrests for drug offenses in 1960; ten years later there were over 230,000 arrests (Wald & Hutt, 1972). In 1972 over one-quarter of the federal money spent on drug abuse programs was spent for the enforcement of drug laws.

Antidrug legislation continues to be enacted, despite the fact that most observers of the American drug scene regard legal controls as ineffectual. Antidrug laws have not made drug use less likely; they have merely made it criminal. Unfortunately, in addition to being ineffective, most drug laws have had many deleterious effects. For example, in addition to the criminal status associated with drug possession, distribution or delivery, drug use is related to other criminal behavior. Most addicts turn to criminal means of acquiring the money necessary to support their $100-to-$200-a-day habits. More criminalization occurs as the addict is brought into contact with the skills and support of the criminals he, or she, will encounter in prison. Perhaps the most devastating effect of drug laws is their destructive impact on the legal system itself. Police corruption flourishes in the context of enforcing narcotic laws. Beyond this, the resources of law enforcement are continuously diverted from the protection of persons and properties to activities such as entrapment, surveillance, and petty seizures.

Increasingly, behavior therapy techniques are being applied to a wide range of drug abuse problems. Specific treatments have been developed under three general therapeutic paradigms: aversive conditioning, contingency management, and a mixed or multimodal approach.

Aversive Conditioning. The most frequently applied behavioral treatments to drug offenses are ones in which the major therapeutic element is some form of aversion therapy. Most aversive treatments have used electrical or chemical stimuli; recently some treatments have employed verbal or covert stimuli.

Covert sensitization offers several advantages over the use of shock or chemically induced aversion (Cautela & Rosenstiel, 1975). Few side effects have been observed, although some investigators have reported the generalization of aversive responses to nontargeted stimuli (Ashem & Donner, 1968). Special equipment or medical personnel is not required, and the procedure can be applied repeatedly in multiple environments. An additional benefit is that ''because the subject's own visualized experiences are used, a wide variety of conditioned and unconditioned stimuli are available and the conditioned stimuli presented in imagery may better approximate his behavior in the natural environment'' (Droppa, 1973, p. 147). These assets are balanced by the recognition that some patients report difficulty in maintaining vivid images thereby necessitating imagery training, and that precise therapist control of imagery is often problematic.

The first use of covert sensitization with a drug abuser was reported by Anant (1968). The patient was a 32-year-old female ''addicted to tranquilizers'' and displaying a history of alcohol abuse. Imagination of drug use and the desire for drugs were paired repeatedly with visualization of nausea. Another stage of treatment involved ''aversion relief'' in which the imagery of drug-control behaviors was paired with termination of visualized illness. The client reported no drug use at an assessment conducted three months after the termination of treatment.

Steinfeld (1970) and his colleagues (Steinfeld, Rautio, Rice & Egan, 1973) have used group covert sensitization with correctional inmates who were primarily heroin users. Evaluation of this program is difficult because some patients were receiving several treatments (e.g., encounter and traditional group therapy) and no followup assessment was conducted. Self reports, however, revealed no drug use at the end of treatment for seven of eight patients.

Contingency Management. The most comprehensive use of a contingency management approach to drug abusers is represented by the work of Polakow and Doctor (1974); Polakow and Peabody (1975) and Polakow (1975) which is described in detail in Chapter 7. Another example of a contingency-based approach is reflected in the work of Boudin, Valentine, Ingraham, Brantley, Ruiz, Smith, Catlin, and Regan (1974) who reported an impressive community-based extension of a contracting approach with a large group of drug dependent individuals the majority of whom were opiate addicts. This work is also described in Chapter 7.

Multimodal Approaches. Multimodal treatment of addicts reflects an increased appreciation of the fact that drug abuse is multiply determined, and that addicts are usually characterized by a number of problems including physiological dependence, social anxiety, interpersonal deficits, and an impoverished self-concept. The most typical multimodal behavioral approach involves the use of some form of aversion therapy to reduce drug use in combination with other procedures intended to develop the addict's ability in other critical areas.

A few studies have combined behaviorally based procedures with methadone maintenance for the treatment of herion addicts. Liebson and Bigelow (1972) supplied methadone contingent on continued disulfiram therapy by a client with an 18-year history of alcohol abuse and a 12-year history of opiate addiction. The reinforcing properties of methadone rendered it an ideal consequence for the contingency management of disulfiram-taking. Despite previous failures with hospitalization, Alcoholics Anonymous, and disulfiram therapy alone, the client had not resumed either opiate or alcohol abuse after three years on this contingency schedule.

Bigelow, Lawrence, Harris, and D'Lugoff (1973) have evaluated the contributions of contingency management (the major reinforcer being the privilege of taking home medication) and "behavior therapy" (anxiety reduction technique) to a methadone maintenance and supportive counseling program. A factorial combination of these approaches yielded the following four treatment cells: behavior therapy, contingency management, combined behavior therapy and contingency management, and supportive counseling only.

At the time of the report 80 volunteers had participated in the program. Most patients were between 20 and 25 years of age, had a drug abuse history of over five years in duration, had not finished high school, and had a record of multiple arrests but had not served time in prison. The majority of clients from whom preliminary data had been gathered had been in their assigned treatment condition for less than 20 weeks. Small group size and shortened treatment precluded many meaningful between-group comparisons, however, some evidence which suggested relative treatment effects was discussed. First, the percentage of clients engaged in activities such as work or school increased as time in treatment increased. For those who had participated in their assigned treatment for at least 20 weeks, the two modalities utilizing contingency management were associated with the largest percentage of full time employment. Urinalyses indicated that the rate of multiple drug use remained quite high among participants and was not reliably differentiated among different treatments. However, the great majority of positive urinalysis tests were sedative-tranquilizer positives rather than narcotic-quinine positives. Increasing the sample sizes and lengthening the posttreatment time enough to allow adequate followup will undoubtedly permit the necessary parametric and long-term evaluations of these outcomes.

EVALUATION

Clinical Adequacy

The major clinical shortcoming of intervention with nonincarcerated offenders is obvious. There is an excessive reliance on aversion therapy as the apparent treatment of choice. This has been particularly true with sex offenders (see also Barlow, 1973; Barlow & Abel, 1976). Of the many studies involving sexual deviations reviewed in this chapter, all but a handful included an aversive technique of some sort.

While there is some evidence that unintended but positive side effects, such as increased heterosexual arousal, are occasionally associated with unassisted aversion therapies (Bancroft, 1971; Barlow, Leitenberg, & Agras, 1969), the primary justification for their popularity remains their expedient suppression of objectionable behavior. At the same time, this preoccupation with suppression has evoked considerable conceptual disenchantment, even among many behavior therapists who realize that aversion therapy does very little to promote the acquisition of competencies commonly believed to be lacking or underdeveloped in many kinds of offenders.

Recognition of the limitations of aversion therapy has been accompanied by some encouraging developments which should enable clinicians to provide increasingly more sophisticated interventions that will decrease the probability of illegal conduct, and increase the likelihood of competent, prosocial behavior as well. These developments have occurred on three dimensions, each of which is described briefly below.

One development, occurring primarily at the technological level, has been the expanded knowledge in the use of physiological assessment. This has been true particularly in research on sexual deviance, where penile plethysmography has become a valuable technique for differential diagnosis, the monitoring of clinical improvement, and as a therapy adjunct (Bancroft, 1971). For example, changes in penile circumference (Quinsey, Steinman, Bergersen, & Holmes; 1975), and penile volume (Freund, 1965) have been used to diagnose child molesters where, at least in the former study, subjective ratings of sexual attractiveness did not allow such identification.[7] Less exotic measures such as the GSR also have demonstrated diagnostic utility. Kercher and Walker (1973) reported that GSR responses (but *not* changes in penile volume) successfully discriminated convicted rapists from inmates convicted for nonsexual offenses. Additional research (e.g., Abel, Barlow, Blanchard, & Mavissakalian, in press) has suggested modifications in basic plethysmographic technique that can make voluntary control, or distortion of penile response (Quinsey & Bergersen, 1976) more difficult. In addition to their frequent use in monitoring the effects of aversion therapy, penile-arousal measures might be used at a preliminary stage of therapy to select those clients who might profit most from aversion, as opposed to those whose arousal patterns contraindicate the need for aversion.

A second important trend has been at the theoretical level where a broadening of etiological explanations of sexual deviance has occurred. The traditional explanation of deviant arousal and behavior has followed a Pavlovian paradigm wherein a formally neutral stimulus or activity develops its positive valence on the basis of an intensive, single trial association (or multiple lesser intense associations) with an erotic stimulus. McGuire, Carlisle, and Young (1965) cite Jasper's (1963) succinct statement of this theory: "Perversion arises through the accidents of our first experience."

McGuire, et al. (1965) provide an alternative to the notion that deviant arousal is learned on the basis of a few, initial conditioning trials. Their view is that the initial associative experience provides particularly strong arousal and the continuing basis for erotic fantasies which, when subsequently used during masturbation, increases the habit strength of the deviant behavior. The strength of the deviant fantasies is likely to incubate due to both memory distortions and their repeated association with masturbatory arousal and orgasm. Indirect evidence for the supportive role of deviant fantasies is provided by the demonstration that exhibitionists treated successfully ($n = 10$), and unsuccessfully ($n = 10$) by aversion therapy were differentiated by the greater frequency of masturbation to deviant fantasies in the failure group (Evans, 1970). Additionally, Evans (1968) reported that aversion treatment of five exhibitionists with normal masturbatory fantasies progressed more rapidly than an identical treatment for five exhibitionists with deviant fantasies accompanying masturbation.

One of the most important implications of this conceptualization is that its primary clinical derivative, orgasmic reconditioning, has emerged as a viable alternative to aversion therapy, even in cases where deviant arousal is quite strong. The orgasmic reconditioning technique, in which fantasies of heterosexual intercourse are substituted for deviant fantasies just seconds before masturbation-induced orgasm, illustrates the advantages of a theoretical paradigm that is more receptive to the importance of mediational events in the acquisition of new behaviors.

Finally, the growing appreciation that many offenders are characterized by numerous, often independent deficits has spawned the advocation of what has been termed broad-spectrum behavior therapy. In his well-known account of the behavioral treatment of a middle-aged alcoholic, Lazarus (1965; see also Lazarus, 1971) introduced the broad-spectrum term and identified the following ingredients of the approach: (1) procedures aimed at reestablishing the client's physical well-being; (2) aversion and anxiety relief conditioning to eliminate compulsive habits; (3) evaluation of a client's social interaction with a special emphasis on determining anxiety antecedents to problem behaviors; (4) anxiety reduction techniques such as desensitization, assertion training, behavioral rehearsal, and hypnosis; (5) auxiliary therapy with a client's spouse; (6) socioeconomic interventions with past or potential employers; (7) establishment of new reinforcing activities, including hobbies or new forms of social participation; and (8) other adjunctive measures such as drugs or chemotherapy.

With regard to sexual deviance, Barlow (1973) has discussed four distinct treatment goals which, when pursued in combination, could provide a comprehensive, multimethod approach for most offenders. First, several varieties of aversion therapy can be directed at the suppression of deviant sexual arousal and behavior. The second goal is illustrated by such techniques as relaxation training, desensitization, and cue-controlled relaxation, all of which aim at the reduction of fear associated with heterosexual behavior. The objective of a third set of procedures (aversion relief, orgasmic reconditioning, intensive exposure to erotic stimuli) is an increase in arousal to heterosexual stimuli and fantasies. Finally, adequate heterosexual responsiveness depends on the availability of competent, instrumental heterosocial skills.

Social skills training, role playing, and guided *in vivo* practice are techniques intended to train or retrain clients in social approach behaviors necessary for heterosexual functioning. As behavioral researchers' inclinations become more sensitive to the heterogeneity of offender populations, one would anticipate an increase in the systematic, preplanned selection of techniques clinically indicated for an individual case. As an example, aversion would not appear to be a treatment of choice for sexual deviance which stems primarily from intense anxiety regarding heterosexual activities. On the other hand, conditioned sexual anxiety, accompanied by severe heterosocial limitations, might require the use of some anxiety relief measure as well as a skill training component.

Methodological Status

Empirical evaluations of behavior therapy with offenders are typified by methodological unsophistication. The literature consists, almost exclusively, of a series of confounded case studies yielding consistently optimistic results about the efficacy of behavior therapy with offenders, many of whom had been unresponsive to previous rehabilitative efforts.

Given the social undesirability, and the condemnation of the usual target behaviors discussed in this chapter, it is doubtful that the minimum elements of experimental design required to establish causality (e.g., treatment reversals, random assignment, control groups) will be attempted. The rarity of certain types of these offenders imposes an additional burden on between-subject designs which, of course, require several times as many subjects as their within-subject counterparts.

Currently, the equally compelling needs for clinical integrity, and methodological adequacy would be satisfied best by the use of single-subject, multiple-baseline designs. In the usual multiple-baseline design, two or more behaviors of the same subject are chosen for examination. The logic of this design depends on a demonstration that the effects of an intervention are specific to the behavior to which the intervention is applied. Behaviors not treated should not change, thereby serving as a continuing baseline against which the intervention's impact can be measured. While the most common type of multiple-baseline design is one in which treatment is presented across different behaviors, other versions sequentially introduce treatment across different individuals or situations.

Although the multiple-baseline design's assumption that interventions produce specific change while extraneous factors produce generalized ones has been criticized (Kazdin & Kopel, 1975), the same authors have offered three recommendations that could sustain the ability of multiple-baseline designs to demonstrate cause-effect relationships. The recommendations include: (1) the selection of baselines maximally independent of one another; (2) the use of several rather than few baselines; (3) a temporary reversal phase on one of the baselines. The first two recommendations seem especially well-suited for interventions with sex offenders, who usually present a set of partially independent problems including heterosexual anxiety, deviant sexual arousal and fantasy, and a lack of necessary heterosocial skills (Barlow, 1973). An additional advantage of the multiple-baseline strategy is that the effect of an intervention can be demonstrated without withdrawing treatment, a not-inconsiderable asset over the reversal or ABAB design which predicts recovery of the target behavior when treatment is withdrawn.

Ideally, an era of well-controlled multiple-baseline studies would be followed by the use of factorial designs that could allow an unconfounded evaluation of numerous variables' contributions to therapeutic change. The most economical use of the subjects necessary for these factorial designs will depend, of course on asking the most crucial research questions. Currently, the use of a factorial design to demonstrate the superiority of some behavioral intervention to a no-treatment control condition would be trivial. The accumulated weight of both controlled and uncontrolled case studies indicates that, for most offenders treated outside of a penal institution, any of a variety of behavior therapies will be more effective than doing nothing.

Two areas of inquiry would derive maximum benefits from future factorial experimentation. First is to identify which treatment, delivered by what kind of therapist, is most effective with what type of clients, under which conditions (Kielser, 1971; Paul, 1969). Ultimately, behavior therapists must face the fact that offenders' individual differences are likely to interact with alternative behavioral techniques to produce differential levels of effectiveness. To date, there are few exceptions (see Best, 1975) to behaviorists' persistent neglect of the variance-reducing potential of individual differences (Berzins, 1977). Second, factorial research should be directed at isolating the components of treatment packages which contribute the most to positive outcomes. This is especially important for offenders because of the frequency with which *potpourri* of techniques are embedded in the context of aversive conditioning. As an example, Barlow (1973) comments that aversion relief has been combined with aversive conditioning in over 150 cases, despite no empirical confirmation that the relief technique enhances clinical outcomes. With regard to the dimensions of the current chapter, an inspection of Tables 6-1, 6-2, 6-3, and 6-6 reveals that over 50 percent of the cases reviewed combined more than one type of technique in the complete intervention. None of these studies employed a design which was sufficient to estimate the relative importance of the separate intervention components.

The current limitations of methodology should obscure neither the efficacy of behavior therapy with nonincarcerated offenders, nor deter clinicians from applying techniques that have appeared at the case history level to exceed the impact of previous treatment. On the other hand, case study successes are not equivalent to methodologically adequate demonstrations of causality. Such demonstrations, on at least a single-subject basis, are an ambitious mandate for research with offender populations which, if realized, will enable the development of more successful therapies for noninstitutionalized offenders than has been the rule.

NOTES

[1]With respect to overall effects, the association between socioeconomic class and treatment outcome remains unclear. On the one hand, Lorion (1973, 1974) has concluded that there is not

an established relationship between social class and treatment outcome, while Heitler (1976) maintains that lower-class psychotherapy participants are likely to benefit less from therapy. Despite the lack of consensus on this issue, the consistency of disadvantages encountered by lower class psychotherapy clients has prompted a number of extra- or pre-therapy attempts, either to prepare these clients for the role requirements of psychotherapy (Heitler, 1976), or to adapt psychotherapy services to the cultural requirements of lower-class clients (Kelly, Snowden & Munoz, 1977).

[2] Additional accounts of behavioral treatments for fetishists, voyeurs, and transvestites who apparently had not experienced any contact with the adult criminal justice system for their sexual misbehavior may be found in Blakemore, Thorpe, Barker, Conway, and Lavin (1963), Bond and Evans (1967), Cooper (1963), Gaupp, Stern and Ratliff (1971), Hallam and Rachman (1972), Marks and Gelder (1967), Morgenstern, Pearce and Reis (1965), and Pinard and Lamontagne (1976).

[3] It is not clear what proportion of these patients had been represented in an earlier report on electrical aversion with sexual deviations (Bancroft & Marks, 1968).

[4] It is not clear which of the earlier described exhibitionists (Wickramasekera, 1972) are included in the Wickramasekera (1976) report.

[5] For other reports of behavioral treatments with pedophiles, see Bancroft, Jones and Pullman (1966), Bancroft and Marks (1968), Beech, Watts and Poole (1971), Hallam and Rachman (1972), and Laws (1974).

[6] Abel, Barlow, Blanchard and Guild (in press) identify the following developments as crucial for the more objective assessment of rapist behavior: (1) a physiological measure specific to sexual arousal; (2) a suitable rape stimulus to present to the rapist while measuring his arousal and (3) an experimental design that would allow a separation of the different elements of rapists' sexual arousal.

[7] The concern that clients might distort the outcomes of their treatments is not without some justification. Rosen and Kopel (1977) reported a case of a married man who had been arrested for cross-dressing and then exposing himself, in female attire, to males he encountered in a public parking lot. His choice of this location was, at least partly, influenced by his wife's command that he never cross-dress in their home again. (Obviously, some behaviors are not entirely situationally specific.).

The patient's arousal to a transvestite-exhibitionist videotape was eliminated by the use of biofeedback conditioning procedures. Penile measures, and assessments of related clinical changes confirmed the durability of improvements over a four-month followup period. Despite the patient's report of apparent successful adjustment for two years following treatment, he and his wife subsequently admitted that they had deceived the therapists for more than a year, hiding the facts that he had resumed cross-dressing and exposure, and had once again been arrested.

What the determinants of this deception were, and how it might have been detected or prevented, are open to inquiry. In the authors' own words, "the events in this case provide a striking demonstration of the unreliability of self-report data as a clinical outcome measure" (Rosen & Kopel, 1977, p. 915). This problem is probably most pronounced in instances where the original targets of treatment, if redetected, are subject to severe, punitive sanctions.

Chapter 7
Community-based Behavior Modification

The first prison I ever saw had
inscribed on it "Cease to do
evil: learn to do well," but the
inscription was on the outside:
the prisoners could not read it.

— George Bernard Shaw,
Imprisonment

The integration of behavior modification with officially and formally organized, community-based corrections for adults has been an infrequent accomplishment. This state of affairs contrasts dramatically with juvenile corrections where numerous applications of behavioral principles in community settings consistently have produced specific behavioral changes and positive outcomes on recidivism measures (Davidson & Seidman, 1974; Nietzel, Winett, MacDonald & Davidson, 1977).

The characteristics that have led to the greater amenability of the juvenile justice system to community corrections exceed the obvious one of age. The beginning of a separate justice system for juveniles originated in the belief that flexible, somewhat informal procedures would maximize the possibilities for individualized care. Ideally, the court was viewed as providing the supervision and attention of responsible parents, a role which seemed to require few of the legal safeguards so typical of the adult justice system. A second distinction involved the belief that adult behavior patterns are more ingrained and more unchangeable thereby limiting correctionists' optimism that purely rehabilitative efforts in any setting will have much impact on the older offender.

Finally, there is a rather pervasive notion that juvenile offenses are less violent or felonious than those committed by adults, therefore decreasing the need for institutional confinement or constant surveillance of younger offenders. In fact, available data suggest the contrary. In 1973, over one-third of all cases cleared by law enforcement agencies involved offenders under the age of

18 (F.B.I., 1973). More recent figures confirm the youthfulness of offenders charged with serious crimes. Table 7-1 presents the percentage of offenders under 15, 18, and 21 who had been arrested for one of the F.B.I. index crimes. Of particular interest is the fact that over 60 percent of individuals arrested for an index offense were younger than 21 years of age.

PROBATION

Probation has been heralded as America's distinctive contribution to modern penology (Newman, 1968). While it is true that probation was first instituted, legally and officially, in this country, it had several important forerunners in legal history. One of the most important was the English common law tradition that the courts could suspend temporarily the imposition of criminal sentences. Presumably, the motivation for this policy was a desire to reduce the brutal punishment, or lengthy imprisonment, of offenders for whom such sentences seemed unwarranted.

Table 7-1 Arrests of Persons Under 15, 18, and
21 Years of Age, 1975*

Offense	Total Arrests (all ages)	Percentage of Persons Arrested		
		Under 15	Under 18	Under 21
Criminal Homicide:				
a) murder and nonnegligent manslaughter	16,485	1.1	9.5	25.2
b) manslaughter by negligence	3,041	2.6	12.1	32.0
Forcible rape	21,963	3.9	17.6	37.0
Robbery	129,788	9.6	34.3	57.7
Aggravated assault	202,217	5.2	17.6	32.3
Burglary	449,155	20.1	52.6	72.6
Larceny	958,938	20.1	45.1	62.8
Motor vehicle theft	120,224	14.4	54.5	73.1
Violent crime**	370,453	6.5	23.1	41.2
Property crime***	1,528,317	19.6	48.0	66.5
All index offenses	1,901,811	17.0	43.1	61.5

* Based on Tabel 37 of Federal Bureau of Investigation, *Uniform Crime Reports,* United
States Department of Justice, Washington, D.C., 1975.
** Murder, forcible rape, robbery, and aggravated assault.
*** Burglary, larceny, and motor vehicle theft.

There were seveal legal devices during the nineteenth century which could accomplish the temporary suspension of a sentence (See Carney, 1977, pp. 76-79; Newman, 1968, pp. 3-12). At least four judicial practices have been viewed as direct precursors of probation. Each of these procedures is reviewed briefly below.

1. Benefit of clergy. Benefit of clergy involved a claim by the church that since clerics were subject to church law, their punishment, even for secular violations, should be left to the church rather than the state. Newman (1968) claims the primary objective of this plea was avoidance of capital punishment. Apparently some nonclerics began to take advantage of the ''benefit,'' and the procedure fell into disuse in the middle of the nineteenth century.

2. Judicial reprieve. Judicial reprieve referred to the discretionary power of a judge to suspend temporarily a sentence when he was dissatisfied with the verdict or when the convicted party applied for a pardon. Newman (1968) argues that this method was never intended to involve an indefinite suspension, as is the case with probation.

3. Recognizance and Bail. Recognizance developed in the fourteenth century as a preventive measure by which someone suspected of wrongdoing gave assurance by entering a bond or promise with the state that offenses would not occur. Apparently, this device was used both for suspected troublemakers, and for those individuals actually arraigned in court for some criminal offense.

Bail originated in medieval England, where pretrial release of an accused was deemed necessary to eliminate prolonged periods of incarceration before trial. Minor offenses were tried in court only twice a year, and serious offenses required traveling justices, often resulting in a delay of years. For this reason, sheriffs were allowed to release a prisoner conditional upon his promise, or a promise of a third party, that the accused would appear for his trial. If the accused did not appear, the third party could be arrested; in effect, the third party was given custodial power over the defendant. From the outset, bail relationships in England were characterized by their personal nature. Social and geographical conditions in America necessitated a fortification of these methods. Stable personal relationships were less frequent among recently formed settlements; added to this was the great expanse of the American Frontier to which the accused could flee. As a result, the commercial bail-bondsman appeared in America as a replacement for the third-party surety in England. It is interesting to note that the conditions of bail as practiced in ancient England closely approximate some of the conditions of our modern-day probation system.

4. Filing of cases. The "filing" of a case involved the suspension of a sentence when for any of several reasons the court felt that an immediate sentence was not required. Its implementation necessitated the consent of the defendant, and whatever special condition the court chose to impose. It seems very likely that sentences were suspended indefinitely in some cases, similar to the current practice of filing away cases in large metropolitan jurisdictions.

The legal thread which unifies these judicial devices was the common-law tradition that courts could *temporarily* suspend sentences for specific purposes. The emerging procedure of probation, however, assumed a judicial prerogative to suspend a sentence *indefinitely* on the basis of several types of conditional criteria. This view was denied in the *Killits* decision,[1] in which the Supreme Court rejected the proposition "that those courts possessed the arbitrary discretion to permanently decline to enforce the law." In spite of the Supreme Court's objection to indefinite suspension, the flexibility provided by a system of common law, and the general approval of the public, enabled conditional (and indefinite) suspensions of sentence to continue.

The first statute legitimizing probation was passed in 1878 by Massachusetts, which had pioneered several forms of sentence suspension, and under the leadership of John Augustus[2] had, as early as 1841, placed offenders on probationary status. Probation was not enacted by statute at the federal level until 1925. At the present time, all 50 states have laws that empower probation services.

The demand that corrections rehabilitate rather than merely incarcerate offenders has led to a greatly expanded use of probation. Among available correctional dispositions, probation represents the preferred settlement for most juveniles, first-time offenders, some categories of misdemeanants, and offenders who pose little hazard to community safety or stability. Along with parole, probation accounts for the bulk of community treatment available in the criminal justice system. It offers the advantages of community placement and continued supervision of the offender, but does not involve a period of confinement as does parole. More than one-half of all criminal sentences ordered in this country involve probation (Carney, 1977).

Carney (1977) proposes five theoretical and practical justifications for probation's popularity. (1) It maximizes the normalizing influences available in the community but absent in most correctional institutions; (2) it minimizes the physical and psychological degradation that accompany imprisonment; (3) it attempts to "humanize" rehabilitation; (4) it is cheaper than the cost of institutional confinement; and (5) it is regarded as a more effective correctional procedure than incarceration.

Although the concept of probation is widely endorsed, its actual practice is broadly criticized. A frequent criticism is directed at the unmanageably large probation caseloads. While the recommended ratio is 35 offenders per officer, over two-thirds of probated adults are seen by officers with caseloads in excess of 100 (U.S. President's Commission, 1967).[3] One result of this overloading is that community supervision is often only nominal. For this reason, many periods of probation are really unsupervised suspended sentences. Another objection to probation is that the goals for the probationer are either vague or concerned only with identifying behaviors that should not occur. In lieu of adequate case management and supervision, probation officers often are forced to rely on aversive control of their clients' behavior.

Probation Effectiveness

An unequivocal judgment about the effectiveness of probation is precluded by several problems. First, there are disagreements about suitable criteria by which to measure success. Many programs monitor arrests for new criminal offenses; others examine probation violations in addition to rearrest data. In some instances recidivism figures are limited to actual convictions. A second difficulty involves the great diversity of programs that are subsumed under the rubric of probation. Although some probation services offer community-based educational, vocational, and counseling programs, many others are able to provide only the most superficial levels of intervention devoted largely to surveillance of probationers' activities.

Carney (1977) discusses several empirical studies (Empey & Rabow, 1970; Irving & Sandhu, 1973; Rumney & Murphy, 1968; and Sparks, 1971) that have claimed lower recidivism rates for probation than for commitment to prison. Whether these differences are due to the special effects of probation, or to the preselection of offenders less likely to recidivate under any conditions remains unclear. Even in the absence of demonstrations that probation produces lower recidivism, continuation or expansion of probation could be justified on economic grounds. If one assumes, as most correctional experts do, that probation is no less effective than imprisonment in lessening future criminal conduct, the reduced expense of probation (approximately one-tenth of the cost of institutional commitment) renders it a generally preferred alternative to incarceration.

Behavioral Approaches to Probation

The augmentation of adult probation services with behavioral techniques is an innovative development in correctional behavior modification. It represents a welcome demonstration of behavior modification's utility in noninstitutional settings.

To date, the most comprehensive investigation of a behavioral approach to probation has been a well-controlled study by Polakow and Doctor (1974; see also Doctor & Polakow, 1973, for an abbreviated description of this research). The subjects were 26 adults (15 females, 11 males) who had served an average of 12.5 months on probation prior to the initiation of the study. They had been transferred to the program because previous probation officers, using traditional case management procedures, had found them too difficult to work with. The vast majority of the crimes for which these subjects had been convicted were drug related.

The probation period consisted of three graduated contingency phases. In Phase One, the probationer earned a credit for weekly meetings with his or her probation officer. Accumulation of eight points allowed the participant to advance to Phase Two, where points were earned for attendance at a group meeting with other probationers. These group meetings were devoted to "experience sharing within the social context, discussion of problems, and support for positive self-correction of deviant behavior." Phase Two lasted a minimum of ten weeks.

Phase Three required a participant to execute a written, individualized contract with his, or her, officer that specified new behaviors which the probationer felt he, or she, needed to develop (e.g., obtaining employment, new social activities). In most instances, contracts were confined to the one class of behavior which was considered to be the offender's most crucial deficit. Successful completion of contracted behaviors resulted in predetermined reductions in the remaining probation time. Aversive control was deliberately minimized throughout the program. The only "punishment" was demotion to Phase One for violations of written probation conditions.

Using an own-control design, the authors compared participants' performance on traditional probation to that achieved during the contingency management period. Program evaluation focused on four outcomes: number of probation violations, number of new arrests, proportion of probation time in which the participant was employed, and attendance at scheduled probation meetings. The results for the first three measures are presented in Table 7-2 and clearly indicate the superior effectiveness of the contingency based probation. Attendance at meetings also increased significantly during the contingency program. The rearrest data are especially impressive in light of the fact that no systematic contingencies were applied to the occurrence of illegal conduct, including drug usage.

Results achieved during the contingency management program also were contrasted with outcomes produced by an intensive supervision program (The Community Oriented Youthful Offenders Program; COYOP) in which the probation officer was responsible for a reduced caseload, thereby allowing more frequent contact with clients. The contingency management and intensive supervision caseloads were matched in size and amount of time spent with each probationer. The mean ages of the two caseloads were virtually equivalent. The outcomes of this comparison were quite similar to that of the own-control study. Contingency management probation was more effective than intensive probation in decreasing the mean number of probation violations and new arrests, and in increasing the number of months employed.

Contingency management probation has been applied to a number of other drug related offenses. Polakow (1975) treated a probated barbiturate addict

Table 7-2 Mean Scores and Associated *t* Tests for Number of
Probation Violations, Arrests, and Months Employed While on
Intensive Probation and Contingency Management

Dependent variable	Type of probation	Sex		Total	*t*Diff
		M	F		
Mean number of probation viola-	Regular	1.43	2.05	1.75	
					5.05*
tions/year	Contingency	0.00	.26	.15	
Mean number of arrests while on	Regular	2.64	1.53	2.00	
					4.22*
probation	Contingency	.18	.13	.15	
Percentage of months em-	Regular	51.9	38.6	44.6	
ployed while					3.30*
on probation	Contingency	74.7	78.9	76.9	

*p < .001.

(From Doctor & Polakow, ''A Behavior Modification Program for Adult Probationers,''
Proceedings, 81st Annual APA Convention, 1973, Copyright 1973 by the American Psychological Association. Reprinted by Permission.)

with the simultaneous use of covert sensitization, behavioral rehearsal, and
contingency contracting. The participant was a 24-year-old female who had
been sentenced to three years of probation for a recent felony conviction
involving the possession of dangerous drugs. The contract was similar to that
of the Polakow and Doctor (1973) report in which successful completion of
therapy assignments resulted in one-week reductions in total probation time.
Initially, the contract required performance of one non-drug activity per week.
This criteria was increased gradually until by the 35th week of treatment the
client was completing at least seven non-drug activities each week. Thirty
weeks of covert sensitization (sessions 7 through 37) produced a strong aversive reaction to imagined drug use, and enabled the client to stop her barbiturate use completely. Behavioral rehearsal was used to strengthen the client's
ability to deal more effectively with events that could be anxiety provoking for
her.

After one year of treatment, the client had been drug free for three months
and was employed. At the end of 15 months, she had maintained these
improvements and was dismissed from probation. Self-report and agency
records indicated that the client remained drug free and continued to be
employed 18 months after treatment termination.

Another example of a contractual approach to probation was introduced by Polakow and Doctor (1973) in their attempt to decrease a young married couple's use of barbiturates and marijuana. The participants were a 21-year-old man and his 23-year-old wife both of whom had been sentenced to three years of probation for possession of marijuana. While it was the woman's first arrest, the husband had a long record of drug-related arrests. A contingency contract was negotiated between the therapist and the couple which specified that the couple must perform one non-drug related social activity per week, the verifiable completion of which would be reinforced by shortening their total probation time by a matching week. The wife agreed, further, to reinforce her husband's attempts to reduce drug use and gain employment. He in turn contracted to attempt to secure a job, which he accomplished successfully two weeks later. Over the 36 sessions of treatment, the number of required non-drug activities was increased gradually to seven per week. The couple also participated in group-based training in social skills and received instructions on how to negotiate their own marital contracts. Neither individual reported any drug use at a one-year followup; the husband had retained his employment, and marital adjustment was satisfactory.

Behaviorally based probation has been successfully extended to other targets besides drug abuse. For example, Polakow and Peabody (1975) reported the treatment of a 30-year-old woman who had been placed on probation for child abuse involving her young son. Therapy was multifaceted, and included (a) negotiation of a behavioral contract between the mother and son that set limits on the permissible behaviors for both parties (satisfactory performance of this contract resulted in a reduction of total probation time); (b) discrimination training to improve the mother's disciplinary control of her son's aggressive behavior; and (c) assertion training designed to develop a more effective interpersonal repertoire for the mother. An 18-month followup revealed sustained improvement for both mother and son. Child abuse had not reccurred in this interval.

The initial successes of behavioral approaches to probation suggest that future efforts in this area might examine the extent to which behavioral techniques could permit a redefinition of other probation functions. Table 7-3 contrasts several activities as they would be implemented with behavioral or traditional probation methods. At this time there is no empirical support for the usefulness of all such behavioral redefinitions. However, the preliminary data which have compared typical probation counseling with contingency contracting would seem to encourage further investigations of the efficacy of acquainting probation officers with the behavioral alternatives discussed in Table 7-3.

PORT

PORT (an acronym for Probation Offenders Rehabilitation and Training) is a community-based, residential program for adult offenders requiring a correc-

Table 7-3 A Comparison of Standard and Behavioral Approaches to Probation Practice*

Institutional Activity	Probation Method	Behavioral Method
Record Keeping	Enter descriptive information about client, what he says about what he is doing.	Definition and charting of target behavior. Identify goals in behavioral terms. Enter objective information, as well as impressions about the client. Objective sources of information would involve proof of activities, visits to client in natural environment, visits or calls to significant others in environment. Changes in behavior would be monitored.
Plans for work with client	Develop generalized nonbehavioral goals that have good social value such as reduce acting-out behavior, improve self-image, and ability to get along with others.	Develop organized sequential plan to work with client. Define your goals in objective behavioral terms and secondary steps toward goals. Behavioral plan as an educational function.
Structure of contact with client	Be open, responsive, inactive listener. The client is responsible for making self-corrections, you provide warm atmosphere and reflection. Probation officer is positive, and client is acting appropriately for contingent verbal response upon appropriate client verbal behavior.	Consequation rules are clearly defined, as well as behavioral expectations within each sequential step. Client controls reinforcements. Behavior outside of office is reinforced, regardless of relationship with probation officer.
Accountability	Report psychological status of client and how hard you are working with him. Try not to get pinned down to specifics. Focus on terminal goals and deficits.	Keep accurate records of target behaviors. Baseline and continual recording provide evidence on speed of change.
Incentives	Use aversive control via threats, punishment by incarceration, fines, or continued probation if behavioral demands are not made.	Use of natural reinforcers in the system such as time off probation, sequence of behavioral expectations show probability of successful responses.

(Reprinted with permission from Robert L. Polakow, "Establishing Behavior Therapy in a Public Agency," presented at the convention of the Association for the Advancement of Behavior Therapy, Chicago, 1974.)

tional alternative with more structure than that provided by traditional probation, but with less restrictions than institutional confinement. Originated in
Rochester, Minnesota, in 1969, PORT is distinguished by two innovative
elements (Keve, 1974; Schoen, 1972).

First, the program represents a combination of behavior modification procedures and group therapy. Progress through the five levels of the program is
determined jointly by group (i.e., residents) and staff decisions, and the
accumulation of points for performance in such areas as budget management,
social activities, educational achievement, and work completion. This emphasis on group decision making in a token economy framework is reminiscent
of Fairweather's very successful work with chronic psychiatric patients (Fairweather, Sanders, & Tornatzky, 1974). This programmatic affirmation of
self-direction and social responsibility is a unique characteristic that differentiates PORT from many prison token economies.

The second unusual variation in PORT is that it simultaneously serves
juvenile and adult offenders (age range, 13-47). Such an age integration is
avoided vigorously in most institutions because of the suspected danger of
criminalizing younger residents. In the case of PORT, however, the direction
of influence is intended to be reversed so that older residents benefit from the
decriminalizing efforts extended to juveniles. An additional attempt to make a
PORT placement less stigmatizing for its residents is provided by a staff
consisting largely of live-in college students.

The available descriptions of the PORT program suggest that it closely
approximates an optimal alliance of community corrections with behavior
modification techniques, but, to date, confirmatory outcome research is minimal. An early review of the program (Schoen, 1972) revealed that of the first
60 residents, 34 had been discharged. Six of these ultimately were returned to a
correctional institution but 28 were living successfully in the community.

Probation Subsidy

One systems-level attempt to strengthen probation services is California's
subsidy program. Initiated in 1966, probation subsidy is a system in which the
state pays counties for each juvenile and adult offender placed on probation
rather than incarcerated in a penal institution. The amount of payment is based
on the product of the computed cost of institutional care times the amount by
which a county reduces its commitments to the state's prison system. Pre-1966
commitment rates are the baseline against which current commitment practices
are measured.

This program illustrates a broad-scale contingency management approach to
institutional change, founded on the simple but pragmatic principle of reinforcing a system for the results that are desired. Generally, the California
project has been viewed as a success, and other states are beginning to
experiment with their own versions of probation subsidy. Clearly, the program

has saved the state millions of dollars.[4] Whether subsidy has resulted in more effective rehabilitation of offenders, or increased protection of the public is less clear and awaits further evaluation.

PAROLE

After probation, parole is the most common form of community corrections. Although they are both examples of community-based dispositions, parole and probation have many differences. Probation is administered through the judicial branch of government, while parole is considered an executive responsibility, and is often administered from departments of correction or social services. Parole can be defined as the selective and supervised release of offenders who have served a portion of their prison sentence. Ideally, the usual conditions of restriction imposed on the parolee are directed at two goals: (1) the continued protection of society, and (2) the continued rehabilitation of the offender. In addition to some set of restrictive conditions, most parole programs provide correctional counseling for their clients.

Parole had its origin in a combination of eighteenth and nineteenth century penal policies exemplified by the work of two men, Captain Alexander Maconochie and Sir Walter Crofton (Carney, 1977). Alexander Maconochie was a nineteenth century governor of Norfolk Island, a British penal colony to which English convicts were transported to relieve the overcrowded conditions in British prisons. Convinced that the deplorable conditions of the island required reform, Maconochie developed a plan by which a prisoner could earn his early release through the accumulation of a good prison record. Maconochie's plan also employed the "ticket-of-leave," a device allowing the appropriate executive officer (e.g., a governor) to exempt a convict from a penal-work sentence on the condition that the convict was able to secure and maintain other civil employment in a given area. Tickets-of-leave were also granted for good behavior, marriage, and special services. After a number of years, a system was adopted by which a ticket-of-leave could be obtained only after a convict had served a certain set period of time. Carney (1977) summarized the following two elements of the Maconochie system:

(1) A "marks" system which allowed inmates to earn their way out of confinement through "industry and good conduct."

(2) A five-phase system leading to unconditional freedom. These phases were: (a) rigid discipline and absolute confinement; (b) labor on government chain gangs; (c) limited freedom within prescribed areas; (d) a ticket-of-leave or conditional freedom; and (e) total freedom.

The Maconochie program was never employed extensively beyond Norfolk Island because it did not allow for the supervision of released inmates. An additional problem was the lack of a sufficient labor market in which to integrate inmates after their release. These deficiencies were addressed in Sir

Walter Crofton's rehabilitation program which he termed the "intermediate system" but which has generally come to be known as the "Irish system."

Crofton's program consisted of three phases: (1) strict imprisonment; (2) intermediate imprisonment, and (3) ticket-of-leave. The first stage lasted approximately eight to nine months, and required very arduous and boring work by inmates who were kept in solitary confinement. During the second stage, prisoners were able to earn "marks" for a good employment record. After proving his reform during this stage, and having an offer of employment outside the institution, an inmate was promoted to the third, or ticket-of-leave, phase. Crofton developed a set of restricted conditions which were in effect during this phase, and which, if broken, could result in the reimprisonment of the violator.

While Newman (1968) has suggested a number of other historical forerunners of parole, the most important development, in addition to the programs by Maconochie and Crofton, was the indeterminate sentence, a concept that actually accompanied parole rather than preceded it. The indeterminate sentence is one in which the offender is committed to prison for an indefinite period of time, the precise time of release being contingent on the amount of correctional progress displayed by the prisoner. In practice, indeterminate sentences usually are bounded by minimum and maximum periods of incarceration (e.g., one to five years) that are sufficiently broad to allow considerable flexibility in the length of sentence served.

For a number of years, the indeterminate sentence has been considered an almost essential counterpart of successful parole in that release could be conditional on the inmate's demonstration of reformation rather than the mere passage of time.[5] At present, the honeymoon between professional correctionists and the indeterminate sentence appears to have ended. Many authorities, including those who had been original supporters of the indeterminate sentence are now calling for its abolition (see Carney, 1977, pp. 146-148) and replacement with determinate sentences or "flat time." The main criticisms of the indeterminate sentence have focused on the mental hardship it works on inmates who remain uncertain as to when their release might be allowed, and the lack of empirical evidence that indeterminate sentences make any unique therapeutic contribution to an offender's rehabilitation.

The first formal system of parole was administered from the Elmira Reformatory in 1876 under the direction of Superintendent Zebulon Brockway who, not surprisingly, was also an early advocate of the indeterminate sentence. Currently, all states, as well as the federal government, have a parole system. Despite numerous objections to both the administration of parole and the accompanying indeterminate sentence, parole continues to be a very heavily used component of the correctional system. In recent years more than 70 percent of inmates released from prison were released on parole; in 1974 there were approximately 130,000 offenders on active parole (Carney, 1977).

It is ironic that this increasing utilization of parole is contemporaneous with intensifying challenges to the existence of the parole system itself. A major target of these objections has been the parole board, the body primarily responsible for parole-release decisions. These boards have been criticized as being arbitrary, subject to political patronage, inefficient, unprofessional, conservative, too liberal, and fundamentally unfair. Proposed changes in the parole board system have included: (1) the use of explicit, formalized criteria, or a formula on which to base release decisions; (2) increased professionalization of the board, to be achieved by discontinuing the practice of political appointments; (3) more diligent judicial surveillance of parole board procedures with regard to potential violations of inmates' constitutional rights; and (4) transfer of parole board functions to the courts. Although the complete future of the parole board is not clear at this time, one factor seems certain. Unless the quality of parole board justice is improved through some fundamental modifications in procedure, administrative pressures and judicial reviews may converge on the necessity of abolishing not only the parole board, but the parole system as we now know it.

Parole Effectiveness

The same problems that plague the evaluation of probation services complicate empirical assessments of the effectiveness of parole. Definitions of recidivism vary greatly, as do the followup periods during which the outcome data are collected. There are no uniform criteria upon which release decisions are made rendering any comparisons between different parole systems or between parole and continued incarceration a very hazardous venture. In an attempt to remedy these difficulties, a system of unified record keeping, the Uniform Parole Reports, was begun in 1974. Carney (1977, p. 207) cites Uniform Parole Reports figures which indicate that although the percentage of recommitment to prison for new offenses has stabilized at 8 percent in recent years, the percentage of parole "successes" has increased consistently up to 81 percent in 1972. These data suggest that the "increase" in parole successes may be an illusory one, derived primarily from a shift in agency policies in the handling of the "technical violations" of parole.

One of the first evaluations of the Federal prison and parole system was conducted in 1956 by Glaser (1969) who surveyed every tenth male adult releasee, 31 percent of whom were parolees. Over the duration of an approximately four-year followup, 31 percent of those released were returned to prison. Twenty-eight percent had been convicted or accused of a new felony. This figure is consistent with a more recent federal survey (U.S. Department of Justice, 1974) of 1,800 inmates released in 1970 which found that 67 percent of those released had not recidivated after two years. In this study, recidivism included either parole revocation or a new conviction, resulting in a jail sentence of 60 days or more. In general, the success rate for parolees after one to two years of release is 60-70 percent. There is no adequate evidence that this success rate is produced by any specific element of parole such as supervision or case counseling. Carney (1977) argues that recidivism for a randomly selected control group that received no parole supervision but who were released from prison would be equal, or less, than that of parolees under active supervision.

Behavioral Approaches to Parole

Unlike probation, parole programs have made infrequent use of behavioral techniques in their services for released offenders. The reasons for this are not entirely clear. Perhaps the fact that parole represents the last portion of the correctional process rather than the initial phase, as is the case with probation, minimizes the enthusiasm for such rehabilitative embellishments as behavioral contracting or social skills training. In addition, probationers and parolees might be distinguished by the types of crimes they have committed, as well as other characteristics (prior record, age) that would indicate the appropriateness of different types of interventions for them.

Boudin, Valentine, Ingraham, Brantley, Ruiz, Smith, Catlin, and Regan (1974) reported an impressive community-based program for a large group of drug dependent individuals, the majority of whom were opiate addicts. The recipients of the program had experienced substantial contact with the criminal justice system. Ninety-one percent had been arrested on at least one occasion, and 76 percent had received at least one conviction for a criminal charge. Forty-two percent were nonvoluntary participants, having been required to take part in the program as a condition of their parole, probation, or work release. The report did not indicate what percentage of the nonvoluntary group were on parole, but 64 percent had served at least one prior prison sentence.

The program was based on an extension of the behavioral contracting approach that other research (Polakow & Doctor, 1974; Polakow, 1975; Polakow & Doctor, 1973) had indicated was effective with probated drug offenders. Four types of contracts were employed in the course of the treatment program. The first was a *precontract agreement* in which the participants were requested to make a material commitment to the project as a demonstration of their motivation. This commitment often took the form of depositing either a sum of money or a highly valued personal item. Participants were also asked to undertake several responsibilities, including frequently contacting the project staff by phone and in person, writing daily diaries, seeking or continuing employment, and supplying several urine samples per week.

Following this phase, which also served as a baseline period, a *managerial contract* was written that established an "individualized behavior program" in five areas: responsibilities, consequences, privileges, bonuses, and special considerations. Client responsibilities included such tasks as job procurement or job maintenance, attendance at all meetings with treatment staff, drug abstinence, self-monitoring of several dependent measures, making frequent phone contacts with the staff, daily preparation of a diary, and adherence to a urine collection schedule. Participants also were required to establish a joint bank account with their contract manager. These bank accounts were used in two ways. First, they enabled participants to learn some basic budgeting skills. Second, they provided the treatment team with a mechanism for reinforcing adaptive behaviors. For example, participants were able to earn a weekly allowance by complying with the conditions of their contract.

Breaches of contracts resulted in specific penalties (usually a fine) while privileges and bonuses were earned by compliance with the conditions of the contracts. "Special considerations" involved changes in client status necessitated by such demands as parole conditions or leaves of absence. Krasnegor and Boudin (1973) also reported the adjunctive provision of aversive conditioning, behavioral rehearsal, and marital counseling as needed by certain individuals throughout the project.

Transitional contracts were introduced as a means of reducing project structure and increasing individual responsibility for those participants who demonstrated successful performance during the managerial contract phase. In the final stage of treatment, participants constructed *personal contracts* that established their individual long-term objectives and the behavioral means for attaining them.

Status of case outcomes was determined on the basis of four criteria: (1) work and school performance, (2) personal and social adjustment, (3) drug use, (4) arrest and conviction history. Multiple sources of criteria evaluation were employed, including clinical observation, self-report, agency records, urinalyses, peer reports, and participant diaries. For a participant to be judged a positive case outcome, he, or she, had to demonstrate satisfactory performance in at least three of the four criteria areas. Any occurrence of extremely maladaptive adjustment (a felony arrest) precluded a judgment of positive case outcome.

Data were reported on 33 clients who had participated in the project for at least 15 days. Of these, 14 were current participants while 19 had terminated treatment. Of the terminators, six were program graduates, all of whom were evidencing positive case outcomes. Eleven of the terminators had stopped treatment against staff advice. Of these, seven were meeting positive case criteria, two were classified as negative outcomes, and the status for the other two was unknown. Two participants terminated treatment for "other reasons"; both were classified as negative outcomes. The successful adjustment of the self-terminators was interesting, especially in light of the fact that some "occasional discreet use" of drugs was reported by this group while drug use was very rare among program graduates. It is possible that this difference was an artifact of the drug preferences for the two groups. Program graduates were all primarily opiate users while self-terminators tended to prefer barbiturates, a category of drugs which is both more easily obtained and less subject to severe social surveillance and sanction than the opiates. Whatever the explanation for this finding, the results do suggest that both abstinence and controlled drug use might be indicative of equally positive treatment outcomes with different types of addicts. A followup of program graduates, ranging from 12 to 453 days, indicated maintenance of positive effects.

Two aspects of the Florida project demand particular attention. First, it demonstrated that a comprehensive, well-integrated treatment package could be applied to a large group of quite diverse drug abusers (some of whom were parolees) in a natural setting. Second, this is the only behaviorally oriented program of this type that has systematically prepared paraprofessional volunteers to implement the bulk of the intervention. The use of paraprofessionals in an ecologically representative treatment setting is likely to increase the range of the addict population that perceives these programs as viable. In fact, Boudin, et al. (1974) reported data that the percentage of younger and non-white participants has increased over the levels reflected by the initial program group.

NOTES

[1] Ex parte United States, 242 U. S. 27-53 (1916).

[2] Augustus is generally regarded as the "Father of Probation," although Carney (1977) reviews evidence that the procedure had been employed more than 150 years earlier in Albany, New York.

[3] For a long period of time, the ideal caseload was estimated to be 50 per officer. While there is considerable tradition behind this recommendation, there are few data to support it. Lipton, Martinson and Wilk's (1975) review of probation studies did not find a positive relationship between reduced caseload and reduced recidivism. In fact, one study (Lohman, 1967) revealed a higher rate of probation violations with smaller caseloads. This outcome may be due to the fact that reduced caseloads permit more time for surveillance, therefore more technical violations can be detected. On the other hand, there is some evidence that intensive probation may contribute to a lower rate of new criminal offenses (Lohman, 1967).

[4] Carney (1977) cites an estimate that probation subsidy saved California $126,000,000 in its first five years of operation.

[5] As a matter of fact, continuation of parole programs does not require the indeterminate sentence. In practice, there is nothing incompatible with parole, and fixed or determinate sentences. Specified reductions of sentences, known in advance to the offender, can be made contingent on prescribed prison behavior (Singer, 1977). In this way, the fixed sentence can be reduced by fixed amounts of time, thereby objectifying the basis by which parole can be earned. This type of solution has sometimes been referred to as the flexibility determinate sentence (Carney, 1977, pp. 145-146).

Chapter 8
The Ecology of Correctional Behavior Modification

> If we mean to thrive and do good,
> break open the gaols and let out
> the prisoners.
>
> — Shakespeare, *Henry VI*

> The more laws and order are made
> prominent, the more thieves and
> robbers there will be.
>
> — Lao Tzu

The effective application of behavior modification principles to the control, alteration and prevention of adult criminal behavior is a promise that has yet to be fulfilled. This discrepancy between current accomplishment and potential promise is attributable to the failure of behaviorally inclined professionals in the correctional arena to confront effectively five major limitations of their craft. The remaining chapters of this book involve an evaluation of the ecological, conceptual, methodological, legal, and ethical status of correctional behavior modification.

Before examining each of these criteria in detail, it is important to attend to their interrelationships. The first three perspectives (ecological, conceptual, and methodological) converge on the question, "Can behavior modification be used effectively to rehabilitate or to control adult crime?" The last two (legal and ethical) ask essentially "Should it be?" Despite the obvious importance of the second question, it is premature, unless one is interested in the morality or the legality of unverified, often ill-conceived procedures. The present chapter is concerned with the first of these criteria, the ecological settings in which correctional behavior modification is usually conducted.

COMMUNITY CORRECTIONS

Despite its relatively recent history, the community based corrections movement has exerted a momentous impact on the American criminal justice system. It has been heralded consensually as the single most important innovation in prisoner rehabilitation. Considerable legislative and administrative energy has been directed at manipulating federal funding and other financial incentives so as to increase the use of community corrections programs. While the initial panacean proclamations have now become somewhat muted and the virtues of "the community" progressively deromanticized, the concept of community corrections still retains a very high status among correctional officials. In fact, this standing continues to rival that bestowed on its recent psychological sibling—the community psychology movement.

Both orientations share many conceptual components: an emphasis on environmental-sociological explanations of conduct; the use of social labeling theory (Becker, 1963), in which deviance is seen not as a characteristic of the individual but as the end result of social processes initiated by influential officials—a preference for prevention rather than reparation of social dysfunction, creation of noninstitutional modes of helping, increased employment of nonprofessionals, and attempts at system-level rather than individual change (Cowen, 1973). These diverse principles have been operationalized into three general strategies for effective offender programming via community corrections. I shall refer to these three strategies as deinstitutionalization, decriminalization, and diversion. The rationales for and examples of these efforts will be discussed in the remaining sections of this chapter.

Deinstitutionalization

Institutionalization is much maligned in every field of rehabilitation. Many criticisms of institutions are inspired primarily by the observation that the special medical or correctional or mental health services they are intended to provide become subservient to the maintenance of the institution or the organization itself. Accompanying this objection is the view that, at their worst, custodial institutions often brutalize their residents both physically and psychologically, and stigmatize them as officially deviant in a way which is almost immune to reversal. While the emphasis on the corrupting power of institutionalization no doubt reflects a social reality, it also obscures the possible benefits of these establishments. Three effects of institutions generally are positive in nature. First is the ability to preserve or to sustain certain patterns of valued behavior. For example, the family exemplifies a cultural institution which supports a continuity of values and moral behavior across relatively long periods of time. Second, institutions, by their structure, are able to insure a predictability of events without which most social policies would be impossible. Although a less charitable point of view regards this force as little more than a blind resistance to reorganization or institutional change, it does provide a stability of function and responsibility necessary for the administration of most social programs. Finally, custodial institutions segregate from society those individuals whose behavior is so threatening or violent to others as to require special care. The fact that the same institutions concurrently protect deviant populations from particularly vicious or revengeful persons in the community should not be overlooked.

It is apparent that the possible positive contributions of correctional institutions have been outweighed by their commonly recognized negative influences. The reasons for the persistent failure of correctional structures are neither new, nor surprising. American penology in general has been plagued by the lack of a coherent and consistent correctional philosophy that has resulted in prisons being effective neither as instruments of punishment, nor of rehabilitation. Conrad (1965) has referred to the constant accommodation of rehabilitative programs to the overriding demands of custodial security as the "irrational equilibrium" in corrections. Attempts to punish criminals in a swift and judicious manner, while at the same time using the semantics of treatment to justify the policy, may be just as irrational and unworkable. The deleterious effects of a "will o' the wisp" correctional theory are extended by the pervasive apathy of a public that demands little more of its correctional institutions than the avoidance of inmate rioting. As recent events have unfortunately indicated, even the goal of protecting inmates from one another, perhaps the most basic objective of any custodial establishment, is rendered difficult within the modern American prison.

Deinstitutionalization as a correctional goal rests on two assumptions. First, the restoration of the offender will be maximized to the extent that institutional confinement is minimized. Second, the preferred correctional settings possess the greatest similarity to the social milieu in which the adjustment of the offender should occur. Scull (1977) has introduced the term *decarceration* as a synonym for public efforts to deinstitutionalize deviant populations. While the concept of decarceration is virtually equivalent to that of deinstitutionalization, Scull has focused his analysis of this procedure on the handling of mentally disturbed patients rather than persons in legal jeopardy.

There are, of course, numerous alternatives to institutionalization having considerable historical recognition. Certainly, probation and parole are the most common decarceration procedures. As Chapter 7 has indicated, the use of probation has become almost standard for first offenders. The U.S. President's Commission (1967) reported that some jurisdictions employed probation for as much as 70 percent of their felony convictions. The suspended sentence is another judicial decarceration procedure used very frequently with first-time offenders. Unfortunately, the lack of systematic supervision associated with this method has reduced its correctional potential. Probably its major effect on the criminal justice system is that it lessens the size of probation and prison populations. Not surprisingly, this increasing reliance on noncustodial alternatives has been associated with a declining U.S. prison population. Scull (1977) reports that the prison rate of 120.8/10,000 in 1961, dropped to 96.7/10,000 just ten years later in 1970, despite sharp increases in both reported crime and actual arrest rates.[1]

Deinstitutionalization efforts have taken a number of other forms involving the basic principle of graduated release. For example, work-release has been in existence dating from Wisconsin's passage of the Huber Act in 1913. These programs permit the offender to attain or to retain standard civil employment in the community during the day while returning to institutional custody at night. This process continues until the expiration of sentence. The general success of work-release has led to its widespread use in many prison systems (Root, 1973). One of the first large-scale programs began in 1959 in North Carolina where adult felons were considered for work-release after having served a small portion of their sentences. Revocation or violations of work-release conditions occurred in only 15 percent of the cases (U.S. President's Commission, 1967). Work-release was introduced to the federal system by the Prisoner Rehabilitation Act of 1965. Federal revocation rates are quite low for participants who usually enter the program about six months before their expected time of parole (U.S. President's Commission, 1967).

Work-release is thought to serve a number of purposes. It eases the abruptness of transition from institution to community. It provides a mechanism for meaningful vocational training that may increase the possibility of obtaining employment following total release from the institution. It is responsive to demands for governmental economy (Root, 1973) in that participants reimburse the state for at least a portion of their incarceration costs. Finally, it is thought to have a positive "psychological" impact on the inmate who is able to assume more autonomy and responsibility for himself than is allowed in total custody.

One of the most comprehensive investigations of work-release was performed by Rudolff and Esselstyn (1971) and Rudolff, Esselstyn and Kirkham (1973) who evaluated 2,360 inmates confined between 1968 and 1970 at California's minimum security Elmwood Rehabilitation Center. Forty-two percent of these inmates had participated in a work-release program while 58 percent had not. Among several other findings it was discovered that, 18 months after their full release from prison, work-furlough inmates had significantly fewer arrests than nonfurlough participants. Further analyses were performed to determine whether these differences were produced by work-release or merely reflected prior differences between participating and nonparticipating inmates. A comparison of work-release inmates with a group of nonparticipants, matched on marital status, alcohol and drug use, age, attitudes, and personality characteristics, revealed that nonparticipants were still arrested twice as often, and recommitted to prisons two and a half times more frequently than work-release inmates.

Related to work-release is the more recent example of study, or educational-release (Leeke & Clements, 1973), in which inmates have the privilege of leaving prison for short periods of time to attend academic or vocational training programs. Connecticut was the first state to establish study-release, beginning its project in 1959. A recent survey revealed 40 states with formal study-release programs (Smith, McKee, & Milan, 1974); no doubt, that number has increased somewhat in the intervening time. While there appears to be little empirical evidence regarding the rehabilitative effects of study-release, available figures do indicate that such programs can be administered with little danger to local communities. Smith, McKee, and Milan (1974) reported that only slightly more than two percent of the 3,000 participants covered by their survey had absconded while on study-release.

Furlough programs are another form of graduated release from institutional custody. Furlough involves "any unsupervised visit away from the correctional facility for the purpose of visiting the offender's family, job interview, school inverview or test, funeral trip, etc." (Markley, 1973). It should be distinguished from the frequent practice of "special leave" where the prisoner is accompanied by a guard or special agent in whose custody he remains. Mississippi was the first state with a formalized furlough program, initiating its system in 1918. More than one half of the states now have furlough programs, and the vast majority of them report that administrative problems associated with such projects are minimal (Markley, 1973).

Furlough is believed to accomplish a number of rehabilitative objectives. The opportunity to experience the freedom associated with even short periods of release should increase self-esteem and independence, as well as enable the inmate to anticipate better the sources of some post-release adjustment stresses. Community visitation is also intended to strengthen family ties, an important goal, in consideration of some data that suggest a positive relationship between family affiliations during incarceration, and more successful post-release adjustment (Glaser, 1964). Although there are few data supporting these specific claims, two states have evaluated their furlough programs and found them to be generally successful. Markley (1973) cites Holt's (1969) (Holt & Miller, 1972) evaluation of the California system which revealed that 60 percent of inmates taking part in the furlough program experienced "no problem" during their initial year of parole, while only 42 percent of nonparticipants were problem free. Chambers (1971) indicated the rate of misconduct among Oregon inmates on furlough to be 1.34 percent, and the rate of escape to be only 1 percent.

A final graduated release program is the halfway house which many states have introduced as a transitional facility between full incarceration and total freedom (Killinger & Cromwell, 1974). In many ways, halfway houses function almost as a form of residential parole in which increased levels of structure, control, and surveillance are made possible by requiring participants to live together for a number of months after prison discharge. Fox (1977) summarizes the programs of several halfway houses operated by the United States Bureau of Prisons, and the states of Texas, Massachusetts, and Kentucky and concludes that halfway houses are a viable correctional alternative, despite a chronic lack of funding and community support. The operation and organization of halfway houses has been strengthened in recent years by the establishment of the International Halfway House Association and the publication of *The Guidelines and Standards for Halfway Houses and Community Treatment Centers* (McCartt & Mangogna, 1973; see Fox, 1977).

It should be obvious that, with the exception of probation, the so-called deinstitutionalization procedures do not result in the total decarceration of offenders. The gradual release procedures are not so much a radical alternative to custodial confinement as they are a means of hastening former inmates' reintegration and return to the community. While such methods do not eliminate imprisonment, they do lessen it and, it is hoped, also constrain the negative impact of institutionalization.

Decriminalization

Decriminalization involves a set of strategies intended to reverse the stigmatization process that accompanies the criminal justice system's processing of the accused and the convicted. The movement through the justice system of an individual accused of a criminal offense can be viewed as a series of procedures whereby the accused either exits from, or is retained by that system. A general, comprehensive view of the movement of a case through the criminal justice system is presented in Fig. 8-1. As revealed in Fig. 8-1, there are few available "exit points" from the machinery of the interrelated bureaucracies which compose the criminal justice system. "Exit points" can be considered as any point of discretion where law enforcement, judicial, or correctional personnel authorize the interruption or the termination of an individual's processing within the criminal justice system.

Of course, the process involving the greatest degree of discretion is arrest. It is well known that police do not arrest all the offenders they either observe or encounter after a complaint; in fact, it is apparent that they do not arrest most of them. Following an arrest, there are few mechanisms by which the accused can be extricated from the system, especially during its initial stages. There are, basically, five exit points by which an individual can terminate, or temporarily interrupt his or her, contact with the criminal justice system: (1) release on bail or some form of nonfinancial surety providing a temporary exit, (2) dismissal of criminal charges, (3) acquittal, (4) reversal of conviction or sentence by a reviewing court, and (5) completion of correctional disposition after a finding or plea of guilty. At a conceptually simple level, decriminalization can be thought of as a collection of procedures for increasing the alternatives to existing exit points from the system. Special emphasis has been placed on the development of exits during the early stages of processing the accused.

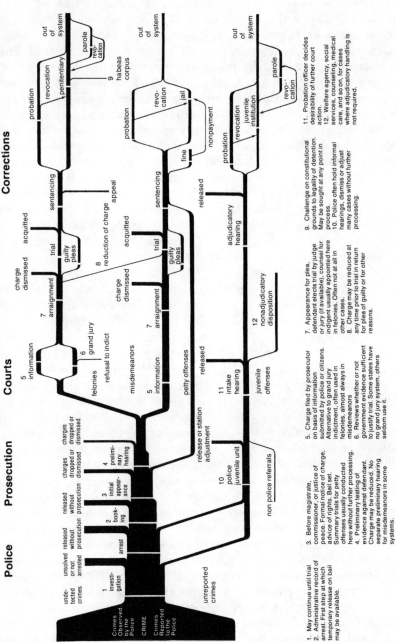

Fig. 8-1. Overview of the Criminal Justice System. Source President's Commission on Law Enforcement and Administration of Justice. *The Challenge of Crime in Free Society.* Washington, D.C.: USGPO, 1967.

A recent popular proposal, designed to minimize the legal system's tendency to create deviance, is the dismantling of portions of the substantive criminal law. This is the boldest and most straightforward example of decriminalization, because it redefines major areas of conduct as noncriminal, thereby eliminating them from the purview of law enforcement agencies. From this perspective, decriminalization occurs at the statutory level.

Statutes against drunkenness, acquisition and possession of drugs, gambling, and varieties of sexual behavior between consenting adults are generally recognized as ineffective controls of socially unpopular conduct, because they attempt to enforce a morality to which many people do not adhere. It has been suggested that this flowering of moral prohibitions is a reflection of a "too ready notion that the way to deal with any kind of reprehensible conduct is to make it criminal" (U.S. President's Commission, 1967). Whatever their origins, these "victimless crimes" (Schur, 1965) create a host of difficulties (Morris & Hawkins, 1970). They represent over one half of all nontraffic arrests in this country, and impose an unworkable burden on law enforcement, administrative, and judicial agencies. Decisions to regard these behaviors as "unlawful" result in the association of those engaged in such activities with more violent and felonious offenders. Such associations are among the most powerful sources of criminalization. In addition, they divert law enforcement resources from the control of more dangerous crime and, at the same time, provide unusually fertile grounds for bribery and police corruption.

Morris and Hawkins (1977) recommend the decriminalization of two other categories of behavior currently subject to criminal statutes. The first of these is "public welfare offenses" which include the "application of the criminal law to the regulation of traffic, pure foods, housing conditions, dangerous drugs and alcohol, industrial safety, and discrimination in employment, and the regulation of business practice generally . . ." (p. 16). The second category involves corporate criminality, defined as "the plunder of the marketplace and of the consumer by some of our contemporary 'overmighty subjects,' the nationwide and sometimes multinational corporations" (p. 16).

The decriminalization of victimless crimes, business crime, and offenses against public welfare need not be construed as a sanction or encouragement of such behavior. A search for alternative procedures to control or to discourage such conduct, coupled with a systematic reexamination of the appropriateness of many of our criminal statutes, might reduce objectionable behavior as well as objectionable means of regulating it. In this regard, Morris and Hawkins (1977) propose a tripartite categorization of illegitimate conduct with differential models of legislation, regulation, enforcement, and punishment associated with each type of conduct. The purpose of this division is to allow the criminal justice system to concentrate its resources on high-priority or dangerous crime while simultaneously providing more efficient, but noncriminalizing controls of objectionable commercial and moral behavior.

The three categories of conduct are defined in the following manner:

Crime Type A: Predation, including homicide, forcible rape, robbery, aggravated assault, arson, burglary, household breaking, and traditional types of stealing.

Crime Type B: Illicit Practices, including embezzlement, corporate crime, price fixing, fraudulent conversion, tax offenses, bribery, forgery, passing of worthless checks, counterfeiting, "con" games, obtaining money or property by false pretenses, buying, receiving, and possessing stolen property, trafficking in drugs, pilferage, simple assaults, weapon carrying, vandalism, and a variety of minor offenses and deceptive practices.

Crime Type C: Illegitimate Activities, including "public welfare" offenses such as violations of regulations or statutes governing the sale of pure food and drugs, industrial safety, public health and safety, housing, zoning, fair business practices, discrimination in employment, environmental protection, licensing, the sale and manufacture of dangerous narcotic drugs and alcohol, gambling, statutory rape and acts contrary to the public decency, nonsupport, neglect, desertion or abuse of family or children, prostitution and commercialized vice, public drunkenness, disorderly conduct, vagrancy, begging, and loitering.

The recommended procedures for regulating each of the three types of conduct are presented in Table 8-1. This model restricts the full impact of the criminal justice system to the investigation, adjudication, and penalization of predatory crime. Criminal adjudication and penalization would be retained for illicit practice offenses, while an entirely noncriminal system would be employed for the regulation of the so-called illegitimate activities.[2]

A second form of decriminalization efforts has been directed at the creation of alternatives to police arrests, the official procedure by which the operations of the criminal justice system are initiated. One type of problem for which a police intervention often occurs is the family dispute or interpersonal crisis, in which a citizen argument often erupts into a violent confrontation. The "family disturbance call" is also a dangerous activity for police; Bard (1971) cites figures that 40 percent of on-duty police injuries occur while responding to this type of call.

Bard (1969, 1970; Bard & Berkowitz, 1967) was the first to develop a program by which a special group of New York City policemen (nine black, and nine white volunteers) were trained to intervene in the typical family disturbance call without making an arrest. The training program focused on the development of interpersonal skills which would allow the officer to intervene in the dispute in such a way as to minimize the possibility of citizen or police violence. Whenever possible, the argument was pacified by crisis intervention

Table 8-1

Crime Type	Investigators	Adjudicators	Maximum Penalty
A	Police	Criminal courts	Imprisonment
B	Civilian agents, inspectors, and undercover 'enforcement officers	Criminal courts	Imprisonment
C	Civilian agents, inspectors, and undercover enforcement officers	Administrative boards, commissions, etc. (criminal courts only for persistent offenders)	Fines and license withdrawal

(Reprinted with permission from Morris & Hawkins, Letter to the President on Crime Control, Chicago: University of Chicago Press, 1977.)

techniques, and the disputants were referred to an appropriate social service agency for further assistance.

Methodological problems precluded the comparison of the special officers' performance with that of nonparticipating police. None of the 18 officers, however, suffered any injuries stemming from their many family crisis interventions. Another project (Driscoll, Meyer, & Schanie, 1973) included a followup assessment of families who had received assistance either from officers with special crisis training or untrained police. Citizens who had their calls responded to by trained officers evaluated their assistance significantly more favorably than those individuals whose calls were answered by regular police.

Goldstein, Monti, Sardino and Green (1977) have prepared a manual which can be used to train police officers in the skills of crisis intervention. Future research might investigate the feasibility of training the police in alternatives to typical arrest procedures for racial disturbances, mass demonstrations, and other incidents in which police and citizen violence are too often precipitated (Chevigny, 1969).

A third point at which decriminalization efforts have been concentrated is the interval between arrest and final case disposition. During this time, the primary vehicle by which persons charged with crime secure their release is financial bail. Failure to gain release has been associated with numerous deleterious effects for those detained, including loss of job, restrictions on the preparation of an adequate defense, and lengthy imprisonment. More germane to the issue of criminalization is the ubiquitous finding that a person who is living in the community at the time of adjudication has an improved chance of acquittal, or of receiving a suspended sentence or probation if convicted than a person who is being detained in jail (Foote, 1965; Nietzel & Dade, 1973; Rankin, 1964). These consequences have fallen most frequently to indigent defendants who do not have the means to purchase their release.

The past decade has witnessed many bail reform (Nietzel & Dade, 1973) and supervised release (Oxberger, 1973) projects[3] intended to mitigate the effects of pretrial incarceration by developing nonfinancial methods of assuring that the accused will appear in court whenever required. The release of accused persons on their own recognizance (ROR) has proven to be as reliable a method as financial bail in certifying the return of criminal defendants. ROR has also reduced the amount of criminalizing incarceration to which indigents otherwise would be exposed.

The Manhattan Bail Project (Ares, Rankin, & Sturz, 1963) was the first recent attempt to modify bail procedures so as to eliminate (or at least lessen) the hardships faced by the indigent. Project workers conducted a quick interview with the accused prior to the setting of his bail. This inquiry assessed five areas assumed to be related to the probability that a defendant would appear for his trial: the defendant's roots in the community, residence factors, employment status, contact with friends and relatives, and past record. This information was verified through telephone or field contact with relatives or friends of the accused. Objective point values were assigned to the degree to which a given person satisfied the above criteria. If the person met the minimum number of points, the magistrate was given the recommendation by the interviewer to release the accused without money or property bail. The findings indicated that in the pretrial situation the rate of ROR "jumping" was less than the failure-to-appear under traditional bail procedures. Of the defendants released on their own recognizance, only 1.6 percent failed to appear for the trial; of those released on bail bond, three percent failed to appear (Goldfarb, 1965).

The importance of the Manhattan Project was that it not only demonstrated that a large number of defendants could be released without money bail, but also led to similar projects in many major jurisdictions. Currently, almost every major urban center in the country has developed a program patterned after the Manhattan experience. Many innovations have been introduced, one of the most important being the use of a wide range of professionals and volunteers to gather information from defendants, verify it, and present it to magistrates (Goldfarb, 1965; Kennedy, 1968; Scott, 1966; Smith, 1965).

At its beginning, the Manhattan Project excluded several types of offenders from consideration. Defendants charged with homicide, assault on a police officer, rape, and narcotics offenses were among those not considered. Gradually, most projects (including Manhattan) have come to consider all defendants (Scott, 1966). Along with the liberalization of types of offenders considered has come a relaxation in the requirements for ROR release. Many projects no longer employ strictly objective factors for their recommendation decisions.

Nietzel and Dade (1973) interviewed 80 persons charged with criminal violations in Champaign County, Illinois. The procedures were not limited to indigents or misdeameanants, but were extended to all defendants. Recommendations for an ROR release were based on the Manhattan Bail Project criteria. The project was in effect for one month.

Decisions regarding ROR release during the project were compared to 231 preproject cases and 100 postproject cases. The results indicated a significant increase in the use of nonfinancial release (ROR) during the project. Postproject data revealed that the frequency of ROR release returned to its preproject level. Of those defendants released on recognizance, the failure to reappear rate was lowest during the project (2.3 percent) as compared with preproject (10.1 percent) and postproject (15.8 percent). Finally, convicted defendants who had been released on their own recognizance received a significantly lower (p < .02) number of prison or jail sentences than did those defendants either released by some other means, or detained previous to a final decision, or pleading guilty at their first appearance.

Diversion

The decriminalization venture which has gained the widest support is the pretrial intervention or diversion project. Diversion refers to the early suspension of the arrest-arraignment-prosecution sequence, and the referral of the accused to a community-based, short-term (often 90 days) treatment program that provides resources such as individual counseling, career development, and job finding. Fox (1977) lists a number of other projects virtually synonymous with the procedures and aims of pretrial diversion: pretrial intervention programs, probation without adjudication, deferred prosecution, accelerated rehabilitative disposition, and deferred sentencing.

Pretrial diversion is innovative only in that what was most often known as "prosecutorial discretion" has been publicized and exploited for rehabilitative purposes (DeGrazia, 1974). Peterson (1973) describes a prototypical program involving a five-step process by which (1) eligible participants are identified and interviewed by the staff shortly following arrests; (2) a rehabilitation plan is formulated by the project staff; (3) consent to the program is requested from the accused, prosecutor, arresting officer, and crime victim; (4) assuming consent, the filing of criminal charges is suspended during participation in the project; and (5) at the conclusion of participation, one of four recommendations is made to the court concerning disposition of the case (dismissal of charges, filing of charges, extension of program participation, or filing of charges accompanied by a report of successful involvement in the program).

The establishment of criminal restitution programs has often been associated with the concept of diversion or deferred sentencing (Fox, 1977). Laster (1970) has described several examples of restitution at the preadministrative (before arrest), administrative (police or prosecution), adjudicatory, and probationary levels. The goals of restitution are twofold: the crime victim's condition (either physical or financial) should be restored to the level enjoyed prior to the offense, and participation in the restitution effort should be therapeutic for the criminal. The "enforcement of responsibility" on the offender (Schafer, 1968) requires his continued presence in the community in lieu of institutional confinement. Essentially, restitution offers a set of quasi-civil remedies for illegal activities. One of its distinct advantages is that it can furnish the socially desirable goal of offender reform while reducing the individually ruinous result of offender stigmatization.

Diversion programs are the beneficiaries of numerous claims for their rehabilitative power. Among their supposed advantages are flexibility, economy, the minimization of stigma associated with prosecution and adjudication, the maintenance of the accused in the community, and increased responsibility by offenders for their behavior. In fact, two recent reviews (Mullen, Carlson, Earle, Blew, & Li, 1974; Roesch, 1976) of diversion projects lament the lack of empirical evidence supporting the specific positive effects of diversion. Nonetheless, diversion projects continue to proliferate. There are now at least 50 formalized pretrial diversion programs in over 20 states (Chatfield, 1974; Fox, 1977).

The critics of diversion have concentrated their objections on a number of practical and legal imbroglios. For example, Balch (1974) regards them as fundamentally coercive in that arrested individuals volunteer only because of their fear of subsequent prosecution. Associated with this concern are fears that due process protections, the right to counsel, and the presumption of innocence may be jeopardized by a too hasty decision to participate in a diversion project. Despite these several empirical and legal questions, the prevailing belief is that pretrial diversion projects constitute a valuable intervention. Recidivism rates are thought to be lower for diverted individuals than for those receiving either probation or prison sentences (Peterson, 1973). Diversion is also considerably more cost-effective than probation/incarceration alternatives. Finally, pretrial interventions respond equally well to the often incompatible ambitions of swift, efficient case processing, and judicious decriminalization (Roesch, 1976).

ECOLOGICAL CONVENTIONALITY

The "ecological conventionality" of behavior modification refers to the restriction of behavioral techniques to institutional settings, where the usual conditions of custody limit both the objectives of the intervention as well as the ability of inmates to participate meaningfully in it. As previous chapters have indicated, most noninstitutional forms of correctional behavior modification are offered in a traditional one-to-one psychotherapy context, a type of intervention about which more will be said in the next chapter.

The ecological conventionality of correctional behavior modification elicits a number of appropriate concerns. First, it should give pause to those apologists who discredit criticisms that behavior modification often functions as a source of coercive control over behavior that may be compatible with administrative preferences but has little relevance to extra-institutional adjustment. It is precisely in this "total institution" context (Goffman, 1961), in which equity in competing sources of influence and adversary confrontations are minimized, that the potential for coercive and irrelevant behavioral requirements is maximized. There is a monotonous regularity to prison token economies rewarding such inmate behaviors as cell maintenance, politeness, and promptness, a set of requirements that has been described as "convenience behaviors" (DeRisi, quoted in Geller, 1974). In this respect, it is also revealing that the most systematic behavioral programs have been applied to inmates described by program developers in terms such as "men whose activities, while not aggressive, were continually disrupting the administration of other programs and threatening the good order of the institution" (Oliver, 1974, p. 2).

A frequently articulated advantage of behavior modification is its adaptability to *in vivo* assessments and applications (O'Leary & Wilson, 1975). In comparison with other therapeutic approaches, behaviorally oriented techniques are considered to be more suitable to diverse target populations (Ullmann & Krasner, 1975), more understandable to important socializing agents (Tharp & Wetzel, 1969), and more easily implemented by third-party mediators such as teachers, volunteers, or parents (Tharp & Wetzel, 1969). Despite these claims, behavior modification has remained disturbingly restricted to institutional settings in the adult correctional system. With the exception of the previously described work on probation and parole (Chapter 7), correctional behavior modification has been minimally influenced by the press for community corrections.

There is sufficient anecdotal evidence to suggest that the ease with which a control technology is learned is related to the ease with which it can be corrupted. Commenting on the CMP with which he was associated, Geller has said, "perhaps the lawyer's most appropriate criticism of our program was that we would introduce into the penal system a new technique for manipulating behavior, a technique that would be eventually misused or abused by unsupervised prison staff" (Trotter, 1975, p. 10). In a certain sense, behavior modification has become institutionalized. In exchange for administrative acceptance, behaviorists often have legitimized, and even routinized management techniques by the introduction of a therapeutic lexicon (Page, Caron, & Yates, 1975).

Another concern with the orientation of correctional behaviorism is that behavior modifiers have not evidenced the strong commitment to active, prevention oriented, system level change that characterizes the evolving role models of community psychologists (Rappaport & Chinsky, 1974). Too often, they have appeared to be content with making bad prisoners into good ones. The conventionality of behavioral interventions extends beyond the issue of physical location to a more central factor involving the traditionalism of roles which psychologists have played in the criminal justice system. The typical functions of psychologists have included preparations of competency, probation and sentencing reports, expert trial testimony (usually regarding the mental status of a defendant), and the assessment and treatment of individual inmates in prisons (Nietzel & Moss, 1972). These services reflect an emphasis on the etiological significance of mental illness, emotional disturbance, and personality problems to criminal behavior. One implication of this position is that rehabilitation of criminals should rest with mental health professionals who, supposedly, have the special expertise necessary to identify and to treat such disorders. Consequently, psychologists historically have restricted themselves to interventions intended primarily for the individual offender or for small groups of offenders. Rappaport (1977) has presented a model for interventions in the various components of the criminal justice system intended to broaden the level of analysis and services provided by psychologists (see Table 8-2). Rappaport has recommended the expansion of organizational and institutional, as opposed to individual levels of intervention. Inspection of the six intersections in Table 8-2, involving organizational and institutional levels or operation, reveals a substantial convergence between the activities depicted there and the interventions espoused by the present chapter.

Ultimately, the issue of ecological conventionality will force psychologists to reverse their continuing reluctance to confront seriously the most basic problem of behavior modification within penal institutions: *it is not possible for a prison to be both an institution of punishment and of rehabilitation.* I would contend that the primary purpose of a prison should be the punishment of the individuals sent to it. By their construction, staffing, and organization prisons are best suited to be institutions of punishment. Further, we need be neither apologetic nor embarrassed about this recommendation. Punishment is justified on the simple grounds that society has decided an offender deserves it. Ultimately, this moral injunction is a cornerstone of the criminal law: people who deliberately break society's laws should be punished.

Imprisonment happens to be an effective form of punishment; effective, not because it necessarily changes the offender, but because the loss of freedom is perceived, almost universally, as very punitive. Both psychologically and physically, sustained institutional custody is an uncomfortable, degrading, and upsetting experience. In fact, with the exception of very infrequently employed capital punishment, imprisonment is the harshest form of punishment our society deliberately imposes. All behavioral scientists should be very clear about the fact that imprisonment is a form of punishment. It needs no further justification. This is not to say that prisoners could not, or should not be "corrected" or "reformed" or "rehabilitated" as a consequence of their imprisonment. There is no question that some prisoners are reformed during their incarceration; however, such occasional reformation should not result, as it has so often, in attempts to masquerade prisons as institutions of correction or treatment.

An endorsement of the fact of punishment by incarceration need not be accompanied by a tolerance for any conditions which make the experience unnecessarily frequent, lengthy, or cruel. The recent report of the Commission for the Study of Incarceration (von Hirsch, 1976) has suggested a goal of mitigating "the harshness and caprice of the penal system without losing whatever usefulness in crime prevention it now has" (p. XIX). Toward this end, the Committee has recommended the following reforms intended to allow a just system of punishments: (a) use of prison confinement for only the most serious criminal offenders; (b) limitations on length of sentence so that few would exceed three years; (c) development of alternative punishments (fines, limited deprivations of freedom) for offenders convicted of lesser offenses; (d) reductions in disparity of sentence length; (e) elimination of the indeterminate sentence.

What professional role does this use of prison suggest for psychologists employed in a penal institution? In my opinion, it leaves very little. First of all, as psychologists we need not and should not be administrators of punishment. On the other hand, neither should we obscure the fact of punishment by seducing inmates' participation in "correctional" or "therapeutic" programs, which, in the typical prison environment, are almost always implicitly coercive (see Morris & Hawkins, 1977). This argument does not require the elimination of institutional treatment programs. What it does require is that an inmate's participation in any treatment program, whether it be educational, vocational, or psychological *must be* fully voluntary and *must not be* seen as the reason for imprisonment. A psychologist should not be part of any prison treatment program that coerces inmate participation.

There are two major alternatives to institutional versions of "correctional" psychology. First, psychologists should attempt to identify and modify those components of the entire criminal justice system that exacerbate the criminalization of the individuals it processes. Second, psychologists should attempt to develop and evaluate community-based programs with the avowed purpose of assisting those persons whose legal jeopardy is apparent but has not yet resulted in their institutional confinement. These recommendations are consistent with Rappaport's (1977) contention that the crucial task for the community psychologist in the legal system is neither rehabilitation nor punishment. Rather it is the mobilization of "actual and potential environmental processes so as to reduce the involvement of persons in the apparatus of the criminal justice system" (p. 327).

Table 8-2 Selected Examples of Interventions at Multiple Levels (Points of Intervention) in the Three Components of the Criminal Justice System.

Level of Analysis and Possible Points of Intervention	Component of the Criminal Justice System		
	Corrections Agencies	Administration of Justice (Courts)	Police and Law Enforcement
Individual* and Small-Group	Socialization programs and various forms of psycho-therapy for inmates.	Assessment of competency to stand trial, dangerousness, etc.	Individual counseling for both law enforcement agents and people they refer for assistance.
	Training in vocational skills		Communication skills training (e.g., police-community relations programs). Police selection procedures.
Organizational	Development of more "humane" prisons (e.g., behavior modification and organizations development in prison settings).	Pretrial interventions (e.g., bail-bond reforms, adult treatment or "true" diversion programs, intensive probation for juveniles).	Diversion programs for juveniles prior to court referral.
			Consultation and police training programs (e.g., in crisis intervention skills).
Institutional	Probation and parole alternatives; community-based treatment settings (e.g., behavior modification based, or autonomous alternative settings). Liberalization of prison rules (e.g., work release programs).	Reform of laws and procedures (e.g., jury procedures, sentencing); decriminalization of victimless crimes; elimination of juvenile status offenses.	Reform or redirection of police procedures such as neighborhood control and/or recruiting of local policemen. Educational and informational exchanges on values, mores, and lifestyle of local neighborhoods. Prevention of violence by means of situational or environmental changes. Enforcement of gun control, environmental, and safety laws. Radical nonintervention; removal of social control functions.

*Note: Although interventions at this level are included for the sake of completeness, they are not recommended as a direction for community psychology.

(From *Community Psychology: Values, Research and Action* by Julian Rappaport. Copyright © 1977 by Holt, Rinehart, and Winston. Reprinted by permission by Holt, Rinehart, and Winston).

The remainder of this chapter proposes several specific functions and activities for psychologists in the criminal justice system which would exemplify and extend the above two principles for ecologically appropriate correctional interventions.

Decriminalization of the Criminal Justice System

1. One area of social policy analysis that would benefit from the evaluation skills of the psychologist is the frequently recommended strategy of modifying certain portions of the substantive criminal law. At present, the criminalization of the so-called victimless crimes appears to be a harmful and expensive policy for which better alternatives could be created. Psychologists could participate in the development of programs and legislation designed to minimize the present legal system's tendency to create or to impose deviance by the labels and methods it employs. Statutes against drunkenness, the acquisition and possession of drugs, gambling, prostitution, abortion, and sexual behavior between consenting adults, all invade the private domain of an individual's decision as to how to live his or her own life. Whatever deterrent value these laws may have (and none has been demonstrated) is overshadowed by the multitude of difficulties they create. A reexamination of the appropriateness of these criminal statutes is an immediate necessity. As an example, it might be possible to conduct a pilot level evaluation of the impact of the Morris and Hawkins (1977) plan, in which the different types of offensive behavior are regulated through alternative investigatory and adjudicatory agencies.

2. The police are engaged in many functions which detract from their primary assignment of crime prevention and control. Many of these service functions, or enforcements of "convenience norms" (Myren, 1968), could be performed better, and more cheaply by some agency other than the police. The behavioral scientist could become a consultant for how to modify some aspects of present police behavior. Recent programs (Bard, 1969; Glaser & Ross, 1969) have demonstrated substantial success in training patrolmen to intervene in the typical family disturbance call without making an arrest. Alternatives to the typical procedures could be developed for other incidents in which police and citizen violence are too often an outcome.

3. The criminal justice system will reap the full advantage of the participation of mental health professionals, particularly psychologists, only when they commit themselves to the required evaluative research. There is a need for research by which the procedures of all phases of the judicial-legal system can be evaluated. Certainly research-sophisticated psychologists, in conjunction with other mental health professionals and social scientists, can have a primary role to play in this area.

Expansion of Community-based Components in the Criminal Justice System

Psychologists' greatest impact on this area would be derived from their creation and evaluation of criminal justice system procedures that reflect a combination of *early interventionism* and *localism of setting* while retaining all necessary due process protections for the accused. The preferred settings for correctional, as opposed to punitive, efforts should be community-based programs, offered at initial stages of the criminal justice system.

4. The benefit of applying behavioral procedures to probation services (Ray & Kilburn, 1970) could be duplicated by a merger of behavioral techniques with deinstitutionalization, diversion, and decriminalization efforts. Diversion often is maligned for being unobservable, unsystematic, and too informal (Brakel, 1971). The use of explicit contingency contracting, for example, could be useful in specifying behaviors to be both developed and resisted for a diversion participant. The contingencies that would support these changes would be made public and, ideally, would involve naturally occurring reinforcers such as employment benefits, movement privileges, expungement of an official police record, reductions in sentence length, and the like. Finally, contingency contracts could prescribe increased participation of significant social mediators (e.g., peers, spouse, nonprofessionals) in the offender's diversion or restitution program.

At a minimum, behavioral contributions to diversion or decriminalization projects should increase the use of functional analyses of the environmental or interpersonal situations in which an individual's unlawful conduct is most likely. This type of systematic, individualized assessment has been represented infrequently in community correctional efforts. When individual assessments have been utilized, they have focused on the specification of behavioral "excesses" that need to be reduced. Assessment efforts might be redistributed more profitably to the identification of behavioral deficits as correctional targets (Shah, 1970).

5. Behavioral techniques should also be extended to the variety of gradual release procedures intended to ease the transition from prison confinement to residence in the community. Currently, work release, educational release, furlough, and halfway houses are operated with little theoretical guidance about how they could produce positive behavioral changes in their participants. As a result, most forms of graduated release remain content with claims that the public is no more endangered by conditions of partial, rather than total, incarceration.

One example of such an approach is Ellsworth House, operated by the San Mateo County (California) Probation Department (Lamb & Goertzel, 1975). Serious offenders (77 percent had committed felonies) who had received a jail sentence of at least four months were selected for placement in this residential program intended as a full (not "halfway") community-based alternative to jail confinement. The program provided a variety of services, such as vocational counseling, job placement assistance, and individual and group counseling, but the central ingredient was a "behavior modification system of rewards and punishment." This system involved three important elements: provision of rewards (weekend passes) and penalties (jailed for a weekend) contingent on specific program accomplishments or misbehaviors; the use of group contingencies, in which a previously formed small group of inmates would lose one half of its available privileges contingent on proscribed conduct by any one of its members; and a division of the program into three phases, with each phase introducing more responsibilities and increased privileges. Phase One lasted at least 30 days, and restricted a resident to the facility, except for attendance at his job or school. Promotion to Phase Two was determined by a vote of residents and staff, and resulted in greater freedom for the resident, mainly in the form of longer weekend passes. During Phase Three, the offender is released from the facility, and returns only for a regular visit with his probation officer.

Results for participants in Ellsworth House were contrasted with a group of offenders assigned to either an honor camp or a work furlough facility. All of these men had been eligible for an assignment to Ellsworth House; the basis upon which a particular disposition was chosen was determined randomly. The random assignment of eligible inmates to the experimental and comparison conditions was an unusual feature of this study, and permitted a more objective evaluation of the program than is usually the case. At a one-year post-release followup, recidivism was 30 percent for Ellsworth House participants and 32 percent for members of the comparison group. While the program obviously has not been associated with differential recidivism rates, it has resulted in substantial employment differences. At the same one-year followup, 15 percent of Ellsworth House men were unemployed, in contrast to 29 percent of the comparison group.

6. As with other areas affecting the quality of the criminal justice system, a major contribution of psychologists concerned with community-based corrections would be to conduct social policy research on the immediate and extended effects of these community projects. Beyond directing such research, the psychologist should attempt to stimulate whatever social changes his, or her, data mandate. One potential vehicle for this type of impact is dissemination research, in which the researcher not only focuses attention on the development of empirically validated social change procedures, but engages in systematic efforts to initiate the adoption of successful procedures in other communities or settings. Coupled with this charge is the responsibility for the researcher to monitor the quality of the implanted program, promote the replication of the original research, and assist in needed modifications.

To date, behaviorists have demonstrated an insufficient affinity for the broad spectrum, prevention-directed programs that would involve them in new ecological settings. Until this affinity becomes apparent, the very relevance of behavior modification to the rehabilitation of offenders should be questioned. One hopes for the liberation of behavior modifiers from their institutions and offices to the environments in which crime actually occurs. It is in these settings that crime also can be controlled.

NOTES

1 However, Silberman (1978) has observed that during the 1970s the trend has again reversed, so that since 1972 the number of incarcerated inmates has increased at an annually accelerating rate.

2 A related ingredient in this decriminalization effort would be to relieve police of most of their traffic control, and traffic law responsibilities, thereby enabling them to concentrate on the prevention and control of predatory crimes. Morris and Hawkins (1977) recommend the creation of a Traffic Control Corps "whose responsibilities would include field duties such as point duty, the supervision of pedestrian crossings, and controlling traffic congestion, as well as the enforcement of the laws relating to the parking of automobiles, speeding, careless driving, and accidents not involving personal injury" (p. 48).

3 The Polk County (Iowa) Department of Court Services provides, as part of its comprehensive community-based correctional program, a Community Corrections Project, intended for defendants who are unable to secure either bail or recognizance releases. Two features of this project are unique. First, it attempts to secure the release of the high-risk defendant (for whom many bail-reform projects do not recommend release) by providing more intensive supervision of him during the release. Second, it emphasizes the initiation of a correctional effort during the pretrial release period by "the exploration and utilization of community roots through employment, family psychiatrists, drug and/or other types of counseling programs."

Chapter 9
Conceptual and Methodological Adequacy of Behavioral Corrections

> He who does not prevent a crime
> when he can, encourages it.
>
> — Seneca

On both conceptual and methodological grounds, social learning approaches to criminal rehabilitation are deficient. In this chapter, specific conceptual and methodological deficiencies are identified, and suggestions for their remediation are provided.

CONCEPTUAL ADEQUACY

Conceptually, behavior modification in corrections bears little resemblance to the methods employed in other settings. No doubt, this is due in part to marked differences in the recipient populations and the parameters of their disturbing behavior. As a group, officially defined offenders may be less likely to benefit from individual or group forms of therapy; likewise, the coercive quality surrounding most institutional "treatment" probably reduces its ability to rehabilitate inmates who are resentful and suspicious of those programs in which they are forced to participate. It should not be surprising that this combination of factors results in the development and delivery of therapies that motivate neither their recipients nor their providers.

A larger proportion of this conceptual problem is due, however, to the basic theoretical poverty that pervades the field. Correctional behavior modification has proven notably resistant to the advances that have been reflected in other areas of behavioral application. This problem is particularly pronounced with institutional forms of behavior modification (Chapter 5), but has manifested itself with out-patient behavioral interventions (Chapter 6) as well.

Often, the terminology of behavioral principles is used as an ad hoc justification for correctional procedures that are not primarily rehabilitative in intent. As Bottrell (1974) has indicated, "any human (or animal) interaction with the environment can be conceptualized according to operant or respondent principles of learning as seen in behavior modification. This does not mean, however, that all such techniques represent behavior modification as a therapeutic technique" (p. 1). We should resist these temptations to misrepresent unplanned, often retributive manipulations of the environment as "behavior modification," and, in the process, to falsely elevate them to the otherwise undeserved status of "treatment." The conceptual sterility of behavior modification will continue as long as behavioral terminology is employed as semantic gloss for the correctional status quo. The initial portion of this chapter presents five principles intended to bolster the conceptual adequacy of correctional behavior modification. Increased attention to these five issues should contribute to those behavioral conceptualizations concerned primarily with planned principles of effective intervention.

Cognitive Control

Recent conceptualizations of behavior therapy have emphasized the importance of mediational events in the acquisition of new behavior. Procedures emphasizing attentional shifts, self-monitoring, and imaginal processes have been elaborated into such treatment packages as systematic desensitization (Paul & Bernstein, 1971), covert modeling (Kazdin, 1973, 1974; Nietzel, Martorano, & Melnick, 1977), covert sensitization (Polakow, 1975), thought stopping (Wisocki, 1973), and other methods of self-control (Thoresen & Mahoney, 1974). Systematic attempts to assist offenders in augmenting cognitive or self-control abilities have been reported infrequently. Applications of covert sensitization to sex offenders (see Chapter 6), and drug addicts (Polakow, 1975), are very occasional exceptions. Most other examples (Bond & Hutchinson, 1960; Marzagao, 1972; and Wickramasekera, 1968) have involved systematic desensitization. Despite the recent social learning emphasis on the informational value of reinforcement, the prevailing practice of correctional behavior modification remains tied to a conditioning paradigm, in which contingencies are manipulated for the regulation of overt performance only.

Individualized Treatment

The concept of individualized treatment procedures has not been adequately pursued in this area. For example, even if one accepts the elimination of prisoner aggression as a desired, uniform target, it is not at all clear why graduated token economies, or tier systems would be the preferred strategy to accomplish this for all prisoners. Laws (1974) has attributed the failure of a token economy at the Atascadero State Hospital, in part, to the fact that it was applied to a heterogeneous group of inmates who were not all deficient in the targeted behaviors. Uniformity of treatments reflects, in most cases, an earlier inattention to the assessment of the conditions that are maintaining unlawful conduct.

A related issue is the degree to which inmates could be paired with treatment techniques that are uniquely optimal for them. Client-technique matching would require pretesting to determine the nature of an appropriate pairing. Unfortunately, present conceptual understandings of patient-therapist, or patient-technique interactions, are minimal and provide few guidelines for the preintervention parameters that should be evaluated (Berzins, 1977). Beyond this, behavior modifiers in particular have ignored the variance-reducing potential that might be derived from a more deliberate concern with patient-technique or patient-therapist matching.

Attempts at matching offenders with various therapy alternatives will require both a careful delineation of a particular offender's behavioral patterns and a functional analysis of the environmental and interpersonal situations in which the individual's illegal conduct has been most likely. This type of systematic, individualized assessment has been used infrequently in the re-habilitation of adult offenders. Shah's (1970) work is an excellent example of individualized assessment efforts that focus on a determination of both be-havioral excesses and deficits underlying a given offender's problem behavior. The ensuing treatment package represents what many therapists would recognize as "broad spectrum" behavior therapy. The immediate goal of Shah's behavioral treatment is "cessation of the antisocial activities." Attainment of this goal is related to therapeutic activity in three treatment areas, the emphasis of which is determined by the prior assessment efforts.

Elimination of Behavioral Deficits. Some offenders are seen as lacking appropriate educational, interpersonal, vocational, or sexual skills. Deficiencies in these areas may result in a performance of alternative behaviors, followed periodically by positive outcomes, but nonetheless legally prohibited. Interventions, such as job training, assertion training, and therapist modeling of social skills, are frequently directed at the acquisition of responses needed in these areas.

Discrimination Training. Certain behaviors (e.g., sexual offenses) are socially disturbing because "they occur at the wrong time, with the wrong people, or in socially inappropriate situations" (Shah, 1970). The treatment goal in these instances is to bring the behaviors under adequate stimulus control. Techniques such as desensitization, cognitive restructuring, and aversive conditioning are often employed to accomplish this aim.

Development of Self-control. Related to problems in stimulus control is inept self-control of certain responses. Some offender's behavior is offensive because of its inappropriate frequency, duration, or intensity. In these cases, development of self-control over these parameters may be facilitated via modeling, role-playing, contingency contracting, or aversive methods.

Constructional Approaches

Goldiamond (1974) has contrasted what he terms the *pathological* and *constructional* orientations toward offender rehabilitation. The former emphasizes the alleviation of distress by the elimination of certain repertoires, while the latter seeks solution via "the construction of repertoires (or their reinstatement or transfer to new situations)" (Goldiamond, 1974; p. 14). The institutional treatment of adult offenders has relied almost exclusively on the pathological orientation. Constructional approaches are more typical of outpatient or community-based versions of behavior modification. In one sense that is paradoxical, since institutional offenders are likely to be characterized by more restricted repertoires that would benefit from a constructional emphasis. Increased attention should be directed at cultivating programs that seek to construct new, lawful repertoires for those offenders whose severe behavioral or self-control deficits have required institutional care.

Programming of Generalization

For some time, behavioral therapists have stressed that generalization and maintenance of therapy changes require the deliberate programming of generalization procedures (Keeley, Shemberg & Carbonell, 1976; Nietzel & Moore, in press). Generalization implies that therapeutic changes appear in multiple situations *(stimulus generalization* or *transfer of training)*, or involve the development of related, but untreated, behaviors *(response generalization)*. *Maintenance* of treatment-instigated changes over time is usually measured by followup assessments, and can be considered either a special instance of stimulus generalization or distinct from generalization (Bandura, 1969). Procedurally, the assessment of generalization vs. maintenance is not as distinct as the prior definitions might suggest. Maintenance can be measured by a readministration of a posttest in the original treatment setting, in a nontreatment context, or in the natural setting where change is primarily desired. Stimulus generalization can be assessed during treatment (most often in the case of within-subjects' designs), at posttest, and/or at a followup by varying the tasks, surroundings, personnel or salient cues from those present during the treatment. Followup measurement of stimulus generalization can also serve as a maintenance measure of generalized treatment effects. Response generalization is usually measured at either the posttest, the followup, or both, by establishing before and after measures of nontarget behaviors.

Issues pertaining to maintenance and generalization would seem crucial for offenders whose lengthy periods of incarceration are justified partly on the basis of their supposed potency for bringing about long-term change. There is, of course, great skepticism that prison programs (including institutional behavior modification) produce any lasting changes in "real world behavior" (Opton, 1974).

A review of the behavioral correctional literature reveals a rather substantial neglect of techniques aimed at increasing either generalization or maintenance. The majority of "outpatient" behavioral interventions have included some maintenance or generalization technique, but most of these techniques have been unduly restricted at both the conceptual and practical levels. The most frequently employed procedures have been (1) to instruct clients in the *in vivo* use of aversive conditioning, covert sensitization, or relaxation, and (2) to reintroduce treatment trials in the form of "booster sessions" following the termination of treatment. For the most part, these procedures are introduced near the end of treatment or during the followup interval, and involve little more than an extension of the treatment process across time, or to different settings.

Very few institutional programs have included deliberate generalization programming. In its last two phases, the CMP did fade the use of credits concomitant with a greater reliance on social supports; however, few subjects ever progressed to those levels.

Community-based interventions have the advantage of providing treatments in the environment in which continued behavior change is to be displayed. Issues of generalization, however, are not entirely circumvented by such *in vivo* treatments. It is still necessary to achieve transfer of training when treatment contingencies are discontinued, even if the physical-social surroundings remain constant.

Other generalization procedures, such as group contingencies (Hindelang, 1970), cognitive restructuring, delayed reinforcement, role-playing, and distributed (or massed) practice, have not been pursued systematically in the rehabilitation of adult offenders. One possibility for increasing the durability of behaviors incompatible with criminal conduct would be to develop techniques which strive to strengthen complex, sequential repertoires that would allow a client to maintain a desired position, in spite of social pressure to the contrary. For example, Nietzel, Martorano and Melnick (1977) incorporated "reply training" (learning effective responses to condemnation or noncompliance with initial assertive behaviors) into a basic covert modeling treatment package for social unassertiveness. In essence, participants were asked to imagine noncompliance to their initial assertive response. After imagining a second assertive reply to this noncompliance, participants visualized compliance to the second example of modeled assertion. Participants receiving such "reply training" evidenced significantly more assertion on role-playing scenes for which they were trained than that displayed by controls or by participants receiving covert modeling without the "reply training." In addition, this advantage generalized to nontrained situations and extended interactions where a sequence of different assertive responses was demanded. No significant differences were detected on a followup phone call requiring sustained assertiveness.

Prevention and System-level Interventions

For the most part, correctional behaviorists have aimed their interventions at the individual or small group level. Consequently, their services have reflected an emphasis on an adjustment model rather than one which is directed at preventive, system-level changes in the criminal justice system (Rappaport, 1977). Correctional behaviorists have yet to pursue the integration of behavioral and systems analyses which has typified mental health programming in other areas (Harshberger & Maley, 1974). A "systems" approach to crime has found expression in the suggestion that crime control would be best achieved by making unlawful behavior more difficult to accomplish. In this approach, both the locus of control and the timing of the interventions are altered. The "correction" of the individual is redirected to the "anticipatory prevention" (Sykes, 1972) of the criminal act itself. There is less concern with the deterrence or apprehension or correction of the criminal, and more with the physical or social environmens under which certain types of crime flourish and are even encouraged.

A collection of technological advances, environmental redesign (Jeffery, 1971; Newman, 1972), architectural changes, improved means of surveillance, and legislative action exemplifies a type of social engineering that has been termed "hardening the target" (Sykes, 1972). Specific examples of such target hardening include gun control legislation, monetary incentives for the voluntary surrender of privately owned firearms, payment of incentive wages to police officers contingent on decreases in the incidence of crimes in their jurisdictions (Time, 1974), community planning (Fabbri, 1974), deterrent patrols and team policing (Anderson, 1974; Bloch & Speckt, 1973), and increased citizen involvement in law enforcement (Owens & Elliott, 1974). Jacobs (1961) has suggested developing multiple social uses of unsupervised space in high crime areas, thereby diminishing the opportunities for illegal activity that would otherwise have a low risk of detection.

Another very controversial application of anticipatory crime prevention involves the electronic monitoring of the location and activities of potential law breakers. Schwitzgebel (1968) has developed an "electronic rehabilitation system" that allows the continual monitoring of the location of parolees (or probationers, diverted offenders, or defendants released on recognizance).

This system requires the subject to wear two small electronic transmitters that activate a network of repeater stations which, in turn, retransmit the signals to a base station. In this manner, the precise tracking of individuals across large areas is possible. This monitoring system could greatly increase the control of crucial, *in vivo* behaviors. For example, a contract clause which proscribes certain high risk areas as off-limits for the offender could be easily and reliably enforced.

The common element of all strategies is the community elimination, disruption, or constraint of criminal resources. Additionally, in most instances, certain parameters of the environment are modified so as to make the commission of crime physically more difficult. Such system level responses to crime problems offer much promise as efficient, well integrated control procedures. As such, they also represent procedures that will require persistent, legal, and public scrutiny of their application. Special vigilance should extend to the use of sophisticated monitoring systems, and their potential violations of constitutional protections set forth in the First and Ninth Amendments (see A. Miller, 1971, for a discussion of the objections to governmental surveillance of its citizens).

The prevention of crime has become one of the major objectives of many law enforcement agencies. The enthusiasm evoked by the notion of crime prevention is, in many ways, reminiscent of the optimistic fervor which, several years ago, greeted the concept of community-based corrections. The primary funding agency for crime prevention efforts has been the National Institute of Law Enforcement and Criminal Justice (NILECJ), which, in recent years, has provided for 31 crime prevention programs at an expense of more than $3 million (Matthews, 1973). The appearance, in 1973, of a professional journal *(Crime Prevention Review)* is further testimony to the growth of this field.

In their ideal form, crime prevention programs are based on a combination of social and physical sciences. Their objective is seldom total prevention in the sense of guaranteeing the complete absence of crime. Rather, they are aimed at decreasing the incidence of crime; reducing the frequency of certain types of crime; and disrupting the pattern of criminal behavior of certain offenders, or groups of offenders. In practice, it is questionable that crime prevention achieves the theoretical integration claimed by its proponents. Often, it seems to have an almost exclusive emphasis on insuring the physical security of property. Further, many efforts at crime prevention give the impression of not so much preventing crime as displacing it to new areas or victims.

There have been very few behavioral approaches to crime prevention. Mastria and Hosford (1976) reported the use of assertion training and self-defense in a rape prevention program. Incorporation of assertion training into the program was based on the hypothesis that "the inability to control occurrences and the sense of helplessness may be seen in the behavior of the victim before the attack and that this may have influenced the rapist in choosing that particular victim'' (p. 3). While assertion training and assertion training plus self-defense were more effective than self-defense only or no-treatment conditions in increasing behavioral and self-report manifestations of social assertiveness, there were no data to show that participants in these conditions were better able to handle situations in which a sexual assault might occur.

Behavior analytic methodology has been employed to compare the effects of two types of prevention strategies for shoplifting, one of the most frequent and costly crimes in the United States (McNees, Egli, Marshall, Schnelle, & Risley, 1976). Two separate studies, each using an ABA design, evaluated the effects of general antishoplifting signs (''shoplifting is not uplifting''; Study I) and the effects of a procedure that increased the threat of detection (Study II).

In Study I, a 26-day (23 observations) baseline was followed by a 20-day (17 observations) intervention period during which five antishoplifting signs were placed in the merchandise department of interest (young women's clothing). The final phase was a five-day return to baseline (no signs). The results indicated that the placement of warning signs was associated with a moderate (approximately one-third) decrease in stealing, while the amount of total sales was unaffected.

Study II employed a multiple baseline design to assess the impact of more specific signs which identified particular types of merchandise frequently taken by shoplifters. For two different types of merchandise (marked with a red star) threre was a large (approximately 90 percent) reduction in shoplifting from baseline levels after the introduction of the warning signs. There was no appreciable change in theft rates for ''control merchandise,'' which was not marked by the special signs for the duration of the study.

These results confirm data from other areas of applied behavior analysis, such as environmental protection, in which specific forms of antecedent stimulus control, or ''prompts,'' exert greater effects than do their generalized counterparts (Geller, Witmer & Orebaugh, in press). Beyond its data on shoplifting prevention, the greater importance of the McNees, et al. study is to be found in its demonstration that applied behavior analysis can provide a measurement-evaluation system which will be able to assess the effects of a number of alternative crime prevention strategies.

RESEARCH METHODOLOGY

The research methodology of correctional behavior modification is at an embryonic stage of development. For the most part, the rationales of the research designs in this area appear to be an indiscriminate amalgamation of single-subject and group methodology. Of the many outpatient studies presented in Tables 6-1, 6-2, 6-3, and 6-6, the great majority were case studies. Only four studies employed group designs; in two of these there were no controls, and in the other two, control subjects differed in many ways from the recipients of the experimental treatments. Three other studies employed single-subject methodology, which did not permit an adequate evaluation of treatment effectiveness.

Evaluations of institutional behavior modification have yet to reveal a single instance in which an adequate no-treatment control group has been included. Only a few research programs (Andrasik, McNamara & Abbott, 1977; Milan, et al., 1974 and Polakow, 1975) contain enough of the rudiments of an experimental design to allow statistical comparisons. In one of these cases, the appropriateness of the comparisons that were performed was questionable. Milan, et al. (1974) applied analysis of variance to data gathered in a sequential reversal design, despite the fact that the necessary assumptions of homogeneity of variance, normal distribution of error, and independence of observations are probably violated in such designs.

The minimal requirements of single-subject methodology are also infrequently represented. Reversal data are reported in few instances. Very few studies report baseline data. Those that do (McNamara & Andrasik, 1977) often suffer from unstable baselines which do not provide an acceptable source of experimental comparison. The selection of multiple baselines, or highly specific behaviors, that could permit some statements about functional control has not occurred except on a very limited basis (research conducted at the Draper Institute and by McNees, et al., 1976 are exceptions).

The majority of correctional behavior modification research would appear to have virtually no scientific value. According to Paul's (1969) schema, they would be classified as nonfactorial, single-group designs without comparative measurements. As such, the existing literature provides very little compelling support for belief in the specific effectiveness of behavior modification techniques in rehabilitating adult offenders. At an anecdotal level, there is widespread agreement that offender behavior change is associated with the presence of some behavioral procedures. Nonetheless, isolation of the mechanisms responsible for such changes is not now possible.

Investigators who wish to confirm the functional relationship between some change in behavior and some specific behavioral intervention will have to attend to the following *minimum* design requirements: (1) randomized or matched subject assignment to experimental and control groups (alternatively, in single-subject designs, reversal or multiple baseline procedures should be used); (2) collection of preintervention or stable baseline assessments against which the later effects of experimental interventions can be compared; (3) employment of observers or assessors who are blind to the experimental status of participants; (4) factorial inclusion of the domains likely to be influential in behavior change (treatment techniques, therapist characteristics, time, and dimensions of the physical-social environment); and (5) empirical monitoring of both intentionally manipulated and unintentionally occurring independent variables.

Programmatic evaluation of any social institution is a troublesome enterprise. Evaluation-outcome research in correctional environments has proven to be an especially formidable task. Political, economic, and professional limitations consistently impinge on the evaluator, and reduce the level of product associated with program evaluation research (Wortman, 1975). While high quality program evaluation is a difficult undertaking, the growth of alternatives to standard experimental methodology has increased the potential for conducting scientifically meaningful research on complex and changing social programs. One important response to the usual set of methodological obstacles has been to advocate the use of quasi-experimental designs (Campbell & Stanley, 1966) that allow tentative conclusions about program effects after ruling out as many alternative explanations ("threats") for the results as possible.

One can sympathize with the plight of correctional program evaluators and, at the same time, recognize that quasi-experimental methods have been underutilized. One illustration of this approach is Schnelle and Lee's (1974) use of an interrupted time-series design to evaluate the effects of a disciplinary intervention on the behavior of 2,000 adult inmates. The design involved an extension of a single-group "before" and "after" design. Data were monitored for seven months prior to the implementation of the policy (transfer of disruptive prisoners to a new institution) and for 23 months subsequent to the change. Statistical analyses were based on those described by Glass, Wilson, and Gottman (1973) who proposed an "integrated moving average" model which allows probability estimates of the changes in slope and level between different treatment phases in a sequential research design. (Another example of a behavior analytic approach to program evaluation is illustrated by the McNees, et al. (1976) study reported previously in this chapter.)

I am not advocating that quasi-experimental procedures be regarded as a replacement for experimentally controlled investigations, but this type of methodology can provide applied behavior analysts with pilot data upon which their later social experimentation can build. Unfortunately, correctional research from any theoretical perspective has yet to demonstrate this kind of scientific continuity. The infrequent use of techniques such as time-series analyses or quasi-experimental designs may be due to their relative newness to most behavioral scientists. If this is the case, efforts to become better acquainted with these methods would be an initial step in upgrading the level of product which can be obtained from correctional behavior modification research.

Chapter 10
Legal and Ethical Challenges to Correctional Behavior Modification

> It is of more importance to the
> community that innocence should
> be protected than it is that guilt
> should be punished.
>
> — John Adams

This chapter reviews the ethical and legal status of behavior modification as a rehabilitation strategy for adult offenders. Case law relevant to the legality of behavior modification in correctional settings is presented, and several principles of professional ethics which bear on these issues are discussed.

LEGAL CHALLENGES

Historically, the courts have been disinclined to pass judgment on what constitutes adequate treatment for rehabilitation. Recently this reluctance has given way to a greater willingness to evaluate the legality of both psychiatric and correctional care. It is apparent that the courts are no longer willing to permit violations of inmate (or patient) rights, despite the difficulties inherent in nonexpert review of rehabilitation and treatment methods. Litigation designed to challenge the application of behavior therapy within prisons frequently has been successful (Saunders, 1974). Decisions in lawsuits (most often initiated by the National Prison Project of the American Civil Liberties Union) have resulted in the termination of several institutional behavior modification programs, including the Federal Bureau of Prisons' START Program, Virginia's Contingency Management Program, and the Special Program Unit and Control Unit Treatment Program in the state of Illinois. For detailed presentation and analysis of one such case (*Armstrong v. Bensinger*), see Goldberger (1975).

A comprehensive review of the legal status of correctional therapy would exceed the present chapter's intentions. The reader interested in a complex exploration of the legal issues of correctional behavior modification and the more general problems of enforced treatments is referred to excellent reviews by Damich (1974), Friedman (1975), Gobert (1975), Martin (1975), Moya and Achtenberg (1974), Rubin (1976), Schwitzgebel (1972, 1974b), Shapiro (1971), Singer (1977a & b), Spece (1972) and Wexler (1973, 1974a). This section addresses itself to six of the most frequently cited legal principles upon which challenges to correctional behavior modification are based. Selective annotations to recent case law accompany a brief description of each of the legal precedents.

Right to Treatment

First advocated by Birnbaum (1960), the right to treatment for patients committed to psychiatric hospitals found legal support in the landmark *Rouse v. Cameron* (1966) decision. Subsequent cases have strengthened this doctrine through successful due process arguments (*Wyatt v. Stickney*, 1971; later *Wyatt v. Aderholt*, 1974; *Donaldson v. O'Connor*, 1974). *Donaldson* has been upheld by the Supreme Court with its decision that a state may not constitutionally confine without treatment those nondangerous individuals who are capable of surviving by themselves, or with the help of others, outside the institution (*Donaldson v. O'Connor*, 1975). Since *Rouse*, one federal court has extended the right to treatment for the mentally ill to the right to rehabilitation applicable to prison offenders (*Holt v. Sarver*, 1970). Specifically, the *Holt* court held that the absence of affirmative rehabilitation programs, where there also are conditions that militate against reform and rehabilitation, may violate constitutional requirements.

The most important aspects of the *Wyatt* decision included the court's ban on involuntary labor by patients, unless compensated by the minimum wage, and specification of the physical and psychological resources to which patients are entitled by constitutional right. The thrust of *Wyatt* is found in the directive that a patient is entitled to the "least restrictive conditions necessary to achieve the purposes of commitment."

The doctrine of the least restrictive alternative originated in *Shelton v. Tucker* (1960). One of its most fundamental implications is that a person should not be incarcerated for treatment or rehabilitation if there are less drastic means for accomplishing the desired objective. Similarly, deprivations other than confinement would be prohibited if less restricted but equally effective conditions were available (see *Wyatt*). The least restrictive alternative doctrine has been championed as a more effective check on the inadequacy of institutional care than the more general right-to-treatment requirement (Foianini, 1975), because it focuses critically on the basic problem of involuntary confinement. Further elaboration of the least restrictive alternative mandate can be found in *Lake v. Cameron* (1966), *Lessard v. Schmidt* (1972), *Welsch v. Likins* (1974), and, of course, *Wyatt v. Stickney* (1971).

Although the *Wyatt* case does not involve a direct attack on a behavior modification program it obviously has far reaching implications for the legally acceptable reinforcers that can be used in hospital and (by implication) prison token economies (see *Clonce v. Richardson*, 1974).[1] While based on the principle of reward, reinforcement programs require, in fact, an initial state of deprivation to insure their motivational potency. *Wyatt* would require, however, the noncontingent availability of the following constitutionally protected rights:

1) payment of the minimum wage for therapeutic or nontherapeutic institutional work;
2) a right to privacy, including a bed, closet, chair, and bedside table;
3) meals meeting minimum daily dietary requirements;
4) the right to visitors, religious services, and clean personal clothing;
5) recreational privileges (e.g., television in the day room); and
6) an open ward and ground privileges when clinically acceptable.

Understandably, psychologists have viewed the *Wyatt* precedent with considerable concern. Berwick and Morris' (1974, p. 436) view is a typical one: "The field of law is beginning to step in and demand that mental patients get fair treatment; however, they may inadvertently be undermining attempts to establish adequate treatments." There can be no doubt that *Wyatt* jeopardizes traditional token economies operated in institutional settings. At the same time, the decision is not irreconcilable with all possible behavior modification programs.

Wexler (1973) has recommended the contingent use of "idiosyncratic reinforcers," nonbasic items which patients differentially prefer (e.g., eating hardboiled rather than softboild eggs, viewing *Kojak* rather than *Columbo*). Token economies utilizing idiosyncratic reinforcers would probably be legally permissible, because, by definition, idiosyncratic reinforcers are not equivalent to general, absolute rights. Another alternative (Wexler, 1974a, 1975) would be to continue to use the "*Wyatt* basics" as reinforcers, but require fully informed consent of all participants in the program. A problem with this solution is that courts have held that informed consent to "drastic therapies" can be revoked at any time. This requirement would permit residents, by their own choosing, to convert contingent privileges into noncontingent rights, thereby usurping the program of its motivational impact.

Informed Consent

The claim that institutional residents have a right to treatment is complicated by the fact that they also may have a right to refuse it (Damich, 1974).

Operationally, an individual's control over his or her treatment often takes form through the notion of informed consent. Fully informed consent involves several elements, including full specifications of the nature of treatment; a description of its purpose, risks, and likely outcomes; advisement that consent may be terminated at any time without prejudice to the individual; and a demonstration of a capacity to consent. The question of capacity is a very complex one (Singer, 1977b). Friedman (1975) discusses three possible criteria for determining competence to consent: the ability to reach a reasonable conclusion; the capacity to reach a decision based on rational reason; and the capacity to make a decision. None of these standards is without problems pertaining to the operationalization of concepts such as rationality or reasonableness. After a review of the advantages and disadvantages of available standards, Friedman (1975) offered a standard based on "the ability to understand and knowingly act upon the information provided" (p. 80).

Obtaining written informed consent is usually required for experimental, intrusive (e.g., psychosurgery; *Kaimowitz & Doe v. Department of Mental Health*, 1973), and aversion therapies (e.g., apomorphine-based conditioning; *Knecht v. Gillman*, 1973). At least one court (*Kaimowitz*) has found that the process of institutionalization reduces an inmate's decision-making abilities to the extent that truly voluntary informed consent cannot be obtained from involuntarily confined individuals.[2] The court argued that neither knowledge of the process nor voluntary consent could be insured with institutionalized persons. The court held, in principle, that participation in programs without necessary participant knowledge and voluntariness was coercive, therefore illegal.

The full importance of the *Kaimowitz* decision remains to be seen. Its ultimate impact depends on whether the decision is interpreted as meaning that an involuntarily confined patient or inmate can never give legally adequate consent to any treatment, or whether its restrictions are limited to particular factual situations, where the nature of the setting, the dangerousness or intrusiveness of the procedure, and the amount of coercive pressure to submit to the intervention are all considered before an absolute ban is imposed.

As of now, there is no legal doctrine that an inmate may refuse all rehabilitation, or even refuse all but his most preferred mode of treatment (Wexler, 1974a). There is clear precedent that inmates may refuse methods which violate their privacy (Spece, 1972), which are unduly drastic (Damich, 1974), or which are no more than cruel and unusual punishment (*Knecht v. Gillman*, 1973). Any extension, however, of the reasoning of the *Kaimowitz* decision could result in the doctrine that institutionalization robs the inmates of volitional decision making with respect to participation in less drastic therapies — for example, group therapy or token economies. Wexler (1974b) has commented on the irony of such a development: "If involuntary confinement itself creates coercion, administering any therapy to the patient violates his right *not* to be treated without consent — which obviously vitiates entirely the right *to* treatment" (p. 679).

At the other extreme, there is the question of whether an inmate may consent to receive a procedure that could otherwise be prohibited via statutory, common law, or constitutional control. Obviously, there are numerous precedents involving the waiver of constitutional rights put forth in the Fourth, Fifth, Sixth, and Seventh Amendments (see Rubin, 1976). Usually, the courts have not allowed a person to agree to his own injury (Friedman, 1975). Similarly, an individual may not be allowed to waive a constitutional protection against certain procedures which the general public has an interest in prohibiting. As an example, this suggests that an inmate might not be permitted to waive Eighth Amendment protections against cruel and unusual punishment, since one of the standards for applying the Eighth Amendment is whether the procedure in question offends the general community's current sense of decency (see also the section on "Treatment as Punishment" below).

The very existence of the informed consent requirement in this area bespeaks the often coercive nature of rehabilitation and psychiatric treatment. From the legal point of view, however, coercion is acceptable when it is "reasonable" or "constructive," and limited (Wexler, 1974b, 1975). For example, the legality of plea bargaining has been upheld. If it is the court's desire to prohibit unreasonable coercion in offender rehabilitation, it will need to exceed the level of precision evidenced in the *Kaimowitz* decision (Singer, 1977a & b.). From the standpoint of the mental health professional, the problem might be mitigated somewhat by attempts to replace the consent model of treatment with the more ethically appealing contract model (Ayllon, 1975; Schwitzgebel, 1974a), or with a hierarchy of protections requiring differential levels of consent (Davison & Stuart, 1975). Whatever mechanism predominates, behavior modifiers should resist the use of hazardous or experimental techniques without the informed consent of their intended recipients. In instances of inmates judged incompetent to consent, intrusive treatments are justified only when they promote some compelling public purpose, and are no more restrictive than necessary to accomplish that purpose.

Due Process

Due process attacks on institutional behavior modification have taken two forms.[3] The first is known as *procedural due process*, which is generally concerned with the manner by which certain deprivations of life, liberty, or property are ordered by the state or the federal government. In those cases most relevant to institutional behavior modification, the issue has focused on the necessary due process standards applicable to transfers or assignments to special prison programs. The successful litigation brought by the ACLU National Prison Project against the START program was based, in part, on a procedural due process attack. Problem prisoners in other institutions of the Federal Bureau of Prisons were transferred to treatment in START. Given the very restrictive nature of the first level of the START program (e.g., limitations on visitation, exercise, etc.), petitioners argued that placement in START was tantamount to placement in a segregation unit, and actually constituted a form of punishment. The procedural issue involved "whether, in the absence of notice, charges and hearing, the selection and forceable transfer of a prisoner into START violates the constitutional rights of the prisoner by denying him due process and equal protection of the law" (Saunders, 1974, p. 9).

In *Clonce v. Richardson* (1974, summarized by Saunders, 1974) the court found that because of the changes in the condition of confinement, the "START prisoners were entitled, prior to administrative transfer, to a due process hearing guaranteed by the Fifth Amendment" (p. 24). In this case, the court rejected the respondent's claim that because START was a treatment program due process criteria were obviated. Essentially, the same procedural due process argument was raised successfully by petitioners in the *Armstrong v. Bensinger* (1972) case.

The second form of due process requirements is known as *substantive due process*. It applies not to the procedures by which certain deprivations occur, but to the extent, fairness, or reasonableness of these deprivations. For example, a substantive due process restriction on institutional forms of behavior modification would require that involuntary treatment bear some *reasonable* relationship to the purpose for which coercion is being applied. More specifically, this would include the previously mentioned right to the least intrusive treatments (Wexler, 1975), and to the least restrictive treatment available (*Armstrong v. Bensinger*, 1972; *Jackson v. Indiana*, 1972; *Kaimowitz and Doe v. Department of Mental Health*, 1973; *Lake v. Cameron*, 1966; and *Wyatt v. Stickney*, 1971).

The Right to Physical and Mental Privacy, and Autonomy

One substantial basis for the right to refuse treatment or rehabilitation rests on the right to privacy and its closely aligned doctrine, the right to mental autonomy. The origin of the right to privacy principle is usually attributed to Justice Louis Brandeis' famous dissent in *Olmstead v. United States* (1928) in which he claimed that American citizens have a right to be left alone. Subsequent court opinions have established the existence of "zones of privacy" which protect the privacy of marital conduct (*Griswold v. Connecticut*, 1965) and the right of a woman to have an abortion (*Roe v. Wade*, 1973). The right to mental autonomy is an extension of the First Amendment protection of free speech to freedom to think as one pleases (Friedman, 1975; see *Whitney v. California*, 1927).

Several cases have ratified the right to privacy and mental autonomy as a limitation on permissible institutional treatment techniques. In *Mackey v. Procunier* (1973), the court found the Vacaville succinylcholine conditioning program (see Chapter 5) to raise questions regarding "impermissible tinkering with the mental processes." In *Kaimowitz and Doe v. Department of Mental Health* (1973), the court recognized that the First Amendment protected not only the communication of ideas but their generation as well. With respect to mental privacy, the court held that intrusions into the intellect of involuntarily confined subjects was a violation of their right to privacy that included the inviolability of thoughts, behavior, personality, and identity. Similar issues were raised in plaintiff briefs in *Armstrong v. Bensinger* (1972), a case which was decided ultimately on procedural due process grounds.

Treatment as Punishment

A developing legal-medical controversy is the contention that the distinction between punishment and some forms of treatment (aversive conditioning, time out, token economies, and the indeterminate sentence) is spurious (Opton, 1974; Rubin, 1976). Preservation of a treatment-punishment distinction is not without important consequences. While courts are reluctant to intervene in practices classified as treatment, punishment is regulated constitutionally, statutorily, and administratively. Elimination of the distinction could result in First, Fourth, Fifth, Eighth, and Ninth Amendment attacks on coercive or violent therapies (Opton, 1974).

Rubin (1976) proposes five factors that should be considered in any attempt to distinguish treatment from punishment. First, what is the purpose of the procedure in question? While there are several perspectives from which to evaluate the objectives of a challenged procedure, one of the most crucial concerns the permanence of any changes which the technique is intended to promote. A technique of treatment should aim at more durable, permanent, or maintainable changes than would a procedure of punishment, whose application is directed at a more immediate modification of behavior. A second consideration involves the prognosis for success in achieving the technique's presumably therapeutic objectives. Greater protection and scrutiny are warranted for those procedures that are highly experimental, and therefore lacking suitable empirical testimony to their effectiveness. A third factor is the professional acceptance of the technique as being an instrument of treatment. Techniques regarded consensually by professionals as therapeutic in nature should enjoy a higher status than those which do not have a professional endorsement. This criterion should be considered cautiously, since history indicates that professionals often make premature judgments about the effectiveness of their "treatments." The most traditional consideration involved in assessing the possible punitive qualities of any technique is its intrusiveness. The extent to which an intervention is forced upon an unwilling recipient increases the aversiveness of that technique while concomitantly reducing whatever lasting rehabilitative value its unforced application might have had. Related to this criterion is the final factor, which would hold suspect the use of any procedure for which an inmate has not given his fully informed consent. While obtaining a prisoner's consent would not preclude a technique from being punitive, the failure to obtain consent would invalidate the therapeutic status of most procedures. None of these factors should predominate in a determination of a procedure's status. Rather, the decision should be a cumulative one which considers the interdependence of the above factors on a case-by-case basis.

The most obvious source of constitutional influence on this issue is derived from the Eighth Amendment's proscription of cruel and unusual punishments, but the extent to which that amendment's protections will be applied to institutional behavior modification is questionable (Friedman, 1975). First of all, its prohibition does not pertain to punishment in general, only to those punishments found to be cruel *and* unusual (see Rubin, 1976). A determination that a particular punishment is both cruel and unusual has not been a routine judicial decision. Use of the Eighth Amendment has usually been reserved for procedures that are ''barbarous'' or ''shocking to the conscience'' (Friedman, 1975). Rubin (1976) has offered three criteria for defining the conjunctive status of ''cruel and unusual punishment'': the application of the procedure is excessive in reference to the goal it seeks to achieve; the procedure offends a community's contemporary sense of decency; and the adverse effects of the procedure are disproportionate to its beneficial results. With the exception of some forms of aversive conditioning (*Knecht v. Gillman*, 1973), most current examples of institutional behavior modification would not qualify as barbarous or shockingly offensive and therefore are unlikely to be prohibited on Eighth Amendment grounds.

A related objection to a reliance on Eighth Amendment controls of behavior modification is that it might not constitute the most stringent test of a procedure's acceptability. As Friedman (1975) has warned, ''This false confidence in the Eighth Amendment protections could lead to a judicial disinterest in recognizing other rights to refuse treatment theories which might ultimately provide a higher standard of protection'' (p. 65).

Opton (1974) contends that there has not been ''a single case in which a treatment has been ruled as unconstitutionally cruel and unusual punishment'' (p. 609). The issue has been raised, to some degree, in several cases (*Adams v. Carlson*, 1973; *Clonce v. Richardson*, 1974; *Knecht v. Gillman*, 1973; *Mackay v. Procunier*, 1973; *Sanchez v. Ciccone*, 1973; and *Wyatt v. Aderholt*, 1974). The *Knecht* court did find injection of apomorphine for behaviors such as swearing, or not getting up when ordered, to be cruel and unusual punishment, but did not object to the procedure when used for other rule violations (Opton, 1974). In *Holt v. Sarver*, 1970, a federal court applied the Eighth Amendment to certain prison conditions which it described as ''shocking to the conscience.''

The goal of treatment-as-punishment arguments would seem to be that aversive treatments be subject to the same judicial scrutiny and legal controls as acknowledged punishment. Realization of this objective might be attained best by adhering to Opton's (1974) suggestion that ''Opponents of involuntary, punitive therapy oppose it not on the grounds that it is 'really' punishment rather than therapy, but on the grounds that it is both punishment and therapy, hence meriting the constitutional and other legal safeguards of both'' (p. 644).

Violation of Other Substantitive Constitutional Rights

Another constitutional source for judicial intervention into certain prison programs is the Bill of Rights' guarantees of certain personal freedoms. Although First Amendment rights are not unconditional, their violation is usually tolerated only for some compelling public interest (Moya & Achtenberg, 1974). For example, petitioners in the START case claimed that the following constitutional rights were violated by the imposition of the START program upon them (Saunders, 1974; see also *Sanchez v. Ciccone*, 1973):

(1) Freedom of speech and association;
(2) Freedom of religion;
(3) Freedom from search and seizure; and
(4) Freedom from invasion of privacy (see previous section on the right to privacy and mental autonomy).

In *Armstrong v. Bensinger* (1972), petitioners raised similar objections to the Special Program Unit at the Stateville-Joliet Prison Complex in Illinois.

For its part, the government argued in response to the START petition that the contingent availability of such "rights" was the most essential component of the treatment because they constituted the most powerful reinforcers. Although the court held that these points were moot because of the termination of START, its analyses of petitioners' claims anticipates the eventual success of future litigation based on such attacks. (Likewise, *Armstrong* was decided on procedural due process grounds.) Of future importance was the court's rejection of the government's claim that assignment to START was an internal matter of the Bureau of Prisons not reviewable by the court.

ETHICAL CONSIDERATIONS

Behavior modification is confronted by a public that has become increasingly apprehensive about the ethics of its use. Historically, in the area of adult corrections, there has been great tolerance for intrusive techniques because of the promise of controlling very threatening behavior that is strongly disapproved of by most of us. Yet, recent discussions of the morality of behavior modification, in both the professional (Opton, 1975; Schwitzgebel, 1974a; Wexler, 1973, 1974a) and lay media (Hilts, 1974; Mitford, 1973), have provoked new skepticism and concern from a public whose ethical sensibilities have been tenderized in this post-Watergate era. Clearly this ferment has removed ethical considerations from a "merely academic" context to a position where vested and public interests have been mobilized into legislative or executive action. At this time, at least two federally funded prison token economies have been disbanded by their originating agencies or local officials, and several more face impending discontinuation. The Law Enforcement Assistance Administration has announced that it no longer will support any program involving behavior modification, psychosurgery, or chemotherapy research. Additionally in 1974, Congress passed the National Research Service Award Act which mandated the formation of the Commission for the Protection of Human Subjects of Biomedical and Behavioral Research. The tasks for this body were to identify basic ethical principles underlying human research, and to establish procedures and guidelines insuring that such research be conducted in accord with these standards.

Ethical objections to behavior modification techniques are, in fact, only part of a larger concern with a host of behavior control or behavior influence (Krasner & Ullmann, 1973) technologies. Most potent sources of control (economic, political, surgical, pharmacological, and genetic) have evoked heated debates concerning the ethics of their use. The association of behavior modification with these influences has been a two-edged sword. On the one hand, behavior modification often is attributed a degree of influence which has not been empirically demonstrated. Many commentators on penal behavior modification exaggerate the effects of behavior techniques in controlling the action and "minds" of inmates who are portrayed as helpless to resist the force of these supposedly overwhelmingly powerful procedures. At the same time, some of the more objectionable aspects of organic interventions (irreversibility, intrusiveness, etc.) have been inaccurately associated with behavioral methods. Bandura (1974) has argued that behavioral technology is not the puissant, irresistible means of control often portrayed by both its advocates and its detractors. Neither is it irreversible, subliminal, or especially intrusive in most of its forms. The professionals' disclaimers aside, ethical challenges to behavior modification do continue to be vigorously expressed. For purposes of this discussion, these ethical objections are addressed under the following five topics: ethical misconceptions, behaviorists' "image" of man, behavior control, aversion techniques, and ethical "prompting."

Ethical Misconceptions

Ethical objections to correctional behavior modification are frequently generated by descriptions in the media that are, at best, outdated and, at worst, misinformed or distorted. It would be tempting to diminish the importance of such misconceptions by representing them merely as differences in the semantic preferences of behaviorists and their adversaries. This temptation should be resisted because it obscures the basis upon which many of the most fundamental protests are founded.

Professionals have jeopardized, in part, the general public's understanding of behavior modification by their earlier nonjudicious choices of terminology. One of the most unfortunate and misleading of designations has been that of "conditioning." This term suggests a procedure of behavior change which is insidious, reflexive, and mechanical. In fact, as Bandura (1974) has indicated, behavior theory has outgrown the conditioning model, and now increasingly emphasizes such processes as mediation (Bandura, 1969), self-regulation (Thoresen & Mahoney, 1974), and attentional control (Maher, 1975).

These advances aside, "conditioning" has been the appellation of choice for many critics of behavioral corrections. Descriptions of behavior modification programs have been linked inappropriately with the ethics and outcomes of psychosurgery (Gobert, 1975), and pharmacological treatments (Shapiro, 1974). A related error is the partitioning of behavior therapy into inaccurate theoretical divisions. For example, Gaylin and Blatte (1975) claim there are only two major categories of behavioral interventions: those based on aversion therapy, and those derived from operant conditioning. Heldman (1973) was moved to describe behaviorists as "come lately technocrats, who see all the world as their laboratory and individual man as little more than a rat in a maze" (p. 13). Following some attempts to associate Skinner with Hitler and Mao, Heldman concludes, "in one naive stroke, he (Skinner) would destroy the ediface or protection we have built up against totalitarianism" (p. 18). This level of polemic has been equalled by a prisoner's description of applied behavior analysis in prisons as "a concerted genocidal attack upon ethnic minorities, not much different from the types of procedures that were employed by the Nazis during their politico-fanatic war against the Jews" (Clemons, 1975, pp. 129-130). Thankfully, positions as gratuitious and poorly reasoned as these are infrequent. Other, less strident attributions persist, however.

One connotative implication of the conditioning paradigm has been that behaviorists are reluctant to consider (if not deliberately inattentive to) internal events. In fact, systematic desensitization, modeling, and covert sensitization are all techniques which conceptually and procedurally require the self-regulation of imagination, cognition, and attention. Careful philosophical scrutiny of even the extreme operant orientation of Skinner reveals a reliance on distinctly intentional, teleological, and purposive constructs (Rychlak, 1973).

Behaviorists increasingly are acknowledging man's ultimate intentional nature and, at the same time, maintaining that intentions are explainable and modifiable (Nietzel, 1974). This position requires generation of empirical laws of behavior which do not violate a belief in individual responsibility for particular actions (Caplan & Nelson, 1973). As psychologists have progressed in their efforts to understand and modify subjective experiences, the goals of some behavioral interventions have begun to stress development or facilitation of an individual's repertoire of self-regulation skills. A recent example of this emphasis in corrections would be Abel's work with nonincarcerated offenders (see Chapter 6). Unfortunately, it is the case that almost all institutional programs have continued relatively unencumbered by developments concerning self-control, or cognitive processing.

Even successful attempts to correct some of the misattributions directed at behavior modifiers will not eliminate the ethical dilemmas posed by their treatments. Indeed, revised attributions will generate new and potentially more intense concerns. For example, effective modification of mediational events appears to be much more intrusive than the alteration of discrete responses. As we have already seen, a number of recent court decisions have confirmed the existence of a constitutional protection of cognition and the right to mental privacy. If the expectation that behaviorists will increasingly identify self-control processes as treatment targets is accurate, then one could also anticipate a replacement of charges of "simplemindedness" with those of "invasion of privacy."

Image of Man

The foregoing set of ethical objections may converge upon the realization that many people find behaviorists' implied image of man to be objectionable (Friedman, 1975). One very good indication of a profession's views of human nature is the degree of concern evidenced for the process of change as well as the final outcomes. Despite this fact, behavior modifiers have been consistently inattentive to the *process* of change, which their correctional efforts have illustrated. Shapiro (1974) has distinguished between procedures intended to do something *for* or *with* an individual and those intended to do something *to* him. Commenting on the treatment of Alex, the "hero" in *Clockwork Orange*, Shapiro suggests, "something was done *to* Alex, not *for* him, and his conforming conduct was not something for which he is likely to be praised. The way in which the conformity was achieved was an assault on personal autonomy rather than an enhancement of it" (p. 299).

In this respect, correctional psychologists have not explored sufficiently the opportunities to exploit ethical requirements such as informed consent, or treatment contracts for the goal of maximizing client inputs into the change process. Behavior therapists in other areas have recognized the importance of an active, collaborative relationship between the professional and the client. This collaboration is often operationalized by a therapeutic contract (Karoly, 1975) that specifies desired changes, procedures to be employed, potential risks, and the responsibilities of both the client and therapist. The client then becomes an active agent, a planner of his or her own change. If "consent" were obtained within the context of a negotiated contract that would allow the offender to reach informed decisions about his own rehabilitation, it could function not only as a necessary legal safeguard but as a potential therapeutic tool as well.

The issue is not simply that for rehabilitation to be ethical it must be voluntary. More importantly, what is required are interventions that take seriously the notion that offenders assume "roles as active, informed and informative participants rather than as passive recipients of programs" (Brodsky, 1973b, p.18).

Active inmate-professional collaboration in rehabilitation programming could be promoted by any one of a number of procedures. For example, Brodsky (1973b) has advocated the use of a voucher system similar to those employed in public schools (Weiler, 1974). The voucher system would allow inmates to purchase that form of rehabilitation which they prefer among several competing alternatives, thereby increasing their freedom in choosing a treatment and, at the same time, offering incentives to correctional professionals for treatment innovations. Other recommendations designed to increase inmate participation in the treatment process are the employment of ex-offenders as correctional staff (Nietzel & Moss, 1972), participatory management (Brodsky, 1973b), and peer-group decision making (Schoen, 1972).

A more deliberate concern with the processes by which unlawful behavior is changed is justified on both ethical and therapeutic grounds. Such a concern is also likely to foster an image of man that is more appreciative of his abilities and his desire for self-modification.

The Control of Behavior

A frequent ethical objection is that behavior control procedures can and may be used for totalitarian, freedom-limiting ends. In a more general discussion of behavior modification morality, Kazdin (1975) has identified three issues related to this general fear: "the *purpose* for which behavior is to be controlled, *who* will decide the ultimate purpose and exert control, and whether behavioral control entails an abridgement of individual *freedom*" (p. 230). While this set of concerns is more intense for efforts such as the redesign of society (Skinner, 1971) or educational reprogramming (Winett & Winkler, 1972), questions about the appropriate rehabilitation goals for adult offenders are increasingly encountered by correctional officials.

A continuing problem is the feeling that professionals are used to legitimize retribution, control, and induced passivity by making them appear to be instruments of treatment (Opton, 1974, 1975). Conrad (1965) has referred to the constant accommodation of therapeutic programs to the overriding requirements of public safety and protection as the "irrational equilibrium." The distressing fact is that virtually any procedure within a prison can be made to appear like treatment. Often, the equilibrium is maintained by a strategic substitution of informal means of control for a more formalized, centralized set of disciplinary rules. Informal control may take the form of interpersonal or material rewards and deprivations from staff to inmate (Cressey, 1969). It may also be formalized via the token or graduated tier systems described in Chapter 5.

The ease with which line staff can acquire the principles of contingency management portends the possibility of informal means becoming much more systematic in application. The fate of the Contingency Management Program (see Chapter 5) provides an example of this outcome. Following legal challenges from the ACLU, the supervisory psychological staff has been removed from the Virginia Program; "the CMP has now been converted into a static program without graduated steps, whose intent is to modify the behavior of inmates who disrupt institutional routine by venting aggression, cowering, or simply refusing to obey rules and regulations according to the latest description by prison officials" (Trotter, 1975, p. 10). Certainly, it would be unfair to characterize all guards as "villains," or all psychologists as "saints," to use Skinner's (1971) terminology. Nonetheless, the use of behavior control techniques by prison guards has been shown repeatedly to further self-serving aims of managerial control and inmate docility.

Behavior control is often equated with the loss of freedom, or a diminishment of personal autonomy. From a forensic perspective, this sentiment has found expression in the "right to be different" ideology (Shapiro, 1974), and its "right against treatment" corollary (Damich, 1974). The ethical considerations involved in "treat" vs. "no treat" decision are more complex than the rhetoric of mandatory treatment proponents and opponents has allowed. Philosophical discussions of whether there "really is" freedom has yielded agreement only on the position that the *perception* of freedom is crucial to human adjustment (Lefcourt, 1973). The extent to which correctional behavior modification has enhanced or weakened the perception of individual freedom has yet to be determined empirically. It is to be hoped that this question will persist. On the face of it, most institutional forms of behavior modification do not appear to strengthen their sometimes involuntary participants' sense of freedom and personal autonomy.

Of course, control via behavior modification is not without its defenders. The hackneyed claims that behavior modification is value free or morally neutral are not as frequently heard today as in the past. There is, of course, no value free intervention in any setting (Kazdin, 1975). The very decision to work in a correctional institution reflects a number of moral decisions regarding what constitutes changeworthy behavior and what are the best procedures for changing it. Frankly, it would be best to put to rest the pretense of ethical neutrality. Certainly, it does not appease critics. Neither does it potentiate thoughtful considerations of the ethical dilemmas that are necessarily encountered by behavioral practitioners.

Undoubtedly, behavior modifiers are accurate in their claim that their procedures are consistent with public norms and preferences. Indeed, behavior modification possesses the unique capacity to satisfy, simultaneously, advocates of both correctional "permissiveness" and "harshness." At a conceptual level, therapeutic principles are emphasized; however, the ensuing procedures are not so nurturant as to offend law and order sympathizers. At the least, there is tacit societal endorsement for current correctional practice. Nonetheless, professional interests and discussion of the ethics of intervention should not be restricted to instances in which an often apathetic public's tolerance is exceeded.

One advantage over other sources of control which behavior modification may possess, is the explicitness and overtness of its techniques and of its objectives (Friedman, 1975). Manipulation of environmental or interpersonal consequences typically results in an individual's cognizance of the operating contingencies. In fact, there is an extensive literature which suggests that behavior is not changed much by contingencies of which subjects are unaware (Dulany, 1968). Therefore, regulation of behavior through reinforcement procedures can be of informational value to clients (Bandura, 1974). This type of cognitive input and influence may be of special importance to lawbreakers whose behavior is troublesome, often because of its situational inappropriateness or the unavailability of alternative nonoffensive behaviors.

One feature which distinguishes available technologies of control is the degree to which they allow reciprocal control to be exercised. For example, the methods of genetic or medical influence are largely inaccessible to the public, thus restricted to a small number of professional users. On the other hand, we are taught that our society extends a degree of political influence to each adult. In principle, behavior modification provides methods of countercontrol for its recipients. For example, people can learn to be more systematic in their attempts to modify the systems in which they live. Likewise, they can withhold certain social or tangible reinforcers from those who seek to modify their behavior by the use of similar types of contingencies. However, countercontrol will be effective only to the extent that there is some equity in the distribution and possession of reinforcers among system members. In this regard, the prospects for inmate efforts at (nonviolent) countercontrol in correctional institutions remain largely illusory. Reciprocity of control is more tenable for offenders whose intended rehabilitation occurs in more open, community settings.

Perhaps the greatest restriction on personal freedom is a limited behavioral repertoire and the attending reduction in attainable outcomes (Bandura, 1974; Kazdin, 1975). An overriding goal of most behavior modifiers is to increase the number of functional, adaptive skills from which an individual may select a certain behavioral strategy. Such "repertoire expansion" can free a person from his own behavioral deficits and allow for the development of a greater confidence in living. The notion of limited repertoires is obviously salient to offender populations who are largely uneducated, unemployed, and unsocialized. Behaviorists can argue persuasively that when their interventions emphasize the enhancement of performance, they are actually amplifying rather than stultifying individual freedoms.

Aversive Control

Despite the fact that most of our existing social systems have institutionalized the use of aversive control, the application of aversive procedures in correctional settings usually arouses the most energetic of ethical protests (see Opton, 1974; Saunders, 1974). Friedman (1975) proposes a number of factors that may account for the extra attention and concern of which behavior modification is the recipient: (1) its origin in experimental laboratory work with animals; (2) its preference for detached, mechanistic, and scientific descriptions; (3) its frequent, but inappropriate association with organic therapies; (4) its highly visible techniques, and explicit, specific objectives; and (5) the fact that its use has experienced a rapid growth among a variety of mental health professionals. Another problem, relevant to the "discriminatory regulation of applied behavior analysis," is that many abuses attributed to behavior modifiers occur in programs administered by professionals not well trained in behavioral principles (Goldiamond, 1975). Although the training of program staff is an important ingredient in evaluating the adequacy of both aversive and nonaversive rehabilitation techniques, it may be an inadequate criterion for deciding what is behavior modification, and what is not.

Aversive control can be manifest in diverse ways. *Punishment* can take one of two procedural forms: the application of an aversive stimulus contingent on the occurrence of unwanted behavior, or the withdrawal of a positive reinforcer following a proscribed behavior. Most prison punishment is of the latter type although "direct" punishment is not unknown (Opton, 1974). *Aversive counter conditioning* is a third variety of aversive control involving the application of a negative reinforcer simultaneously with either the perception of the stimulus that elicits the problem behavior or the performance of that behavior itself. It is typified by components of some penal programs and by many outpatient treatments for sexual, drug, and alcohol-related problems.

Behaviorists are fond of indicating that the majority of their interventions avoid aversive control and rely instead on the use of positive influences. While this may be true in many clinical settings, it is less characteristic of adult corrections. Most institutional programs, behaviorally oriented or not, abound with punishable behaviors running the gamut from cursing (Opton, 1974) to a noncooperative attitude (Saunders, 1974). This misuse of aversive techniques is compounded by the fact that the stimuli used on prisoners are among the most potent available. At a time when most clinicians have sought to employ minimal levels of aversive stimulus intensity, or to replace actual stimulus presentations with imaginal versions of the noxious event, e.g., covert sensitization (Polakow, 1975), prisoners are being subjected to injections of succinylcholine and apomorphine.

A continuing conceptual criticism of punishment procedures is that they merely suppress behavior and do not promote the new learning of more acceptable responses. Based on the early work of Estes (1944), this view has been tempered somewhat by the recognition of Solomon's work (1964) which suggests that new instrumental behaviors can be learned in response to the classically conditioned fear that may accompany punishment (see Rimm & Masters, 1974, for a clinically oriented discussion of two-factor learning theory). Nonetheless, the accepted clinical judgment is that the maintenance of punishment-generated change is related to the extent that alternative responses, replacing those that were suppressed, are acquired. Unfortunately, few prison programs have combined efforts of building desirable repertoires with their efforts toward eliminating undesirable ones (Goldiamond, 1974).

Another common objection to aversive procedures is that their consistent administration results for the recipients in negative side effects that include fear, anger, and helplessness. There is no reason to assume inmates to be any more resistant than other target groups to these side effects; nor should they be expected to be any more tolerant of punishment as a means of control. Indeed, the special behavioral history of prisoners is usually predictive of their ability to execute very effective counteraggression against their punishers (Sage, 1974).

It is paradoxical that certain parameters of aversive treatments are used both to justify and to condemn their use. Many aversive stimuli are very painful; not a few introduce the risk of injury. For those reasons, aversive techniques possess the greatest potential for human harm of all the treatments in psychology's armamentarium. At the same time, the intensity of many aversive procedures accounts for one of their main advantages. They are capable of bringing behavior under rapid, resolute and complete control. In some instances (inmate violence) decisive control is required; however, it is probably the case that the "successful" use of necessary aversion procedures make future application in nonessential situations more likely. The question of how to limit the escalation of punishment is a critical one for those professionals who would advocate even its very circumscribed use.

A reliance on professional ethics for the control of punishment procedures would appear to be an insufficient restraint. Numerous objectionable aversive methods have been sustained in prison with professional tolerance (Sage, 1974). It would be just as futile to argue for an across-the-board prohibition of aversive techniques which, in some limited situations, are probably necessary. In lieu of these two extremes, adherence to a set of formal guidelines for the use of aversive methods with offenders might be the most reasonable alternative. Development of these could be the responsibility of judicial panels, citizens' review boards, local bar associations, or specially created advisory boards composed of lawyers, inmates, and correctional agents. A basis for these guidelines is suggested by Kazdin's (1975) discussion of minimal ethical requirements surrounding the clinical use of aversive techniques. He identified four issues that should be confronted seriously before any decision to proceed with an aversive technique: careful determination of the stimulus intensity to be used (ideally, this might be somewhere between detection and pain thresholds); specification of the time limits on an aversive program; prior examination of the availability of nonaversive procedures for modification of the targeted behavior; and an empirical demonstration of the correctional utility of the proposed method. In light of a prison system that has had difficulty documenting the efficacy of 200 years of punishment, this last requirement is likely to prove particularly onerous.

Ethical Prompting

The ethical questions posed by correctional behavior modification should not remain restricted to adversarial debates between special interest groups, be they prisoners or behavioral psychologists. Correctional policy has yet to elicit the intensity of concern and involvement that the public has demonstrated on other issues related to criminal justice (capital punishment). Similarly, many behavioral scientists have not evidenced an enthusiasm for contingencies that increase the likelihood of broader public participation in the development and review of correctional programs.

A much needed "ethical" contribution from the professionals would be a behavioral analysis of the means by which the public can increase its inputs into discussions of values, ethics, and policy as they relate to offender rehabilitation. With respect to the implementation of community corrections, a solicitation of the local milieu's involvement in program definition is essential (Atthowe, 1973). This recommendation is based on the assumption that programs which begin with maximal citizen and inmate input are likely to yield the most meaningful outcome. A number of related procedures could contribute to the realization of this goal. They include early prompting of citizen participation in the development of programs; the establishment of citizen-professional review boards for local correctional programs; development of positive community resources in an attempt to stimulate creative, alternative social systems (Rappaport, Davidson, Wilson, and Mitchell, 1975); and local publication of the process, and outcome of local programs.

Legitimate behavior modification programs should have no qualms about exposure to public, legislative, or judicial inquiry. Neither should they resist the informed scrutiny of those inmates they are intended to serve. If concerns or criticisms are the results of misunderstandings, misinterpretations, or inaccurate information, educative efforts are indicated. If, on the other hand, the program is revealed to be misapplied, ineffective, inadequate, or destructive, there would be a need for corrective action, perhaps to include legal sanctions against program administrators and advisors who continue programs judged to be unsatisfactory.

Another suggestion would be that behavior modification funding decisions should be based on a demonstrated adherence to a codified set of ethical standards for correctional treatment (see Braun, 1975, for guidelines for one such code). As an initial attempt to provide professional self-regulation, Ayllon (1975) has suggested the following set of guidelines for the practice of behavior modification in institutional settings: (1) participants should be informed of the possible outcome of treatment interventions; (2) inmates should be informed of all procedures that will be employed during the intervention; (3) participation should be voluntary; (4) participants should be free to discontinue the program at any time; (5) participants should be informed of the progress they are making; (6) inmates are entitled to individualized treatment techniques; (7) inmates should have the opportunity to express their feelings and attitudes about the interventions; and (8) techniques should not be employed which would impoverish the environment below certain base guarantees of social and personal rights. Related specifically to the issue of aversive control is the caveat that "only when the patient's actions present a clear and imminent danger to his own or others' physical integrity may aversive or noxious stimuli be justified" (Ayllon, 1975).

Finally, the recommendation that behavioral scientists should shape specific ethical decisions that increase governmental and public acceptance of behavior modification procedures seems ill-conceived. For example, Bornstein, Bugge, and Davol (1975) contend that the task for behaviorists is "formulating an intervention program to increase governmental and public acceptibility regarding the practice of and research in behavior modification" (p. 65). It is incumbent upon behaviorists to consider ethical debate as desirable, independent of the ultimate opinions reached by the participants. One's doubts about the ethics of systematic behavioral control are unlikely to be mitigated by professionals whose primary aim appears to be the reinforcement of the "right values."

NOTES

[1] The *Wyatt* court did specifically require that behavior modification programs utilizing aversive or noxious stimuli be approved by the institution's Human Rights Committee and have the consent of patients, or the consent of patients' guardians if patients were unable to give consent.

[2] See also *Aden v. Younger*, 57 Cal App. 3d 662, 129 *Cal. Rptr.* 535 (1976).

[3] The difficulties in discussing the boundaries of the due process clause are discussed in Gunther and Dowling (1970, pp. 796-840).

Chapter 11
Prescriptions for the Effective Modification of Criminal Behavior

> Moral habits induced by public
> practices are far quicker in making
> their way into men's private lives
> than the failings and faults of
> individuals are in infecting the
> city at large.
>
> — Plutarch

In addition to reviewing a number of theoretical positions on the causes of crime, this book has attempted to represent the current status of rehabilitative interventions that are derived from a social learning perspective on criminal behavior. Behavioral approaches toward the treatment of adult criminals have occurred in one of three settings: penal institutions, nonresidential therapies, and community corrections. Each of these settings has posed particular problems for the delivery of effective and ethical correctional services as well as attempts to evaluate these interventions in a scientifically rigorous manner.

SOCIAL LEARNING THEORY AND CRIME

Several features of the literature surveyed in the previous chapters merit our consideration. First, with respect to the various theoretical explanations of crime, we should resist the temptation to regard theories of crime as either "right" or "wrong." Theories of crime are neither right nor wrong, however, they do differ on a number of dimensions which permit several meaningful evaluations. All theories possess a range of explanatory convenience whereby the focus of their conceptualizations apply particularly well to certain types of crime but not at all well to other types. Many forms of sociological theory appear well suited for an understanding of crimes against property; but, biological explanations may be more appropriate for a formulation of episodic, extreme violence against persons.

Theories also differ in the type of data they seek to explain. Some theories restrict their attention to "official" criminals, those who are formally apprehended and convicted by the criminal justice system. With other positions, the primary concern is self-reported acts of illegal conduct, regardless of official detection and consequences. In the case of social labeling or conflict theories, the focus is not on original, individual acts of deviance at all, but on the often selective manner by which the justice system imposes the status of "criminal" on certain people.

Theories of crime also differ in the extent to which they generate practical implications for effective rehabilitation. Sociological positions frequently suggest programs of social reform intended to mitigate economic, educational or employment disadvantages which are assumed to be criminogenic. For the most part, biological theories do not engender very many useful techniques for the rehabilitation of adult offenders. Rehabilitation is not a crucial concern of either social labeling or conflict theories. These two positions regard crime as a status created by the criminal justice system, rather than particular, offensive acts by individuals; the practical implication of this view is not that criminals need correction, rather, crime needs a new name which would remove the stigma from those who behave deviantly.

On each of these three criteria (the range of explanatory convenience, the nature of the data explained, and the derivable implications for rehabilitation) learning theories of crime fare reasonably well. The concepts of learning theory apply equally to crimes of aggression and transgression; in fact, one of the major assumptions of this position is that all behavior, criminal or noncriminal, is subject to identical conditions of learning. Another asset of learning theory is its focus on how specific criminal acts, detected or not, are developed by individual offenders, officially apprehended or not. Finally, the belief that crime is learned is usually accompanied by an optimism that it can be unlearned. Behavioral learning theory implies several practical procedures for crime control and correction.

This is not to say that learning accounts of crime are without any limitations. Obviously, they are not. They do not adequately explain why some people who behave illegally are officially treated as criminals while others, who commit the same proscribed acts, escape the impact of the criminal justice system. Neither do most learning theories give sufficient attention to the fact that individuals differ in their susceptibility to virtually identical opportunities to learn criminal behavior. In most cases, learning is a necessary, rather than a sufficient, explanation of crime.

As we have seen, Feldman's (1977) view has attempted to avoid these limitations by considering the importance of personality differences and social labeling processes. As such, it confronts the reality of criminal phenomena more adequately than a theory exclusively restricted to learning concepts. Its inclusion of personality predispositions accounts for the selective manifestation of the learning opportunities that can lead to crime. Secondly, its consideration of social labeling influences can explain how occasional offensive behaviors are inadvertently amplified into criminal careers through the harmful consequences of the stereotypes imposed by the criminal justice system itself.

PRESCRIPTIONS FOR EFFECTIVE BEHAVIORAL CORRECTIONS

In Chapter 1, I proposed several criteria against which we could evaluate behavioral approaches to the problems of crime. These criteria were derived from a community psychology orientation toward social-problem solving, and involved the following five dimensions: (a) ecology; does the environment in which the intervention takes place enhance or limit the impact of the intervention? (b) prevention; does the intervention strive for some preventive impact? (c) system-change orientation; does the intervention aim to produce some degree of institutional change, rather than, or in addition to, the adaptation of persons? (d) generalizability; is the intervention conceptualized and delivered in ways that maximize the potential for its effects to be generalized to new settings and across time? and (e) multidisciplinary focus; is the intervention enriched by an active consideration of legal, sociological, political, economic, and organizational variables?

In this final chapter I wish to prescribe a number of innovations which could improve the quality of correctional behavior modification practiced in institutions, individual therapy, or community settings. Most of these prescriptions have been presented more fully in Chapters 8, 9, and 10. In this chapter, I have organized them under the five criteria for effective interventions from the perspective of behavioral community psychology.

Ecology

The primary principle here is straightforward. Behavioral corrections should be delivered in the environments where most crime actually occurs. Crime occurs in communities; whenever possible, so should corrections. Unfortunately, most offenders have been exposed to behavioral techniques in penal institutions. Chapter 8 suggested several methods for introducing behavioral corrections to new ecological settings. Among the most important were the following:

1. Behavioral techniques for rehabilitation should be integrated with the three general strategies of community corrections — deinstitutionalization, decriminalization, and diversion.

2. Such an integration will require that behavior modifiers become more concerned with the effects of the early stages of the criminal justice system, such as arrest, bail, and arraignment, so that they can develop programs whose purpose is not so much rehabilitation as the reduction of persons' contact with the criminal justice system itself.

3. We should recognize that prisons will continue to exist in some form, and that they are best suited to be institutions of punishment rather than rehabilitation. However, behavior modifiers should not participate in penal institution programs which, despite their rehabilitative intentions, coerce the participation of inmates.

4. Behavior modifiers should develop and evaluate community-based programs for the explicit purpose of assisting people whose legal jeopardy is apparent, but who have yet to be imprisoned for their misconduct.

Prevention

Behaviorists have not developed many prevention-directed programs for the problems of crime. Certainly, this deficiency is not limited to the field of crime. Cowen (1977) has argued that within the entire arena of community psychology there are precious few bonafide examples of primary prevention. At present, primary prevention is more rhetoric than accomplishment. Nonetheless, there are some opportunities for behaviorists to exert more of a preventive influence on the problems of crime than has previously been the case.

5. Social learning theory's emphasis on the role of televised violence as an instigator of interpersonal aggression suggests that the mass media could also be used to provide exemplary, nonaggressive models who contribute to the vicarious development of nonaggressive repertoires.

6. Behavior analytic methodology can be used to compare the effects of various manipulations of the environment that are meant to have preventive impact. One example of this research was McNees, Egli, Marshall, Schnelle, and Risley's (1976) evaluation of two alternative prevention strategies for shoplifting (Chapter 9).

7. An emphasis on competence building, on the development of behaviors which decrease the necessity of crime, is another approach to prevention. Behavioral treatment of adult offenders has relied on what Goldiamond (1974) termed the *pathological* orientation, an emphasis on the elimination of certain behaviors. Increased attention should be given to programs with a *constructional* orientation that attempts to prevent future crime by providing individuals with new repertoires of socially productive behavior.

System-oriented Change

For the most part, correctional behavior modification has reflected an emphasis on an adjustment model, rather than one which is directed at system-level changes. Most examples of behavioral corrections have produced "first-order change" in individuals, rather than changes of the "second order" (Watzlawik, Weakland & Fisch, 1974) that involve modification of some system's functioning (Emery & Marholin, 1977; Seidman, 1977). Chapter 9 offered several examples of programs that tried to curb crime by eliminating, disrupting, or constraining the criminal resources that exist in any community. The following interventions are examples of programs that aim at "second-order changes" in criminogenic systems.

8. The locus of control and the timing of interventions should be altered so that the correction of individuals is redirectd to the "anticipatory prevention" (Sykes, 1972) of criminal acts themselves.

9. This calls for a type of social engineering, or "hardening of the target," which requires the integration of behavioral and systems analyses. The result of this integration would involve efforts at crime control rather than criminal correction.

Generalizability

Behavioral correctional literature reveals a substantial neglect of techniques intended to increase the generalizability and maintenance of some intervention's effects. Several chapters discussed these issues as they pertain to the area of correctional behavior modification. The following recommendations were emphasized.

10. There is too much emphasis on aversive techniques notorious for their short-lived effects. Whenever possible, techniques that aim at competence building are to be preferred over techniques directed at behavioral suppression.

11. Generalization will be extended by treatments that are delivered in the environments where the desired changes are expected to occur. As with the case of ecological criteria, community-based programs are preferable to those that are implemented within institutions.

12. Some authors have suggested that token economies can have a generalizable effect even when operated within an institution because one of the values of contingency management is that it introduces "real world" consequences to the prison. This effect is limited to token economies whose objectives are ethically defensible, where residents participate on a voluntary rather than compulsory basis, and whose general orientation is favorable to human development, rather than accommodation to the institution.

13. The effects of correctional techniques could be amplified by involving nonprofessionals and peers in interventions so that the conditions introduced during treatment could be continued in posttreatment environments, or in natural settings during treatment itself.

Multidisciplinary Focus

It is essential that behavioral approaches to any social problem consider the role of multiple determinants of the problem. Among the variables most likely to influence problems of crime are legal, political, sociological, and economic. This book concentrated on several legal and ethical issues that impinge on attempts to modify criminal behavior. There are four emerging legal-ethical standards that will increasingly be applied to correctional behavior modification.

14. Participation in correctional programs, especially when the programs are delivered to institutional offenders, should be voluntary.

15. Behavior modifiers should avoid the use of hazardous, aversive, or experimental techniques without the informed consent of their recipients.

16. Only when these techniques promote some compelling public interest, and are no more intrusive than necessary to accomplish their purpose are they justified for use on offenders who lack the capacity to consent.

17. Institutional behavior modification must conform to the expanding doctrine of the *least restrictive alternative*, which currently holds that *patients* are entitled to the least restrictive conditions necessary to achieve the purposes of their commitment. It is anticipated that this doctrine will be extended more firmly to prisoner rehabilitation in future cases.

There is a Hungarian proverb to the effect that ''Adam ate the apple, and our teeth still ache.'' Among the many interpretations which may be given to this message, the most pertinent for our present interests is that wrongdoing will not be eliminated. All crimes will not be prevented. Nor will all criminals be cured. This is an important perspective to hold when evaluating the accomplishments of any correctional practice, including behavior modification.

The orientation of this book has been a critical one. Its emphasis has been on the deficiencies of behavioral practice as currently conceptualized and evaluated. These criticisms, however, have been motivated more by optimism for the future of correctional behavior modification than by pessimism about its past. The fact that correctional behavior modification suffers from many limitations should not obscure its frequent successes, which have been surveyed throughout this book.

The task at hand is to build these initial successes into a more systematized science of crime prevention and offender change while at the same time replacing ineffectual, even harmful, procedures with more productive alternatives. This task is made easier by the fact that the major criteria for successful behavioral approaches to crime all point in compatible directions. The development of community-based interventions that prevent the opportunities or the need for crime, and/or produce positive, generalizable changes in offenders will also satisfy the requirements that offenders are entitled to rehabilitation that is neither coercive, restrictive, nor unduly intrusive but which encourages their well-informed, active participation. A simultaneous responsiveness to this field's needed ecological-conceptual innovations as well as its emerging legal-ethical requirements should produce new procedures with great capacity for influencing criminal behavior.

REFERENCES

Chapter 1

Albee, G. W. *Mental health manpower trends.* New York: Basic Books, 19.

Arens, R. *Insanity defense.* New York: Philosophical Library, 1974.

Bandura, A. *Principles of behavior modification.* New York: Holt, Rinehart, Winston, 1969.

Bard, M. Family intervention police teams as a community mental health resourc. *Journal of Criminal Law, Criminology, and Police Science,* 1969, *60,* 247-250.

Barocas, H. A. A technique for training police in crisis intervention. *Psychotherapy Theory, Research and Practice,* 1971, *8,* 342-343.

Bazelon, D. L. Psychologists in corrections — Are they doing good for the offender or well for themselves? In S. L. Brodsky (Ed.), *Psychologists in the criminal justice system.* Urbana, Ill.: University of Illinois Press, 1973.

Bennett, C. C., Anderson, L. S., Cooper, S., Hassol, L., Klein, D. C., & Rosenblum, G. (Eds.). *Community psychology: A report of the Boston conference on the education of psychologists for community mental health.* Boston: Boston University and South Shore Mental Health Center, 1966.

Bermant, G., Nemeth, C., & Vidmar, N. *Psychology and the law.* Lexington, Mass.: Lexington Books, 1976.

Bernstein, D. A. Modification of smoking: An evaluative review. *Psychological Bulletin,* 1969, *71,* 418-440.

Blinder, M. G. Understanding psychiatric testimony. *Judicature,* 1974, *57,* 308-311.

Bloom, B. L. *Community mental health: A historical and critical analysis.* Morristown, N.J.: General Learning Press, 1973.

Bolman, W. M. An outline of preventive psychiatric programs for children. *Archives of General Psychiatry,* 1968, *17,* 5-8.

Boring, E. G. *A history of experimental psychology* (2nd ed.). New York: Appleton-Century-Crofts, 1950.

Briscoe, R. V., Hoffman, D. B., & Bailey, J. S. Behavioral community psychology: Training a community board to problem solve. *Journal of Applied Behavioral Analysis,* 1975, *8,* 157-168.

Brodsky, S. L. *Psychologists in the criminal justice system.* Urbana, Ill.: University of Illinois Press, 1973.

Brooks, A. D. *Law, psychiatry, and the mental health system.* Boston: Little, Brown, 1974.

Burtt, M. E. *Legal psychology.* Englewood Cliffs, N.J.: Prentice-Hall, 1931.

Cloward, R. A., & Ohlin, L. E. *Delinquency and opportunity: A theory of delinquent gangs.* New York: Free Press, 1960.

Cohen, A. K /inquent boys: the culture of the gang. Glencoe, Ill.: Free Press,
1955. lothers in the classroom. Psychology Today, 1969, 2, 36-39.

Cowen, E Social and community interventions. Annual Review of Psychology,
Cowen, E 423-472.

197 Psychologists and primary prevention: Blowing the cover story. An
Cowen American Journal of Community Psychology, 1977, 5, 481-490.

e., Dorr, D., Izzo, L. D., Madonia, A. J., & Trost, M. A. The primary
Cowhealth project: A new way of conceptualizing and delivering school mental
services. Psychology in the schools, 1971, 5, 216-225.

, W. E., Kazdin, A. E., & Mahoney, M. J. Behavior modification: Princi-
issues, and applications. Boston: Houghton-Mifflin, 1976.

/ H., Bray, R. M., & Holt, R. W. The empirical study of social decision
ess in juries. In J. L Tapp and F. J. Levine (Eds.), Law, justice, and the
ividual in society. New York: Holt, Rinehart, and Winston, 1976.

nd, B. L. Criminal responsibility of the mentally ill. Stanford Law Review,
51, 14, 59-86.

n v. U.S. [214 F. 2d. 862 (D. C. Cir. 1954)].

, R. The effect of olfactory stimuli in arresting uncinate fits. Brain, 1956, 79,
267-281.

senck, H. J. The effects of psychotherapy: An evaluation. Journal of Consulting
Psychology, 1952, 16, 319-324.

Eysenck, H. J. Crime and personality. Boston: Houghton-Mifflin, 1964.

Eysenck, H. J. The effects of psychotherapy. New York: International Science Press,
1966.

Feldman, M.P. Criminal behavior: A psychological analysis. New York: Wiley,
1977.

Fingarette, H. The meaning of criminal insanity. Berkeley: University of California
Press, 1972.

Foucault, M. Madness and civilization. New York: Pantheon Books, 1965.

Franzini, L. R., & Tilker, H. A. On the terminological confusion between behavior
therapy and behavior modification. Behavior Therapy, 1972, 3, 279-282.

Gardner, W. Behavior modification in mental retardation. New York: Aldine, 1971.

Goldstein, A. P. Structured learning therapy: Toward a psychotherapy for the poor.
New York: Academic Press, 1973.

Goldstein, A. P., Heller, K., & Sechrest, L. B. Psychotherapy and the psychology of
behavior change. New York: Wiley, 1966.

Goldstein, A. S. The insanity defense. New Haven, Conn.: Yale University Press,
1967.

Gormally, J., & Brodsky, S. L. Utilization and training of psychologists in the
criminal system. American Psychologist, 1973, 28, 926-928.

Halberstam, D. The best and the brightest. New York: Random House, 1969.

Ince, L. P. The use of relaxation training and a conditioned stimulus in the elimination
of epileptic seizures in a child: A case study. Journal of Behavioral Therapy and
Experimental Psychiatry, 1976, 7, 39-42.

Iscoe, I., Bloom, B. L., & Spielberger, C. D. Community psychology in transition.
New York: Wiley, 1977.

Jacobs, F. G. Criminal responsibility. London: Weidenfeld and Nicholson, 1971.

Jeffery, C. R. *Criminal responsibility and mental disease*. Springfield, Ill.: Charles C. Thomas, 1967.

Kazdin, A. E. *Behavior modification in applied settings*. Homewood, Ill.: Dorsey Press, 1975.

Kessler, M., & Albee, G. W. Primary prevention. *Annual Review of Psychology*, 1975, *26*, 557-592.

Kittrie, N. N. *The right to be different*. Baltimore: Johns Hopkins Press, 1971.

Korman, M. National conference on levels and patterns of professional training in psychology: The major themes. *American Psychologist*, 1974, *27*, 441-449.

Lazarus, A. A. *Behavior therapy and beyond*. New York: McGraw-Hill, 1971.

Lazarus, A. A. Has behavior therapy outlived its usefulness? *American Psychologist*, 1977, *32*, 550-554.

Leon, G. R. Current directions in the treatment of obesity. *Psychological Bulletin*, 1976, *83*, 557-578.

Livermore, J., & Meehl, P. E. The virtues of M'Naghten. *Minnesota Law Review*, 1967, *51*, 804-808.

Locke, E. A. Is "behavior therapy" behavioristic? An analysis of Wolpe's psychotherapeutic methods. *Psychological Bulletin*, 1971, *76*, 318-327.

Lorion, R. P. Patient and therapist variables in the treatment of low income patients. *Psychological Bulletin*, 1974, *81*, 344-354.

Lovaas, O. I., Koegel, R., Simmons, J. Q., & Long, J. Some generalization and follow-up measures on autistic children in behavior therapy. *Journal of Applied Behavior Analysis*, 1973, *6*, 131-166.

Margolies, P. Behavioral approaches to the treatment of early infantile autism: A review. *Psychological Bulletin*, 1977, *84*, 249-264.

Marshall, J. *Law and psychology in conflict*. New York: Bobbs-Merrill, 1966.

Monahan, J. Toward undergraduate education in the interface of mental health and criminal justice. *Journal of Criminal Justice*, 1974, *2*, 61-65.

Munsterberg, H. *On the witness stand*. New York: Doubleday, Page, 1908.

Murchinson, C. A. *Criminal intelligence*. Worcester, Mass.: Clark University, 1926.

Nietzel, M. T., & Moss, C. S. The role of the psychologist in the criminal justice system. *Professional Psychology*, 1972, *3*, 259-270.

Nietzel, M. T., Winett, R. A., MacDonald, M. L., & Davidson, W. S. *Behavioral approaches to community psychology*. New York: Pergamon Press, 1977.

O'Connor, R. D., & Rappaport, J. Application of social learning principles to the training of ghetto blacks. *American Psychologist*, 1970, *25*, 659-661.

O'Leary, K. D., & Wilson, G. T. *Behavior therapy: Application and outcome*. Englewood Cliffs, N.J.: Prentice-Hall, 1975.

People v. Goedecke, 65 Cal. 2d 850, 423 p. 2d 777, 56 Cal. Rptr. 625 (1967).

Peterson, D. R. *The clinical study of social behavior*. New York: Appleton-Century-Crofts, 1968.

Quinney, R. *Critique of legal order*. Boston: Little, Brown, 1974.

Rappaport, J. *Community psychology: Values, research, and action*. New York: Holt, Rinehart, and Winston, 1977.

Reckless, W. C. *The Crime Problem*. New York: Appleton-Century-Crofts, 1961.

Riesman, D. Some observations on law and psychology. *University of Chicago Law Review*, 1951, *19*, 30-44.

Rimm, D. C., & Masters, J. C. *Behavior therapy: Techniques and empirical findings.* New York: Academic Press, 1974.

Rokeach, M., & Vidmar, N. Testimony concerning possible jury bias in a Black Panther murder trial. *Journal of Applied Social Psychology*, 1973, *3*, 19-29.

Rosenhan, D. L. On being sane in insane places. *Science*, 1973, *179*, 250-258.

Sarason, S. B. *The psychological sense of community: Prospects for a community psychology.* San Francisco: Jossey-Bass, 1974.

Scharf, P., Kohlberg, L., & Hickey, J. Ideology and correctional interventions: The creation of a just prison community. In J. Monahan (Ed.) *Community mental health and the criminal justice system.* New York: Pergamon Press, 1976.

Shapiro, D., & Schwartz, G. E. Biofeedback and visceral learning: Clinical applications. *Seminars in Psychiatry*, 1972, *4*, 171-184.

Seidman, E., & Rappaport, J. The educational pyramid: A paradigm for training, research, and manpower utilization in community psychology. *The American Journal of Community Psychology.* 1974, *2*, 119-130.

Skinner, B. F. *Science and human behavior.* New York: Macmillan, 1953.

Spielberger, C. D., Megargee, E. I., & Ingram, G. L. Graduate education. In S. L. Brodsky (Ed.), *Psychologists in the criminal justice system.* Urbana, Ill.: University of Illinois Press, 1973.

Sutherland, E. H. *Principles in criminology* (4th ed.). Philadelphia: Lippincott, 1947.

Szasz, T. S. *Psychiatric justice.* New York: Macmillan, 1965.

Szasz, T. S. *The manufacture of madness; a comparative study of the Inquisition and the mental health movement.* New York: Harper and Row, 1970.

Tapp, J. L. Psychology and the law: An overture. *Annual Review of Psychology*, 1976, *27*, 359-404.

Temerlin, M. K. Diagnostic bias in community mental health. In O. Milton and R. G. Wahler (Eds.), *Behavioral disorders: Perspectives and trends* (3rd ed.). Philadelphia: Lippincott, 1973.

Tharp, R. G., & Wetzel, R. J. *Behavior modification in the natural environment.* New York: Academic Press, 1969.

Thibaut, J., & Walker, L. *Procedural justice: A psychological analysis.* Hillsdale, N.J.: Lawrence Erlbaum Associates, 1975.

Toch, H. (Ed.). *Legal and criminal psychology.* New York: Holt, Rinehart, and Winston, 1961.

Turk, A. T. *Criminality and legal order.* Chicago: Rand-McNally, 1969.

Ullmann, L. P., & Krasner, L. *A psychological approach to abnormal behavior.* Englewood Cliffs, N.J.: Prentice-Hall, 1969.

Ullmann, L. P., & Krasner, L. *A psychological approach to abnormal behavior* (2nd ed.). Englewood Cliffs, N.J.: Prentice-Hall, 1975.

United States President's Commission on Law Enforcement and the Administration of Justice. *The challenge of crime in a free society.* Washington, D.C.: U.S. Government Printing Office, 1967.

U.S. v. Freeman, 357 F. 2d 606, 622-625 (2d Cir. 1966).

U.S. v. Pollard, 171 F. Supp. 474 (E. D. Mich. 1959).

Winett, R. A. Disseminating a behavioral approach to energy conservation. *Professional Psychology*, 1976, *7*, 222-228.

Wolpe, J. *Psychotherapy by reciprocal inhibition.* Stanford: Stanford University Press, 1958.

Yochelson, S., & Samenow, S. E. *The criminal personality,* (vol. 1). *A profile for change*. New York: Jason Aronson, 1976.
Zax, M., & Specter, G. A. *An introduction to community psychology*. New York: Wiley, 1974.

Chapter 2

Akman, D., & Normandeau, A. Towards the measurement of criminality in Canada: A replication study. *Acta Criminologica*, 1968, *1*, 135-260.
Beattie, R. H. Problems of criminal statistics in the United States. *Journal of Criminal Law, Criminology, and Police Science*, 1955, *46*, 178-186.
Biderman, A. D. Report on a pilot study in the District of Columbia on victimization and attitudes toward law enforcement. Field Survey I.: *United States President's Commission on Law Enforcement and Administration of Justice*. Washington, D.C.: U.S. Government Printing Office, 1967.
Black, D. J., & Reiss, A. J., Jr. Patterns of behavior in police and citizen transactions. Section I of *Studies of crime and law enforcement in major metropolitan areas* (Vol. 2). Washington, D.C.: U.S. Government Printing Office, 1967.
Bloom, B. L. A census tract analysis of socially deviant behaviors. *Multivariate Behavioral Research*, 1966, *1*, 307-320.
Clark, J. P., & Wenninger, E. P. Socioeconomic class and area as correlates of illegal behavior among juveniles. *American Sociological Review*, 1962, *27*, 826-834.
Clinard, M. A cross-cultural replication of the relation of urbanism to criminal behavior. *American Sociological Review*, 1960, *25*, 253-257.
Cohen, A. K. *Delinquent boys: The culture of the gang*. Glencoe, Ill.: The Free Press, 1955.
Dentler, R. A., & Monroe, L. J. Social correlates of early adolescent theft. *American Sociological Review*, 1961, *26*, 733-743.
Ennis, P. H. *Criminal victimization in the United States: A report of a national survey*. United States President's Commission on Law Enforcement and Administration of Justice. Washington, D.C.: U.S. Government Printing Office, 1967.
Erickson, M. L., & Empey, L.T. Court records, undetected delinquency and decision-making. *Journal of Criminal Law, Criminology, and Police Science*, 1963, *54*, 456-469.
Fox, V.B. *Community-based corrections*. Englewood Cliffs, N.J.: Prentice-Hall, 1977.
Glaser, D. *Crime in the city*. New York: Harper and Row, 1970.
Gold, M. Undetected delinquent behavior. *Journal of Research in Crime and Delinquency*, 1966, *13*, 27-46.
Goldman, N. *The differential selection of juvenile offenders for court appearance*. New York: National Council on Crime and Delinquency, 1963.
Hann, R. G. Crime and the cost of crime: An economic approach. *Journal of Research in Crime and Delinquency*, 1972, *9*, 12-30.
Harries, K.D. *The geography of crime and justice*. New York: McGraw-Hill, 1974.
Harris, L. *The public looks at crime and corrections*. Washington, D.C.: Joint Commission on Correctional Manpower and Training, 1968.
Hindelang, M. J. The uniform crime reports revisited. *Journal of Criminal Justice*, 1974, *2*, 1-17.

Hirschi, T. *Causes of delinquency*. Berkeley: University of California Press, 1969.

Kalish, C. B. *Crimes and victims: A report on the Dayton-San Jose pilot survey of victimization*. National Criminal Justice Information and Statistics Service, Law Enforcement Assistance Administration, United States Department of Justice, Washington, D.C., 1974.

Laster, R. Criminal restitution: A survey of its past history and an analysis of its present usefulness. *University of Richmond Law Review*, 1970, *5*, 71-98.

Maltz, M. D. Crime statistics: A mathematical perspective. *Journal of Criminal Justice*, 1975, *3*, 177-194.

McCandless, B. R., Persons, W. S., III, & Roberts, A. Perceived opportunity, delinquency, race, and body build among delinquent youth. *Journal of Consulting and Clinical Psychology*, 1972, *38*, 281.

McEachern, A., & Bauzer, R. Factors related to disposition in juvenile police contacts. In M. W. Klein (Ed.), *Juvenile gangs in context: Theory, research, and action*. Englewood Cliffs, N.J.:Prentice-Hall, 1967.

Miller, W. B. Lower-class culture as a generating milieu of gang delinquency. *Journal of Social Issues*, 1958, *14*, 5-19.

Miller, W. B. Theft behavior in city gangs. In M. W. Klein (Ed.), *Juvenile gangs in context: Theory, research, and action*. Englewood Cliffs, N.J.: Prentice-Hall, 1967.

Mitford, J. *Kind and usual punishment*. New York: Knopf, 1974.

Morris, N., & Hawkins, G. *The honest politician's guide to crime control*. Chicago: University of Chicago Press, 1970.

Nettler, G. *Explaining crime*. New York: McGraw-Hill, 1974.

Nye, F. I., & Short, J. F., Jr. Scaling delinquent behavior. *American Sociological Review*, 1957, *22*, 326-331.

Palmer, J., & McGuire, F. L. The use of unobtrusive measures in mental health research. *Journal of Consulting and Clinical Psychology*, 1973, *40*, 431-436.

Piliavin, I., & Briar, S. Police encounters with juveniles. *American Journal of Sociology*, 1964, *70*, 206-214.

Reasons, C. E., & Kuykendall J. L., (Eds.). *Race, crime, and justice*. Pacific Palisades, Calif.: Goodyear Publishing, 1972.

Reid, S. T. *Crime and criminology*. Hinsdale, Ill.: Dryden Press, 1976.

Reiss, A. J., Jr. *Measurement of the nature and amount of crime*. U.S. Government Printing Office, Washington, D.C., 1967.

Reiss, A. J., Jr., & Rhodes, A. L. The distribution of juvenile delinquency in the social class structure. *American Sociological Review*, 1961, *26*, 720-732.

Robison, S. M. A critical view of the uniform crime reports. *Michigan Law Review*, 1966, *64*, 1031-1054.

Rosenthal, R., & Rosnow, R. *Artifact in behavioral research*. New York: Academic Press, 1969.

Schafer, S. *The victim and his criminal: A study in functional responsibility*. New York: Random House, 1968.

Schellhardt, T. D. Arresting forecast: U.S. crime will drop as population matures. *The Wall Street Journal*, Oct. 3, 1977, *1*, 20.

Seidman, D., & Couzens, M. Getting the crime rate down: Political pressure and crime reporting. *Law and Society Review*, 1974, *8*, 457-493.

Sellin, T. Crime in the U.S. *Life*, Sept. 9, 1957, p. 49.

Sellin, T., & Wolfgang, M. E. *The measurement of delinquency.* New York: Wiley, 1964.

Sellin, T., & Wolfgang, M. E. Measuring delinquency. In T. Sellin and M. E. Wolfgang (Eds.), *Delinquency: Selected studies.* New York: Wiley, 1969.

Shaw, C. R., & McKay, H. D. Social factors in juvenile delinquency. National Commission on Law Observance and Enforcement, *Report on the Causes of Crime,* No. 13. Washington, D.C.: U.S. Government Printing Office, 1931.

Skogan, W. G. Measurement problems in official and survey crime rates. *Journal of Criminal Justice,* 1975, *3,* 17-32.

Torok, L. A. A convict looks at crime and criminals. *Catholic Viewpoints,* 1971, *27,* 17.

Uniform crime reporting handbook. Washington, D.C.: F.B.I. Government Publications, 1976.

United States President's Commission on Law Enforcement and Administration of Justice. *The challenge of crime in a free society.* Washington, D.C.: U.S. Government Printing Office, 1967.

Voss, H. L. Ethnic differentials in delinquency in Honolulu. *Journal of Criminal Law, Criminology, and Police Science,* 1963, *54,* 322-327.

Waldo, G. P., & Chiricos, T. G. Perceived penal sanction and self-reported criminality: A neglected approach to deterrence research. *Social Problems,* 1972, *19,* 522-540.

Wallerstein, J. A., & Wyle, C. J. Our law-abiding lawbreakers. *Federal Probation,* 1947, *25,* 107-112.

Warner, S. B. Crimes known to the police — An index of crime? *Harvard Law Review,* 1931, *45,* 307.

Webb, E. J., Campbell, D. T., Schwartz, R. D., & Sechrest, L. *Unobtrusive measures: Nonreactive research in the social sciences.* Chicago: Rand-McNally, 1966.

Wilkins, L. T. New thinking in criminal statistics. *Journal of Criminal Law, Criminology, and Police Science,* 1965, *56,* 277-284.

Wolfgang, M. E. Uniform crime reports: A critical appraisal. *University of Pennsylvania Law Review,* 1963, *111,* 708-738.

Wolfgang, M. E., Figlio, R. M., & Sellin, T. *Delinquency in a birth cohort.* Chicago: University of Chicago Press, 1972.

Zeisel, H. F.B.I. statistics — A detective story. *American Bar Association Journal,* 1973, *59,* 510-512.

Chapter 3

Alexander, F., & Healy, W. *Roots of crime.* New York: Knopf, 1935.

Alexander, F., & Staub, H. *The criminal, the judge, and the public.* New York: Macmillan, 1931.

Arieti, S. *The intrapsychic self.* New York: Basic Books, 1967.

Banfield, E. C. *The unheavenly city.* Boston: Little, Brown, 1968.

Bowlby, J. In *Why delinquency?* Report of the conference on the scientific study of juvenile delinquency. London: National Association for Mental Health, 1949.

Bowlby, J. *Child care and the growth of love.* Baltimore: Penquin, 1953.

Bowlby, J., & Salter-Ainsworth, M. D. *Child care and the growth of love*. London: Penguin, 1965.

Buss, A. H. *Psychopathology*. New York: Wiley, 1966.

Chambliss, W. J., & Seidman, R. B. *Law, order, and power*. Reading, Mass.: Addison-Wesley, 1971.

Chesno, F. A., & Kilmann, P. R. Effects of stimulation on sociopathic avoidance learning. *Journal of Abnormal Psychology*, 1975, *84*, 144-150.

Christiansen, K. O. Threshold of tolerance in various population groups illustrated by results from the Danish Criminologic Twin Study. Cited by S. T. Reid, *Crime and criminology*. Hinsdale, Ill.: Dryden Press, 1976, p. 137.

Cleckley, H. *The mask of sanity* (4th ed.). St. Louis: Mosley, 1964.

Cloward, R. A., & Ohlin, L. E. *Delinquency and opportunity: A theory of delinquent gangs*. New York: Free Press, 1960.

Cohen, A. K. *Delinquent boys: The culture of the gang*. Glencoe, Ill.: Free Press, 1955.

Cohen, A. K. *Deviance and control*. Englewood Cliffs, N.J.: Prentice-Hall, 1966.

Cohen, A. K., & Short, J. F. Research in delinquent subcultures. *The Journal of Social Issues*, 1958, *14*, 20-37.

Coleman, J. C. *Abnormal psychology and modern life* (5th ed.). Glenview, Ill.: Scott, Foresman, 1976.

Cortes, J. B. *Delinquency and crime: A biopsychosocial approach*. New York: Seminar Press, 1972.

Crowe, R. R. The adopted offspring of women criminal offenders: A study of their arrest records. *Archives of General Psychiatry*, 1972, *27*, 600.

Dahrendorf, R. Toward a theory of social conflict. *Journal of Conflict Resolution*, 1958, *2*, 170-183.

Dahrendorf, R. *Class and class conflict in an industrial society*. London: Routledge and Kegan Paul, 1959.

Dugdale, R. L. *The Jukes: A study in crime, pauperism, disease, and heredity* (4th ed.). New York: Putnam, 1942.

Ellingson, R. J. The incidence of EEG abnormality among patients with mental disorders of apparently nonorganic origin. *American Journal of Psychiatry*, 1954, *111*, 263-275.

Eysenck, H. J. *Crime and personality*. Boston: Houghton Mifflin, 1964.

Feldman, M. P. *Criminal behavior: A psychological analysis*. London: Wiley, 1977.

Freud, S. *The complete psychological works of Sigmund Freud* (Vol. 19). London: Hogarth, 1961.

Glover, E. *The roots of crime*. New York: International Universities Press, 1960.

Glueck, S., & Glueck, E. *Unravelling juvenile delinquency*. Cambridge, Mass.: Harvard University Press, 1950.

Glueck, S., & Glueck, E. *Physique and delinquency*. New York: Harper, 1956.

Glueck, S., & Glueck, E. *Predicting delinquency and crime*. Cambridge, Mass.: Harvard University Press, 1959.

Goddard, H. H. *The Kallilak family; a study in the heredity of feeblemindedness*. New York: Macmillan, 1916.

Greer, S. Study of parental loss in neurotics and sociopaths. *Archives of General Psychiatry*, 1964, *11*, 177-180.

Hare, R. D. *Psychopathy: Theory and research*. New York: Wiley, 1970.

Healy, W., & Bronner, A. F. *New light on delinquency and its treatment.* New Haven, Conn.: Yale University Press, 1936.

Hooton, E. A. *Crime and the man.* Cambridge, Mass.: Harvard University Press, 1939.

Jacobs, P. A., Brunton, M., Melville, M. M., Brittain, R. P., & McClemont, P. B. Aggressive behavior, mental subnormality, and the XYY male. *Nature,* 1965, *208,* 1351.

Jacobs, P. A., Price, W. H., Court-Brown, W. M., Brittain, R. P., & Whatmore, P. B. Chromosome studies on men in a maximum security hospital. *Annals of Human Genetics,* 1968, *31,* 339-347.

Jarvik, L. F., Klodin, V., & Matsuyama, S. S. Human aggression and the extra Y chromosome: Fact or fantasy? *American Psychologist,* 1973, *28,* 674-683.

Johnson, A. M., & Szurek, S. A. The genesis of antisocial acting out in children and adults. *Psychoanalytic Quarterly,* 1952, *21,* 323-343.

Kessler, S., & Moos, R. H. XYY chromosomes: Premature conclusions. *Science,* 1969, *165,* 442.

Kitsuse, J. I., & Dietrick, D. C. Delinquent boys: A critique. *American Sociological Review,* 1959, *24,* 208-215.

Kranz, H. *Lebenschicksale krimineller Zwillinge.* Berlin: Springer-Verlag OHG, 1936.

Kranz, H. Untersuchungen an Zwillingen in Furosorgeerjiehungsanstalten. *Z. Induktive Abstammungs-Vererbungslehre,* 1937, *73,* 508-512.

Lange, J. *Crime and destiny,* New York: Charles Boni, 1930.

Legras, A. M. Psychose en criminaliteit bij tweelingen. Utrecht, 1932; cited by D. Rosenthal, *Genetics of psychopathology.* New York: McGraw-Hill, 1971.

Loomis, S. D. EEG abnormalities as a correlate of behavior in adolescent male delinquents. *American Journal of Psychiatry,* 1965, *121,* 1003.

Maher, B. A. *Principles of psychopathology.* New York: McGraw-Hill, 1966.

Mannheim, H. *Comparative criminology.* London: Routledge and Kegan Paul, 1965.

Matza, D. *Delinquency and drift.* New York: Wiley, 1964.

Mays, J. B. *Crime and the social structure.* London: Faber, 1963.

McCord, W., & McCord, J. *The psychopath: An essay on the criminal mind.* Princeton, N.J.: Van Nostrand, 1964.

Megargee, E. I. Undercontrolled and overcontrolled personality types in extreme antisocial aggression. *Psychological Monographs,* 1966, *80.*

Merton, R. K. *Social theory and social structure.* Glencoe, Ill.: Free Press, 1957.

Miller, W. B. Lower-class culture as a generating milieu of gang delinquency. *Journal of Social Issues,* 1958, *14,* 5-19.

Nettler, G. *Explaining crime.* New York: McGraw-Hill, 1974.

Peterson, D., & Thomas, C. Review of relevant research in correctional rehabilitation. In J. Cull and R. Hardy (Eds.), *Fundamentals of criminal behavior and correctional systems.* Springfield, Ill.: Charles C. Thomas, 1973.

Price, W. H., & Whatmore, P. B. Criminal behavior and the XYY male. *Nature,* 1967, *213.*

Quay, H. C. *Personality and delinquency.* In H. C. Quay (Ed.), *Juvenile delinquency.* Princeton, N.J.: Van Nostrand, 1965.

Quinney, R. *Critique of legal order.* Boston: Little, Brown, 1974.

Reid, S. T. *Crime and criminology.* Hinsdale, Ill.: Dryden Press, 1976.

Rosenthal, D. *Genetic theory and abnormal behavior.* New York: McGraw-Hill, 1970.

Rossi, P. H. The city as purgatory. *Social Science Quarterly,* 1971, *51,* 817-820.

Schafer, S. *Theories in criminology.* New York: Random House, 1969.

Schulsinger, F. Psychopathy, heredity, and environment. In L. Erlenmayer-Kimling (Ed.), *International Journal of Mental Health,* 1972, *1,* 190.

Sheldon, W. H. *The varieties of temperament: A psychology of constitutional differences.* New York: Harper and Brothers, 1942.

Sheldon, W. H. *Varieties of delinquent youth: An introduction to constitutional psychiatry.* New York: Harper and Brothers, 1949.

Sutherland, E. H. *Principles in criminology* (4th ed.). Philadelphia: Lippincott, 1947.

Sutherland, E. H., & Cressey, D. R. *Criminology* (9th ed.), New York: Lippincott, 1974.

Sykes, G. M., & Matza, D. Techniques of neutralization: A theory of delinquency. *American Sociological Review,* 1957, *22,* 664-670.

Taylor, I., Walton, P., & Young, J. *The new criminology: For a social theory of deviance.* New York: Harper and Row, 1973.

Turk, A. T. *Criminality and legal order.* Chicago: Rand-McNally, 1969.

Ullmann, L. P., & Krasner, L. *A psychological approach to abnormal behavior* (2nd ed). Englewood Cliffs, NJ.: Prentice-Hall, 1975.

Vold, G. B. *Theoretical criminology.* New York: Oxford University Press, 1958.

Yochelson, S., & Samenow, S. E. *The criminal personality,* vol. 1. *A profile for change.* New York: Jason Aronson, 1976.

Chapter 4

Akers, R. L. Problems in the sociology of deviance: Social definitions and behavior. *Social Forces,* 1967, *46,* 455-465.

Azrin, N. H., & Hutchinson, R. R. Conditioning of the aggressive behavior of pigeons by a fixed-interval schedule of reinforcement. *Journal of Experimental Analysis of Behavior,* 1967, *10,* 395-402.

Azrin, N. H., Hutchinson, R. R., & Hake, D. F. Attack, avoidance, and escape reactions to aversive shock. *Journal of the Experimental Analysis of Behavior,* 1967, *10,* 131-148.

Bandura, A. *Principles of behavior modification.* New York: Holt, Rinehart, and Winston, 1969.

Bandura, A. *Aggression: A social learning analysis.* Englewood Cliffs, N.J.: Prentice-Hall, 1973.

Bandura, A. Social learning analysis of aggression. In E. Ribes-Inesta and A. Bandura (Eds.), *Analysis of delinquency and aggression.* Hillsdale, N.J.: Lawrence Erlbaum, 1976.

Bandura, A., & McDonald, F. J. The influence of social reinforcement and the behavior of models in shaping children's moral judgments. *Journal of Abnormal and Social Psychology,* 1963, *67,* 274-281.

Bandura, A., Ross, D., & Ross, S. A. Imitation of film-mediated aggressive models. *Journal of Abnormal and Social Psychology,* 1963, *66,* 3-11.

Becker, H. S. *Outsiders: Studies in the sociology of deviance.* Glencoe, Ill.: Free Press, 1963.

Berkowitz, L. The concept of aggressive drive: Some additional considerations. In L. Berkowitz (Ed.), *Advances in experimental social psychology*, (Vol. 2). New York: Academic Press, 1965.

Burgess, R. L., & Akers, R. L. A differential association-reinforcement theory of criminal behavior. *Social Problems*, 1966, *14*, 128-147.

Campbell, D. T. On the conflicts between biological and social evolution, and between psychology and moral tradition. *American Psychologist*, 1975, *30*, 1103-1126.

Christie, R. Some abuses of psychology. *Psychological Bulletin*, 1956, *53*, 439-451.

Clinard, M. B. The process of urbanization and criminal behavior. *American Journal of Sociology*, 1942, *48*, 202-213.

Clinard, M. B. Rural criminal offenders. *American Journal of Sociology*, 1944, *50*, 38-45.

Clinard, M. B. Criminological theories of violations of war time regulations. *American Sociological Review*, 1946, *11*, 258-270.

Cohen, A. K. *Deviance and control*. Englewood Cliffs, N.J.: Prentice-Hall, 1966.

Cowan, P. A., Langer, J., Heavenrich, J., & Nathanson, M. Social learning and Piaget's cognitive theory of moral development. *Journal of Personality and Social Psychology*, 1969, *11*, 261-274.

Cowan, P. A., & Walters, R. H. Studies of reinforcement of aggression, I: Effects of scheduling. *Child Development*, 1963, *34*, 543-551.

Dinitz, S., Scarpetti, F., & Reckless, W. C. Delinquency vulnerability: A cross group and longitudinal analysis. *American Sociological Review*, 1962, *27*, 515-517.

Dollard, J., Doob, L. W., Miller, N. E., Mowrer, O. H., & Sears, R. R. *Frustration and aggression*. New Haven, Conn.: Yale University Press, 1939.

Erikson, K. T. Notes on the sociology of deviance. *Social Problems*, 1962, *9*, 307-314.

Eron, L. D., Huesmann, L. R., Lefkowitz, M. M., & Walder, L. O. Does television violence cause aggression? *American Psychologist*, 1972, *27*, 253-263.

Eysenck, H. *Crime and personality*. Boston: Houghton-Mifflin, 1964.

Feldman, M. P. *Criminal behavior: A psychological analysis*. London: Wiley, 1977.

Fodor, E. M. Delinquency and susceptibility to social influence among adolescents as a function of level of moral development. *Journal of Social Psychology*, 1972, *86*, 253.

Friedrich, L. K., & Stein, A. H. Aggressive and prosocial television programs, and the natural behavior of preschool children. *Monographs of the Society for Research in Child Development*, serial No. 151, 1973.

Geen, R. G., & Stonner, D. Effects of aggressiveness habit strength on behavior in the presence of aggression-related stimuli. *Journal of Personality and Social Psychology*, 1971, *17*, 149-153.

Gibbs, J. P. Conceptions of deviant behavior: The old and the new. *Pacific Sociological Review*, 1966, *9*, 9-14.

Hirschi, T. *Causes of delinquency*. Berkeley: University of California Press, 1969.

Hogan, R. Moral conduct and moral character: A psychological perspective. *Psychological Bulletin*, 1973, *79*, 217-232.

Hogan, R., & Dickstein, E. Moral judgment and perceptions of injustice. *Journal of Personality and Social Psychology*, 1972, *23*, 409-413.

Homans, G. C. Output restriction, norms, and social sanctions. In W. A. Rushing (Ed.), *Deviant behavior and social process*. Chicago: Rand McNally, 1969.

Jeffery, C. R. Criminal behavior and learning theory. *The Journal of Criminal Law, Criminology, and Police Science*. 1965, *56*, 294-300.

Kaplan, R. M., & Singer, R. D. *Psychological effects of televised fantasy violence: A review of the literature*. Unpublished manuscript, Riverside, Calif.: University of California, 1972.

Kittrie, N. N. *The right to be different*. Baltimore: Johns Hopkins Press, 1971.

Kohlberg, L. The development of children's orientations toward a moral order. *Vita Humana*, 1963, *6*, 11-33.

Kohlberg, L. State and sequence: The cognitive developmental approach to socialization. In D. A. Gosler (Ed.), *Handbook of socialization theory and research*. New York: Rand McNally, 1969.

Kurtines, W., & Greif, E. B. The development of moral thought: Review and evaluation of Kohlberg's approach. *Psychological Bulletin*, 1974, *81*, 453-470.

Lagerspetz, K. M. J. *Studies on the aggressive behavior of mice*. Helsinki: Suomalinen Tiedeakatemia, 1964.

Lemert, E. M. Isolation and closure theory of naive check forgery. *Journal of Criminal Law, Criminology, and Police Science*, 1953, *44*, 293-307.

Lemert, E. M. *Human deviance, social problems, and social control*. Englewood Cliffs, N.J.: Prentice-Hall, 1967.

Liebert, R. M., & Baron, R. A. Short-term effects of televised aggression on children's aggressive behavior. In J. P. Murray, E. H. Rubinstein, & G. A. Comstock (Eds.), *Television and social behavior, v. 2: Television and social learning*. Washington, D.C.: U.S. Government Printing Office, 1972.

Loew, C. A. Acquisition of a hostile attitude and its relationship to aggressive behavior. *Journal of Personality and Social Psychology*, 1967, *5*, 335-341.

MacDonald, M. L. The forgotten Americans: A sociopsychological analysis of aging and nursing homes. *American Journal of Community Psychology*, 1973, *1*, 272-294.

Mercer, J. R. Social system perspective and clinical perspective: Frames of reference for understanding career patterns of person labeled mentally retarded. *Social Problems*, 1965, *13*, 18-34.

Milgram, S. Behavioral study of obedience. *Journal of Abnormal and Social Psychology*, 1963, *67*, 371-378.

Milgram, S. *Obedience and authority: An experimental view*. New York: Harper and Row, 1974.

Mischel, W. *Introduction to personality*. New York: Holt, Rinehart, and Winston, 1976.

Nettler, G. *Explaining crime*. New York: McGraw-Hill, 1974.

Nye, F. I. *Family relationships and delinquent behavior*. New York: Wiley, 1958.

Patterson, G. R., Littman, R. A., & Bricker, W. Assertive behavior in children: A step toward a theory of aggression. *Monographs of the Society for Research in Child Development*, serial No. 113, 1967, *32*.

Patterson, G. R., Ludwig, M., & Sonoda, B. *Reinforcement of aggression in children*. Unpublished manuscript, University of Oregon, 1961.

Piaget, J. *The moral judgment of the child*. London: Routledge and Kegan Paul, 1932.

Reckless, W. C. *The crime problem.* New York: Appleton-Century-Crofts, 1961.

Reckless, W. C., Dinitz, S., & Murray, E. Self-concept as an insulator against delinquency. *American Sociological Review,* 1956, *21,* 744-746.

Reid, S. T. *Crime and criminology.* Hinsdale, Ill.: Dryden Press, 1976.

Reiss, A. J. Delinquency as the failure of personal and social controls. *American Sociological Review,* 1951, *16,* 196-207.

Rimm, D. C., & Masters, J. C. *Behavior therapy: Techniques and empirical findings.* New York: Academic Press, 1974.

Rosenthal, R., & Jacobsen, L. *Pygmalion in the classroom: Teacher expectation and pupil's intellectual development.* New York: Holt, Rinehart, and Winston, 1968.

Ruma, E. H., & Mosher, D. L. Relationship between moral judgment and guilt in delinquent boys. *Journal of Abnormal Psychology,* 1967, *72,* 122-127.

Scheff, T. J. *Being mentally ill.* Chicago, Ill.: Aldine, 1966.

Schur, E. *Labeling deviant behavior: Its sociological implications.* New York: Random House, 1971.

Short, J. F., Jr. (Ed.). *Gang delinquency and delinquent subcultures.* New York: Harper and Row, 1968.

Skinner, B. F. *Science and human behavior.* New York: Macmillan, 1953.

Singer, J. L. The influence of violence portrayed in television or motion pictures upon overt aggressive behavior. In J. L. Singer (Ed.), *The control of aggression and violence.* New York: Academic Press, 1971.

Sutherland, E. H. *Principles of criminology.* Philadelphia: Lippincott, 1939.

Sutherland, E. H. *Principles of criminology* (4th ed.). Philadelphia: Lippincott, 1947.

Sutherland, E. H. Development of the theory. In A. K. Cohen, A. R. Lindesmith, and K. F. Schuessler (Eds.), *The Sutherland papers.* Bloomington, Ind.: Indiana University Press, 1956.

Sutherland, E. H., & Cressey, D. R. *Criminology* (9th ed.). Philadelphia: Lippincott, 1974.

Taylor, I., Walton, P., & Young, J. *The new criminology: For a social theory of deviance.* London: Routledge and Kegan Paul, 1973.

Trasler, G. *The explanation of criminality.* London: Routledge and Kegan Paul, 1962.

Ward, R. H. The labeling theory: A critical analysis. *Criminology,* 1971, *9,* 268-290.

Chapter 5

Azrin, N. H., & Holz, W. C. Punishment. In W. K. Honig (Ed.), *Operant behavior: Areas of research and application.* New York: Appleton, 1966.

Bassett, J. E., Blanchard, E. B., Harrison, H., & Wood, R. Applied behavior analysis on a county penal farm: A method of increasing attendance at a remedial education center. *Proceedings of the 81st annual convention of the American Psychological Association.* Washington, D.C.: APA, 1973.

Bassett, J. E., Blanchard, E. B., & Koshland, E. Applied behavior analysis in a penal setting: Targeting "free world" behaviors. *Behavior Therapy,* 1975, *6,* 639-648.

Boren, J. J., & Colman, A. D. Some experiments on reinforcement principles within a psychiatric ward for delinquent soldiers. *Journal of Applied Behavior Analysis,* 1970, *3,* 29-38.

Brodsky, S. L. *Psychologists in the criminal justice system*. Urbana, Ill.: University of Illinois Press, 1973.

Clements, C. B., & McKee, J. M. Programmed instruction for institutionalized offenders: Contingency management and performance contracts. *Psychological Reports*, 1968, *22*, 957-964.

Colman, A. D., & Baker, S. L. Utilization of an operant conditioning model for the treatment of character and behavior disorders in a military setting. *American Journal of Psychiatry*, 1969, *125*, 1395-1403.

Colman, A. D., & Boren, J. J. An information system for measuring patient behavior, and its use by staff. *Journal of Applied Behavior Analysis*, 1969, *2*, 207-214.

Dirks, S. J. Aversion therapy: Its limited potential for use in the correctional setting. *Stanford Law Review*, 1974, *26*, 1327-1341.

Feldman, M. P., MacCulloch, M. J., Mellor, V., & Pinschoff, J. The application of anticipatory avoidance learning to the treatment of homosexuality. III. The sexual orientation method. *Behaviour Research and Therapy*, 1966, *4*, 289-299.

Geller, E. S. Attempts to implement behavioral technology in Virginia corrections. Colloquium presentation at Florida State University, October 1974.

Geller, E. S., & Johnson, D. F. Letter to the *APA Monitor*, November 1974, *5*, 3, 18.

Geller, E. S., Johnson, D. F., Hamlin, P. H., & Kennedy, T. D. Behavior modification in a prison: Issues, problems, and compromises. *Criminal Justice and Behavior*, 1977, *4*, 11-43.

Glaser, D. *The effectiveness of a prison and parole system*. Indianapolis: Bobbs-Merrill, 1964.

Goldfarb, R. L., & Singer, L. R. Maryland's defective delinquency law and the Patuxent Institution. *Bulletin of the Menninger Clinic*, 1970, *34*, 223-234.

Hodges, E. F. Crime prevention by the indeterminate sentence law. *American Journal of Psychiatry*, 1971, *128*, 291-295.

Holland, J. G. *Behavior modification for prisoners, patients, and other people as a prescription for the planned society*. Paper presented at the meeting of the Eastern Psychological Association, Philadelphia, 1974.

Johnson, D. F., & Geller, E. S. *Operations manual: Contingency management program*. Blacksburg, Va.: Virginia Polytechnic Institute and State University, 1973.

Keith, C. *Specialized treatment for homosexuals in institutions*. Paper presented at the 82nd annual convention of the American Psychological Association, New Orleans, 1974.

Kennedy, R. E. Behavior modification in prisons. In W. E. Craighead, A. E. Kazdin, & M. J. Mahoney (Eds.), *Behavior modification: Principles, issues, and applications*. Boston: Houghton-Mifflin, 1976.

Knecht v. Gillman, 488F. 2nd 1136-1137 (8th cir. 1973).

Levin, S. M., Barry, S. M., Gambaro, S., Wolfinsohn, L. & Smith, A. Variations of covert sensitization in the treatment of pedophilic behavior: A case study. *Journal of Consulting and Clinical Psychology*, 1977, *45*, 896-907.

Levinson, R. B. *Behavior modification programs in the Federal Bureau of Prisons*. Paper presented at the 82nd annual convention of the American Psychological Association, New Orleans, 1974.

Marshall, W. L. A combined treatment method for certain sexual deviations. *Behaviour Research and Therapy*, 1971, *9*, 293-294.

Marshall, W. L. The modification of sexual fantasies: A combined treatment approach to the reduction of deviant sexual behavior. *Behaviour Research and Therapy*, 1973, *11*, 557-564.

Marshall, W. L. A combined treatment approach to the reduction of multiple fetish-related behaviors. *Journal of Consulting and Clinical Psychology*, 1974, *42*, 613-616.

Marshall, W. L., & McKnight, R. D. An integrated treatment program for sexual offenders. *Canadian Psychiatric Association Journal*, 1975, *20*, 133-138.

Mattocks, A., & Jew, C. *Assessments of an aversive treatment program with extreme acting-out patients in a psychiatric facility for criminal offenders.* Unpublished manuscript, Vacaville Medical Facility, 1970.

McCray v. Maryland, Misc. Pet. No. 4363, Montgomery City, Maryland District Court, 1971 (excerpted in 40 U.S. L.W. 2307).

McKee, J. M. The Draper experiment: A programmed learning project. In G. Ofiesh and W. Meierhenry (Eds.), *Trends in programmed instruction.* National Education Association, 1964.

McNamara, J. R., & Andrasik, F. Systematic program change — its effects on resident behavior in a forensic psychiatry institution. *Journal of Behavior Therapy and Experimental Psychiatry*, 1977, *8*, 19-23.

McNamara, J. R., Andrasik, F., & Abbott, D. M. *Short-term recidivism rates for residents released from a forensic psychiatry behavior change program: A preliminary analysis.* Unpublished manuscript, 1977.

Milan, M. A. *Behavior modification for the disadvantaged: The token economy as a basis for effective correctional management.* Paper presented at the 1972 convention of the American Personnel and Guidance Association, Chicago, March 1972.

Milan, M. A., & McKee, J. M. Behavior modification: Principles and applications in corrections. In D. Glaser (Ed.), *Handbook of criminology.* Chicago: Rand McNally, 1974.

Milan, M. A., Wood, L. F., Williams, R. L., Rogers, J. G., Hampton, L. R., & McKee, J. M. *Applied behavior analysis and the imprisoned adult felon project I: The cellblock token economy.* Montgomery, Ala.: Experimental Manpower Laboratory for Corrections, 1974.

Monahan, J. Personal communication, 1977.

Oliver, R. M. *The Virginia program from an administrator's perspective.* Paper presented at the 82nd annual convention of the American Psychological Association, New Orleans, 1974.

Opton, E. Psychiatric violence against prisoners: When therapy is punishment. *Mississippi Law Journal*, 1974, *45*, 605-644.

Rappaport, J. *Community psychology: Values, research, and action.* New York: Holt, Rinehart, and Winston, 1977.

Reimringer, M. J., Morgan, S., & Bramwell, P. Succinylcholine as a modifier of acting and behavior. *Clinical Medicine*, July 1970, 28-29.

Reppucci, N. D., & Saunders, T. J. Social psychology of behavior modification: Problems of implementation in natural settings. *American Psychologist*, 1974, *29*, 649-660.

Sage, W. Crime and the clockwork lemon. *Human Behavior*, September 1974, 16-23.

Saunders, A. G. *Behavior therapy in prisons: Walden II or clockwork orange*. Paper presented at eighth annual convention of Association for Advancement of Behavior Therapy, Chicago, 1974.

Saunders, A. G., Milstein, B. M., & Roseman, R. *Motion for partial summary judgment*. Filed in United States District Court for the Western District of Missouri, Southern Division, January 7, 1974. Available from the National Prison Project, Washington, D.C.

Serber, M., & Keith, C. The Atascadero project: Model of a sexual retraining program for incarcerated homosexual pedophiles. *Journal of Homosexuality*, 1974, *1*, 87-97.

Spece, R. Conditioning and other technologies used to "treat?," "rehabilitate?," "demolish?" prisoners and mental patients. *Southern California Law Review*, 1972, *85*, 616-684.

Trotter, S. Token economy program perverted by prison officials. *APA Monitor*, February 1975a, *6*, 10.

Trotter, S. Patuxent: "Therapeutic" prison faces test. *APA Monitor*, 1975b, *6*, 1, 4, 12.

Von Holden, M. H. *A behavioral modification approach to disciplinary segregation*. Paper presented at the 99th Congress of Corrections, Minneapolis, August, 1969.

Chapter 6

Abel, G. G., Barlow, D. H., & Blanchard, E. B. *Developing heterosexual arousal by altering masturbatory fantasies: A controlled study*. Paper presented at the Association for the Advancement of Behavior Therapy, Miami Beach, Florida, December, 1973.

Abel, G. G., Barlow, D. H., Blanchard, E. B., & Guild, D. The components of rapists' sexual arousal. *Archives of General Psychiatry*, in press.

Abel, G. G., Barlow, D. H., Blanchard, E. B., & Mavissakalian, M. Measurement of sexual arousal in male homosexuals: The effect of instructions and stimulus modality. *Archives of Sexual Behavior*, in press.

Abel, G. G. & Blanchard, E. B. The role of fantasy in the treatment of sexual deviation. *Archives of General Psychiatry*, 1974, *30*, 467-475.

Abel, G. G., Blanchard, E. B., Barlow, D. H., & Flanagan, B. *A controlled behavioral treatment of a sadistic rapist*. Paper presented at the Association for Advancement of Behavior Therapy, 4th annual convention, San Francisco, 1975.

Abel, G. G., Blanchard, E. B., & Becker, J. V. An integrated treatment program for rapists. In R. Rada (Ed.) *Clinical aspects of the rapist*. New York: Grune and Stratton, in press.

Abel, G. G., Levis, D. J., & Clancy, J. Aversion therapy applied to taped sequences of deviant behavior in exhibitionism and other sexual deviations: A preliminary report. *Journal of Behavior Therapy and Experimental Psychiatry*, 1970, *1*, 59-66.

Adams, S. N. *Evaluative research in corrections: A practical guide*. U.S Department of Justice, Law Enforcement Assistance Administration, 1975.

Anant, S. S. Treatment of alcoholics and drug addicts by verbal conditioning techniques. *International Journal of the Addictions*, 1968, *3*, 381-388.

Ashem, B., & Donner, L. Covert sensitization with alcoholics. A controlled replication, *Behaviour Research and Therapy*, 1968, *6*, 7-12.

Bancroft, J. H. *Deviant sexual behavior*. Oxford: Oxford University Press, 1974.

Bancroft, J. H. Application of psychophysiological measures to the assessment and modification of sexual behavior. *Behaviour Research and Therapy*, 1971, *9*, 119-130.

Bancroft, J. H., Jones, H. C., & Pullman, B. P. A simple transducer for measuring penile erections with comments on its use in the treatment of sexual disorders. *Behaviour Research and Therapy*, 1966, *4*, 239-241.

Bancroft, J. H., & Marks, I. Electrical aversion therapy in sexual deviations. *Proceedings of the Royal Society of Medicine*, 1968, *61*, 796-799.

Barlow, D. H. Increasing heterosexual responsiveness in the treatment of sexual deviation: A review of the clinical and experimental evidence. *Behavior Therapy*, 1973, *4*, 655-671.

Barlow, D. H., & Abel, G. G. Recent developments in assessment and treatment of sexual deviation. In W. E. Craighead, A. E. Kazdin, and M. Mahoney (Eds.), *Behavior modification: Principles, issues, and applications*. Boston: Houghton-Mifflin, 1976.

Barlow, D. H., Abel, G. G., Blanchard, E. B., Bristow, A., & Young, F. A heterosocial skills checklist for males. *Behavior Therapy*, in press.

Barlow, D. H., Leitenberg, H., & Agras, W. S. The experimental control of sexual deviation through manipulation of the noxious scene in covert sensitization. *Journal of Abnormal Psychology*, 1969, *74*, 596-601.

Beech, H. R., Watts, F., & Poole, A. D. Classical conditioning of sexual deviation: A preliminary note. *Behavior Therapy*, 1971, *2*, 400-402.

Berzins, J. I. Therapist-patient matching. In A. S. Gurman & A. M. Razin (Eds.), *Effective psychotherapy*. New York: Pergamon Press, 1977.

Best, J. A. Tailoring smoking withdrawal procedures to personality and motivational differences. *Journal of Consulting and Clinical Psychology*, 1975, *43*, 1-8.

Bigelow, G. E., Lawrence, C., Harris, A., & D'Lugoff, B. *Contingency management and behavior therapy in a methadone maintenance program*. Paper presented at the 82nd convention of the American Psychological Association, Montreal, 1973.

Blakemore, C. B., Thorpe, J. G., Barker, J. C., Conway, C. G.,& Lavin, N. I. The application of faradic aversion conditioning in a case of transvestism. *Behaviour Research and Therapy*, 1963, *1*, 29-34.

Bond, I. K., & Evans, D. Avoidance therapy: Its use in two cases of underwear fetishism. *Canadian Medical Association Journal*, 1967, *96*, 1160-1162.

Bond, I. K., & Hutchinson, H. C. Application of reciprocal inhibition therapy to exhibitionism. *Canadian Medical Association Journal*, 1960, *83*, 23-25.

Boudin, H., Valentine, V., Ingraham, R., Brantley, J., Ruiz, M., Smith, G., Catlin, R., & Regan, E. *Contingency contracting with drug addicts in the natural environment*. Unpublished manuscript, University of Florida, 1974.

Brill, N. Q., & Storrow, H. A. Social class and psychiatric treatment. *Archives of General Psychiatry*, 1960, *3*, 340-344.

Brownmiller, S. *Against our will: Men, women, and rape*. New York: Simon and Schuster, 1975.

Callahan, E. J., & Leitenberg, H. Aversion therapy for sexual deviation: Contingent shock and covert sensitization. *Journal of Abnormal Psychology*, 1973, *81*, 60-73.

Cautela, J. R., & Rosenstiel, A. K. Use of covert sensitization in treatment of drug abuse. *The International Journal of the Addictions*, 1975, *10*, 277-303.

Coleman, J. C. *Abnormal psychology and modern life*, 5th edition. Glenview, Ill.: Scott, Foresman, 1976.

Cooper, A. A. A case of fetishism and impotence treated by behavior therapy. *British Journal of Psychiatry*, 1963, *109*, 649-652.

Davison, G. C. The elimination of a sadistic fantasy by a client-controlled counter-conditioning technique: A case study. *Journal of Abnormal Psychology*, 1968, *73*, 84-90.

Davison, G. C., & Wilson, G. T. Goals and strategies in behavioral treatment of homosexual pedophilia: Comments on a case study. *Journal of Abnormal Psychology*, 1974, *83*, 196-198.

Diamond, B. L. The psychiatric prediction of dangerousness. *University of Pennsylvania Law Review*, 1974, *123*, 439-452.

Driver v. Hinnant, 356 F. 2d 761 (4th Cir. 1966).

Droppa, D. Behavioral treatment of drug addiction: A review and analysis. *The International Journal of the Addictions*, 1973, *8*, 143-162.

Easter v. District of Columbia, 361 F. 2d 50 (D.C. Cir. 1966).

Edwards, N. B. Case conference: Assertive training in a case of homosexual pedophilia. *Journal of Behavior Therapy and Experimental Psychiatry*, 1972, *3*, 55-63.

Epstein, L. H., & Peterson, C. L. Control of undesired behavior by self-imposed contingencies. *Behavior Therapy*, 1973, *4*, 91-95.

Evans, D. R. Masturbatory fantasy and sexual deviation. *Behaviour Research and Therapy*, 1968, *6*, 17-19.

Evans, D. R. Subjective variables and treatment effects in aversion therapy. *Behaviour Research and Therapy*, 1970, *8*, 147-152.

F.B.I. *Uniform Crime Reports*. Washington, D.C.: U.S. Government Printing Office, 1975.

Fookes, B. H. Some experiences in the use of aversion therapy in male homosexuality, exhibitionism and fetishism-transvestism. *British Journal of Psychiatry*, 1960, *115*, 339-341.

Forgione, A. G. The use of mannequins in the behavioral assessment of child molestors: Two case reports. *Behavior Therapy*, 1976, *7*, 678-685.

Foy, D. W., Eisler, R. M., & Pinkston, S. Modeled assertion in a case of explosive rages. *Journal of Behavior Therapy and Experimental Psychiatry*, 1975, *6*, 135-137.

Fredericksen, L. W., & Eisler, R. M. *Control of explosive behavior: A skill development approach*. Unpublished manuscript, University of Mississippi Medical Center, Jackson, Miss., undated.

Fredericksen, L. W., Jenkins, J. O., Foy, D. W., & Eisler, R. M. Social-skills training to modify abusive verbal outbursts in adults. *Journal of Applied Behavior Analysis*, 1976, *1*, 117-125.

Freund, K. Diagnosing heterosexual pedophilia by means of a test for sexual interest. *Behaviour Research and Therapy*, 1965, *3*, 229-234.

Garfield, S. L. Values: An issue in psychotherapy: Comments on a case study. *Journal of Abnormal Psychology,* 1974, *83,* 202-203.

Gaupp, L. A., Stern, R. M., & Ratliff, R. G. The use of aversion-relief procedures in the treatment of a case of voyeurism. *Behavior Therapy,* 1971, *2,* 585-588.

Hallam, R.S., & Rachman, S. Some effects of aversion therapy on patients with sexual disorders. *Behaviour Research and Therapy,* 1972, *10,* 171-180.

Hare, R. D. *Psychopathy: Theory and research.* New York: Wiley, 1970.

Heitler, J. B. Preparatory techniques in initiating expressive psychotherapy with lower-class, unsophisticated patients. *Psychological Bulletin,* 1976, *83,* 339-352.

Horos, C. V. *Rape.* New Canaan, Connecticut: Tobey Publishing, 1974.

Imber, S. D., Nash, E. H., Jr., & Stone, A. R. Social class and duration of psychotherapy. *Journal of Clinical Psychology,* 1955, *11,* 281-284.

Jaspers, K. *General psychopathology.* Manchester, England: Manchester University Press, 1963.

Kazdin, A. E., & Kopel, S. A. On resolving ambiguities of the multiple-baseline design: Problems and recommendations. *Behavior Therapy,* 1975, *6,* 601-608.

Kellam, A. M. Shoplifting treated by aversion to a film. *Behaviour Research and Therapy,* 1969, *7,* 125-127.

Kelly, J. G., Snowden, L. R., & Munoz, R. F. Social and community interventions. *Annual Review of Psychology,* 1977, *28,* 323-362.

Kercher, G. A., & Walker, C. E. Reactions of convicted rapists to sexually explicit stimuli. *Journal of Abnormal Psychology,* 1973, *81,* 46-50.

Kiesler, D. J. Experimental designs in psychotherapy research. In A. E. Bergin and S. L. Garfield (Eds.), *Handbook of psychotherapy and behavior change: An empirical analysis.* New York: Wiley, 1971.

Kohlenberg, R. J. Treatment of a homosexual pedophiliac using *in vivo* desensitization: A case study. *Journal of Abnormal Psychology,* 1974, *83,* 192-195.

Kushner, M. The reduction of a long-standing fetish by means of aversive conditioning. In L. P. Ullmann and L. Krasner (Eds.), *Case studies in behavior modification.* New York: Holt, Rinehart, and Winston, 1965.

Laws, D. R. *Non-aversive treatment alternatives of hospitalized pedophiles: An automated fading procedure to alter sexual responsiveness.* American Psychological Association Convention, New Orleans, August, 1974.

Lazarus, A. A. Towards the understanding and effective treatment of alcoholism. *South African Medical Journal,* 1965, *39,* 736-741.

Lazarus, A. A. *Behavior therapy and beyond.* New York: McGraw-Hill, 1971.

Liebson, I., & Bigelow, G. E. A behavioral-pharmacological treatment of dually addicted patients. *Behaviour Research and Therapy,* 1972, *10,* 403-405.

Lipton, D., Martinson, R., & Wilks, J. *The effectiveness of correctional treatment: A survey of treatment evaluation studies.* New York: Praeger, 1975.

Lorion, R. P. Socioeconomic status and traditional treatment approaches reconsidered. *Psychological Bulletin,* 1973, *79,* 263-270.

Lorion, R. P. Patient and therapist variables in the treatment of low income patients. *Psychological Bulletin,* 1974, *81,* 344-354.

Marks, I. M., & Gelder, M. G. Transvestism and fetishism: Clinical and psychological changes during faradic aversion. *British Journal of Psychiatry,* 1967, *113,* 711-729.

Marks, I. M., Gelder, M. G., & Bancroft, J. Sexual deviants two years after electric aversion. *British Journal of Psychiatry*, 1970, *117*, 73-85.

Marks, I. M., Rachman, S., & Gelder, M. G. Methods for assessment of aversion treatment in fetishism with masochism. *Behaviour Research and Therapy*, 1965, *3*, 253-258.

Marquis, J. N. Orgasmic reconditioning: Changing sexual object choice through controlling masturbation fantasies. *Journal of Behavior Therapy and Experimental Psychiatry*, 1970, *1*, 263-271.

Marshall, W. L. The modification of sexual fantasies: A combined treatment approach to the reduction of deviant sexual behavior. *Behaviour Research and Therapy*, 1973, *11*, 557-564.

Marzagao, L. R. Systematic desensitization treatment of kleptomania. *Journal of Behavior Therapy and Experimental Psychiatry*, 1972, *3*, 327-328.

McGuire, R. J., Carlisle, J. M., & Young, B. G. Sexual deviation as conditioned behavior: A hypothesis. *Behaviour Research and Therapy*, 1965, *2*, 185-190.

Mees, H. L. Sadistic fantasies modified by aversive conditioning and substitution: A case study. *Behaviour Research and Therapy*, 1966, *4*, 317-320.

Miller, P. M. A behavioral intervention program for chronic public drunkenness offenders. *Archives of General Psychiatry*, 1975, *32*, 915-918.

Miller, P. M., Hersen, M., & Eisler, R. M. Relative effectiveness of instructions, agreements, and reinforcement in behavioral contracts with alcoholics. *Journal of Abnormal Psychology*, 1974, *83*, 548-553.

Mohr, J. W., Turner, R. E., & Ball, R. M. Exhibitionism and pedophilia. *Corrective Psychiatry and Social Therapy*, 1964, *8*, 4.

Monahan, J. The prediction of violence. In D. Chappell and J. Monahan (Eds.), *Violence and criminal justice*. Lexington, Mass.: Lexington Books, 1975.

Monahan, J. The prevention of violence. In J. Monahan (Ed.), *Community mental health and the criminal justice system*. New York: Pergamon Press, 1976.

Monahan, J., & Cummings, L. The prediction of violence as a function of its perceived consequences. *Journal of Criminal Justice*, 1974, *2*, 239-242.

Morgenstern, F. S., Pearce, J. F., & Reis, W. L. Predicting the outcome of behavior therapy by psychological tests. *Behaviour Research and Therapy*, 1965, *2*, 191-200.

Nietzel, M. T., Winett, R. A., MacDonald, M. L., & Davidson, W. S. *Behavioral approaches to community psychology*. New York: Pergamon Press, 1977.

Paul, G. L. Behavior modification research: Design and tactics. In C. M. Franks (Ed.), *Behavior therapy: Appraisal and status*. New York: McGraw-Hill, 1969.

Pinard, G., & Lamontagne, Y. Electrical aversion, aversion relief and sexual retraining in treatment of fetishism with masochism. *Journal of Behavior Therapy and Experimental Psychiatry*, 1976, *7*, 71-74.

Polakow, R. Covert sensitization treatment of a probation barbiturate addict. *Journal of Behavior Therapy and Experimental Psychiatry*, 1975, *6*, 53-54.

Polakow, R., & Doctor, R. A behavioral modification program for adult drug offenders. *Journal of Research in Crime and Delinquency*, 1974, *11*, 63-69.

Polakow, R., & Peabody, D. Behavioral treatment of child abuse. *International Journal of Offender Therapy and Comparative Criminology*, 1975, *19*, 100-103.

Quinsey, V. L., & Bergersen, S. G. Instructional control of penile circumference in assessments of sexual preference. *Behavior Therapy*, 1976, *7*, 489-493.

Quinsey, U. L., Steinman, C. M., Bergersen, S. G., & Holmes, T. F. Penile circumference skin conductance, and ranking responses of child molesters and "normals" to sexual and nonsexual visual stimuli. *Behavior Therapy*, 1975, *6*, 213-219.

Raymond, M. J. Case of fetishism treated by aversion therapy. *British Medical Journal*, 1956, *2*, 854-857.

Reitz, W. E., & Keil, W. E. Behavioral treatment of an exhibitionist. *Behavior Therapy and Experimental Psychiatry*. 1971, *2*, 67-69.

Rooth, F. G., & Marks, I. M. Persistent exhibitionism: Short-term response to aversion, self-regulation, and relaxation treatments. *Archives of Sexual Behavior*, 1974, *3*, 227-247.

Rosen, R. C., & Kopel, S. A. Penile plethysmography and biofeedback in the treatment of a transvestite-exhibitionist. *Journal of Consulting and Clinical Psychology*, 1977, *45*, 908-916.

Schaffer, L., & Myers, J. K. Psychotherapy and social stratification. *Psychiatry*, 1954, *17*, 70-76.

Serber, M. Shame aversion therapy. *Journal of Behavior Therapy and Experimental Psychiatry*, 1970, *1*, 213-215.

Shah, S. A. A behavioral approach to outpatient treatment of offenders. In H. C. Rickard (Ed.), *Unique programs in behavior readjustment*. New York: Pergamon Press, 1970.

Speer, D. C. *The role of the crisis intervention model in the rehabilitation of criminal offenders*. Erie County Suicide Prevention and Crisis Service, unpublished manuscript, 1972.

Steadman, H. Some evidence on the inadequacy of the concept and determination of dangerousness in law and psychiatry. *The Journal of Psychiatry and Law*. Winter 1973, 909-926.

Steinfeld, G. The use of covert sensitization with institutionalized narcotic addicts. *The International Journal of the Addictions*, 1970, *5*, 225-232.

Steinfeld, G., Rautio, E., Rice, A., & Egan, M. *The use of covert sensitization with narcotic addicts (further comments)*. Danbury, Conn.: Federal Correction Institute, Narcotics Unit, 1973.

Stevension, J., & Jones, I. H. Behavior therapy techniques for exhibitionism. *Archives of General Psychiatry*, 1972, *27*, 239-241.

Stevenson, I. & Wolpe, J. Recovery from sexual deviations through overcoming nonsexual neurotic responses. *American Journal of Psychiatry*, 1960, *116*, 739-742.

Strupp, H. H. Some observations on the fallacy of value-free psychotherapy and the empty organism: Comments on a case study. *Journal of Abnormal Psychology*, 1974, *83*, 199-201.

Thorpe, J. G., Schmidt, E., & Castell, D. A comparison of positive and negative (aversive) conditioning in the treatment of homosexuality. *Behaviour Research and Therapy*, 1963, *1*, 357-362.

United States President's Commission on Law Enforcement and Administration of Justice. *The challenge of crime in a free society*. Washington, D.C.: U.S. Government Printing Office, 1967.

Wald, P., & Hutt, P. The drug abuse survey project: Summary of findings, conclusions, and recommendations. In P. Wald & P. Hutt (Eds.), *Dealing with drug abuse*. New York: Praeger, 1972.

Wallace, C. J., Teigen, J. R., Liberman, R. P., & Baker, V. Destructive behavior treated by contingency contracts and assertive training: A case study. *Journal of Behavior Therapy and Experimental Psychiatry*, 1973, *4*, 273-274.

Wickramasekera, I. The application of learning theory to the treatment of a case of sexual exhibitionism. *Psychotherapy: Theory, Research, and Practice*, 1968, *5*, 108-112.

Wickramasekera, I. A technique for controlling a certain type of sexual exhibitionism. *Psychotherapy: Theory, Research, and Practice*, 1972, *9*, 207-210.

Wickramasekera, I. Aversive behavior rehearsal for sexual exhibitionism. *Behavior Therapy*, 1976, *7*, 167-176.

Winick, C., & Nyswander, M. Psychotherapy of successful musicians who are drug addicts. *American Journal of Orthopsychiatry*, 1962, *32*, 622-636.

Wolken, G., Moriwaki, S., & Williams, K. Race and social class as factors in orientation towards psychotherapy. *Journal of Counseling Psychology*, 1973, *20*, 312-316.

Zax, M., & Cowen, E. L. *Abnormal psychology: Changing conceptions*. New York: Holt, Rinehart, and Winston, 1972.

Chapter 7

Boudin, H., Valentine, V., Ingraham, R., Brantley, J., Ruiz, M., Smith, G., Catlin, R., & Regan, E. *Contingency contracting with drug addicts in the natural environment*. Unpublished manuscript, University of Florida, 1974.

Carney, L. P. *Probation and parole: Legal and social dimensions*. New York: McGraw-Hill, 1977.

Davidson, W. S., & Seidman, E. Studies of behavior modification and juvenile delinquency: A review, methodological critique, and social perspective. *Psychological Bulletin*, 1974, *81*, 998-1011.

Doctor, R., & Polakow, R. L. A behavior modification program for adult probationers. *Proceedings of the 81st Annual Convention of the American Psychological Association*. Washington, D.C.: APA, 1973.

Empey, L. T., & Rabow, J. The Provo experiment in delinquency rehabilitation. In T. E. Laswell, J. H. Burma, and S. H. Aronson (Eds). *Readings in sociology*. Glenview, Ill.: Scott Foresman, 1970.

Ex parte United States, 242 U.S., 27-53 (1916).

Fairweather, G. W., Sanders, D. H., & Tornatzky, L. G. *Creating change in mental health organizations*. New York: Pergamon Press, 1974.

F.B.I. *Crime in the United States, 1973: Uniform Crime Reports*. United States Department of Justice, Washington, D.C., 1973.

F.B.I. *Crime in the United States, 1975: Uniform Crime Reports*. United States Department of Justice, Washington, D.C., 1975.

Glaser, D. *The effectiveness of a prison and parole system*. New York: Bobbs-Merrill, 1969.

Irving, L. H., & Sandhu, H. S. *Offender typology and family interaction: An evaluation of probation success in Oklahoma*. LEAA Criminal Justice Monograph, Reintegration of the Offender into the Community, U.S. Government Printing Office, June 1973.

Keve, P. *Prison life and human worth.* Minneapolis: University of Minnesota Press, 1974.

Krasnegor, L., & Boudin, H. Behavior modification and drug addiction: The state of the art. *Proceedings of the 81st convention of the American Psychological Association, Montreal.* Washington, D.C.: APA, 1973.

Lipton, D., Martinson, R., & Wilks, J. *The effectiveness of correctional treatment: A survey of treatment evaluation studies.* New York: Praeger, 1975.

Lohman, J. D., et al. *The intensive supervision caseloads: A preliminary evaluation.* The San Francisco Project: A study of Federal probation and parole. Research Report No. 11. University of California, March 1967. Cited in D. Lipton, R. Martinson and S. Wilks. *The effectiveness of correctional treatment: A survey of treatment evaluation.* New York: Praeger, 1975.

Newman, C. L. (Ed.) *Sourcebook on probation, parole and pardons* 3rd ed. Springfield, Ill.: Charles C. Thomas, 1968.

Nietzel, M. T., Winett, R. A., MacDonald, M. L., & Davidson, W. S. *Behavioral approaches to community psychology.* New York: Pergamon Press, 1977.

Polakow, R. L. Covert sensitization treatment of a probationed barbiturate addict. *Journal of Behavior Therapy and Experimental Psychiatry,* 1975, *6,* 53-54.

Polakow, R. L., & Doctor, R. M. Treatment of marijuana and barbiturate dependency by contingency contracting. *Journal of Behavior Therapy and Experimental Psychiatry,* 1973, *4,* 375-377.

Polakow, R. L., & Doctor, R. M. A behavioral modification program for adult drug offenders. *Journal of Research in Crime and Delinquency,* 1974, *11,* 63-69.

Polakow, R. L., & Peabody, D. Behavioral treatment of child abuse. *International Journal of Offender Therapy and Comparative Criminology,* 1975, *19,* 100-103.

Rumney, J., & Murphy, J. P. *Probation and social adjustment.* New York: Greenwood Press, 1968.

Schoen, K. PORT: A new concept of community-based correction. *Federal Probation,* September 1972, *36,* 35-40.

Singer, R. Consent of the unfree: Medical experimentation and behavior modification in the closed institution. Part I. *Law and Human Behavior,* 1977, *1,* 1-43.

Sparks, R. F. The effectiveness of probation. In L. Radzinowicz and M. E. Wolfgang (Eds.), *The criminal in confinement.* New York: Basic Books, 1971.

United States Department of Justice, Bureau of Prisons, Success and Failure of Federal Offenders Released in 1970. *Advance Copy,* April 11, 1974.

United States President's Advisory Commission on Law Enforcement and Administration of Justice, Task Force Report. U.S. Government Printing Office, 1967.

Chapter 8

Ares, C. E., Rankin, A., & Sturz, H. The Manhatten Bail Project: An interim report on the use of pre-trial parole. *New York University Law Review,* 1963, *38,* 67-95.

Balch, R. W. Deferred prosecution: The juvenilization of the criminal justice system. *Federal Probation,* June 1974, *38,* 46-50.

Bard, M. Family intervention teams as a community mental health resource. *Journal of Criminal Law, Criminology, and Police Science,* 1969, *60,* 247-250.

Bard, M. *Training police as specialists in family crisis intervention.* Washington, D.C.: National Institute of Law Enforcement and Criminal Justice, U.S. Government Printing Office, 1970.

Bard, M. The role of law enforcement in the helping system. *Community Mental Health Journal,* 1971, *7,* 151-160.

Bard, M., & Berkowitz, B. Training police as specialists in family crisis intervention: A community psychology action program. *Community Mental Health Journal,* 1967, *3,* 315-317.

Becker, H. *Outsiders: Studies in the sociology of deviance.* Glencoe, Ill.: Free Press, 1963.

Brakel, S. Diversion from the criminal process: Informal discretion, motivation, and formalization. *Denver Law Journal,* 1971, *48,* 211-227.

Chambers, D. R. *Temporary leaves for male felons? Oregon's experience.* Unpublished manuscript, Salem, Oregon, 1971.

Chatfield, S. Pretrial disposition in the Twin Cities. *American Bar Association Journal,* 1974, *60,* 1089-1092.

Chevigny, P. *Police power.* New York: Pantheon Books, 1969.

Conrad, J. *Crime and its correction.* Berkeley: University of California Press, 1965.

Cowen, E. L. Social and community interventions. *Annual Review of Psychology,* 1973, *24,* 423-472.

DeGrazia, F. Diversion from the criminal process: The "mental health" experiment. *Connecticut Law Review,* 1974, *6,* 432-528.

Driscoll, J. M., Meyer, R. G., & Schanie, C. F. Training in family crisis intervention. *Journal of Applied Behavioral Sciences,* 1973, *9,* 62-82.

Foote, C. The coming constitutional crisis in bail. *University of Pennsylvania Law Review,* 1965, *113,* 959-999.

Fox, V. *Community-based corrections.* Englewood Cliffs, N.J.: Prentice-Hall, Inc., 1977.

Geller, E. S. *Attempts to implement behavioral technology in Virginia corrections.* Colloquium presentation at Florida State University, 1974.

Glaser, D. *The effectiveness of a prison and parole system.* Indianapolis: Bobbs-Merrill, 1964.

Glaser, E., & Ross, H. *A program to train police officers to intervene in family disturbances.* Unpublished manuscript, Redondo Beach, California, 1969.

Goffman, E. *Asylums.* Garden City, N.J.: Anchor Books, 1961.

Goldfarb, R. *Ransom: A critique of the American bail system.* New York: Harper and Row, 1965.

Goldstein, A. P., Monti, P. J., Sardino, T. J., & Green, O. J. *Police crisis intervention.* Kalamazoo, Mich.: Behaviordelia, 1977.

Holt, N. *California pre-release furlough program for state prisoners.* California Department of Corrections, Sacramento, Calif., 1969.

Holt, N., & Miller, D. *Explorations in inmate-family relationships.* Research report No. 46. Sacramento, California, 1972.

Kennedy, P. VISTA volunteers bring about successful bail reform in Baltimore. *American Bar Association Journal.* 1968, *54,* 1093-1096.

Killinger, G., & Cromwell, P. (Eds.), *Alternatives to imprisonment: Corrections in the community.* St. Paul, Minn.: West, 1974.

Lamb, R. H., & Goertzel, V. A community alternative to county jail: The hopes and the realities. *Federal Probation*, 1975, *39*, 33-39.

Laster, R. Criminal restitution: A survey of its past history and an analysis of its present usefulness. *University of Richmond Law Review*, 1970, *5*, 71-98.

Leeke, W., & Clements, H. Correctional systems and programs — An overview. In J. Cull and R. Hardy (Eds.), *Fundamentals of criminal behavior and correctional systems*. Springfield, Ill.: Charles C. Thomas, 1973.

Markley, C. W. Furlough programs and conjugal visiting in adult correctional institutions. *Federal Probation*, March 1973, *37*, 19-25.

McCartt, J.M., & Mangogna, T.J. *Guidelines and standards for halfway houses and community treatment centers*. Washington, D.C.: United States Department of Justice, 1973.

Morris, N., & Hawkins, G. *The honest politician's guide to crime control*. Chicago: University of Chicago Press, 1970.

Morris, N., & Hawkins, G. *Letter to the President on crime control*. Chicago: University of Chicago Press, 1977.

Mullen, J., Carlson, K., Earle, R., Blew, C., & Li, L. *Pretrial services: An evaluation of policy related research*. Cambridge, Mass.: Abt Associates, 1974.

Myren, R. A. *The role of the police*. Task force report to the United States President's Commission on Law Enforcement and the Administration of Justice. Washington, D.C.: United States Department of Justice, 1968.

Nietzel, M. T., & Dade, J. Bail reform as an example of a community psychology intervention in the criminal justice system. *American Journal of Community Psychology*, 1973, *1*, 238-247.

Nietzel, M. T., & Moss, C. The psychologist in the criminal justice system. *Professional Psychology*, 1972, *3*, 259-270.

O'Leary, K. D., & Wilson, G. *Behavior therapy: Application and outcome*. Englewood Cliffs, N.J.: Prentice-Hall, 1975.

Oliver, R. *The Virginia program from an administrative perspective*. Paper presented at the 82nd Annual Convention of the American Psychological Association, New Orleans, 1974.

Oxberger, L. Revolution in corrections. *Drake Law Review*, 1973, *22*, 250-265.

Page, S., Caron, P., & Yates, E. Behavior modification methods and institutional psychology. *Professional Psychology*, 1975, *6*, 175-181.

Peterson, T. The Dade County pretrial intervention project: Formalization of the diversion function and its impact on the criminal justice system. *University of Miami Law Review*, 1973, *28*, 86-114.

Rankin, H. The effects of pretrial detention. *New York University Law Review*, 1964, *39*, 642-646.

Rappaport, J. *Community psychology: Values, research, and action*. New York: Holt, Rinehart, and Winston, 1977.

Rappaport, J., & Chinsky, J. M. Models for delivery of service from a historical and conceptual perspective. *Professional Psychology*, 1974, *5*, 42-50.

Ray, E., & Kilburn, K. Behavior modification techniques applied to community behavior problems. *Criminology*, 1970, *8*, 173-184.

Roesch, R. Predicting the effects of pre-trial intervention programs on jail populations: A method for planning and decision making. *Federal Probation*, 1976, *40*, 32-36.

Root, L. S. State work release programs, an analysis of operational policies. *Federal Probation*, December 1973, *37*, 52-57.

Rudoff, A., & Esselstyn, T. C. Evaluating work furlough: A followup. *Federal Probation*, June 1973, *37*, 48-53.

Rudoff, A., Esselstyn, T. C., & Kirkham, G. L. Evaluating work furlough. *Federal Probation*, March 1971, *35*, 34-38.

Schafer, S. *The victim and his criminal: A study in functional responsibility.* New York: Random House, 1968.

Schur, E. M. *Crimes without victims: Deviant behavior and public policy.* Englewood Cliffs, N.J.: Prentice-Hall, 1965.

Scott, R. Bail factfinding project at San Francisco. *Federal Probation*, 1966, *30*, 39-43.

Scull, A. T. *Decarceration, community treatment and the deviant: A radical view.* Englewood Cliffs, N.J.: Prentice-Hall, 1977.

Shah, S. A. A behavioral approach to outpatient treatment of offenders. In H. Rickard (Ed.), *Unique programs in behavior readjustment.* New York: Pergamon Press, 1970.

Silberman, C. E. *Criminal violence, criminal justice.* New York: Random House, 1978.

Smith, R. A new approach to the bail practice. *Federal Probation*, 1965, *29*, 3-6.

Smith, R. R., McKee, J. M., & Milan, M. A. Study-release policies of American correctional agencies: A survey. *Journal of Criminal Justice*, 1974, *2*, 357-363.

Tharp, R. G., & Wetzel, R. J. *Behavior modification in the natural environment.* New York: Academic Press, 1969.

Trotter, S. Token economy program perverted by prison officials. *APA Monitor*, February, 1975, *6*, 10.

Ullmann, L. P., & Krasner, L. *A psychological approach to abnormal behavior.* (Second Edition) Englewood Cliffs, N.J.: Prentice-Hall, 1975.

United States President's Commission on Law Enforcement and the Administration of Justice. Washington, D.C.: U.S. Government Printing Office, 1967.

von Hirsch, A. *Doing justice: The choice of punishments.* New York: Hill and Wang, 1976.

Chapter 9

Anderson, C. E. The deterrent factor concept: A deployment method for the smaller department. *Crime Prevention Review*, 1974, *1*, 15-20.

Andrasik, F., McNamara, J. R., & Abbott, D. M. *Short-term recidivism rates for residents released from a forensic psychiatry behavior change program: A preliminary analysis.* Paper presented at the meeting of the Midwestern Association of Behavior Analysis, Chicago, Illinois, 1977.

Bandura, A. *Principles of behavior modification.* New York: Holt, Rinehart, and Winston, 1969.

Berzins, J. I. Therapist-patient matching. In A. S. Gurman and A. M. Razin (Eds.), *Effective psychotherapy.* New York: Pergamon Press, 1977.

Bloch, P. B., & Speckt, D. *Neighborhood Team Policing.* United States Department of Justice: Law Enforcement Assistance Administration, Washington, D.C., 1973.

Bond, I. K., & Hutchinson, H. C. Application of reciprocal inhibition therapy to exhibitionism. *Canadian Medical Association Journal,* 1960, *83,* 23-25.

Bottrell, J. *Behavior modification programs: Analogies from prisons to mental institutions.* Paper presented at the 82nd Annual Convention of the American Psychological Association, New Orleans, 1974.

Campbell, D. T., & Stanley, J. *Experimental and quasi-experimental designs for research.* Chicago: Rand McNally, 1966.

Fabbri, J. Crime prevention through physical planning. *Crime Prevention Review,* 1974, *1,* 1-7.

Geller, E. S., Witmer, J. F., & Orebaugh, A. L. Instructions as a determinant of paper disposal behaviors. *Environment and Behavior,* in press.

Glass, E., Wilson, V., & Gottman, J. *The design and analysis of time series experiments.* Boulder, Co.: Laboratory of Educational Research Press, 1973.

Goldiamond, I. Toward a constructional approach to social problems. *Behaviorism,* 1974, *2,* 1-84.

Harshberger, D., & Maley, R. F. (Eds.), *Behavior analysis and systems analysis: An integrative approach to mental health programs.* Kalamazoo, Mich.: Behaviordelia, 1974.

Hindelang, M. A learning theory analysis of the correctional process. *Issues in Criminology,* 1970, *5,* 43-58.

Jacobs, J. *The death and life of great American cities.* New York: Random House, 1961.

Jeffery, C. *Crime prevention through environmental design.* Beverly Hills, Calif.: Sage, 1971.

Kazdin, A. E. Covert modeling and the reduction of avoidance behavior. *Journal of Abnormal Behavior,* 1973, *81,* 87-95.

Kazdin, A. E. Comparative effects of some variations of covert modeling. *Journal of Behavior Therapy and Experimental Psychiatry,* 1974, *5,* 225-232.

Keeley, S. M., Shemberg, K. M., & Carbonell, J. Operant clinical intervention: Behavior management or beyond? Where are the data? *Behavior Therapy,* 1976, *7,* 292-305.

Laws, D. The failure of a token economy. *Federal Probation,* 1974, *38,* 33-37.

Marzagao, L. R. Systematic desensitization treatment of kleptomania. *Journal of Behavior Therapy and Experimental Psychiatry,* 1972, *3,* 327-328.

Mastria, M. A., & Hosford, R. L. *Assertive training as a rape prevention measure.* Paper presented at the Association for the Advancement of Behavior Therapy, New York, N.Y., 1976.

Matthews, D. E. New directions in crime prevention education. *Crime Prevention Review,* 1973, *1,* 20-24.

McNamara, J. R., & Andrasik, F. Systematic program change: Its effects on resident behavior in a forensic psychiatry institution. *Journal of Behavior Therapy and Experimental Psychiatry,* 1977, *8,* 19-23.

McNees, M. P., Egli, D. S., Marshall, R. S., Schnelle, J. F., & Risley, T. R. Shoplifting prevention: Providing information through signs. *Journal of Applied Behavior Analysis,* 1976, *9,* 399-406.

Milan, M., Wood, L., Williams, R., Rogers, J., Hampton, L., & McKee, J. *Applied behavior analysis and the imprisoned adult felon project I: The cell-block token economy.* Montgomery, Ala.: Experimental Manpower Laboratory for Corrections, 1974.

Miller, A. *The assault on privacy.* Ann Arbor: University of Michigan Press, 1971.

Newman, O. *Defensible space: Crime prevention through urban design.* New York: Macmillan, 1972.

Nietzel, M. T., Martorano, R. D., & Melnick, J. The effects of covert modeling with and without reply training on the development and generalization of assertive responses. *Behavior Therapy,* 1977, *8,* 183-192.

Nietzel, M. T., & Moore, D. Generalization and maintenance effects of social-learning therapies for drug abuse: Indications of neglected criteria. *Drug Forum: The Journal of Human Issues,* in press.

Opton, E. Psychiatric violence against prisoners: When therapy is punishment. *Mississippi Law Journal,* 1974, *45,* 605-644.

Owens, R. P., & Elliott, D. D. Burglary prevention by target area. *Crime Prevention Review,* 1974, *1,* 8-14.

Paul, G. L. Behavior modification research: Design and tactics. In C. M. Franks (Ed.), *Behavior therapy: Appraisal and status.* New York: McGraw-Hill, 1969.

Paul, G. L., & Bernstein, D. A. *Anxiety and behavior: Treatment by systematic desensitization and related techniques.* New York: General Learning Press, 1971.

Polakow, R. Covert sensitization treatment of a probationed barbiturate addict. *Journal of Behavior Therapy and Experimental Psychiatry,* 1975, *6,* 53-54.

Rappaport, J. *Community psychology: Values, research, and action.* New York: Holt, Rinehart, and Winston, 1977.

Schnelle, J. F., & Lee, J. F. A quasi-experimental retrospective evaluation of a prison policy change. *Journal of Applied Behavior Analysis,* 1974, *7,* 483-494.

Schwitzgebel, R. Electronic alternatives to imprisonment. *Lex et Scientia,* 1968, *5,* 99.

Shah, S. A. A behavioral approach to outpatient treatment of offenders. In H. C. Richard (Ed.), *Unique programs in behavior readjustment.* New York: Pergamon Press, 1970.

Sykes, G. The future of criminality. *American Behavioral Scientist,* 1972, *15,* 403-419.

Thoresen, C., & Mahoney, M. *Behavioral self-control.* New York: Holt, Rinehart, and Winston, 1974.

Time, September 16, 1974.

Wickramasekera, I. The application of learning theory to the treatment of a case of sexual exhibitionism. *Psychotherapy: Theory, Research and Practice,* 1968, *5,* 108-112.

Wisocki, P. The successful threatment of a heroin addict by covert conditioning techniques. *Journal of Behavior Therapy and Experimental Psychiatry,* 1973, *4,* 55-61.

Wortman, P. Evaluation research: A psychological perspective. *American Psychologist,* 1975, *30,* 562-575.

Chapter 10

Adams v. Carlson, 488 f 2nd 619 (7th Cir. 1973).

Armstrong v. Bensinger, No. 100, 71-2144 (N. D. Ill. 1972). Order vacated and remanded for reconsideration of relief sub nom. United States *ex rel.* Miller v. Twomey, 479 F. 2d 701 (7th Cir.), *cert. denied,* 414 U.S. 1146 (1973).

Atthowe, J.M. Behavior innovation and persistence. *American Psychologist*, 1973, *28*, 34-41.

Ayllon, T. Behavior modification in institutional settings. *Arizona Law Review*, 1975, *17*, 3-19.

Bandura, A. *Principles of behavior modification*. New York: Holt, Rinehart and Winston, 1969.

Bandura, A. Behavior theory and the models of man. *American Psychologist*, 1974, *29*, 859-869.

Berwick, P., & Morris, U. Token economies: Are they doomed? *Professional Psychology*, 1974, *5*, 434-439.

Birnbaum, B. The right to treatment. *American Bar Association Journal*, 1960, *46*, 499.

Bornstein, P., Bugge, I., & Davol, G. Good principle, wrong target — an extension of "Token economies come of age." *Behavior Therapy*, 1975, *6*, 63-67.

Braun, S. H. Ethical issues in behavior modification. *Behavior Therapy*, 1975, *6*, 51-62.

Brodsky, S. L. *Psychologists in the criminal justice system*. Urbana, Ill.: University of Illinois Press, 1973a.

Brodsky, S. L. *Prometheus in the prison: Informed participation by convicted persons*. Paper presented at the 81st annual convention of the American Psychological Association, Montreal, 1973b.

Caplan, H., & Nelson, S. The nature and consequences of psychological research on social problems. *American Psychologist*, 1973, *28*, 199-211.

Clemons, R. Proposed legal regulations of applied behavior analysis in prisons: Consumer issues and concerns. *Arizona Law Review*, 1975, *17*, 127-131.

Clonce v. Richardson, 379 F Supp. 338 (W. D., Mo., 1974).

Conrad, J. *Crime and its correction*. Berkeley: University of California Press, 1965.

Cressey, D. Achievement of an unstated organizational goal: An observation on prisons. In L. Hazelrigg (Ed.), *Prison within society*. Garden City, N.Y.: Anchor Books, 1969.

Damich, E. The right against treatment: Behavior modification and the involuntarily committed. *Catholic University Law Review*, 1974, *23*, 774-787.

Davison, G. C., & Stuart, R. B. Behavior therapy and civil liberties. *American Psychologist*, 1975, *30*, 755-763.

Donaldson v. O'Connor, 493 F. 2d. 507 (SCA 1974).

Donaldson v. O'Connor _____, U.S., _____, 43 L. W. 4929 (1975).

Dulany, D. Awareness, rules, and propositional control: A confrontation with S-R behavior theory. In T. Dixon and D. Horton (Eds.), *Verbal behaviour and general behaviour theory*. Englewood Cliffs, N.J.: Prentice-Hall, 1968.

Estes, W. K. An experimental study of punishment. *Psychological Monographs*, 1944, *57*, (Whole No. 263).

Friedman, P.R. Legal regulation of applied behavior analysis in mental institutions and prisons. *Arizona Law Review*, 1975, *17*, 39-104.

Foianini, R. A. Post commitment: An analysis and reevaluation of the right to treatment. *Notre Dame Lawyer*, 1975, *51*, 287-302.

Gaylin, W., & Blatte, H. Behavior modification in prisons. *American Criminal Law Review*, 1975, *13*, 11-35.

Gobert, J. Psychosurgery, conditioning and the prisoner's right to refuse "rehabilitation." *Virginia Law Review*, 1975, *61*, 155-196.

Goldberger, D. Court challenges to prison behavior modification programs: A case study. *American Criminal Law Review*, 1975, *13*, 37-68.

Goldiamond, I. Toward a constructional approach to social problems. *Behaviorism*, 1974, *2*, 1-84.

Goldiamond, I. Singling out behavior modification for legal regulations: Some effects on patient care, psychotherapy and research in general. *Arizona Law Review*, 1975, *17*, 105-126.

Griswold v. Connecticut, 381 U.S. 479, 485, 85S, ct. 1678, 14 L. Ed. 2d 510 (1965).

Gunther, G., & Dowling, N. *Individual rights in constitutional law* (8th edition). Mineola, N.Y.: Foundation Press, 1970.

Heldman, A. Social psychology v. the first amendment freedoms, due process and limited government. *Cumberland-Samford Law Review*, 1973, *4*, 1-40.

Hilts, P. *Behavior mod*. New York: Harper's Magazine Press, 1974.

Holt v. Sarver, 309F. Supp. 362 (E. D. Ark. 1970).

Jackson v. Indiana, 406 U.S. 715 (1972).

Kaimowitz and Doe v. Department of Mental Health for the State of Michigan, C. A. 73-19434-AW (Cir. Court of Wayne, Michigan, July 10, 1973).

Karoly, P. Ethical considerations in the application of self-control techniques. *Journal of Abnormal Psychology*, 1975, *84*, 175-177.

Kazdin, A. E. *Behavior modification in applied settings*. Homewood, Ill.: Dorsey Press, 1975.

Knecht v. Gillman, 488F. and 1136-1137 (8th Cir. 1973).

Krasner, L., & Ullmann, L. P. *Behavior influence and personality*. New York: Holt, Rinehart and Winston, 1973.

Lake v. Cameron, 364 F. 2d 657 (D. C. Cir. 1966).

Lefcourt, H. The function of the illusions of control and freedom. *American Psychologist*, 1973, *28*, 417-425.

Lessard v. Schmidt, 349 F. Supp. 1078 (E. D. Wis. 1972).

Mackey v. Procunier, 477 F. 2nd 877 (8th Cir. 1973).

Maher, B. *A theory of schizophrenic cognition*. Paper presented at the 47th annual meeting of the Midwestern Psychological Association, Chicago, 1975.

Martin, R. *Legal challenges to behavior modification*. Champaign, Ill.: Research Press, 1975.

Mitford, J. *Kind and usual punishment: The prison business*. New York: Knopf, 1973.

Moya, C. B., & Achtenberg, R. Behavior modification: Legal limitations on methods and goals. *Notre Dame Lawyer*, 1974, *50*, 230-250.

Nietzel, M. T. Psychiatric expertise in and out of court. *Judicature*, 1974, *58*, 39-41.

Nietzel, M. T., & Moss, C. S. The psychologist in the criminal justice system. *Professional Psychology*, 1972, *3*, 259-270.

Olmstead v. United States, 277 U.S. 438, 479, 48S. ct. 564, 572-573, 72 L. Ed. 944 (1928).

Opton, E. M. Psychiatric violence against prisoners: When therapy is punishment. *Mississippi Law Journal*, 1974, *45*, 605-644.

Opton, E. M. Institutional behavior modification as a fraud and sham. *Arizona Law Review*, 1975, *17*, 20-28.

Polakow, R. Covert sensitization treatment of a probationed barbiturate addict. *Journal of Behavior Therapy and Experimental Psychiatry*, 1975, *6*, 53-54.

Rappaport, J., Davidson, W., Wilson, M., & Mitchell, A. Alternatives to blaming the victim or the environment: Our places to stand have not moved the earth. *American Psychologist,* 1975, *30,* 525-528.

Rimm, D. C., & Masters, J. C. *Behavior therapy: Techniques and empirical findings.* New York: Academic Press, 1974.

Roe v. Wade, 410 U.S. 113 (1973).

Rouse v. Cameron, 373 F. 2nd 451, 452 (D. C. Cir. 1966).

Rubin, M. In defense of behavior modification for prisoners: Eighth amendment considerations. *Arizona Law Review,* 1976, *18,* 110-146.

Rychlak, J. *Introduction to personality and psychotherapy.* Boston: Houghton-Mifflin, 1973.

Sage, W. Crime and the clockwork lemon. *Human Behavior,* 1974, 16-23.

Sanchez v. Ciccone, No. 20182-4, 3061-4 (W. D. Mo. 1973).

Saunders, A. *Behavior therapy in prisons: Walden II or clockwork orange.* Eighth annual convention of Association for Advancement of Behavior Therapy, Chicago, 1974.

Schoen, K. PORT: A new concept of community based correction. *Federal Probation,* 1972, *36,* 35-40.

Schwitzgebel, R. K. Limitations on the coercive treatment of offenders. *Criminal Law Bulletin,* 1972, *8,* 267-320.

Schwitzgebel, R. K. A contractual model for the protection of prisoners' rights. Paper presented at the 82nd annual convention of the American Psychological Association, New Orleans, 1974a.

Schwitzgebel, R. K. The right to effective mental treatment. *California Law Review,* 1974b, *62,* 936-951.

Shapiro, M. Legislating the control of behavior control: Autonomy and the coercive use of organic therapies. *Southern California Law Review,* 1974, *47,* 237-356.

Shelton v. Tucker, 364 U.S. 479, 488, 81S. Ct. 247, 252, 5L. Ed. 2d 231 (1960).

Singer, R. Consent of the unfree: Medical experimentation and behavior modification in the closed institution. Part I. *Law and Human Behavior,* 1977a, *1,* 1-44.

Singer, R. Consent of the unfree: Medical experimentation and behavior modification in the closed institution. Part II. *Law and Human Behavior,* 1977b, *1,* 101-162.

Skinner, B. F. *Beyond freedom and dignity.* New York: Knopf, 1971.

Solomon, R. L. Punishment. *American Psychologist,* 1964, *19,* 239-253.

Spece, R. Conditioning and other technologies used to "treat?", "rehabilitate?", "demolish?" prisoners and mental patients. *Southern California Law Review,* 1972, *45,* 616-684.

Thoresen, C., & Mahoney, M. *Behavioral self-control.* New York: Holt, Rinehart and Winston, 1974.

Trotter, S. Token economy program perverted by prison officials. *APA Monitor,* February 1975, *6,* 10.

Weiler, D. *A public school voucher demonstration: The first year at Alum Rock; Summary and conclusions.* A report prepared for The National Institute of Education, Santa Monica: Rand Corp., June 1974.

Welsch v. Likins, 373 F. Supp. 487 (D. Minn. 1974).

Wexler, D. B. Token and taboo: Behavior modification, token economics and the law. *California Law Review,* 1973, *61,* 81-109.

Wexler, D. B. Of rights and reinforces. *San Diego Law Review,* 1974a, *11,* 957-971.

Wexler, D. B. Mental health law and the movement toward voluntary treatment. *California Law Review*, 1974b, *62*, 671-692.

Wexler, D. B. Reflections on the legal regulation of behavior modification in institutional settings. *Arizona Law Review*, 1975, *17*, 132-143.

Whitney v. California, 274 U.S. 357 (1927).

Winett, R. A., & Winkler, R. C. Current behavior modification in the classroom: Be still, be quiet, be docile. *Journal of Applied Behavior Analysis*, 1972, *5*, 499-504.

Wyatt v. Aderholt, 503 F. 2d 1305 (5th Cir. 1974).

Wyatt v. Stickney, 344 F. Supp. 373, 380 (M. D. Alabama, 1971).

Chapter 11

Cowen, E. L. Psychologists and primary prevention: Blowing the cover story. *American Journal of Community Psychology*, 1977, *5*, 481-489.

Emery, R. E., & Marholin, D., II. An applied behavior analysis of delinquency: The irrelevancy of relevant behavior. *American Psychologist*, 1977, *32*, 860-873.

Feldman, M. P. *Criminal behaviour: A psychological analysis*. London: Wiley, 1977.

Goldiamond, I. Toward a constructional approach to social problems. *Behaviorism*, 1974, *2*, 1-84.

McNees, M. P., Egli, D. S., Marshall, R. S., Schnelle, J. F., & Risley, T. R. Shoplifting prevention: Providing information through signs. *Journal of Applied Behavior Analysis*, 1976, *9*, 339-406.

Seidman, E. Justice, values and social science: Unexamined premises. In R. J. Simon (Ed.), *Research in Law and Sociology*, Vol. I, Greenwich, Conn.: JAI Press, 1977.

Sykes, G. The future of criminality. *American Behavioral Scientist*, 1972, *15*, 403-419.

Watzlawik, P., Weakland, J.H., & Fisch, R. *Change: Principles of problem formation and problem resolution*. New York: Norton, 1974.

NAME INDEX

SUBJECT INDEX

ABOUT THE AUTHOR

MICHAEL T. NIETZEL is Associate Professor of Psychology at the University of Kentucky, Lexington. Dr. Nietzel is the author of numerous journal articles in his field of specialization, clinical and community psychology, and is co-author of *Behavioral Approaches to Community Problems*.

PERGAMON GENERAL PSYCHOLOGY SERIES

Editors: Arnold P. Goldstein, *Syracuse University*
Leonard Krasner, *SUNY, Stony Brook*

The terms of our inspection copy service apply to all the above books. A complete catalogue of all books in the Pergamon International Library is available on request.

The Publisher will be pleased to receive suggestions for revised editions and new titles.